Excel 7

A COMPREHENSIVE APPROACH

FOR WINDOWS 95

Carole K. Tobias
Instructor, Microcomputing
Forsyth Technical Community College
Winston-Salem, NC

GLENCOE
McGraw-Hill

New York, New York   Columbus, Ohio   Mission Hills, California   Peoria, Illinois

This program has been prepared with the assistance of Gleason Group, Inc.,
Norwalk, CT.

Editorial Director: Pamela Ross

Developmental Editors: Michael Buchman, Thomas Cain,
Michele Ruschhaupt, Nancy Kaczmarczyk, Katherine Pinard,
Nina Edgmand, Suzanne Weixel, Margaret Marple

Copy Editor: Jill Hobbs

Composition: PDS Associates, Creative Ink

Screens were captured using Pizazz 5 for Windows from Application Techniques, Inc.,
Pepperell, MA.

Glencoe/McGraw-Hill

*A Division of The **McGraw·Hill** Companies*

Excel 7 for Windows 95: A Comprehensive Approach

1 2 3 4 5 6 7 8 9 10 QPH 02 01 00 99 98 97

ISBN 0-02-803340-X

Microsoft, MS, Excel, MS-DOS, and Windows are either registered trademarks or
trademarks of Microsoft Corporation in the United States and/or other countries.

PostScript is a registered trademark of Adobe Systems, Inc.

Contents

UNIT 2

Developing a Worksheet 101

UNIT 3

Changing the Appearance of a Worksheet   *205*

CONTENTS

UNIT 5

Multiple Worksheets and Advanced Printing   *349*

CONTENTS

Appendices

x

Preface

Excel 7 for Windows 95: A Comprehensive Approach has been written to help you master Microsoft Excel for Windows 95. The text is designed to take you step-by-step through the features in Excel that you are likely to use in both your personal and business life.

Case Study

Learning about the features of Excel is one thing, but applying what you've learned is another. That's why a *Case Study* runs throughout the text. It offers you the opportunity to learn Excel within a realistic business context. Take the time to read the Case Study about Kearny-Sansome Accounting, Inc., a fictional business set in San Francisco, California. All of the worksheets for this course will deal with the clients of Kearny-Sansome.

Organization of the Text

The text includes seven *units*. Each unit is divided into smaller *lessons*. There are 21 lessons, each building on previously learned procedures. This building block approach, together with the Case Study and the features listed below, enables you to maximize your learning process.

Features of the Text

- ☑ *Objectives* are listed for each lesson
- ☑ The *estimated time* required to complete the lesson is stated
- ☑ Within a lesson, each *heading* corresponds to an objective
- ☑ *Exercises* that walk you through all procedures in a lesson are titled for easy reference
- ☑ *Key terms* are italicized and defined as they are encountered
- ☑ Extensive *graphics* display screen contents
- ☑ *Toolbar buttons* and *keyboard keys* are shown in the text when they are used
- ☑ *Large toolbar buttons in the margins* provide easy-to-see references
- ☑ Lessons contain important *Notes* and useful *Tips*
- ☑ A *Command Summary* lists the commands learned in the lesson
- ☑ *Using Help* introduces you to a Help topic related to the content of a lesson
- ☑ *Concepts Review* includes True/False, Short Answer, and Critical Thinking questions to focus on lesson content

☑ *Skills Review* provides skill reinforcement for each lesson

☑ *Lesson Applications* ask you to apply your skills in a more challenging way

☑ *Unit Applications* give you the opportunity to use all of the skills you learned throughout the unit

☑ The last application in each Unit Application asks you to create your own worksheet, developing your ability to create worksheets "from scratch"

☑ Appendices

☑ Glossary

☑ Index

Conventions Used in the Text

This text uses a number of conventions to help you learn the program and save your work.

- Text that you are asked to key either in **boldface** or as a separate figure.

- Filenames appear in **boldface**.

- You will be asked to save each document with your initials, followed by the exercise name. For example, an exercise may end with the instruction: "Save the workbook as *[your initials]***5-12.xls**."

- Menu letters you can key to activate a command are shown as they appear on screen, with the letter underlined (example: "Choose <u>P</u>rint from the File menu."). Dialog box options are also shown this way (example: "Click <u>R</u>eplace in the Find dialog box.").

If You Are Unfamiliar with Windows 95

If you're unfamiliar with Windows 95, you'll want to work through *Appendix A: "Windows 95 Tutorial"* before beginning Lesson 1. You may also need to review *Appendix B: "Using the Mouse"* and *Appendix C: "Using Menus and Dialog Boxes"* if you've never used a mouse or Windows before.

Screen Differences

As you read about and practice each concept, illustrations of the screens have been provided to help you follow the instructions. Don't worry if your screen has a somewhat different appearance than the screen illustration. These differences result from variations in system and computer configurations.

Acknowledgments

We would like to thank the many reviewers of this text, and those students and teachers who have used this book in the past, for their valuable assistance. We would particularly like to thank the following reviewers: Susan Olson, Northwest Technical College, East Grand Forks, MN; and Jo Ann Weatherwax, Saddleback College, Mission Viejo, CA.

Installation Requirements

You'll need Microsoft Excel 7 for Windows 95 to work with this textbook. Excel needs to be installed on an IBM or IBM-compatible microcomputer's hard drive (or on a network). To properly install Excel, refer to the manual that came with the program. The following checklist will help you evaluate the requirements for installing Excel.

Hardware

☑ Personal computer with a 386DX or higher processor (486 or higher recommended)

☑ Hard drive

☑ 3.5-inch high-density disk drive (or CD-ROM player)

☑ 8 MB or RAM

☑ 16 MB of hard disk for "Typical" installation; "Custom" or "Complete" installation can require up to 33 MB

☑ VGA or higher-resolution video monitor (SVGA 256-color recommended)

☑ Printer (laser or ink-jet recommended)

☑ Mouse

Software

☑ Excel 7 for Windows 95 or Microsoft Office for Windows 95 (3.5-inch disks or CD-ROM)

☑ Windows 95

Optional Setup Installations

If Excel is already installed on your computer, you may need to add components. The following components may not be included on your computer:

COMPONENT	LESSON TAUGHT
Spreadsheet Templates (Excel option)	13
Microsoft Data Map (Excel option)	17
ClipArt (Office Tools option)	18

Adding New Components

To add new components:

1. Load the CD-ROM or the "Setup" floppy disk originally used in the installation.

2. Click the Start button, choose Settings, and then click Control Panel.

3. Double-click the Add/Remove Programs icon.

4. Click the Install/Uninstall tab.

5. Click the Install button, or the Add/Remove button, whichever is available.

6. Follow the Setup instructions on the screen.

7. When the Excel or Microsoft Office Options are listed, choose an option and click the Change Option button to view the individual components for the option. For example, choose the option Microsoft Excel, click Change Option, and then check components such as Microsoft Data Map or Spreadsheet templates.

8. Click the Select All button to install all components for the particular option.

9. Continue with Setup.

Editorial Advisory Board

CASE STUDY

There's more to learning a spreadsheet program like Microsoft Excel than simply keying data. You need to know how to use Excel in a real-world situation. That's why all the lessons in this book relate to every-day business tasks.

As you work through the lessons, imagine yourself working as an intern for Kearny-Sansome Accounting, a fictional accounting business located in San Francisco, CA.

Kearny Sansome Accounting, Inc.

Kearny-Sansome Accounting, Inc.

240 Montgomery St., San Francisco, CA 94101
(415)555-2000

Kearny-Sansome Accounting, Inc. was formed in 1908 by a group of San Francisco businesspeople to provide accounting services to small San Francisco businesses trying to recover from the earthquake of 1906. The company has grown over the years, but still focuses on smaller businesses. Located in San Francisco's busy Financial District, Kearny-Sansome has clients from all across the nation, although the majority of clients are still from California. The company provides accounting, data processing, and consulting assistance to its clients.

Working As an Intern

You will be working as an intern at Kearny-Sansome Accounting. This involves working with one client for a few weeks, then working with another client for a few weeks, and so on. The managers at Kearny-Sansome feel that it's important for new employees to gain experience working with a variety of clients and tasks, under the direction of an experienced manager, before you begin working on your own. They stress that this period is your "trial period" in which you have an opportunity to demonstrate your skills.

Kearny-Sansome, like other businesses, expects that any incoming employee will have a solid foundation of skills* that includes:

Basic Skills

Reading, writing, arithmetic/mathematics, listening, and speaking

Thinking Skills

Creative thinking, decision making, problem solving, being able to visualize problems and solutions, knowing how to learn, and reasoning

Personal Qualities

Responsibility, self-esteem, sociability, self-management, and integrity/honesty

In addition, Kearny-Sansome believes that the five competencies identified below are the keys to job-performance. The Kearny-Sansome intern program is the company's attempt to evaluate each new employee's level of competency.

Keys to Successful Job-Performance*

1. Resources: Identifies, organizes, plans, and allocates resources

A. *Time*—Selects goal-relevant activities, ranks them, allocates time, and prepares and follows schedules

B. *Money*—Uses or prepares budgets, makes forecasts, keeps record, and makes adjustments to meet objectives

C. *Material and Facilities*—Acquires, stores, allocates, and uses materials or space efficiently

D. *Human Resources*—Assesses skills and distributes work accordingly, evaluates performance and provides feedback

2. Interpersonal: Works with others

A. *Participates as a Member of a Team*—Contributes to the group effort

B. *Teaches Others New Skills*

C. *Serves Clients/Customers*—Works to satisfy customers' expectations

D. *Exercises Leadership*—Communicates ideas to justify a position, persuades and convinces others, responsibly challenges existing procedures and policies

E. *Negotiates*—Works toward agreements involving exchanges of resources, resolves differing interests

F. *Works with Diversity*—Works well with men and women from diverse backgrounds

3. Information: Acquires and uses information

A. *Acquires and Evaluates Information*

B. *Organizes and Maintains Information*

C. *Interprets and Communicates Information*

D. *Uses Computers to Process Information*

4. Systems: Understands complex relationships

A. *Understands Systems*—knows how social, organizational, and technological systems work and operates effectively with them

B. *Monitors and Corrects Performance*—Distinguishes trends, predicts impacts on system operations, diagnoses systems' performance and corrects malfunctions

C. *Improves or Designs Systems*—Suggests modifications to existing systems and develops new or alternative systems to improve performance

5. Technology: Works with a variety of technologies

A. *Selects Technology*—Chooses procedures, tools or equipment including computers and related technologies

B. *Applies Technology to Task*—Understands overall intent and proper procedures for setup and operation of equipment

C. *Maintains and Troubleshoots Equipment*—Prevents, identifies, or solves problems with equipment, including computers and other technologies

* These skills and competencies were identified by the Secretary of Labor and the Secretary's Commission on Achieving Necessary Skills (SCANS). They are included in the report *What Work Requires of Schools: A SCANS Report for America 2000*, published in June, 1991, by the U.S. Department of Labor.

Your Clients During the Intern Period

During your intern period at Kearny-Sansome, you will be working with seven clients.

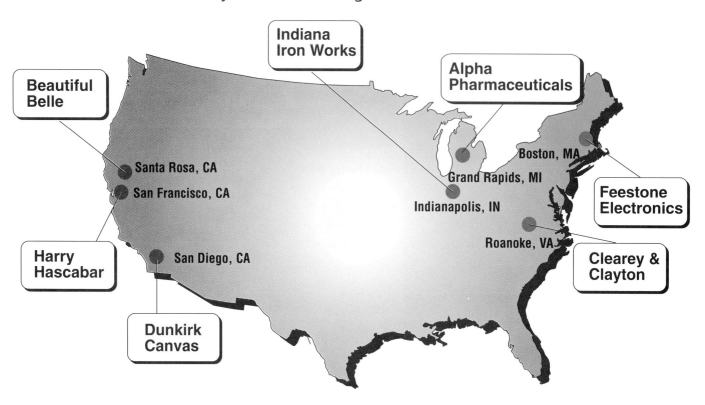

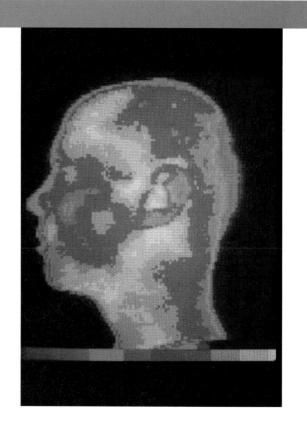

ALPHA Pharmaceuticals

Alpha Pharmaceuticals

145 Bostwick Ave., NE
Grand Rapids, MI 49503
(616)555-4698

Alpha Pharmaceuticals manufactures generic over-the-counter drugs, such as ibuprofen, acetaminophen, and aspirin, for large grocery and drug-store chains. You'll be helping Alpha Pharmaceuticals study historical data about pain relievers. Alpha's president, Mark Latzko, thinks that people are switching from aspirin to ibuprofen. Your worksheets will indicate if he's right.

Beautiful Belle Company

Beautiful Belle Company
103 Professional Center Drive
Santa Rosa, CA 95403
(707)555-2398

The Beautiful Belle Company manufactures a moderately priced line of cosmetics. The company is currently promoting a product called "Sun Soft," a natural, hypo-allergenic lotion that has refined almond and sesame oils as main ingredients. Renata Santo, the Southwest regional sales manager, is test marketing Sun Soft in the Phoenix area. You'll be developing worksheets that track Sun Soft's sales performance against a competing product.

Clearey & Clayton

411 Fort Belknap Dr.
Roanoke, VA 24038
(703)555-0371

Clearey & Clayton got its start by producing scaled-down backpacks and camping gear for small people and children. They now produce camping gear such as backpacks, tents, and kayaks for people of all sizes. You'll be helping Bettina Clearey and John Clayton develop a promotional product list and an order blank for a mail-order catalog.

5

Dunkirk Canvas Company

7270 Mesa Drive
San Diego, CA 9211
(619)555-8954

Dunkirk Canvas Company used to make sails for boats. While they continue to make sails today, their fastest growing business is producing made-to-order canvas boat covers. In fact, the boat cover business has become so big, that the company now finds that it sometimes needs to use independent contractors to make some of their sails. You'll be helping Frank Bouchard and Mickey Finnegan computerize their business records and track independent contractors.

Feestone Electronics

17 New Rutherford Ave.
Boston, MA 02129
(617)555-8700

Feestone Electronics is a nationwide distributor of business machines, such as cellular phones, fax machines, and copy machines. Each of its four regional offices writes its own invoices and keeps track of its own sales and inventory. They provide data to the central office each quarter. You'll be helping Craig Herman, the company's bookkeeper, put together a system that will use e-mail to consolidate data from all the regional offices in one worksheet.

Harry Hascabar's
Hand-Crafted Leather Goods

25529 Taylor St.
San Francisco, CA 94194
(415)555-5895

Harry Hascabar has five shops in San Francisco that sell leather goods such as briefcases, shoes, and handbags. But Harry's first love is running. He's been making special running shoes for long-distance runners for over a decade—and now he wants to start a new company that will sell his shoes and other products for runners. You'll be helping Harry Hascabar create worksheets that present his unique experimental data in attractive charts.

Indiana Iron Works

45 W. 26th St.
Indianapolis, IN 46206
(317)555-4510

Indiana Iron Works is an iron and steel foundry started in 1854 (as "Indiana Horseshoes"). Today, the company specializes in producing beautiful decorative iron work, much of it based on the intricate iron work of the early Renaissance. Over the years, Indiana Iron Works has also acquired quite a bit of property that it now is interested in selling. You'll be helping Dexter Peabody IV, the president of the company, create a customer database, as well as a database of the property holdings of the company.

7

Preview

As you learn Microsoft Excel, you'll be producing professional worksheets, charts, and maps for the clients of Kearny-Sansome Accounting. You'll learn all of the important Excel features, from keying data and creating simple worksheets, to using functions, creating charts and maps, and using Excel's database features. By "working" as an intern at Kearny-Sansome Accounting, you'll gain experience that you can apply to a real-world business.

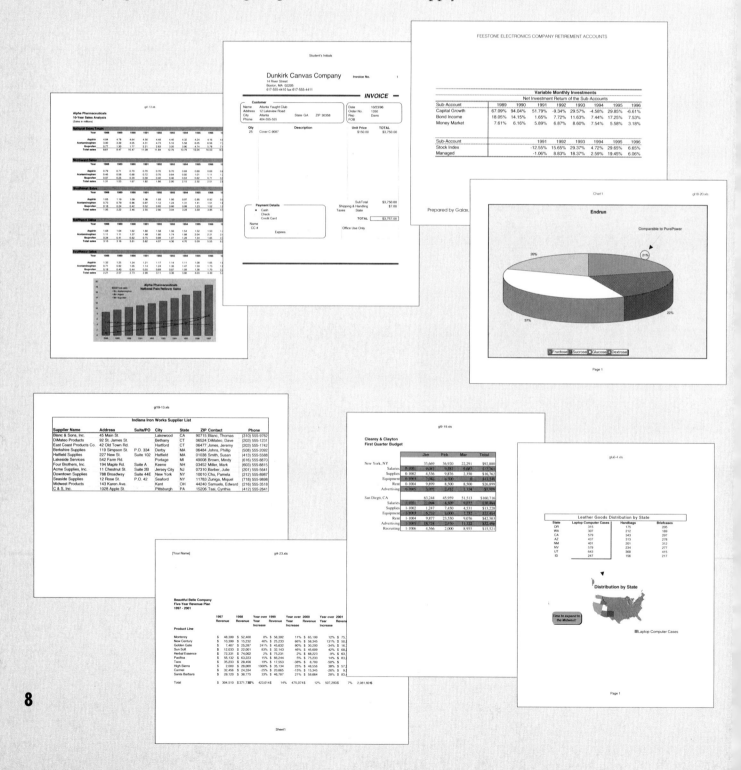

Basic Skills

ALPHA Pharmaceuticals

Drug Company Banks on Growing Pains

Alpha Pharmaceuticals manufactures generic over-the-counter drugs, such as ibuprofen and aspirin, for large grocery and drug-store chains. Because demographic studies are showing that the average age of the general population is trending upward, and since older people tend to have more minor aches and pains than younger people, Alpha anticipates that the pain-reliever business will grow steadily into the 21th century.

Alpha's president, Mark Latzko, has asked his market-research team to study the company's historical data to confirm his belief that people are switching from aspirin to ibuprofen as the pain reliever of choice.

Jean Brody, who heads up the market research team, has requested the following information to fulfill Mark's request:

✔ A detailed worksheet showing sales of aspirin, acetaminophen, and ibuprofen for the past ten years in each of the four national sales regions, with a chart illustrating trends. **(Lesson 1)**

✔ A summary sheet showing Alpha's sales of each product for the last four years and projected sales for the current year **(Lesson 2)**

✔ An attractively styled worksheet showing the five-year sales analyses developed in Lesson 2. **(Lesson 3)**

What Is Excel?

After completing this lesson, you will be able to:

1. **Start Excel.**
2. **Change the active cell.**
3. **Navigate between worksheets.**
4. **Open and close workbooks.**
5. **Navigate within a worksheet.**
6. **Key data in a worksheet.**
7. **Save a workbook.**
8. **Print a workbook and close Excel.**

 Estimated Time: 1½ hours

Microsoft Excel is an electronic workbook that gives you the ability to perform business and scientific calculations effortlessly. It provides powerful charting, database management, and macro programming capabilities. Although Excel is powerful, it's very intuitive and easy to use. Once you learn a few basics, you'll become a productive Excel user very quickly.

Starting Excel

FIGURE 1-1
Shortcut icon to
start Excel

Excel can be started in several ways, depending on how your system is set up. For example, you can use the Start button on the Windows taskbar, the Microsoft Office Shortcut bar, or Windows Explorer. If a shortcut for starting Excel has been created, you can double-click the shortcut icon on the desktop.

NOTE: Windows 95 allows for great flexibility in starting up its applications. If you have any problems, ask your instructor for help.

EXERCISE 1-1 Start Excel

1. Turn on your computer. Windows will load.

2. Click the Start button on the Windows taskbar, and then point to Programs.

3. On the submenu, click Microsoft Excel. (You may have to point first to a program group that contains Microsoft Excel, such as Microsoft Office.) The program is loaded in a few seconds, and the Excel window appears.

FIGURE 1-2
Starting Excel from the Windows taskbar

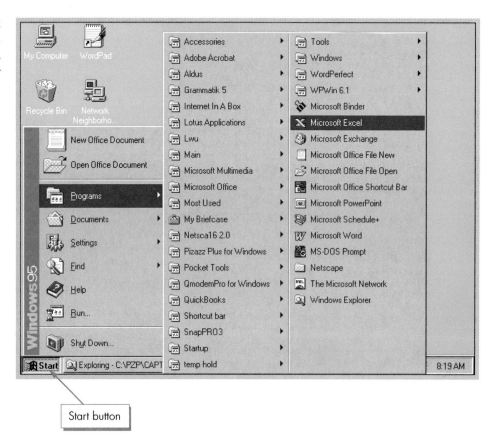

Start button

If you have experience with any other Windows 95 programs, you will feel right at home with the Excel window. It's similar in many respects to the Microsoft Word window, for example. Don't worry if you've never used a Windows 95 program—you'll soon become familiar with the way that the Excel window works.

FIGURE 1-3
The Excel window

Title bar   Menu bar   Standard toolbar

Name box

Column (letter) headings

Formula bar

Formatting toolbar

Worksheet

Worksheet tabs   Status bar   Scroll bars

Row (number) headings

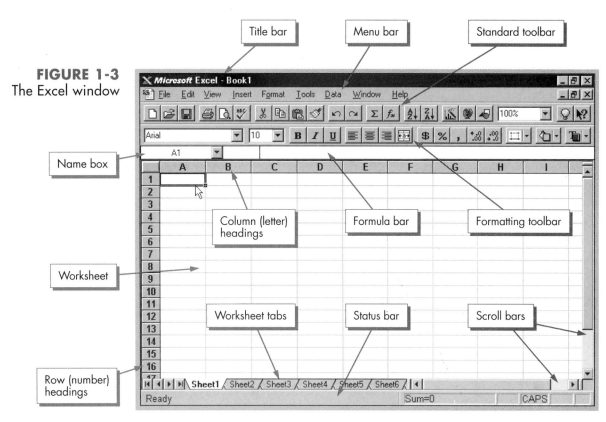

TABLE 1-1   **Parts of the Excel Window**

PART OF THE SCREEN	PURPOSE
Title bar	Contains the name of the workbook. The opening Excel window is always called "Book1."
Menu bar	Displays names of menus that you can use to perform various tasks. You can access menus with either the mouse or the keyboard.
Toolbars	Rows of buttons that allow instant access to a wide range of commands. Each button is represented by an icon and is accessed with the mouse. Excel opens with Standard and Formatting toolbars displayed.
Name box	Indicates the location where data being keyed or edited will appear on the worksheet.
Formula bar	Displays formulas used in the worksheet.
Worksheet	The area where you enter and work with data.
Column headings	Columns on the worksheet. Columns are labeled with letters.

continues

TABLE 1-1   Parts of the Excel Window *continued*

PART OF THE SCREEN	PURPOSE
Row headings	Rows on the worksheet. Rows are labeled with numbers.
Scroll bars	Used with the mouse to move right or left, and up or down, within the worksheet.
Worksheet tabs	Used to move from one worksheet to another.
Status bar	Displays information about the current task or the current status of the worksheet.

EXERCISE **1-2** **Identify Toolbar Buttons**

Some parts of the Excel window, such as toolbar buttons and menu items, can be identified by name when you point to them with the mouse. The status bar provides a more detailed description of the button or menu item.

1. Move the mouse pointer over the TipWizard button 💡 on the Standard toolbar. The button name will appear in a box under the button, and its description will be given in the status bar.

FIGURE 1-4
When you move the mouse pointer over a button, the button name appears.

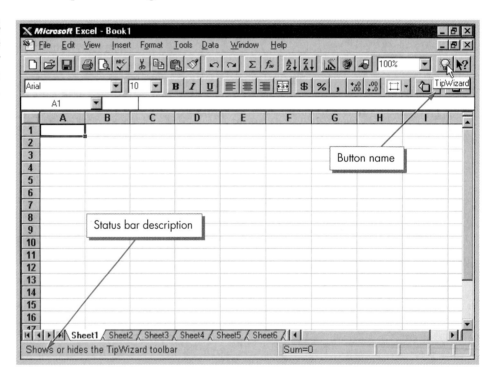

2. Click 💡 with the left mouse button to display the TipWizard box.

TIP: The TipWizard allows you to discover quicker, easier ways to work. When you display the TipWizard, it observes the way that you work and displays tips that can simplify and speed your tasks.

3. Click the button again to hide the TipWizard box.

4. Move the pointer over the New Workbook button 🗋 on the Standard toolbar, but don't click the mouse button. You'll click 🗋 when you want to open a new blank workbook.

5. Point to other toolbar buttons to identify them by name. As you point to each button, notice its description in the status bar.

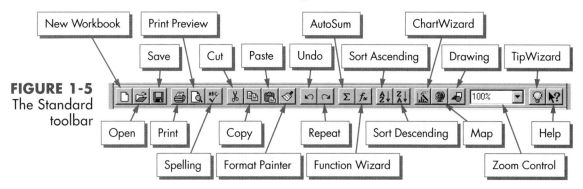

FIGURE 1-5
The Standard toolbar

EXERCISE 1-3 **Identify Menus and Menu Buttons**

1. Move the pointer to File on the menu bar. Click the left mouse button to open the menu. Notice that the status bar describes the File menu options.

FIGURE 1-6
When you point to a menu option, the status bar describes the option.

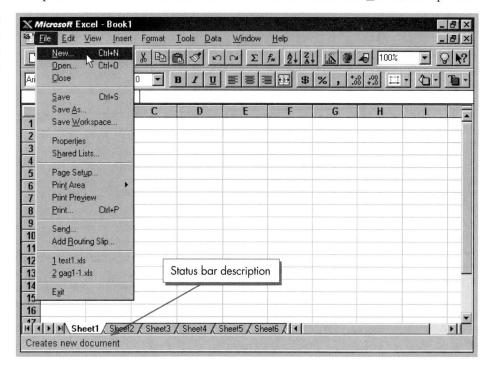

2. Without clicking the mouse button, move the pointer down to one of the File menu options. The option will be highlighted and the status bar will describe it.

3. With the menu open and without clicking the mouse button, move the pointer to Edit on the menu bar. This action opens the Edit menu, and the status bar describes the menu options.

4. Continue moving across the menu bar, observing each description in the status bar.

5. When you are finished, close the open menu by clicking the menu name.

Changing the Active Cell

When you start Excel, a blank *workbook* named "Book1" appears, ready for you to create a new worksheet. The workbook contains 16 *worksheets* that you can visualize as pages bound in a notebook. Worksheets can be added or removed from the workbook, and a workbook can contain from 1 to 255 worksheets.

Each worksheet contains a grid that defines a series of rows and columns. A worksheet can use as many as 16,384 rows and 256 columns to store data. As you've seen, rows are numbered while columns are labeled with letters. Columns start with columns A through Z, then AA through AZ, and so forth, up to column IV.

The intersection of a row and a column forms a box called a *cell*. Each cell in a worksheet has a unique *cell address* that is determined by the column and row in which it is located. A cell address always indicates the column letter first, then the row number (for example, A1, C25, or AF14).

The cell that is current—that is, ready to receive information—is called the *active cell*. The active cell has a heavy border, and its address is displayed in the Name box.

EXERCISE 1-4 Change the Active Cell

1. Press the Down Arrow key ↓ two times. Notice that the active cell changes.

2. Hold down the Ctrl key Ctrl and press the Home key Home. The cell A1 becomes active. You can tell it's active because a heavy border surrounds it. The Name box displays the location of the active cell.

NOTE: Whenever keyboard combinations (such as Ctrl + Delete) are indicated, you should hold down the first key without releasing it, and then press the second key. Release the second key, and then release the first key. An example of the entire sequence is: Hold down Ctrl, press Home, release Home, and then release Ctrl. With practice, you will find it quite natural to execute this sequence.

FIGURE 1-7
The Name box shows the address of the active cell.

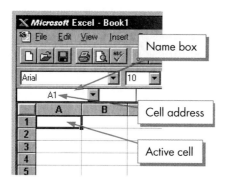

3. Press ⬇ three times, and then press the Right Arrow key ➡ five times. F4 is now the active cell.

Navigating Between Worksheets

You have two options for moving between the worksheets in a workbook:

- Use keyboard commands.
- Use worksheet tabs.

EXERCISE 1-5 **Navigate Between Worksheets Using Keyboard Commands**

1. Press Ctrl + PgDn. The next worksheet appears in the window. The worksheet tab for Sheet2 is highlighted. The active cell is A1.

FIGURE 1-8
The worksheet tab for worksheet 2 is highlighted.

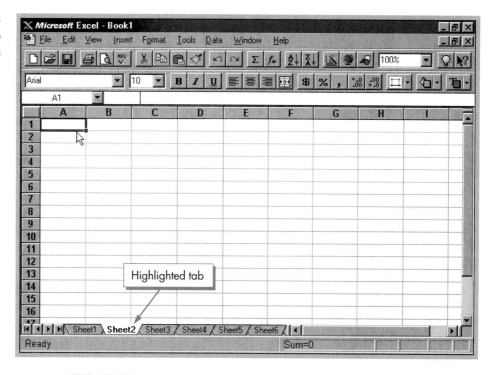

2. Press Ctrl + PgUp to return to Sheet1.

TABLE 1-2 **Keyboard Commands for Navigating Between Worksheets**

KEYSTROKE	ACTION
Ctrl + PgDn	Move to the next worksheet in the workbook
Ctrl + PgUp	Move to the previous worksheet in the workbook

EXERCISE **1-6** **Navigate Between Worksheets Using Worksheet Tabs**

You can use the worksheet tabs to move between worksheets even more quickly. Worksheet tabs also allow you to move to a specific worksheet in a workbook.

1. Click the worksheet tab for Sheet6. Worksheet 6 appears in the window.

2. Click the Right Tab scrolling button ▶ twice. The worksheet tab for Sheet8 appears, but is not highlighted. The tabs for worksheets 1 and 2 are no longer visible.

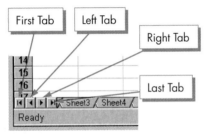

FIGURE 1-9
Tab scrolling
buttons

3. Click the worksheet tab for Sheet8. The tab for Sheet8 is now highlighted.

TIP: The tab scrolling buttons scroll only the worksheet tabs. To open a worksheet, you must click the worksheet tab.

4. Click the Last Tab scrolling button ▶. The tab for Sheet16, currently the last tab in the workbook, appears. Notice that none of the tabs appearing at the bottom of the worksheet is highlighted.

5. Click the Left Tab scrolling button ◀ until you can see the highlighted tab for Sheet8.

6. Click the First Tab scrolling button ◀. You can now see the tab for the first worksheet.

7. Click Sheet1 to return to worksheet 1.

Closing and Opening Workbooks

In the following exercises, you'll have a chance to look at a workbook containing a ten-year sales analysis for Alpha Pharmaceuticals. It gives you an opportunity to learn some basic Excel skills. The worksheet is fairly large, showing historical data for Alpha's four sales regions and each of its products: aspirin, acetaminophen, and ibuprofen.

To open an existing workbook that's stored on a hard disk or floppy disk, you can use one of two methods:

- Choose <u>O</u>pen from the <u>F</u>ile menu.
- Click the Open button on the Standard toolbar.

In the next exercise, you'll use the Open button.

EXERCISE **1-7** **Close and Open Workbooks**

Before you open Alpha's workbook, you will close "Book1," the workbook that you were just examining. Normally, you would also save the file, but since you didn't key any data in "Book 1," it isn't worth saving. (You'll learn how to save a file later in this lesson.)

1. Choose <u>C</u>lose from the <u>F</u>ile menu.

NOTE: If no workbook is open, the workbook window appears gray and the menu bar is reduced to two items, <u>F</u>ile and <u>H</u>elp. You could either open an existing workbook or start a new one.

2. Click on the Standard toolbar. The Open dialog box appears.

FIGURE 1-10
The Open
dialog box

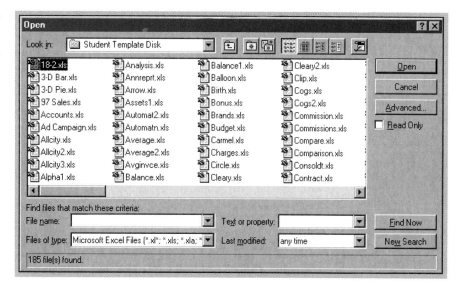

3. Double-click the file **Alpha1.xls** (you could also click it to select it and then click the <u>O</u>pen button). Excel opens the Alpha Pharmaceuticals worksheet.

NOTE: You may have to change the folder or the drive to locate the file. Follow your instructor's directions to find the disk drive and folder of the files that you will open in this lesson and in future lessons.

The Alpha Pharmaceuticals worksheet is formatted using shading, varying column widths, and several type sizes and number formats. These features are easy to use and will be discussed in later lessons.

Navigating Within a Worksheet

You can move to any location in the worksheet by pressing the Arrow keys, but using the scroll bar and keyboard commands allows you to move much more quickly to distant cells.

Notice that "Alpha Pharmaceuticals" appears in both the formula bar and the active cell. The cell address A1 appears in the Name box.

EXERCISE | **1-8** | **Navigate Within a Worksheet Using Keyboard Commands**

1. Press the Down Arrow key ⊡ four times. "National Sales Totals" appears in the formula bar, and the cell address A5 appears in the Name box.

2. Using ⊡ and the Right Arrow key ⊡, move to cell C8. A formula that adds data in cells C17, C25, C34, and C43 appears in the formula bar. The formula result, 4.78, appears in the active cell.

3. Press Home. The active cell moves to column A in the current row.

4. Press the PgDn key PgDn to move down one window. Rows 16 through 31 appear, and rows 1 through 15 disappear.

NOTE: The actual rows or columns that are visible will vary from monitor to monitor, depending on the monitor's size and settings.

5. Press the PgUp key PgUp to move up to the previous window. Rows 1 through 15 become visible again.

6. Press the Alt key Alt+PgDn to move one window to the right. Columns I through Q are displayed, and columns A through H are no longer visible.

7. Press Alt+PgUp. Columns A through H become visible again.

8. Press Ctrl+⊡ four times. Cell A17 is now the active cell. Each time Ctrl+⊡ is pressed, the active cell jumps to the edge of a group of cells containing data.

9. Press Ctrl + ↑ three times. Cell A11 is now active.

10. Press Ctrl + → once. The active cell jumps to cell K11, the last column in the table that starts at cell A5.

11. Press Ctrl + → again. Column IV, the very last column in the worksheet, is now displayed.

12. Press Ctrl + ↓. Row 16384, the last row in the worksheet, appears. Move up or across the worksheet to get an idea of its huge size.

13. Press Ctrl + Home. Pressing this key combination always brings you back to cell A1.

14. Press Ctrl + End. The active cell moves to the cell in the last row in the last column that contains data or formatting instructions.

FIGURE 1-11
Cell K67 is
now active.

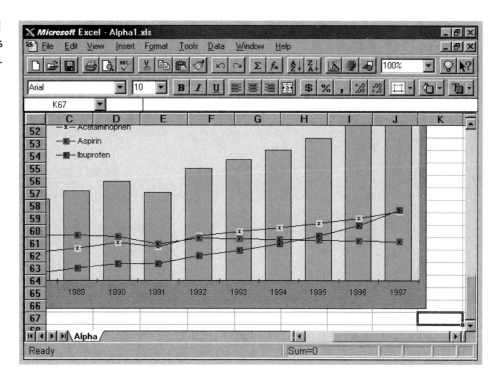

NOTE: A chart showing Alpha Pharmaceutical's sales figures appears at the bottom of the worksheet. The numbers contained in the worksheet are used to create the chart automatically. You'll learn more about using worksheets to generate charts in later lessons.

TABLE 1-3   Keyboard Commands for Navigating Within a Worksheet

KEYSTROKE	ACTION
Arrow keys	Move one cell in the direction of the arrow
Ctrl+Arrow keys	Move to the edge of a group of cells containing data
Home	Move to the beginning of row
Ctrl+Home	Move to the beginning of the worksheet (cell A1)
Ctrl+End	Move to the lower right corner of the worksheet
PgDn	Move down one window
PgUp	Move up one window
Alt+PgDn	Move right one window
Alt+PgUp	Move left one window
Ctrl+Backspace	Move to the active cell

EXERCISE | **1-9** | ## Navigate Within a Worksheet Using Scroll Bars

The scroll bars allow you to move through a worksheet using the mouse. When using the scroll bars, the active cell does not move. You must click a cell to make it active.

1. Press Ctrl+Home to move back to cell A1.

2. Click the down arrow on the scroll bar five times. The active window scrolls out of view. The cell in the top left corner of the worksheet is A6. See Figure 1-12 on the next page.

3. Click cell A6 to make it active. Remember that scrolling in a worksheet doesn't change the active cell. You must click a cell to make it active.

4. Click the up arrow on the scroll bar until you can see cell A1 again. Cell A6 will still be the active cell.

5. Click the right arrow on the horizontal scroll bar six times to move to the right in the worksheet.

6. Drag the scroll box back to the left arrow. Excel displays the column names that you pass over as you move to the left. Column A again becomes visible.

 TIP: To "drag" the scroll box, move the pointer to the box, press the mouse button, and, while holding the mouse button down, move the mouse.

FIGURE 1-12
Scroll bars

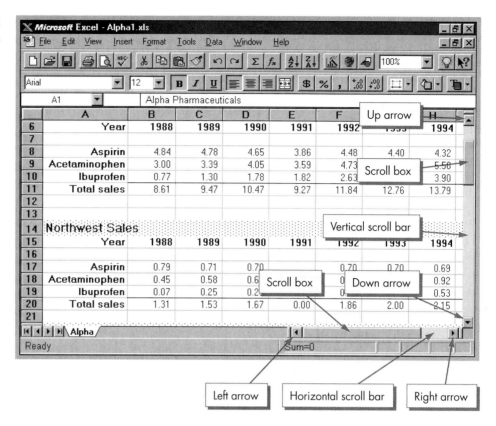

7. On the vertical scroll bar, click between the scroll box and the down arrow. Excel moves down the worksheet one window (13 or more rows, depending on the size of your monitor).

8. Click between the scroll box and the up arrow to move up one window in the worksheet.

9. During steps 4 through 8, cell A6 has remained the active cell. Change the active cell back to cell A1.

TABLE 1-4 | **Navigating with Scroll Bars**

ACTION	RESULT
Click up or down scroll arrow once	Scroll up or down one row
Click left or right scroll arrow once	Scroll left or right one column
Click between scroll arrow and scroll box	Scroll up, down, left, or right one window (at least 9 columns or 13 rows)
Drag scroll box	Scroll a variable amount, depending on the distance the scroll box is dragged

EXERCISE 1-10 Use the Go To Command

The Go To command, which is located on the Edit menu, allows you to move to a specific cell address quickly.

FIGURE 1-13
The Go To dialog box

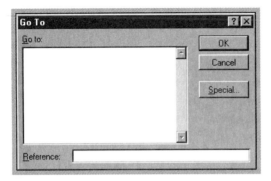

1. Choose Go To from the Edit menu. The Go To dialog box appears.

2. Key **J17** in the Reference text box, and click OK (or press Enter). The dialog box closes, and cell J17 becomes the active cell.

NOTE: Cell J17 displays the number 0.69, but the formula bar displays the number 0.6869. The two differ because the number format for this cell has been set for two decimal places. You'll learn about number formatting in Lesson 3.

3. Press F5. It is the shortcut key for the Go To command.
4. Key **BX94** and press Enter. The active cell moves to column BX, row 94.
5. Press Ctrl + Home to return to cell A1.

Keying Data in a Worksheet

In the following exercises you'll key data in the worksheet for Alpha Pharmaceuticals.

EXERCISE 1-11 Key Data in a Worksheet

1. Click cell E17 to make it active.
2. Key **0.7023**. Notice that the Cancel box, the Enter box, and the Function Wizard button appear in the formula bar, indicating that the formula bar is active.

 TIP: If you make a mistake while keying data, use the Backspace key Backspace to delete the error.

FIGURE 1-14
The formula bar becomes active when you key data.

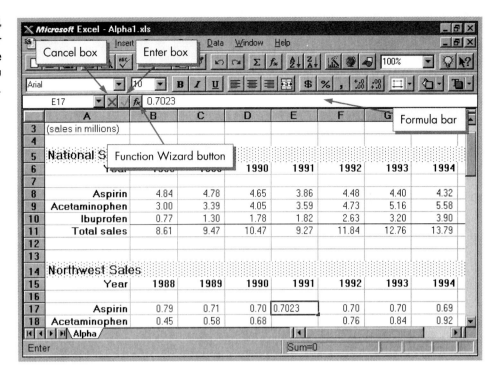

3. Press Enter. The numeric value 0.70 appears in cell E17, and cell E18 becomes active. Notice that the formula bar is no longer active because you haven't yet keyed data in this cell.

4. Key **0.7193** in cell E18, and press ↓. The value 0.72 appears in cell E18, and cell E19 becomes the active cell. You can complete a cell entry by pressing either Enter or an Arrow key. Notice the change in cell E20.

5. Key **3.941** in cell E19 and press Enter. Cell E20 reflects the new total.

EXERCISE 1-12 Change Data in a Worksheet

To change data in a worksheet, move to the cell that contains the incorrect data, key the correct data, and press either Enter or an Arrow key. The old data are replaced automatically.

1. Press ↑ to move to cell E19.

2. Key **0.3941** and press Enter. The new total is 1.82.

3. Press Ctrl + Home to move to cell A1.

Saving a Workbook

In Excel, workbooks are saved as files. When you create a new workbook or make changes to an existing one, you must save the workbook to make your changes permanent. Until your changes are saved, they can be lost if a power failure or a hardware problem occurs.

The first step in saving a workbook for future use is to give it a *filename*. In Windows 95, filenames can be up to 255 characters and generally end with a period and a three-character extension. Filename extensions are used to distinguish between different types of files. For example, Excel workbooks carry the extension .xls and Word documents have the extension .doc.

Throughout the exercises in this book, filenames consist of three parts:

- *[Your initials],* which may be your initials or the identifier your instructor asks you to use, such as **rst**
- The number of the exercise, such as **4-1**
- The **.xls** extension that Excel uses automatically for workbooks
- An example of a filename would be: **rst4-1.xls**

Before saving a new workbook, you should decide where it should be saved. Excel will save a workbook in the current drive and folder, unless you specify otherwise. For example, to save a workbook to a floppy disk, you need to change the drive to either a: or b:, whichever is appropriate for your computer.

 NOTE: Your instructor will advise you on the proper drive and folder for this course.

 When working with an existing file, such as the current file **Alpha1.xls**, choosing the <u>S</u>ave command (or clicking the Save button 🔲 on the Standard toolbar) replaces the file on the disk with the one on which you are working. After the workbook is saved, the old version of the file no longer exists, and the new version contains all of the changes that you made.

When you give an existing workbook a new name using the Save <u>A</u>s command, the original workbook remains on the disk unchanged, and a second workbook is saved as well.

EXERCISE `1-13` **Name and Save a Workbook**

1. Click <u>F</u>ile to open the <u>F</u>ile menu and then choose Save <u>A</u>s. The Save As dialog box appears with the filename **Alpha1.xls** given in the File Name text box.

FIGURE 1-15
The Save As
dialog box

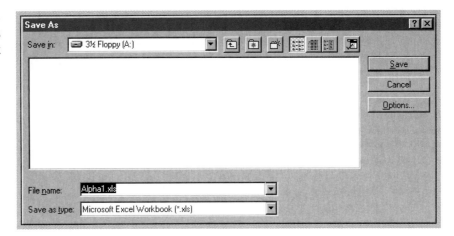

2. In the File name text box, key *[your initials]***1-13.** (You don't have to key the .xls extension. Excel will apply the extension automatically. However, we will show the .xls extension for Excel filenames in the future.)

NOTE: When naming files you can use any combination of uppercase and lowercase letters. Filenames can be up to 255 characters long and can include spaces. For example, a file might be named "Alpha Business Plan.xls."

3. If necessary, change the drive to your data disk by clicking the down arrow in the Save in drop-down list and choosing the appropriate drive. Make sure a formatted disk is inserted in the drive.

4. Click Save, and your workbook is saved and named for future use.

Printing a Worksheet and Closing Excel

Once you have created a worksheet, it's easy to print it. You can use any of these methods:

- Click the Print button 🖨 on the Standard toolbar.
- Choose Print from the File menu.
- Press Ctrl + P.

The menu and keyboard methods open the Print dialog box, which lets you choose different printing options. Pressing 🖨 sends the worksheet directly to the printer using Excel's default settings.

EXERCISE 1-14 **Print a Worksheet**

1. Choose Print from the File menu to open the Print dialog box.

FIGURE 1-16
Print dialog box

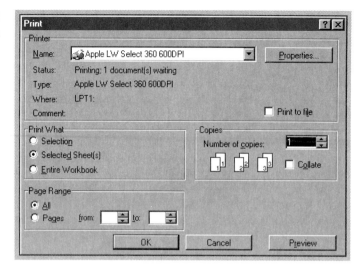

2. The dialog box displays Excel's default settings and shows your designated printer. Click OK or press [Enter] to accept the settings. A printer icon will appear on the taskbar as the workbook is sent to the printer.

 TIP: To print all of the worksheets in the workbook, click the Entire Workbook option in the Print dialog box.

EXERCISE **1-15** **Close a Workbook and Exit Excel**

After you finish working with a workbook and save it, you can close it and open another workbook, or you can exit the program.

There are four ways to close a workbook or to exit Excel:

● Use the File menu. You've already learned how to close a workbook using Close. To exit Excel, choose Exit.

● Use the Close button ⊠ found in the upper right corner of the window.

FIGURE 1-17
Close buttons

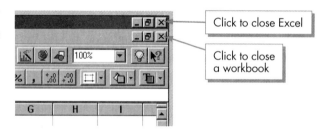

● Use the Control icons, which are located in the upper left corner of the window. Click the Control icon once to view the Control menu. Double-click the appropriate Control icon to close Excel or the current workbook.

FIGURE 1-18
Control menu

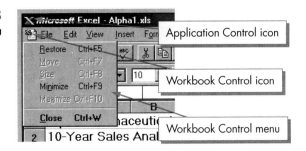

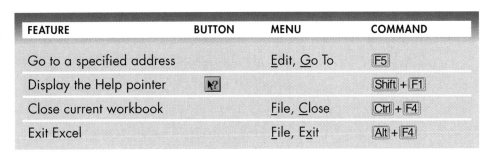

- Use keyboard shortcuts. Ctrl + W closes a workbook and Alt + F4 exits Excel.

1. Double-click the Workbook Control icon to close the workbook.

2. Click the Close button ☒ found in the upper right corner of the window to close Excel and display the Windows desktop.

COMMAND SUMMARY

FEATURE	BUTTON	MENU	COMMAND
Go to a specified address		Edit, Go To	F5
Display the Help pointer	▶?		Shift + F1
Close current workbook		File, Close	Ctrl + F4
Exit Excel		File, Exit	Alt + F4

USING HELP

Excel provides complete on-line Help. You can use it to explain a feature, define a term, or learn about a command or screen element. You'll learn more about Help in future lessons.

This lesson introduced one Help feature: ToolTips. For example, when you move the mouse pointer over a button, Excel displays a ToolTip that identifies the button name. The status bar also describes the button feature.

To identify other parts of the screen, try displaying ScreenTips:

1. Start Excel and click the Help button ▶?. The mouse pointer will appear with a question mark ▶?.

2. Point to a screen area, such as the status bar, and then click. You may also choose a menu item by clicking File, and then clicking Save As. A ScreenTip will appear to describe the screen area or menu item.

3. Click the ScreenTip to close it.

Concept Review

TRUE/FALSE QUESTIONS

Each of the following questions is either true or false. Indicate your choice by circling either **T** or **F**.

T F **1.** There is only one way to start Excel.

T F **2.** The formula bar indicates the location of data being keyed in the active cell.

T F **3.** A workbook can contain up to 255 worksheets.

T F **4.** PgDn moves the screen down one page.

T F **5.** Columns are numbered, while rows are labeled with letters.

T F **6.** The address of the active cell is displayed in the Name box.

T F **7.** Scrolling with the scroll bar doesn't change the active cell.

T F **8.** Moving to a cell using the Go To dialog box doesn't change the active cell.

SHORT ANSWER QUESTIONS

Write the correct answer in the space provided.

1. What is the name of the area on the screen that displays messages that guide you through the menu commands?

_____

2. What is the name of the box formed by the intersection of a row and a column?

_____

3. What is the name of the area within a worksheet that is current, or ready to receive information?

_____

4. Which keyboard command moves you to the beginning of a row?

_____

5. Which keyboard command moves to the beginning of a worksheet?

_____

6. What command allows you to move to a specific cell address quickly?

_____

7. What information appears in the formula bar when you begin to key data?

_____

8. Which filename extension is used for Excel workbooks?

_____

CRITICAL THINKING

Answer these questions on a separate piece of paper. There are no right or wrong answers. Support your answer with examples from your own experience, if possible.

1. What advantages would a spreadsheet program like Excel offer for a business compared with a noncomputerized pen and paper spreadsheet? What advantages for an individual?

2. Excel typically provides three ways to perform a task. You can use menu options, buttons, or keyboard commands. What advantages does each method offer? What disadvantages? Which method do you typically prefer? Why?

3. Excel allows for great flexibility when naming files. Many businesses and individuals establish their own rules for naming files. What kinds of rules would you recommend for naming files in a business? For personal use?

Skills Review

EXERCISE 1-16

Start Excel, change the active cell, navigate between worksheets, and then close the workbook without saving it.

1. Start Excel, if necessary, by following these steps:

   a. Click the Start button 🔳Start on the Windows taskbar.

   b. Point to Programs, and then point to Microsoft Excel (you may need to point first to the program group that contains Microsoft Excel) and click it.

2. Use the Arrow keys to change the active cell to AB15 by following these steps:

   a. Press the Down Arrow key ⬇ until the active cell is A15.

   b. Press the Right Arrow key ➡ until the active cell is AB15.

3. Change to worksheet 3 by pressing [Ctrl]+[PgDn] twice.

4. Make D5 the active cell.

5. Use the tab scrolling buttons to move to worksheet 8 by following these steps:

    a. Click the Right Tab scrolling button ▶ until worksheet 8 appears.

    b. Click the worksheet tab for Sheet8.

6. Use the First Tab scrolling button ◀ to return to worksheet 1.

7. Close the workbook by choosing Close from the File menu. (You won't save this workbook.)

EXERCISE 1-17

Open a file, and then use keyboard commands to navigate within the worksheet.

1. Open the file **Alpha2.xls** by following these steps:

    a. Click 🗁 on the Standard toolbar.

    b. Double-click the file **Alpha2.xls**.

2. Use [↓] and [→] to move to cell L19.

3. Return to cell A1 by pressing [Ctrl]+[Home].

4. Press the PgDn key [PgDn] three times to move down three windows.

5. Press the PgUp key [PgUp] twice to move up two windows.

6. Press [Alt]+[PgDn] four times to move four windows to the right.

7. Press [Alt]+[PgUp] once to move one window to the left. Cell T15 is now active.

8. Press [Ctrl]+[→] to move to the last column in this group of cells.

9. Press [Ctrl]+[↓] to move to the last row in this group of cells.

10. Press [Ctrl]+[End] to move to the cell in the last row in the last cell that contains data or formatting instructions.

11. Press [Ctrl]+[↑]. The active cell jumps to the edge of the previous group of cells containing data.

12. Press [Ctrl]+[↑] two more times. AD6. becomes the active cell.

13. Return to cell A1.

14. Close the workbook without saving it.

EXERCISE 1-18

Open a file, use the scroll bars and the Go To Command to navigate within the worksheet, key data, and then save and close the worksheet.

1. Open the file **Alpha1.xls**.

2. Make cell A1 active (if it isn't already).

LESSON 1 ■ WHAT IS EXCEL?

3. Click the down arrow on the vertical scroll bar seven times to scroll down seven rows.

4. Click the right arrow on the horizontal scroll bar eight times to scroll eight columns to the right.

5. Drag the scroll box on the horizontal scroll bar to the left so that the first column becomes visible again.

6. On the vertical scroll bar, click between the scroll box and the down arrow to move down one window.

7. Use the Go To command by performing the following steps:

   a. Choose Go To from the Edit menu.

   b. Key **E17** in the Reference text box and click OK.

8. Key **0.59** and press Enter.

9. Key **0.55** in cell E18, press ↓, key **0.78** in cell E19, and press Enter.

10. Save the file by following these steps:

   a. Choose Save As from the File menu.

   b. In the File name text box, key *[your initials]***1-18.xls**

   c. If necessary, change the drive to your data disk by clicking the down arrow in the Save in drop-down list and choosing the appropriate drive.

   d. Click Save.

11. Print your workbook by following these steps:

   a. Choose Print from the File menu.

   b. Click OK.

12. Close the workbook and close Excel by following these steps:

   a. Double-click the Workbook Control icon at the left side of the menu bar to close the workbook.

   b. Click the Close button ☒ in the upper right corner of the window to close Excel.

EXERCISE 1-19

Start Excel, open an existing file, change data, and then print and save the workbook.

1. Start Excel.

2. Open the file **Alpha3.xls**.

3. Change the data as shown in Figure 1-19 (on the next page). To change data in a cell, perform the following steps:

   a. Make the cell containing data you wish to change active.

   b. Key the new data.

   c. Move to another cell or press Enter.

FIGURE 1-19

Salesperson	Qtr 1	Qtr 2	Qtr 3	Qtr 4	Total	% of Total
Robert Johnson	65.3	62.7	58.6	52.9		
Ewald Rhiner	61.0	65.5	70.1	75.3	271.9	10.0%
~~Ruth Seuratadot~~	~~81.7~~	~~60.7~~	~~54.0~~	~~47.3~~	243.7	9.0%
Buster Manatee	50.8	56.1	57.5	58.5	222.9	8.2%
Jose Garcia	75.2	77.9	72.4	73.8	299.3	11.0%
Colleen Masterhouse	65.3	70.9	54.6	74.5	265.3	9.8%
Anthony Chen	88.5	74.6	66.4	68.9	298.4	11.0%
Elouise Swift	66.7	73.9	64.7	69.9	275.2	10.1%
~~Lloyd Polaski~~	~~87.5~~	~~42.3~~	~~57.6~~	~~50.3~~	237.7	8.7%
Murray Diamond	61.0	65.8	74.6	74.2	275.6	10.1%
Barbara Bloomberg	70.0	87.7	82.3	90.2	330.2	12.1%
Richard Daniels	53.1	51.1	56.7	72.8		

These will change automatically

4. Save the workbook as *[your initials]***1-19.xls** on your data disk.

5. Click the Print button 🖨 on the Standard toolbar to print the workbook.

6. Close the workbook, and then exit Excel.

Lesson Assignments

EXERCISE 1-20

Start Excel, open an existing file, change the active cell, enter data, use the Save <u>A</u>s command, print the workbook, and then close the workbook and exit Excel.

1. Start Excel.

2. Open the file **Alpha1.xls.**

3. Make cell B17 active.

4. Change the data in cell B17 to 0.6314.

5. Change the data in cell B18 to 0.5563.

6. Add the following data for "Northwest Sales" in 1991:

   Aspirin   **0.7233**

   Acetaminophen   **0.7036**

   Ibuprofen   **0.3179**

7. Save the workbook as *[your initials]***1-20.xls** on your data disk.

8. Print the workbook.

9. Close the workbook, and then exit Excel.

EXERCISE 1-21

Open a file, change data, save the workbook, and then print and close it.

1. Open Excel. Open the file **Alpha4.xls.**

2. Use the Go To command. Move to the following cells and change the data as shown:

Cell	Change Data to:
K10	**6.8431**
D18	**0.6219**
J19	**0.6891**
B25	**1.0618**
K27	**2.0662**
G34	**1.4817**
C36	**0.3993**
K43	**1.4216**
D45	**0.5225**

35

3. Save the workbook as *[your initials]***1-21.xls** on your data disk.

4. Print the workbook.

5. Close the workbook.

EXERCISE 1-22

Open a file, navigate in the spreadsheet, enter data, then save, print, and close the workbook.

1. Open the file **Alpha2.xls**.

2. Verify that no data appear below line 20 or beyond column AE.

3. Go to cell F19, the "National Sales Total." Make a written note of the number in cell for future reference.

4. Make I10 the active cell.

5. Key the following data in cells I10, J10, and K10:

   0.074

   0.071

   0.036

6. Make AA7 the active cell.

7. Key the following data in cells AA7, AB7, and AC7:

   0.135

   0.097

   0.037

8. Return to cell F19. Compare the new value to the figure you wrote down in step 3.

9. Save the workbook as *[your initials]***1-22.xls** on your data disk.

10. Print and close the workbook.

EXERCISE 1-23

Open a file, navigate in the spreadsheet, enter data, then save, print, and close the workbook.

Because the sales volume in Alpha Pharmaceuticals' Northwest region is significantly lower than that in the other regions, the company's president has requested detailed figures for each salesperson. Complete the workbook containing by entering the second- and fourth-quarter numbers shown in Figure 1-20 (on the next page).

FIGURE 1-20

Salesperson	Qtr 2	Qtr 4
Ewald Rhiner	66.4	54.6
Ruth Seuratadot	82.2	86.0
Buster Manatee	73.8	74.1
Jose Garcia	50.3	81.6
Colleen Masterhouse	57.7	74.6
Anthony Chen	81.2	69.7
Elouise Swift	45.9	60.7
Lloyd Polaski	71.0	67.0
Murray Diamond	65.3	70.6
Barbara Bloomberg	79.8	52.4

1. Open the file **Alpha5.xls**.

2. Move to cell C8, and key **66.4** (Ewald Rhiner's second-quarter sales).

3. Press Enter to enter the data and move down one cell.

 TIP: When entering data in more than one column, it's usually easier to press Enter and move down the column than to use the arrow keys to move across a row, especially if you are moving more than one cell.

4. Continue keying the second-quarter data. When you finish entering it, enter all of the fourth-quarter data.

5. When you have finished entering the data, verify that the total figure in cell F19 is 2726.87. If it isn't, check the figures that you keyed, and correct them where necessary.

6. Save the workbook as *[your initials]***1-23.xls** on your data disk.

7. Print and close the workbook.

EXERCISE 1-24

Open a file, key data in four worksheets within one workbook, and then save, print, and close the workbook.

Alpha Pharmaceutical's sales force of is broken down into four regions. The annual sales for the company is shown in a workbook that consists of four worksheets—one worksheet for each region. Some adjustments need to be made in the Annual Sales figures for each region.

1. Open the file **Alpha6.xls**.

2. Add the following data for "May" to Sheet2:

Aspirin	**0.074**
Acetaminophen	**0.070**
Ibuprofen	**0.042**

3. Add the following data for "February" to Sheet3:

Aspirin	**0.126**
Acetaminophen	**0.080**
Ibuprofen	**0.030**

4. Change the amounts for "Ibuprofen" on Sheet4 as shown below:

October	**0.201**
November	**0.210**
December	**0.212**

5. Change the amounts for "September" on Sheet1 as shown below:

Aspirin	**0.132**
Acetaminophen	**0.202**
Ibuprofen	**0.207**

6. Save the workbook as *[your initials]***1-24.xls** on your data disk.

7. Print and close the workbook, and then close Excel.

 TIP: To print all of the worksheets in a workbook, you must click <u>E</u>ntire Workbook in the Print dialog box.

Creating a Simple Worksheet

LESSON

2

OBJECTIVES

After completing this lesson, you will be able to:

1. Enter and edit data in a worksheet.
2. Use Pick from list and AutoComplete to enter labels.
3. Enter data in selected cells.
4. Construct basic formulas.
5. Use the SUM function.
6. Use AutoCalculate.

 Estimated Time: 1½ hours

In Lesson 1, you opened an existing worksheet, examined its contents, and keyed some data. In this lesson, you will create a simple worksheet containing text, numerical values, and formulas from scratch.

Entering Labels and Values in a Worksheet

Excel recognizes text and numbers automatically, and formats them differently. For example:

- An entry that begins with a number or mathematical sign is immediately recognized as a value. Values are aligned at the right margin of the cell by default and are included in calculations.

- An entry that begins with a letter is recognized automatically as a *label*. Labels are aligned at the left of the cell and are excluded from calculations. You can format a number as a label if you begin the entry with an apostrophe ('). The number will then be excluded from calculations.

When you key data, the information appears in both the formula bar and the active cell. Before you complete the entry, you can use the Backspace key `Backspace` to edit the text or the Escape key `Esc` to start over. To complete the entry, you can use one of several mouse or keyboard methods.

TABLE 2-1 Methods for Completing an Entry

ACTION	RESULT
Click another cell	Completes the entry and makes the selected cell active.
Click ☑	Completes the entry. The current cell remains active.
Press `Enter`	Completes the entry and the cell below becomes active.
Press `Tab`	Completes the entry and the cell to the right becomes active.
Press an Arrow key	Completes the entry and the cell above, below, to the right, or to the left becomes active.

EXERCISE **2-1** **Enter Labels and Values in a Worksheet**

1. Start Excel. The workbook Book1 appears, and cell A1 on Sheet1 becomes the active cell.

2. Key **Sales Analysis** in cell A1. (Do not press the Enter key `Enter` yet.) Notice that the status bar indicates that you are in Enter mode. The text appears in both the formula bar and the active cell. Notice also that the Enter box, Cancel box, and Function Wizard button appear on the formula bar in Enter mode. (See Figure 2-1 on the next page.)

3. To delete three of the characters that you entered, press the Backspace key `Backspace` three times.

4. Key **sis** to complete the word "Analysis," and then click the Enter box ☑ in the formula bar. A1 remains the active cell. Notice that the mode returns to *Ready* upon completion of the entry. The text appears in cell A1 and overlaps cell B1.

5. Key **Alpha Pharmaceuticals** and press `Enter`. The new text replaces "Sales Analysis" in cell A1, and cell A2 becomes the active cell. You can change the contents of the active cell by keying a new label or value.

6. In cell A2, key **Regional Sales** and press `Enter` to complete the cell entry. Cell A3 becomes the active cell. Whenever you press `Enter`, the active cell moves down one row.

7. In cell A3, key **Sales in $ millions** and press `Enter`.

8. Press `↑`, and then key **1994**. Do not press `Enter`. Cell A3 now contains "1994," but it should contain "Sales in $ millions."

FIGURE 2-1
Text appears in the formula bar in Enter mode.

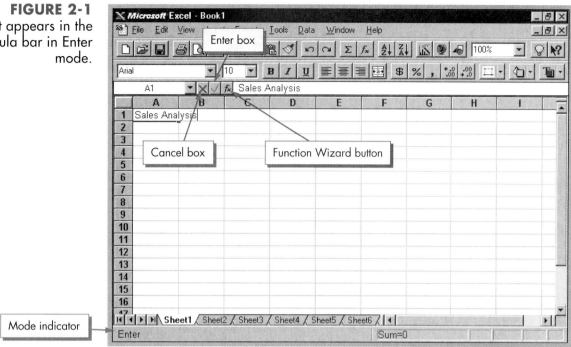

Mode indicator

9. Press the Escape key Esc. The original cell contents is restored.

 TIP: If you overwrite a cell by mistake, do not press Enter. Press Esc or click the Cancel box ✕ on the formula bar to restore the cell's previous contents.

10. Move to cell B7. Key **1994** and press the Tab key Tab. "1994" appears as a right-aligned value and cell C7 becomes the active cell. Pressing Tab activates the cell to the right.

11. Key the text as shown in Figure 2-2.

FIGURE 2-2
The Alpha Pharmaceuticals worksheet layout

	A	B	C	D	E	F	G	H	I
1	Alpha Pharmaceuticals								
2	Regional Sales								
3	Sales in $ millions								
4									
5									
6						Projected	5-year	5-year	
7		1994	1995	1996	1997	1998	Total	% Change	
8	Northeast								
9	Aspirin								
10	Acetaminophen								
11	Ibuprofen								
12	Total								
13									
14									
15									
16									

12. Widen column A to accommodate the column entry "Acetaminophen." To do this, click anywhere in column A, and then choose <u>C</u>olumn from the F<u>o</u>rmat menu. Key **13** in the text box and then click OK. Now 13 characters can fit in the column.

13. Save the workbook as *[your initials]***2-1.xls.**

 NOTE: The text at the top of the worksheet is intended to serve as the worksheet title. Typically, this text is entered in column A and then aligned across the entire worksheet. Aligning text and changing column width is explained in more detail in Lesson 8: "Formatting Text and Numbers."

EXERCISE 2-2 Clear the Contents of a Cell

When you key incorrect data into a cell, you may clear the cell's contents. Simply make the cell active and then press the Delete key Delete. Another way to clear a cell is to use the Cle<u>a</u>r option on the <u>E</u>dit menu, and then choose <u>C</u>ontents.

1. In the current workbook, move to cell A8, which contains "Northeast."

2. Choose Cle<u>a</u>r from the <u>E</u>dit menu. A cascading menu appears.

FIGURE 2-3
<u>E</u>dit menu, Cle<u>a</u>r cascading menu

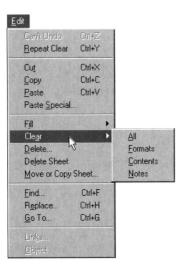

3. Choose <u>C</u>ontents to clear cell A8.

4. Key **Southeast** in cell A8, and then press Enter.

5. Press ↑ to reactivate cell A8, and then press Delete to clear the cell.

6. Key **Northeast** in cell A8, and then press Enter.

 NOTE: The Cle<u>a</u>r cascading menu also allows you to clear formats and notes. Formats, such as bold or italic, are discussed in Lesson 3: "Enhancing a Simple Worksheet." Notes, which explain cell contents and appear as hidden text, are used in Lesson 11: "Advanced Formulas."

EXERCISE 2-3 Edit the Contents of a Cell

If a cell contains a long or complicated entry, you might want to edit the contents rather than rekey the entire entry.

To change to Edit mode you may:

- Double-click the cell.
- Click the cell if it is not active, and then click the formula bar.

1. Double-click cell A3. You are now in Edit mode, as indicated on the status bar. Notice that the pointer changes from a white cross to an I-beam, and the insertion point (the flashing vertical bar) can be positioned to edit text.

2. Click the I-beam between "in" and "$" to position the insertion point.

3. Press ← and → several times. The insertion point moves to the left or right, one character at a time.

4. Press Home. The insertion point moves to the left of "Sales." In Edit mode, keys such as Home and End operate within the cell, rather than within the entire worksheet, as they do in Ready mode.

5. Press Delete nine times to delete "Sales in."

6. Key **(** (open parenthesis), and press End to move to the right of the text.

7. Key **)** (close parenthesis), and press Enter to complete the entry and exit Edit mode. Cell A3 now contains "($ millions)."

TABLE 2-2   Keystrokes in Edit Mode

KEYSTROKE	RESULT
Enter	Completes the entry and returns to Ready mode.
Esc	Restores the previous cell contents and returns to Ready mode.
← or →	Moves the insertion point left or right by one character.
Home	Moves to the beginning of the cell contents.
End	Moves to the end of the cell contents.
Delete	Deletes one character to the right of the insertion point.
Ctrl + Delete	Deletes text to the end of the line.
Backspace	Deletes one character to the left of the insertion point, or deletes selected text.
Ctrl + ← or Ctrl + →	Moves left or right by one word.

Use Pick from list and AutoComplete

Labels for rows are usually keyed in a single column, and often are repeated. For instance, if your worksheet shows sales for three products in four regions, the product names will appear four times, once in each region.

Excel provides two features that make it easier to enter labels:

- Pick from list
- AutoComplete

Both features use information that you have already entered in consecutive cells of a column.

EXERCISE **2-4** **Use the Pick from list and AutoComplete Features**

FIGURE 2-4
Shortcut menu

FIGURE 2-5
Using the Pick from list feature

FIGURE 2-6
AutoComplete suggests an item from the Pick from list.

1. In cell A13, key **Southeast** and press Enter.

2. Right-click cell A14 (position the mouse pointer in cell A14 and click the right button). The shortcut menu appears.

3. Choose Pick from list from the shortcut menu. The list contains the labels that you already keyed in consecutive cells A8 through A13.

4. Click "Aspirin" in the list. Excel automatically inserts this row label in cell A14.

5. Right-click cell A15, choose Pick from list, and click "Acetaminophen" from the list. Excel inserts this label in the active cell.

6. Move to cell A16 and key **I**. The AutoComplete feature highlights "buprofen" as a choice to complete the entry. AutoComplete chooses an item from the Pick from list when you key the first letters of that item. Because "Ibuprofen" is the only item that begins with an "I," you needed to key only one letter in this case.

7. Press Enter to accept "Ibuprofen."

8. Key **As** in cell A17, but do not press Enter. AutoComplete suggests "Aspirin."

9. Press Esc to start over, and key **T**. AutoComplete suggests "Total." Press Enter to complete the entry.

10. Complete the labels in column A as shown in Figure 2-7 on the next page. Key text for the new entries. Use AutoComplete or the Pick from list feature to insert items that you have already keyed.

FIGURE 2-7

	A
18	Northwest
19	Aspirin
20	Acetaminophen
21	Ibuprofen
22	Total
23	Southwest
24	Aspirin
25	Acetaminophen
26	Ibuprofen
27	Total
28	Grand Total

Enter Data in Selected Cells

In many cases, you may find it convenient to work with a group of selected cells. You can select groups of cells as either blocks or ranges. A *block* is a group of cells that are next to one another. A *range* is any group of selected cells.

Excel provides three methods of selecting cells:

● Using the keyboard
● Using the mouse
● Using the Name box

EXERCISE 2-5 **Select a Block of Cells Using the Keyboard**

When you make a cell active, you have actually selected it. To extend the selection using the keyboard, press Shift in combination with the navigation keys.

1. Make cell B9 active.

2. Hold down [Shift], press [→] three times, and release [Shift]. A dark border surrounds the selected cells, B9 through E9. The first cell in the selection, B9, which is also the active cell, appears white. Cells C9 through E9 are highlighted.

3. Press [↓] twice. The selected block now extends from B9 through E11.

FIGURE 2-8
Selected block of
cells

	A	B	C	D	E	F
5						
6	Active cell				Selected cells	
7		1994	1995	1996	1997	1998
8	Northeast					
9	Aspirin					
10	Acetaminophen					
11	Ibuprofen					
12	Total					

4. Key **1.112** and press [Enter]. The value appears in cell B9, and B10 becomes active.

5. Key **1.465** and press [Enter]. The value appears in cell B10, and B11 becomes active.

6. Key **1.085** and press [Enter]. The value appears in cell B11. The next cell in the block, C9, becomes active.

NOTE: Entering data in selected cells can be a very efficient technique, as [Enter] or [Tab] moves only within the selection.

7. Key the remaining data for the selected block as shown in Figure 2-9.

FIGURE 2-9

	A	B	C	D	E
9	Aspirin	1.112	1.082	1.053	1.024
10	Acetaminophen	1.465	1.592	1.73	1.94
11	Ibuprofen	1.085	1.36	1.704	2.225

8. Press [↓]. The block is deselected.

9. Select cell F11 (make it active), hold down [Shift], and press [Home]. The selection extends from F11 through A11.

10. Press [Shift]+[Ctrl]+[Home]. The selection extends from F11 through A1.

11. Press [Shift]+[↓]. The selection shrinks by one row.

12. Press any arrow key to deselect the block.

TABLE 2-3   **Navigation Key Combinations**

SELECTION KEY COMBINATION	ACTION
Shift+Arrow key	Extend the selection one cell in the direction indicated by the Arrow key.
Shift+PgUp or Shift+PgDn	Extend the selection one window up or down.
Shift+Ctrl+Home	Extend the selection to the beginning of the worksheet.
Shift+Home	Extend the selection to the beginning of the row.
Shift+Ctrl+End	Extend the selection to the end of the data in the worksheet.
Shift+Ctrl+Arrow key	Extend the selection to the edge of a block of data in the direction indicated by the Arrow key.
Ctrl+Spacebar	Select an entire column.
Shift+Spacebar	Select an entire row.
Ctrl+A or Ctrl+Shift+Spacebar	Select an entire worksheet.

EXERCISE   **2-6**   **Select Cells Using the Mouse**

Excel provides several ways to select cells using the mouse:

- Click a column heading letter to select an entire column, or click a row heading number to select an entire row.
- Click the Select All button to select the entire worksheet.
- Drag across adjacent cells to select a block.
- Hold down Shift and click a cell to select a block beginning with the active cell and ending at the new location.
- Add a non-adjacent block of cells to a selection by holding down Ctrl and dragging across the additional cells.

FIGURE 2-10
Selecting a column

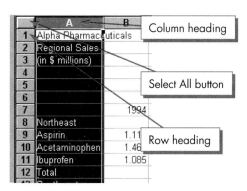

1. Click cell B14, hold down the mouse button, and then drag the pointer diagonally to cell E16.

2. Release the mouse button. Cells B14 through E16 are selected and B14 becomes the active cell.

3. Click any cell to deselect the block.

4. Click column heading A to select the entire column.

5. Click anywhere in the worksheet to deselect the column. Click row heading 1 to select the entire row.

6. Click the Select All button (left of column heading A), to select the entire worksheet.

7. Click cell B7 (containing "1994"), hold down [Shift], and then click cell E7. Cells B7 through E7 are selected.

8. Press [Delete] to clear the cells. The block is still selected, and B7 becomes the active cell.

9. Rekey **1994**, **1995**, **1996**, and **1997** in cells B7, C7, D7, and E7, respectively, pressing [Tab] between each entry.

 TIP: [Tab] moves the active cell to the right. [Shift]+[Tab] moves the active cell to the left.

10. Press [↓] once to deselect the block of cells.

11. Drag from cell B14 to E16 to select this block.

12. Click the down arrow in the vertical scroll bar to display row 28 of the worksheet. Hold down [Ctrl] and drag from B19 to E21. A second block is added to the range.

13. Hold down [Ctrl] and drag from B24 to E26. A third block is added to the range.

14. Hold down [Ctrl] and click B14 to make it the active cell.

FIGURE 2-11
Selected range of non-adjacent blocks

	A	B	C	D	E	F	G	H	I
	B14								
13	Southeast								
14	Aspirin								
15	Acetaminophen								
16	Ibuprofen								
17	Total								
18	Northwest								
19	Aspirin								
20	Acetaminophen								
21	Ibuprofen								
22	Total								
23	Southwest								
24	Aspirin								
25	Acetaminophen								
26	Ibuprofen								
27	Total								
28	Grand Total								

Sheet1 / Sheet2 / Sheet3 / Sheet4 / Sheet5 / Sheet6 /

15. Key **1** and press [Enter]. C15 becomes the active cell.

16. Press [Enter] repeatedly to move through the range. Notice that the active cell moves from the end of one block to the beginning of the next block, and from the end of the range to the beginning of the range.

 TIP: [Enter] moves the active cell down. [Shift]+[Enter] moves the active cell up.

17. Press [Delete] to clear the range contents.

18. Click anywhere in the worksheet to deselect the range.

EXERCISE 2-7 **Select Cells Using the Name Box**

You can select a range of cells by keying in the Name box the first and last cells separated by a colon. For example, you can enter C9:E10 to select the block including cells C9, C10, D9, D10, E9 and E10.

1. Click in the Name box and key **b14:e16**. (Cell references are not case-sensitive, so you can key lowercase letters.)

FIGURE 2-12
Using the Name box
to select cells

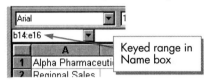

2. Press [Enter]. The cells in the specified range are selected.

3. Click any cell to deselect the block.

4. Save the worksheet as *[your initials]*2-7.xls.

Constructing Basic Formulas

Formulas are instructions that tell Excel how to perform calculations. Formulas may contain mathematical operators, values, cell references, cell ranges, and functions. Excel performs the operations indicated in the formula in a specific order.

TABLE 2-4

Commonly Used Mathematical Operators

OPERATOR	PRECEDENCE	DESCRIPTION
^	1st	Exponentiate
*	2nd	Multiply
/	2nd	Divide
+	3rd	Add
-	3rd	Subtract
( )		Used to control the order of mathematical operations

 NOTE: The exponentiation operator (^) raises a value to a power. The expression 2^3 means "two to the third power," or 2^3, or 2x2x2.

Excel's *order of precedence* defines the order in which it performs formula operations. In a formula, Excel will perform exponentiation operations first, multiplication and division next, and addition and subtraction last. Operations with equal precedence are performed from left to right. You can override the order of precedence by using parentheses (). Excel performs operations inside parentheses first. You can also "nest" expressions—that is, put parenthetical expressions within parentheses. The innermost operations will be handled first. Figure 2-13 shows how parentheses change the order of precedence for operations.

FIGURE 2-13
These two formulas include the same numbers and operators, but parentheses change the order of operations.

$$1 + 2 * 3 - 1 =$$
$$1 + 6 - 1 \quad = \quad 6$$

$$((1+2)*3)-1 =$$
$$((3)*3)-1 =$$
$$9 - 1 \quad = \quad 8$$

You can create formulas using the keyboard, or by entering a combination of keystrokes and mouse clicks. As you key a formula, it appears in both the active cell and the formula bar. When you complete the entry, the result of the calculation appears in the active cell, but the formula bar displays the formula. Excel formulas begin with = (an equals sign). Because cell references in a formula are not case-sensitive, you may enter them in either uppercase or lowercase.

TABLE 2-5   **Typical Excel Formulas**

FORMULA	ACTION
=245+374	Adds the values 245 and 374.
=F4+F5	Adds the values in cells F4 and F5.
=c3+b3-d5	Adds the values in cells C3 and B3, and then subtracts the value in cell D5 from the result.
=(A3+B3)/C9	Adds the values in cells A3 and B3, and then divides the result by the value in cell C9.
=F5*1.02	Multiplies the contents of cell F5 by 1.02 (or 102%).
=F5*C10	Multiplies the contents of cell F5 by the contents of cell C10.

EXERCISE 2-8 Key an Addition Formula

1. In the current workbook, select and clear the contents of cells A13 through A28.

2. Move to cell B12, which should display the total of 1994 sales.

3. Key **=B9+B10+B11** and then press Enter. The result, "3.662," appears in cell B12.

4. Press ↑ to make B12 the active cell. The formula is displayed in the formula bar.

EXERCISE | **2-9** | ## Build an Addition Formula with the Mouse

You can enter a cell reference in a formula by clicking the cell with the mouse. While building a formula, clicking another cell switches the worksheet into Point mode. If you click the wrong cell or make another error, just press Backspace to delete the incorrect characters. You can then continue building the formula.

1. Move to cell C12 and key **=** (the equals sign). Excel changes to Enter mode.

2. Click cell C9. Excel changes to Point mode and a moving dashed border surrounds cell C9. Notice that "=C9" appears in both the active cell and the formula bar.

3. Key **+** (the plus sign). The plus sign is added to the formula, and the moving border disappears. Excel changes to Enter mode.

4. Click cell C10 and then key **+** (the plus sign). The formula "=C9+C10+" appears.

5. Click cell C11, and then press Enter, or click the Enter box ✓ on the formula bar. The result, "4.034," appears in cell C13.

EXERCISE | **2-10** | ## Build Multiplication Formulas

Alpha Pharmaceuticals' sales figures are available for the years 1994 through 1997, but a projection must be calculated for 1998. The company is predicting that aspirin sales will decrease by 5% in 1998, and that acetaminophen and ibuprofen sales will increase by 2% and 3%, respectively.

1. In cell F9, key **=** (the equals sign), and then click cell E9.

2. Key ***** (the multiplication operator), key **.95**, and then press Enter.

3. Press ↑ to return to cell F9. The formula "=E9*0.95" appears in the formula bar, and "0.9728" appears in cell F9. This formula is equivalent to "=E9-E9*0.05" or "5 percent less than E9."

4. Move to cell F10, key **=E10*1.02**, and then press Enter. The result, "1.9788," appears in cell F10. The formula "=E10*1.02" is equivalent to the formula "=E10+E10*0.02."

5. Move to cell F11, key the formula **=E11*1.03** and then press Enter. The result "2.29175" appears.

EXERCISE 2-11 Calculate a Percentage Change

The Alpha Pharmaceuticals worksheet needs calculations to determine the percentage change in each product over the five-year sales period. The general formula for a percentage change is (new-old)/old*100. The subtraction must be performed before division. The resulting decimal must be multiplied by 100 to convert it to a percentage.

1. Move to cell H9 and key **=(**

2. Click cell F9 and then key **-** (the minus sign).

3. Click cell B9 and then key **)**.

4. Key **/** (the forward slash, which is the division operator).

5. Click cell B9, key ***** (the asterisk), key **100**, and then press ⌷Enter⌷.

6. Move back to cell H9. The formula "=(F9-B9)/B9*100" appears in the formula bar, and the result "-12.518" appears in cell H9.

7. In cell H10, enter the formula **=(F10-B10)/B10*100**.

8. In cell H11, enter the formula **=(F11-B11)/B11*100**. The result shows that ibuprofen sales more than doubled over the five-year period, increasing 111.2212 percent.

FIGURE 2-14
Calculating percentage changes

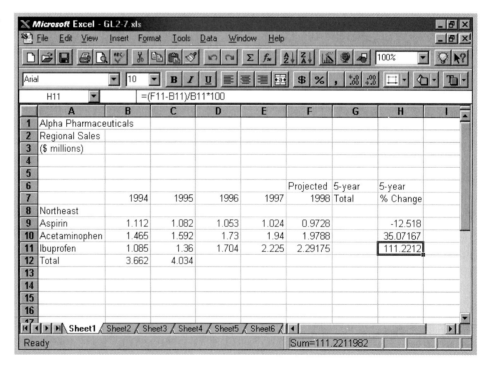

Using the SUM Function

Keying individual cell references is a reasonable way to add two or three cells. It is not practical for adding a long column or row of values, however. Excel's SUM function greatly simplifies the process of adding many values.

In general, a function is constructed with an equals sign and the function name followed by a set of parentheses, with one or more cell references or values placed within the parentheses.

FIGURE 2-15
Structure of a
SUM formula

| Parenthesis | Colon | Parenthesis |

=SUM(E9:E11)

| Equals sign | Function name | Cell references |

In a SUM formula, the cell references can consist of a single cell or a block of cells. Excel refers to these references as a range. Technically, a range is any group of cells specified to be acted upon by a command. To identify a range, key the cell references for two diagonally opposite corners of a group of cells, separated by a colon.

TABLE 2-6   Examples of Ranges

RANGE	DEFINES
C4:C4	A single cell
B5:B10	A range of cells in column B
D3:G3	A range of cells in row 3
C5:F12	A rectangular range of cells in columns C through F, rows 5 through 12

EXERCISE   **2-12**   **Key a SUM Formula**

1. Move to cell E12.
2. Key **=SUM(D9:D11)** and press Enter. The formula adds the contents of cells D9 through D11. The result, "4.487," appears in cell D12.

 NOTE: Like cell references, function names are not case-sensitive, so you can key them in lowercase letters.

EXERCISE   **2-13**   **Enter a SUM Formula Using the Arrow Keys**

1. Move to cell E12.

2. Key **=SUM(**

3. Press ⬆. A moving border surrounds cell E11, and "=SUM(E11" appears in the formula bar.

4. Key **:** (the colon) or **.** (the period) to anchor the border. The formula "=SUM(E11:E11" appears in the formula bar.

5. Press ⬆ twice. The border extends the range from cell E9 through cell E11.

6. Press ⟨Enter⟩ to complete the formula. Excel inserts the closing parenthesis for you automatically. The completed formula is "=SUM(F9:F11)" and the result is 5.189. In this case, you defined the cell range from the bottom to the top. Excel can add cell contents in either direction.

EXERCISE `2-14` **Use the Mouse to Enter a SUM Formula**

You may also create SUM formulas by using the mouse to drag across cells instead of using the Arrow keys.

1. In cell G9, key **=SUM(**

2. Using the mouse, click cell B9.

3. Drag across the row from cell B9 to cell F9, and then release the mouse button. A moving border surrounds the selected range, and the formula "=SUM(B9:F9" appears in the formula bar.

4. Click ✓ on the formula bar, or press ⟨Enter⟩. The formula is completed, and the result, "5.2438," appears in cell G9.

EXERCISE `2-15` **Use the AutoSum Button to Enter a SUM Formula**

The AutoSum button Σ is a shortcut for entering the SUM formula. It enters **=SUM(** and suggests a range to total. At the bottom of a column of values, AutoSum will total the column. At the right of a row of values, AutoSum will total the row.

1. Move to cell G10.

2. Click the AutoSum button Σ on the Standard toolbar. The formula "=SUM(B10:F10)" appears in the formula bar, and a moving border surrounds the cells B10 through F10 on the worksheet.

3. Click the Enter box ✓ on the formula bar, or press ⟨Enter⟩. The result, "8.7058," appears in cell G10.

4. With cell G11 selected, double-click Σ. The SUM formula is entered with the result "13.9496." Notice that the formula range is G9:G10 (for the column) rather than B11:F11 (for the row). The AutoSum feature will automatically add column numbers above a cell before adding row numbers to the left of the cell. Because two values appeared above cell G11, Excel assumed a column SUM formula.

5. To correct the range, click ▣ again. Notice the moving border surrounds the incorrect range.

6. Drag across cells B11 to F11, and then press ⌷Enter⌷. The correct result, "8.66575," appears in cell G11.

7. Enter SUM formulas in cells F12 and G12, using any method. Check that the formulas contain the correct ranges.

FIGURE 2-16
Completed
worksheet

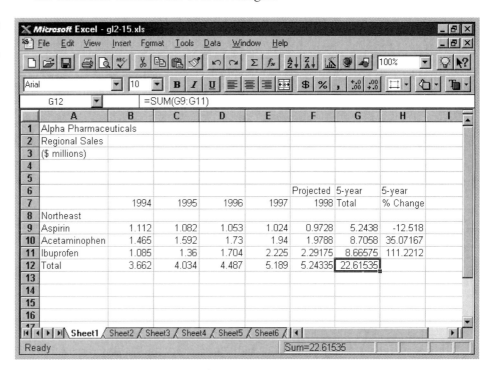

8. Save the workbook as *[your initials]***2-15.xls**.

9. Print the workbook.

Using AutoCalculate

Excel includes an easy-to-use calculator that is built into the program. You can use this calculator, which is called AutoCalculate, to perform simple calculations without entering a formula. For example, if you select a range of cells, AutoCalculate will display the sum of the cells in the status bar.

NOTE: In addition to the SUM function, AutoCalculate can perform other functions, such as Average, Min, and Max. These functions are discussed in Lesson 10: "Using Functions."

EXERCISE 2-16 Use AutoCalculate to Find a Sum

1. Select cells D12 and E12, which contain the total sales for the years 1996 and 1997. At the bottom of the screen, the right portion of the status bar should display "Sum=9.676."

2. Right-click the status bar to display the AutoCalculate menu. Notice the various function names.

3. Choose Sum from the menu, if necessary.

4. Select another range of cells. Notice the sum displayed on the status bar. (See Figure 2-17.)

5. Close the workbook without saving it.

FIGURE 2-17
Using AutoCalculate

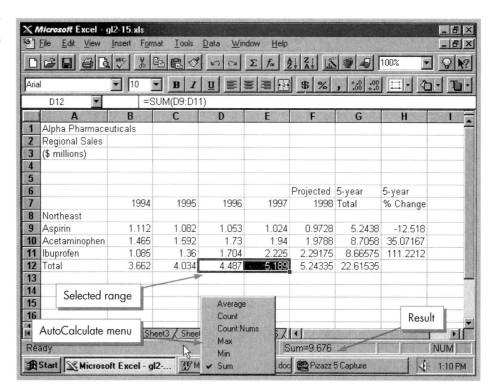

COMMAND SUMMARY

FEATURE	BUTTON	MENU	KEYBOARD
Delete cell contents		Edit, Clear, Contents	Delete
Cancel current entry	✕		Esc
AutoSum	Σ		Alt + =

USING HELP

Excel's online Help feature operates like an interactive teaching tool. One way to explore online Help is to display a list of Help topics. You choose a topic, and Excel will display information or provide a demonstration.

To display a list of Help topics, choose Microsoft Excel Help Topics from the Help menu. You can also press F1 or double-click the Help button ▶?.

Follow these steps to display a Help topic window about selecting cells:

1. Press F1 to display the Help Topics window. Click the Contents tab, if necessary.

2. Browse through the list of topics, each of which is represented by a book icon 📖.

3. Double-click the topic "Entering, Selecting and Editing Data." (You can double-click the icon or the text.)

4. Double-click the topic "Selecting Data."

5. Double-click "Select cells of a worksheet." The question mark page icon ? indicates that Excel will display information about the topic.

6. Review the information in the Help window. Click any term that appears in green with a dotted underline to display a definition box. Click the definition box to close it.

7. Click the first double-arrow button ⏩ to find out how to select cells, rows, and columns.

8. Review the information, scrolling as necessary.

9. Click the Close button ✕ when you're finished.

FIGURE 2-18
The Help Topics window

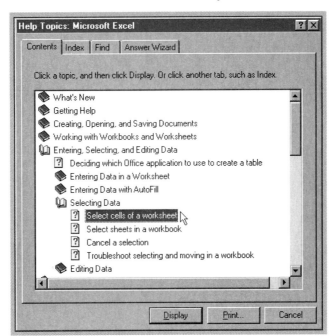

Concepts Review

TRUE/FALSE QUESTIONS

Each of the following statements is either true or false. Indicate your choice by circling either T or F.

T   F   1. The Delete key has the same effect as choosing Cl<u>e</u>ar from the <u>E</u>dit menu, and then choosing <u>C</u>ontents.

T   F   2. If a cell containing a formula is included in another formula, the value of the first formula is included in the calculation.

T   F   3. In Excel, formulas begin with an asterisk (*).

T   F   4. Using parentheses () in a formula allows you to control the order of mathematical operations.

T   F   5. The formula **=SUM(A6:D6)** adds the cells in row 6, from column A to column D.

T   F   6. In formulas, function names must be entered in uppercase letters only.

T   F   7. You can use the AutoSum button to enter a SUM formula.

T   F   8. You can use the SUM function to add the contents of both columns and rows.

SHORT ANSWER QUESTIONS

Write the correct answer in the space provided.

1. Which mode must be displayed in the Status Bar before you begin keying information into a worksheet?

_____

2. When you key information into a cell, where does the information appear on the screen?

_____

3. Which key moves to the first character in the formula bar when in Edit mode?

_____

4. Which mathematical operation is indicated by the use of an asterisk (*)?

_____

5. Which mathematical operations are given last priority in the order of precedence?

_____

6. Which function adds columns and rows?

_____

7. What is the result given by the following formula =(10-4)/2?

_____

8. What is the result given by the following formula =10-4/2?

_____

CRITICAL THINKING

Answer these questions on a separate piece of paper. There are no right or wrong answers. Support your answers with examples from your own experience, if possible.

1. Your boss asks you to proofread a complex worksheet and its printed sources of data. How might AutoCalculate help you verify that data were entered accurately?

2. Last month's sales report worksheet lists products in rows and sales representatives in columns. Your boss asks you to update this report with new data. How can you select cells to speed your work? If your data came from the sales reports of individual sales representatives, would you press Enter or Tab after each entry? Why?

3. Columns in your worksheet are headed with years (for example, 1997, 1998, etc.), and you are keying data beginning in the cell immediately under each column heading. Would you enter the years as labels or values? Why? (Hint: Think about the AutoSum feature.)

Skills Review

EXERCISE 2-17

Enter data, edit data, and enter labels using the Pick from list and AutoComplete features.

1. Click 🗋 to start a new workbook.

2. Key **Alpha Pharmaceuticals** in cell A1, and then press Enter.

3. Key **1997 Sales - Northeast Region** in cell A2, and then press Enter.

4. In cell A3, follow these steps to key a label that indicates that numbers will be shown in thousands of dollars:

  a. Move to cell A3, if necessary, and key **'** (the apostrophe).

  b. Key **($000)** and press Enter.

5. Key **Region** in cell B5, and then press Enter.

6. Label columns for regional data by following these steps:

  a. In cell B6, key **NE** and press Tab.

  b. In cell C6, key **SE** and press Tab.

  c. In cell D6, key **NW** and press Tab.

  d. In cell E6, key **SW** and click ▨ on the formula bar.

7. In cells A7 through A11, key the labels as shown in Figure 2-19.

FIGURE 2-19

	A
7	Q1
8	Aspirin
9	Acetaminophen
10	Ibuprofen
11	Subtotal

8. In cell A12, enter **Q2** (for "second quarter").

9. In cell A13, use the Pick from list feature by following these steps:

  a. Right-click in cell A13 to display the shortcut menu.

  b. Choose Pick from list.

  c. Click "Aspirin" in the list.

10. Use AutoComplete to complete the labels for the second quarter by following these steps:

  a. In cell A14, key **Ac** and then press Enter to enter "Acetaminophen."

  b. In cell A15, key **I** and then press Enter to enter "Ibuprofen."

  c. In cell A16, key **S** and then press Enter to enter "Subtotal."

11. To fit the 13-character row label "Acetaminophen," click any cell in column A, and then choose Column from the Format menu. Choose Width, key **13**, and then click OK.

12. Edit cell A2 to read "1997 Sales" by following these steps:

  a. Double-click cell A2 to switch to Edit mode.

b. Click the I-beam in the text to the right of "Sales" to position the insertion point.

c. Press Shift + End to select the text to the end of the line.

d. Press Delete .

e. Click ✓ or press Enter .

13. Enter the data as shown in Figure 2-20.

FIGURE 2-20

	A	B	C	D	E
6		NE	SE	NW	SW
7	Q1				
8	Aspirin	250	175	150	200
9	Acetaminophen	500	485	390	450
10	Ibuprofen	600	500	480	510
11	Subtotal				
12	Q2				
13	Aspirin	240	180	160	210
14	Acetaminophen	520	470	400	460
15	Ibuprofen	610	640	490	520
16	Subtotal				

14. Clear the word "Subtotal" from cells A11 and A16 by selecting each cell and then pressing Delete .

15. Save the workbook as *[your initials]***2-17.xls**.

16. Print and close the workbook.

EXERCISE 2-18

Select cells, enter data in selected cells, and construct basic formulas.

1. Start a new workbook.

2. Create a heading for the worksheet by keying **Alpha Pharmaceuticals** in cell A1 and **Quality Control Payroll** in cell A2.

3. Create column headings by keying the following text in cells A4 through D4, pressing [Tab] to move across columns:

Name   Salary   Years   Bonus

4. Practice selecting cell ranges by following these steps:

   a. Click column heading B to select that column.

   b. Click row heading 4 to select that row.

   c. Drag from cell A6 to cell A13 to select the range A6:A13.

   d. Click cell A6, hold down [Shift], and click cell C13 to select the range A6:C13.

   e. Select the range A6:C13, hold down [Ctrl], and drag across the range D6:D13 to add it to the selection.

   f. Click anywhere to deselect the block.

5. Select a cell range and then enter data for eight employees by following these steps:

   a. Select the range A6:C13.

   b. Enter the data shown in Figure 2-21, pressing [Enter] to move down each column. Begin with the name "Berenson."

FIGURE 2-21

	A	B	C
6	Berenson	28,000	2
7	Alvarez	33,000	6
8	Czerny	42,000	5
9	Teij	54,100	11
10	Silvers	22,200	3
11	Patino	57,000	9
12	Wang	35,300	2
13	Golden	41,000	6

6. Bonuses are calculated as 2% of salary multiplied by years of service, or (0.02 × Salary × Years). Enter the appropriate bonus formulas by following these steps:

   a. In cell D6, key **=.02*B6*C6** and press [Enter]. Berenson's bonus is $1120, or 2% of $28,000 salary × 2 years of service.

   b. In cell D7, key **=.02***, click cell B7, key *****, click cell C7, and press [Enter].

c. Using either step A or B as your entry method, enter bonus formulas for the rest of the employees.

7. Save the workbook as *[your initials]***2-18.xls**.

8. Print and close the workbook.

Use the SUM function, construct formulas, and use AutoCalculate.

1. Open the file **QCBonus.xls**.

2. In cell A14, key **TOTALS**

3. Key a formula that uses the SUM function to calculate the Salary total by following these steps:

   a. Make B14 the active cell.

   b. Key **=SUM(B6:B13)** and press [Tab].

4. Use the mouse to build a SUM formula that calculates the total years of experience by following these steps:

   a. In cell C14, enter **=SUM(**

   b. Click cell C6, hold down [Shift], and click cell C13.

   c. Press [Tab].

5. Use the AutoSum button to calculate the total of the bonuses by following these steps:

   a. In cell D14, click the AutoSum button [Σ].

   b. Press [Enter].

6. Clear the contents of cell B14.

7. Use AutoCalculate to calculate the salary total by following these steps:

   a. Select cells B6 through B13.

   b. Jot down the number displayed in the status bar. (The number in the status bar should be preceded by "SUM=." If it is not, right-click the status bar, and choose Sum from the AutoCalculate menu.)

   c. Select cell B14, and use the AutoSum button to enter the total. This number should be the same as the number you jotted down.

8. Save the workbook as *[your initials]***2-19.xls**.

9. Print and close the workbook.

Create formulas, print formulas, and interpret formulas.

1. Open the file **Stock.xls**.

2. In cell A21, key **Totals**

3. In cell B21, create a formula that totals the years of experience of the researchers.

4. In cell C21, create a formula that totals the number of shares of stock awarded.

5. Save the workbook as *[your initials]***2-20.xls**.

6. Print the workbook.

7. Examine the formulas in column C to see how the shares of stock were calculated for each researcher. On the printout, write an explanation of how researchers are awarded shares of stock.

8. Close the workbook.

Lesson Applications

Enter data in selected cells and use the SUM function.

1. Open the file **QCPay1.xls**.
2. Select cells B6:C13 and delete their contents.
3. Key the data as shown in Figure 2-22.

FIGURE 2-22

	A	B	C	D
5	Name	Rate	Hours	Pay
6	Berenson	9.25	40	
7	Alvarez	9.46	40	
8	Czerny	10.54	38	
9	Teij	10.64	40	
10	Silvers	9.50	37.5	
11	Patino	10.00	40	
12	Wang	9.88	40	
13	Golden	9.96	40	

4. Create formulas that calculate the Pay for each employee (Rate × Hours).
5. Key **Total** in cell A15.
6. In cell C15, use the SUM function to calculate the total Hours.
7. In cell D15, calculate the total Pay using the AutoSum button. Be sure to adjust the range to add the data in column D.
8. Save the workbook as *[your initials]***2-21.xls**.
9. Print and close the workbook.

Enter data, construct formulas, use the SUM function, and use AutoCalculate.

1. Open the file **QCPay2.xls**.

2. Key the headings and data as shown in Figure 2-23.

FIGURE 2-23

	E	F
5	Overtime	O.T. Pay
6	2	
7	3	
8	0	
9	1.5	
10	0	
11	4.25	
12	2.5	
13	3	

3. Use AutoCalculate to total the number of hours in column C, and then enter this number into cell C15. Use the same method to enter the Pay total in cell D15.

4. In cell E15, use the SUM function to calculate the total Overtime hours. (If you use the AutoSum button, remember to adjust the suggested cell range.)

5. Create a formula for each employee to calculate his or her O.T. Pay. Use the formula "Rate times Overtime times 1.5." (Overtime pay is typically calculated as "time and a half"—that is, at a rate of 1.5 hours.)

6. In cell F15, use the SUM function to calculate the total amount of overtime pay.

7. Save your workbook as *[your initials]***2-22.xls**.

8. Print and close the workbook.

EXERCISE 2-23

Enter data, use AutoComplete and Pick from list, construct formulas, use the SUM function, and use AutoCalculate.

1. Open a file **R&DStaf.xls**.

2. Key the information shown in Figure 2-24, using AutoComplete and Pick from list where possible.

FIGURE 2-24

	B	C	D	E	F
5	Clearance	Level	Vacation Days	Years	Manager
6					
7	None	D15		8	Tang
8	None	C15		15	Richards
9	Top	A43		3	Tang
10	Top	A43		6	Richards
11	None	D15		2	Tang
12	Mid	B23		5	Stevens
13	Top	A43		5	Stevens
14	None	B23		14	Stevens
15	Mid	B23		3	Tang
16	Mid	B23		2	Richards
17	Mid	D15		19	Tang
18	Mid	B23		6	Stevens

3. Calculate the amount of Vacation Days due to each employee using the following information:

For 1 to 5 years: (Years*0.1 + 5)

For 6 to 10 years: (Years*0.1 + 10)

For more than 10 years: (Years*0.15 + 15)

4. Use AutoCalculate to calculate the total Vacation Days, and then enter this number in the appropriate cell.

5. Use the SUM function to calculate the total Years.

6. Save your workbook as *[your initials]***2-23.xls**.

7. Print and close the workbook.

EXERCISE 2-24

Enter data, construct formulas, and use AutoSum.

Alpha Pharmaceuticals' marketing director wants to compare the company's sales with national sales for each product. One way to make this comparison is to calculate market share by dividing Alpha's sales by national sales. Prepare a worksheet that shows market share as a percentage of national sales.

1. Open the file **MktShare.xls**.
2. Key **1997 Market Share** in cell A2.
3. Select the cell range B8:C10, and then key the data shown in Figure 2-25.

FIGURE 2-25

	A	B	C
8	Aspirin	19.671	4.085
9	Acetaminophen	25.093	7.314
10	Ibuprofen	29.384	7.457

4. In cell D8, calculate Alpha's market share for aspirin by creating a formula to divide cell C8 by cell B8.
5. Create formulas to calculate the market share in cells D9 and D10.
6. Using either AutoCalculate or the SUM function, calculate the total pain reliever sales for national sales and Alpha sales in cells B12 and C12, respectively.
7. Calculate Alpha's total market share for pain relievers in cell D12.
8. Save the workbook as *[your initials]***2-24.xls**.
9. Print and close the workbook.

EXERCISE 2-25

Enter data, construct formulas, and use AutoSum.

To prepare for an annual financial planning meeting, the marketing director of Alpha Pharmaceuticals has asked you to create a worksheet that calculates projected national sales for aspirin, acetaminophen, and ibuprofen for 1998 and 1999. These projected sales will be based on 1997 sales information.

1. Create an appropriate heading for the worksheet, with an indicator that the sales figures are expressed in millions.

2. Enter the information in Figure 2-26 as 1997 data. Be sure to widen column A so that the characters in "Acetaminophen" fit.

3. Make sure that the text "1997" is entered as a value, and not a number, so that it will be excluded from calculations. (This step also applies to other cells in the worksheet containing years.)

FIGURE 2-26

```
Product          1997

Aspirin          4.085

Acetaminophen    7.314

Ibuprofen        7.457
```

4. For 1998 and 1999 projected sales, show a 2% increase over the previous year's sales for aspirin and acetaminophen, and a 3% increase each year for ibuprofen.

5. Calculate total sales of pain relievers for each year.

6. Save the workbook as *[your initials]***2-25.xls**.

7. Print and close the worksheet.

LESSON

3

Enhancing a Simple Worksheet

O B J E C T I V E S   After completing this lesson, you will be able to:

1. **Select multiple columns and rows.**
2. **Insert cells, columns, and rows.**
3. **Delete cells, columns, and rows.**
4. **Use the Undo command.**
5. **Use shortcut menus.**
6. **Move data.**
7. **Format numbers.**
8. **Apply text attributes and cell borders.**

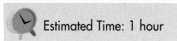
Estimated Time: 1 hour

This lesson teaches easy ways to modify a worksheet by inserting and deleting cells, columns, and rows; changing the number of decimal places displayed; and applying basic text and alignment attributes.

Selecting Multiple Columns and Rows

As you learned in Lesson 2, clicking a row or column heading selects that row or column. You can also select several columns and rows at the same time.

E X E R C I S E   **3-1**   **Select Multiple Columns and Rows with the Mouse**

1. Open the file **USSales1.xls**.

2. Click column heading A to select the column.

3. Click and drag over row headings 2, 3, and 4. The column is deselected and the three rows are selected.

4. Click column heading B, hold down Shift, and click column heading E. Columns B through E are selected.

5. Drag over row headings 2 and 3 to select those rows.

6. Hold down Ctrl and click column heading B. Two rows and one column are selected. (See Figure 3-1.)

7. Click any cell in the worksheet to deselect the columns and rows.

FIGURE 3-1
Selecting columns and rows with the mouse

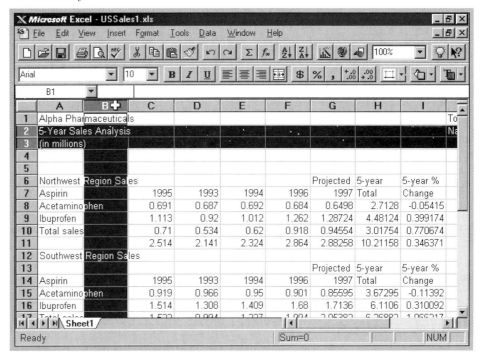

TABLE 3-1 Selecting Columns and Rows

ACTION	RESULT
Click heading	Selects a column or row
Drag across headings	Selects multiple columns or rows
Shift+click heading	Extends the selection to include adjacent columns or rows
Ctrl+click heading	Extends the selection to include nonadjacent columns or rows
Click Select All button	Selects the entire worksheet
Shift+Spacebar	Selects the current row
Ctrl+Spacebar	Selects the current column
Shift+Arrow keys, PgUp, or PgDn	Extends the row or column selection (first select a row or column)

EXERCISE **3-2** **Select Multiple Columns and Rows with the Keyboard**

1. In cell C7, press Shift + Spacebar to select row 7.
2. Select cell D5. Row 7 is deselected.
3. Press Ctrl + Spacebar to select column D.
4. While holding Shift, press → three times. The selection is extended through column G.
5. Select cell B7.
6. Press Shift + → twice to select cells B7 through D7.
7. Press Ctrl + Spacebar to select columns B through D.
8. Use the keyboard to select cells C7 through E9, and then press Shift + Spacebar. Rows 7 through 9 are selected.
9. Press any arrow key to deselect the rows.

Inserting Cells, Columns, and Rows

You can add cells to a worksheet to make room for more data or to make the worksheet easier to read. Use the Insert menu or the keyboard shortcut Ctrl + + (the plus key on the numeric keypad).

EXERCISE **3-3** **Insert a Single Cell**

A section of the **USSales1.xls** worksheet shows ten years of national pain-reliever sales, but contains some errors in it. When the row labels in column J were keyed, "1989" was skipped. Inserting a cell allows you to correct this problem.

1. Press Alt + PgDn to bring columns J through R into view.
2. Select cell J7. Notice that cell J6 contains "1988" and cell J7 contains "1990."
3. Choose Cells from the Insert menu. The Insert dialog box opens.

FIGURE 3-2
Insert dialog box

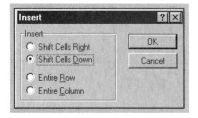

4. Click Cancel, and then press Ctrl + + on the numeric keypad. The Insert dialog box opens again.
5. Choose Shift Cells Down and click OK. An empty cell appears at cell J7. The labels below are shifted down by one cell.
6. Key **1989** in cell J7 and press Enter.

EXERCISE 3-4 **Insert an Entire Column and Row**

You can insert an entire row or column in a worksheet at the position of the active cell. Use the Insert menu or the keyboard shortcut Ctrl + + on the numeric keypad.

1. Select cell A19.

 TIP: Remember, the key combination Alt + PgUp moves one screen left.

2. Choose Rows from the Insert menu. A blank row appears at row 19, and all of the information below this row moves down by one row.

3. Select row 19, and press Ctrl + +. Another row is inserted automatically.

4. Press F5 to open the Go To dialog box.

5. Key **J1** and click OK (or press Enter).

6. Click the column J heading to select the entire column.

7. Choose Columns from the Insert menu (or press Ctrl + +). A blank column appears at column J, and all of the information beyond column J moves right by one column.

EXERCISE 3-5 **Insert Multiple Cells, Columns, and Rows**

To insert several cells, columns, or rows in the same operation, select them before choosing a command. For example, if you select two rows, choosing Rows from the Insert menu (or pressing Ctrl + +) will insert two blank rows.

When inserting rows or columns, be careful not to separate blocks of data by mistake. Rows and columns span the entire worksheet, not just the visible portion of your screen. Rows go 256 cells across, and columns stretch 16,384 cells down.

1. Select rows 28 and 29, and press Ctrl + +. Two blank rows are inserted to separate "Northeast Region Sales" from "Southeast Region Sales."

2. Select rows 12 and 13.

3. Click the right side of the horizontal scroll bar (at the bottom of the screen). Notice that inserting rows here would break up data inappropriately in columns K through O. (See Figure 3-3 on the next page.)

4. Deselect the rows and scroll back to view columns A through I.

5. Select cells A12 through I13, and then press Ctrl + +.

6. In the Insert dialog box, choose Shift Cells Down and click OK. Blank cells appear at cells A12 through I13, and all of the data from cells A12 through I13 move down by two cells.

FIGURE 3-3
Selecting to insert
multiple rows

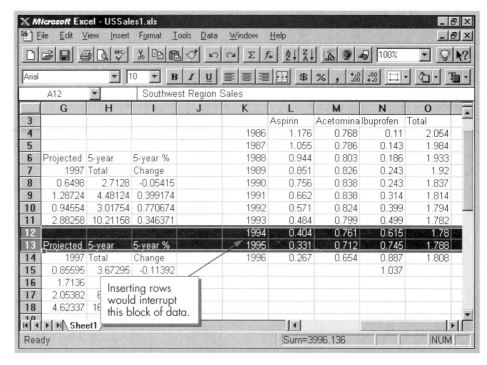

7. Press Alt + PgDn to view the ten-year historical data. Notice that no blank cells interrupt the data.

Deleting Cells, Columns, and Rows

You can delete cells, columns, and rows in much the same way that you insert them. Choose Delete from the Edit menu or press Ctrl + - (the minus sign on the numeric keypad).

When you delete cells, those cells are removed from the worksheet, and the surrounding cells move to fill the space. If the deleted cells contained data, the data is also removed from the worksheet. In contrast, clearing the contents of cells removes the information contained in those cells, but allows the cells to remain in the worksheet.

 NOTE: Never clear contents by keying a blank space in a cell. Although the cell will appear blank, it will actually contain a label. This label may ultimately affect calculations.

EXERCISE   3-6   Delete Cells, Columns, and Rows

1. Select cell N8. This cell contains the same entry as cell N7. The data in column N extends one row below the data in the other columns.

2. Choose <u>D</u>elete from the <u>E</u>dit menu. The Delete dialog box opens.

3. Choose Shift Cells <u>U</u>p and click OK. Cell N8 is deleted, and the cells move up to fill the gap.

FIGURE 3-4
Delete dialog box

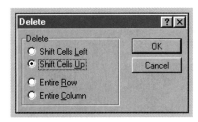

4. Select column B and choose <u>D</u>elete from the <u>E</u>dit menu. Column B is deleted.

5. Select column B, if necessary, and press [Ctrl]+[+] to insert the column.

6. Press [Ctrl]+[-] to delete column B again.

7. Adjust the width of column A to accommodate 13 characters

NOTE: A well-designed worksheet should not contain blank columns, but should have column widths that are adjusted to fit text.

Using the Undo Command

The Undo command reverses the last action performed on the worksheet. If you deleted a column, for example, Undo will bring back the column and its data. If you accidentally overwrite existing data in a cell, Undo can restore the original cell contents.

Undo can reverse only the very last action, meaning that you must undo an incorrect action before you do anything else to the worksheet. Choosing Undo twice in a row reverses, and then restores, the last action. (You can "undo" Undo.)

To use the Undo command, click the Undo button ⟲ on the Standard toolbar, press [Ctrl]+[Z], or choose <u>U</u>ndo from the <u>E</u>dit menu.

NOTE: Undo is a convenient tool, but its usefulness is limited. It is always best to save your worksheet frequently. If you then make an unrecoverable error, you can simply close the worksheet without saving it, and then reopen it.

EXERCISE **3-7** **Use the Undo Command**

1. Save the worksheet as *[your initials]***3-7.xls**.

2. Select column C by clicking its column heading.

3. Choose <u>D</u>elete from the <u>E</u>dit menu. The column is deleted.

4. Choose <u>U</u>ndo from the <u>E</u>dit menu (or press [Ctrl]+[Z]). The column is restored. (If Undo did not work, close the worksheet without saving it, and then open it again.)

5. Click the Undo button 🔄 on the Standard toolbar. The column is deleted again.

6. Click 🔄 again. The column is restored.

Using Shortcut Menus

Shortcut menus provide quick access to frequently used commands, bypassing the menu bar. To display a shortcut menu, select a cell, a cell range, a row, or a column, and then right-click the selection or press ⧏Shift⧐+⧏F10⧐. The commands that you are most likely to use are listed in the shortcut menu. To choose a command, click it with the left mouse button.

EXERCISE `3-8` **Use Shortcut Menus**

FIGURE 3-5
Shortcut menu for cell ranges

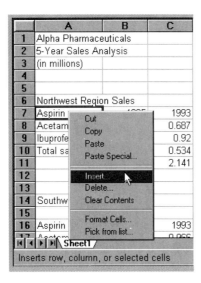

All of the row labels in column A, starting in cell A7, are positioned one cell too high. To correct this problem, a cell can be inserted at cell A7.

1. Make cell A7 the active cell.

2. While pointing to cell A7, click the right mouse button. The shortcut menu appears.

3. Use the left mouse button to choose Insert from the shortcut menu.

4. In the Insert dialog box, choose Shift Cells Down and then click OK. The row labels are positioned correctly.

Moving Data to a New Location

You easily can move the contents of cells to another location without rekeying data. One way is to cut and paste the information, which is a two-step operation. First, you *cut* selected cells. You then move to a new location and *paste* the data in the cells at the new location. You can also copy a selection and paste a copy of it to a new location. Lesson 5 will discuss copying in detail.

Excel provides several ways to issue the cut and paste commands, including:

- The toolbar buttons Cut ✂ and Paste 📋
- Keyboard shortcuts [Ctrl]+[X] to cut and [Ctrl]+[V] to paste
- The shortcut menu

When you cut or copy data from selected cells, it is stored temporarily on the *Clipboard*, an area in the computer's active memory. The Paste command transfers the contents of the Clipboard to the location you choose.

EXERCISE 3-9 Move Data Using Cut and Paste

1. Right-click cell A3.
2. Choose Cut from the shortcut menu. A moving border surrounds cell A3.
3. Click cell A4, and then click the Paste button 📋 on the Standard toolbar. Cell A3 is cleared, the moving border disappears, and the contents of cell A3 appear in cell A4.
4. Click ↶ to undo the Paste command. The moving border marks cell A3, and cell A4 becomes the active cell again.
5. Press [Enter]. The text is moved.

> ✦ **TIP:** Pressing [Enter] has the same effect as the Paste command when the moving border marks a range of cut cells.

6. Click ↶ to restore the text to cell A3. Press [Esc] to remove the moving border.

EXERCISE 3-10 Move Data Using Insert Cut Cells

When you paste data to a cell range, any data contained in the range is over-written by the new data. To insert data at a location that already contains data, use the Insert Cut Cells command. This command causes the existing cells to be shifted down or to the right when data is moved to that location.

1. Save the worksheet as *[your initials]***3-10.xls**.
2. Select cells B7 through B11.
3. Choose Cut from the shortcut menu.
4. Select cell F7.
5. Press [Ctrl]+[V], the keyboard shortcut for Paste. The "1996" data in cells E7 through E11 is overwritten by the "1995" data. Because the formulas in columns F, G, and H referenced the "1996" data, the notation #REF! appears in the cells that contain formulas, indicating a reference error.

6. Click 🔙. The data is restored, and the reference errors are no longer displayed.

7. With the moving border again surrounding cells C7 through C11, and cells E7 through E11 selected, choose Cut Cells from the Insert menu, or choose Insert Cut Cells from the shortcut menu. The "1995" data is inserted between the "1994" and "1996" data. The formulas are not disturbed by the move.

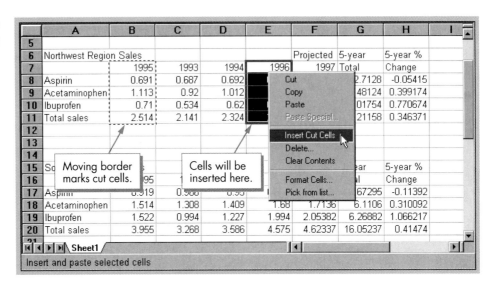

FIGURE 3-6
Inserting cut cells

EXERCISE **3-11** **Move Data Using Drag and Drop**

When you move the white-cross pointer slowly across the border of an active cell or selected cells, it changes to an arrow. This arrow is the drag-and-drop pointer, which allows you to move data to a new location. Old data is replaced with moved data when you release the mouse button.

1. Select cells A1 through A3.

2. Slowly move the white-cross pointer across the selection's border, until the white cross changes into an arrow.

 NOTE: If the arrow pointer does not appear, choose Options from the Tools menu, click the Edit tab, and click the Allow Cell Drag and Drop check box to select the option.

3. Press and hold the left mouse button.

4. Move the arrow to cell D1. A light gray border surrounds cells D1 through D3.

FIGURE 3-7
Using the drag-and-drop method to move data

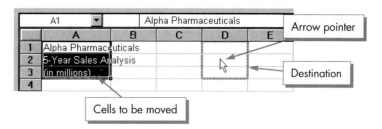

5. Release the mouse button. The data is moved, and cells A1 through A3 are cleared.

6. Select cells B16 through B20.

7. Position the mouse pointer at the border of the selection, until you see the arrow pointer.

8. Hold down Shift, and then drag the I-beam to the vertical gridline between columns D and E, with the top of the I-beam between rows 15 and 16. Notice that you are dragging an I-beam, not a rectangle.

FIGURE 3-8
Using the drag-and-drop method to insert cut cells

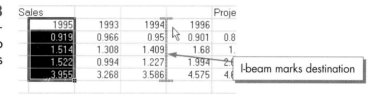

9. Release the mouse button, and then release Shift. You have just inserted the cut cells. The "1995" data is inserted between the "1994" and "1996" data.

EXERCISE 3-12 **Check Cell References and Formulas after Moving Data**

When you move formulas, the cell references in the formulas remain the same, as do the calculations performed by those formulas. When you move cells that are referenced by formulas, Excel updates the formulas automatically, so that they reference the new location of the cells. For example, if a SUM function references the range C5:C10, and you move the contents of cell C10 to cell C12, the SUM function changes automatically to reference the range C5:C12. Always check formulas after moving data to ensure that they are updated correctly.

1. Select cell G8. The correct formula, =SUM(B8:F8), appears on the formula bar.

2. Select cell H8. The correct formula, =(F8-B8)/B8, appears on the formula bar.

3. Check formulas throughout the worksheet.

Formatting Numbers: The Basics

You can format numbers to have a similar appearance without changing their mathematical values. For instance, the values resulting from division often have many decimal places, and decimals may not be aligned. If you format cells to show only two decimal places, the results will be neat and easy to read. Excel still stores all of the undisplayed digits, however, and uses them in future computations. Complete values can be redisplayed at any time.

The Excel Formatting toolbar offers a convenient way to format numbers. More information on number formats, such as dates, fractions, and custom formats, is presented in Lesson 8: "Formatting Text and Numbers."

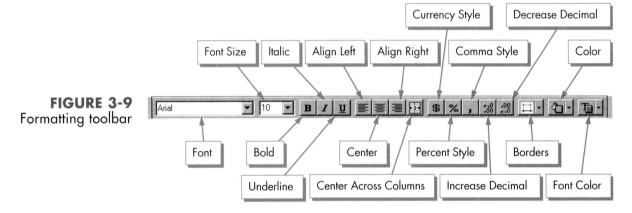

FIGURE 3-9
Formatting toolbar

EXERCISE 3-13 Format Numbers in Comma Style and Percent Style

1. Select cell G8.
2. Click the Comma Style button on the toolbar. Cell G8 is formatted with two decimal places. The Comma Style button inserts commas to separate thousands, if needed, and formats values to have two decimal places.
3. Select cells B8 through G11.
4. Click ⬚ again. All of the selected cells are formatted with two decimal places, and the decimals are aligned.
5. Select cells H8 through H11.
6. Click the Percent Style button ⬚. The selected cells are formatted as percentages with no decimals.

EXERCISE 3-14 Change the Number of Decimals Displayed

You can use the Increase Decimal and Decrease Decimal buttons on the Formatting toolbar to control the number of decimal places displayed in cells.

1. Select cells B17 through G20.

2. Click the Decrease Decimal button . The selected cells display two decimal places.

3. Click the Increase Decimal button . The cells display three decimal places.

4. Select cells H17 through H20.

5. Click ⟨%⟩, and then click ⟨.0⟩. The selected cells are displayed as percentages with one decimal place.

6. Using the Formatting toolbar, format all of the sales region numbers to match the formatting of the "Southwest Region" numbers.

Applying Text Attributes Using the Toolbar

You can use the buttons on the Formatting toolbar to format text as well as numbers. You can control alignment in a cell, apply bold and italics, draw lines, and change the size of text.

 NOTE: Text attributes and borders are discussed in more detail in Unit 3: "Changing the Appearance of a Worksheet."

EXERCISE **Apply Text Attributes Using the Toolbar**

1. Select cells D1 through D3.

2. Click the Center button on the Formatting toolbar. The text in cells D1 through D3 is centered in the cells, but spills over to cells in columns C and E.

3. Select cells D1 and D2.

4. Click the Bold button . The selected text becomes bold.

5. Select cells F6 through H7.

6. Click the Align Right button . The text is aligned with the numbers below it.

 TIP: Column titles should always be aligned with their related data.

7. Select cells A6 through H7 and cells A11 through H11.

8. Click ⟨B⟩ to make the selection bold.

FIGURE 3-10
Formatting the
worksheet

	A	B	C	D	E	F	G	H	I
1			Alpha Pharmaceuticals						
2			5-Year Sales Analysis						
3			(in millions)						
4									
5									
6	Northwest Region Sales					Projected	5-year	5-year %	
7		1993	1994	1995	1996	1997	Total	Change	
8	Aspirin	0.687	0.692	0.691	0.684	0.650	3.404	-5.4%	
9	Acetaminophen	0.920	1.012	1.113	1.262	1.287	5.594	39.9%	
10	Ibuprofen	0.534	0.620	0.710	0.918	0.946	3.728	77.1%	
11	Total sales	2.141	2.324	2.514	2.864	2.883	12.726	34.6%	
12									
13									
14									
15	Southwest Region Sales					Projected	5-year	5-year %	
16		1993	1994	1995	1996	1997	Total	Change	
17	Aspirin	0.966	0.950	0.919	0.901	0.856	4.592	11.4%	

Sheet1

Ready   Sum=0   NUM

EXERCISE 3-16 Use Format Painter to Copy Attributes

Once you've applied a variety of attributes to a cell range—such as bold and
italics, alignment, and number styles—you can copy the attributes from one
cell range to another using the Format Painter button on the Formatting
toolbar.

1. Select cells A6 through H11.

2. Click the Format Painter button ⬚. The selection is surrounded by a
   moving border. You can now copy the formatting of this range to other
   sales region data in the worksheet.

3. Using the Format Painter pointer ⬚, select cells A15 through H20, the
   "Southwest Region Sales" data. The formatting is applied to the data.

FIGURE 3-11
Copying attributes
with Format Painter

	A	B	C	D	E	F	G	H	I
14									
15	Southwest Region Sales					Projected	5-year	5-year %	
16		1993	1994	1995	1996	1997	Total	Change	
17	Aspirin	0.966	0.950	0.919	0.901	0.856	4.592	-11.4%	
18	Acetaminophen	1.308	1.409	1.514	1.680	1.714	7.625	31.0%	
19	Ibuprofen	0.994	1.227	1.522	1.994	2.054	7.791	106.6%	
20	Total sales	3.268	3.586	3.955	4.575	4.623	20.007	41.5%	
21									
22									
23									
24	Northeast Region Sales					Projected	5-year	5-year %	
25		1993	1994	1995	1996	1997	Total	Change	
26	Aspirin	1.544	1.522	1.500	1.480	1.406	7.452	-8.9%	
27	Acetaminophen	1.880	2.039	2.213	2.429	2.478	11.039	31.8%	
28	Ibuprofen	1.275	1.544	1.846	2.301	2.370	9.336	85.9%	
29	Total sales	4.699	5.105	5.559	6.210	6.254	27.827	33.1%	

Selected range

Copy formatting here.

Sheet1

eady   Sum=10087.73464   NUM

Format Painter pointer

4. With the cell range A15 through H20 still selected, double-click ⬚. Double-clicking the button allows you to copy formatting multiple times.

5. Use the Format Painter pointer to select cells A24 through H29, and then select cells A33 through H38. All of the regions now have the same formatting.

6. Press Esc to restore the normal pointer.

EXERCISE **3-17** **Apply Borders to the Bottoms of Cells**

You can create a line that separates data by formatting cells with a bottom border. The easiest way to apply a border is by using the Borders button ⬚▾ on the Formatting toolbar.

1. Select cells A7 through H7.

2. Click the down arrow on the right side of the Borders button ⬚▾. The Borders palette appears.

FIGURE 3-12
Borders palette

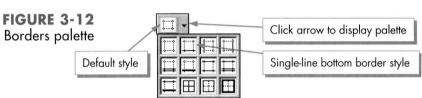

3. Choose the single-line bottom border style (first row, second column) on the palette. The bottom borders of cells A7 through H7 are formatted as a single solid line. The Borders button default is now single-line bottom border.

4. Apply the same border style to separate the headings from data in the other three regions.

5. Save the file as *[your initials]***3-17.xls**.

6. Print the file and close it.

COMMAND SUMMARY

FEATURE	BUTTON	MENU	KEYBOARD
Insert Cells		Insert, Cells, Rows, or Columns	Ctrl + +
Delete Cells		Edit, Delete	Ctrl + -
Cut	✂	Edit, Cut	Ctrl + X
Paste	📋	Edit, Paste	Ctrl + V
Undo	↺	Edit, Undo	Ctrl + Z

83

USING HELP

To find out how to do something in Excel, ask the Answer Wizard. The Answer Wizard lets you ask a question in your own words, and then provides a list of topics to assist you in finding the answer.

To help you complete a task, choose a topic under "How Do I." To understand the task better, choose a topic under "Tell Me About."

Use the Answer Wizard to find out more about moving cells:

1. Choose Answer Wizard from the Help menu.

2. In the first box, key **move data**

3. Click the Search button. Excel displays a list of related topics.

FIGURE 3-13
Using the
Answer Wizard

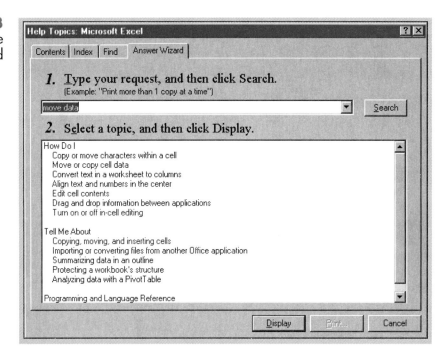

4. Under "Tell Me About," choose the topic "Copying, moving, and inserting cells" and then click Display.

5. Click any of the topics to display a pop-up description box. Click a description box to close it.

6. When you're finished browsing in the Help window, click ⊠ to close Help.

Concepts Review

Each of the following statements is either true or false. Indicate your choice by circling either T or F.

T F **1.** After selecting a column with the mouse, you can extend that selection only by using the mouse.

T F **2.** You can insert an entire row using the Insert dialog box.

T F **3.** When you delete a cell using the Delete dialog box, both the cell and its contents are removed from the worksheet.

T F **4.** Clicking ▣ three times will reverse your last three actions.

T F **5.** Double-clicking a cell displays a shortcut menu.

T F **6.** The Cut, Paste, and Copy buttons are located on the Standard toolbar.

T F **7.** The Comma Style button formats numbers to display two decimal places.

T F **8.** You can use ▨ to copy both alignment and number formatting from one cell range to another.

Write the correct answer in the space provided.

1. To extend a selection using the arrow keys, which key must you hold down?

_____

2. To insert multiple rows, you first select the number of rows to insert, and then press which key combination?

_____

3. Which menu command can restore a column you just deleted by mistake?

_____

4. When you cut a selection, how is it marked onscreen?

_____

5. When you drag to insert cut cells, what do you drag to the new location?

_____

6. How many decimal places does the Percent Style button format numbers to display?

_____

7. On which toolbar is the bold button located?

_____

8. Which keyboard combination selects the current row?

_____

CRITICAL THINKING

Answer these questions on a separate piece of paper. There are no right or wrong answers. Support your answers with examples from your own experience, if possible.

1. You want to add a row of sales data for another product to an existing worksheet. Should you insert a row, or just selected cells? Why?

2. If Excel updates formulas automatically after you move cells, why should you check formulas?

3. Cells B6, B7, and B8 display the values 3.2, 4.0, and 2.9, respectively. Cell B9 contains the formula =SUM(B6:B8) and displays 10.22. How could this be?

Skills Review

EXERCISE 3-18

Select multiple columns and rows; insert and delete cells, columns, and rows; and use the Undo command.

1. Open the file **NWReps1.xls**.

2. Insert a cell to align the labels in column A with the data below by following these steps:

   a. Select cell A8.

   b. Choose Cells from the Insert menu.

   c. Choose Shift Cells Down in the Insert dialog box, and then click OK.

3. Insert a column so that the names in column A can be seen by following these steps:

   a. Select any cell in column B.

   b. Choose Columns from the Insert menu.

4. Delete rows to close up the space between the worksheet heading and the data by following these steps:

   a. Drag over row headings 5 through 8 to select those rows.

   b. Press Ctrl + - (the minus key on the numeric keypad).

5. Choose <u>U</u>ndo from the <u>E</u>dit menu to restore the four rows.

6. Delete three rows by following these steps:

   a. Click row heading 5 to select that row.

   b. Press and hold Shift, and then click row heading 7.

   c. Press Ctrl + - .

7. Adjust column A to accommodate 20 characters.

8. Select and delete column B.

9. Save the workbook as *[your initials]***3-18.xls**.

10. Print and close the workbook.

EXERCISE 3-19

Insert cells, use the shortcut menu, and move data.

1. Open the file **NWReps2.xls**. Some data is missing and the quarterly information was keyed in the wrong order. You will move and insert cells to fix these problems, and then repair formulas, if necessary.

2. Insert cells to make room for new data by following these steps:

   a. Select cells A14:H14.

   b. Right-click the selection to display the shortcut menu.

   c. Choose Insert.

   d. In the Insert dialog box, choose Shift Cells <u>D</u>own and then click OK.

3. Key the data shown in Figure 3-14.

FIGURE 3-14

	Q4	Q3	Q2	Q1	Total	% of Total
Jose Garcia	73.8	72.4	77.912	75.1739	299.286	0.110318

4. Move the "Qtr 1" cells to column B by following these steps:

   a. Select cells F6:F19 and right-click the range.

   b. Choose Cut from the shortcut menu.

   c. Right-click cell B6 and choose Paste from the shortcut menu.

5. Move the "Qtr 4" cells to column F by following these steps:

    a. Select cells C6:C19.

    b. Move the mouse pointer to the border of the range until it becomes an arrow.

    c. Drag the selection to the range F6:F19 and release the mouse button.

6. Move the "Qtr 1" cells from column B to the blank column C.

7. Reverse the positions of the "Qtr 2" and "Qtr 3" information by following these steps:

    a. Select "Qtr 2" cells E6:E19.

    b. Press Ctrl+X to cut these cells.

    c. Select cell D6, which contains "Qtr 3."

    d. Choose Cut C<u>e</u>lls from the <u>I</u>nsert menu (or choose Insert Cut Cells from the shortcut menu).

8. Delete the blank column B.

9. Review the formulas in the "Total" column. Correct them, if necessary. (They should sum the sales in all four quarters for each salesperson.)

10. Review the formulas in the "% of Total" column. (They should divide the total sales for each salesperson by the total sales for all salespersons.)

11. Save the workbook as *[your initials]***3-19.xls**.

12. Print and close the workbook.

EXERCISE 3-20

Move cells, format numbers, apply text attributes, and apply borders.

1. Open the file **NWReps3.xls**.

2. Format the dollar amounts in comma style and displaying only one decimal place by following these steps:

    a. Select cells C8:G19.

    b. Click ⏗ on the Formatting toolbar.

    c. Click ⏗ on the Formatting toolbar.

3. Format the first and last rows of dollar amounts in currency style and displaying only one decimal place by following these steps:

    a. Select cells C8:G8 and C19:G19 (to use Ctrl to select nonadjacent ranges).

    b. Click ⏗ on the Formatting toolbar.

    c. Click ⏗ on the Formatting toolbar.

4. Format amounts in the "% of Total" column in percent style and displaying one decimal place by following these steps:

    a. Select cells H8:H19.

    b. Click ⏗ and then click ⏗.

5. Format and align the column labels by following these steps:

a. Select cells A6:H6 and click ⬛ to make the text bold.

    b. With the cells still selected, click the down arrow on the Borders button ⊞, and then choose the single-line bottom border.

    c. Select cells C6:G6 and click ▤ to right-align the text.

6. Format cells A1:A4 and A19:H19 as bold.

7. Delete the blank row 7.

8. Add a single-line bottom border to the data in row 16 and delete the blank row 17.

9. Delete column B and adjust the column width of column A to 20 characters.

10. Save the workbook as *[your initials]***3-20.xls**.

11. Print and close the workbook.

EXERCISE 3-21

Move cells and rows, format numbers, apply text attributes and borders, copy formats, and use shortcut menus.

1. Open the file **USSales2.xls**.

2. Under "Northwest Region Sales," move row 8 ("Acetaminophen") below row 9 ("Aspirin") to match the sequence in the other three regions. Follow these steps:

    a. Right-click row heading 8, and then click Cut in the shortcut menu.

    b. Right-click row heading 10, and then click Insert Cut Cells in the shortcut menu.

3. Move "Northeast Region Sales" before "Southwest Region Sales" by following these steps:

    a. Select rows 20 through 26 by dragging with the mouse.

    b. Press Ctrl + X to cut the selected rows.

    c. Right-click row heading 13, and then click Insert Cut Cells in the shortcut menu.

4. Format the title in cells A1:A3 as bold.

5. Format text in the "Northwest Region" by following these steps:

    a. Select the row and column labels and the totals (A6:H7, A8:A11, and B11:H11), and make them bold.

    b. Right-align cells G6:H7.

    c. Apply a double-line bottom border to cells A6:H7.

6. Format numbers in the "Northwest Region" by following these steps:

    a. Select the dollar amounts for "Aspirin" (B8:G8) and "Total sales" (B11:G11). Apply the currency style and add one decimal place to these numbers.

    b. To the dollar amounts in cells B9:G10, apply the comma style and add one decimal place. All numbers should have three decimal places.

    c. Apply the percent style to cells H8:H11.

7. Copy the formats for the "Northwest Region" to the other three regions by following these steps:

    a. Select cells A6:H11 and double-click the Format Painter button .

    b. Using the Format Painter pointer, select the "Northeast Region Sales" range (A13:H18) to copy the formatting.

    c. Select the "Southwest Region" range, and then select the "Southeast Region" range.

    d. Press [Esc] to end the process and restore the normal pointer.

8. Save the workbook as *[your initials]***3-21.xls**.

9. Print and close the workbook.

Lesson Applications

Select rows and columns, move cells and columns, insert and delete rows, move data, format numbers, and apply text attributes and cell borders.

1. Open the file **Share1.xls**.

2. Move the information in column E to column B.

3. Check the formulas now in column B to ensure that they divide "Alpha Sales" by "National Sales."

4. Widen column A to 15 characters.

5. Insert two rows at row 4.

6. Format the title cells A1 and A2 as bold.

7. Delete the blank row 12.

8. Format the column labels as centered and bold, and apply a single-line bottom border to cells B7:D7.

9. Apply a single-line bottom border to cells B11:D11.

10. Format the row labels and total numbers as bold.

11. Format the "Market Share" numbers in percent style and displaying two decimal places.

12. Format the "National Sales" and "Alpha Sales" numbers in comma style and displaying two decimal places.

13. Save the workbook as *[your initials]***3-22.xls**.

14. Print and close the workbook.

Select cells, insert rows, use shortcut menus, move data, format numbers and text, and apply cell borders.

Alpha Pharmaceuticals' auditor has reviewed the worksheet that calculates gross pay for the company's Quality Control Division. He noticed that overtime hours were not entered, and that employee Silvers is missing from the list. These errors need to be corrected, and the worksheet needs to be formatted so that it will be easier to read.

1. Open the file **QCPay3.xls**.

2. Insert three blank rows, starting at row 3.

3. Move the data for "Golden" between the data for "Czerny" and "Patino."

4. Under "Patino," insert a new row with the data and formulas for employee Silvers as shown in Figure 3-15. (Leave "Overtime" blank.)

FIGURE 3-15

Name	Rate	Hours	Overtime	Regular Pay	Overtime Pay	Total Pay
Silvers	9.50	37.5		=B13*C13	=D13*B13*1.50	=E13+F13

5. Format cell A1 as bold and italic, and cell A2 as bold.

6. Right-align the text in rows 6 and 7 (except for "Name" in cell A7, which should be left-aligned).

7. Format rows 6, 7, and 16 as bold.

8. Apply a single-line bottom border to cells A7 through G7 and to cells A15 through G15.

9. Apply the comma style to all numbers in the worksheet and display two decimal places.

10. Key the overtime hours for all employees as follows:

Berenson	**2**
Alvarez	**3**
Czerny	**0**
Golden	**3**
Patino	**4.25**
Silvers	**0**
Teij	**1.5**
Wang	**2.5**

11. Use AutoSum to total regular "Hours" and "Overtime" hours. Be sure that the totals appear in bold and display two decimal places.

12. Save the workbook as *[your initials]***3-23.xls**.

13. Print and close the workbook.

EXERCISE 3-24

Select and insert rows and columns, move data, and format text and numbers.

Alpha Pharmaceuticals' president needs to study U.S. population trends to help him make sales forecasts for his company. He is especially interested in the over-40 age group, as this group uses more pain relievers than younger people. His population worksheet should be formatted, and additional data must be inserted.

1. Open the file **PopData1.xls**.

2. Insert three blank rows at row 3.

3. Move the "1990" data, so that it is positioned above the "1991" data.

4. Insert three blank rows below the "1986" data to make room for the "1987," "1988," and "1989" data.

5. Key the missing population figures, as shown in Figure 3-16.

FIGURE 3-16

	Total	Over 40
1987	243.07	91.25
1988	245.35	92.61
1989	247.64	93.97
1995	263.87	105.30
1996	266.75	107.42
1997	269.65	109.55

6. Create formulas in cells D11:D13 and D19:D21 to calculate the percentage of the population over age 40. (Hint: Use one of the existing formulas as a model.)

7. Edit cell A1 so that it reads **U.S. Population**

8. Format cells A1:A2 as bold.

9. Format the column headings in row 6 as right-aligned and bold.

10. Format the numbers in columns B and C to display one decimal place.

11. Format the numbers in column D to be displayed as percentages with one decimal place.

12. Save the workbook as *[your initials]***3-24.xls**.

13. Print and close the workbook.

EXERCISE 3-25

Historical information on pain-reliever sales for the Northwest Region appears in three separate sections of a worksheet. The Marketing Director has asked you to arrange the data into a single table that shows totals by year and by product. The current best-selling product should be shown first.

1. Open the file **NWHist1.xls**.

2. Cut column B and paste it in column D.

3. Cut the data for "Ibuprofen" (D29:D40) and paste it beginning in cell B3.

4. Cut the data for "Acetaminophen" (D16:D27) and paste it beginning in cell C3.

5. Clear the cells below row 15 in column A.

6. Key **Total** in E3 and create formulas in column E to total each year's sales. (Hint: Use AutoSum, but be sure not to add the year.)

7. In cell A15, key **Total**. When AutoComplete suggests "Total Category Sales," press [Delete] to restore "Total," and then press [Enter].

8. Create formulas in row 15 that total individual and total product sales.

9. Clear cells A1:A2, which contain the title, and key the title as shown in Figure 3-17. Insert enough rows to accommodate the title and to leave two blank lines below it.

FIGURE 3-17

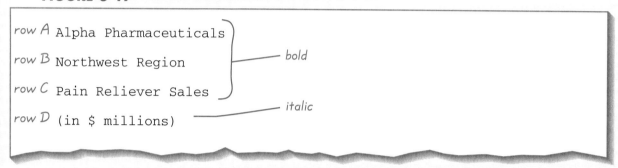

10. Insert the following data above the "Total" row:

    1997   0.209   0.133   0.054

11. Create a formula in column E to total the "1997" sales data.

12. Delete the "1986" data.

13. Right-align the row and column labels and make them bold.

14. Apply a single-line heavy bottom border to the column labels.

15. Apply a double-line bottom border to the sales data for "1997."

16. Format the dollar figures in comma style and displaying two decimal places.

17. Make all totals bold.

18. Save the workbook as *[your initials]***3-25.xls**.

19. Print and close the workbook.

Unit 1 Applications

APPLICATION 1-1

Enter and edit data, use AutoSum, create formulas, move data, and format text and numbers.

You have been asked to prepare a statement of assets for Alpha Pharmaceuticals, listing the things of value that the company owned at the end of 1996. The statement will become part of Alpha's balance sheet and will be included in Alpha's annual report.

1. Open the file **Assets1.xls**.

2. Change the width of column A to 12 characters and column B to 26 characters.

3. In the cell range C7:C10, key the following data:
   2600
   5960
   4710
   600

4. In cell C11, use AutoSum to create a formula for "Total current assets."

5. In cell C13, key **4980**. In cell C14, key **1520**

6. Cut the text in cell C15 and paste it into cell B15.

7. In cell C15, create a formula that subtracts "Depreciation" from "Property, plant, and equipment."

8. In cell C16, key **1390** for "Other Assets."

9. Italicize the amounts for "Total current assets," "Net fixed assets," and "Other Assets." Create a formula in cell C17 that totals these three amounts. Make that total bold.

10. Right-align the labels "Total current assets" and "Net fixed assets." Make both labels italic.

11. Format cells A1 and A2 as bold.

12. Apply a single-line bottom border to cells C10, C14, and C16.

13. Edit the label "(Depreciation)" so that it reads **(Less depreciation)**

14. Edit cells so that only the first letter of the first word of each label is capitalized. (Do not edit the title, however.)

15. Save the workbook as *[your initials]***u1-1.xls**.

16. Print and close the workbook.

APPLICATION 1-2

Enter data, construct formulas, use the Sum function, format text and numbers.

A statement of liabilities and shareholders' equity shows who has claims on the assets of a company. For instance, you can see the amounts owed to outsiders (long-term debt, current debt, accounts payable) and the amounts claimed by the owners (shareholders' equity). You have been asked to prepare such a statement for Alpha Pharmaceuticals. It will later become part of the company's balance sheet.

1. Open **Liablts1.xls**.

2. Change the width of column B to 25 characters.

3. Move the label in cell C13 to cell B13.

4. Enter the data in column C as shown in Figure U1-1, including Sum formulas in cells C8 and C13.

FIGURE U1-1

	A	B	C
5	Long-term liabilities		
6		Long-term debt	690
7		Other long-term liabilities	510
8		Total long-term liabilities	(SUM)
9	Current liabilities		
10		Debt due for repayment	1090
11		Accounts payable	1350
12		Other current liabilities	1760
13		Total current liabilities	(SUM)
14	Shareholders' equity		13320
15	Total liabilities and shareholders' equity		

5. Format cells C8, C13, and C14 as italic, and add a bottom border to cells C7, C12, and C14.

6. Move the current liabilities (rows 9 through 13) before the long-term liabilities (rows 5 through 8).

7. Check to make sure that formulas are still correct.

8. Create a formula in cell C15 that adds "Total current liabilities," "Total long-term liabilities," and "Shareholders' equity." Format the cell as bold.

9. Insert a new row at row 1. Change the first two lines of the title to read as follows:

   Alpha Pharmaceuticals
   Liabilities and Shareholder's Equity

10. Format the first three lines of the title as bold.

11. Save your workbook as *[your initials]*\u1-2.xls.

12. Print and close the workbook.

APPLICATION 1-3

Edit data, move data, insert and delete rows, construct formulas, and use AutoCalculate.

A balance sheet shows that a company's total assets equal the sum of its liabilities and shareholders' equity. You have been asked to construct a balance sheet for Alpha Pharmaceuticals using its asset statement and its statement of liabilities and shareholders' equity. To see the relative size of each item on the balance sheet, you should show the asset ratio for each item. The asset ratio is simply the item divided by the total assets.

1. Open the file **Balance1.xls**.

2. Sheet1 contains Alpha's asset statement. Click the Sheet2 tab to see the statement of liabilities and shareholders' equity.

3. On Sheet2, delete rows 1 through 5, including the title and the blank row.

4. Cut the rest of the material (cells A1:C10).

5. Click the Sheet1 tab, and paste the material below the asset statement, beginning in cell A19.

6. Edit cell A1 to read **Balance Sheet for Alpha Pharmaceuticals**

7. Insert a row at row 19, format blank cell A19 as bold, and key **Liabilities and Owners' Equity**

8. Format cell A5 (which contains the label "Assets") as bold.

9. Insert a new row at row 5.

10. Key $ (dollar sign) in cell C5 and key **% Assets** in cell D5. Format both cells as bold and centered.

11. In cell D8, enter the formula **=C8/C18**. (Cell C18 contains the value for total assets. The formula gives the percentage of total assets represented by the value in cell C8—that is, the asset ratio.)

12. In column D, create asset ratio formulas for all the values in the balance sheet. Be sure to divide by total assets (C18).

13. Format column D in percent style to display one decimal place.

14. Format column C in comma style to display no decimals.

15. Use AutoCalculate to verify the subtotals.

16. Save your workbook as *[your initials]***u1-3.xls**.

17. Print and close the workbook.

APPLICATION 1-4

Enter data in a selected range, construct formulas, use AutoSum, format text and numbers, and insert columns and rows.

In addition to a balance sheet, Alpha Pharmaceuticals' annual report will include an income statement. An income statement shows the revenues, expenses, and net income for a company over a period of time. You have been asked to prepare this statement and to format it attractively.

1. Open a new workbook.

2. Change the width of column A to 28 characters.

3. In the cell range A1:B10, key the data shown in Figure U1-2.

FIGURE U1-2

	A	B
1	Revenue	34050
2	Cost of goods sold	20410
3	Sales expenses	2400
4	Administrative expense	5210
5	Depreciation	480
6	Other expenses	200
7	Earnings before interest and taxes	
8	Interest expense	310
9	Income taxes	1930
10	Net income	

4. Move the entire block of labels and numbers so that "Revenue" appears in cell A7.

5. Starting in cell A1, key the following title:

Income Statement
Alpha Pharmaceuticals
1996
(Dollars in thousands)

6. Format the first three lines of the title as bold.

7. In cell B13, create a formula that subtracts cells B8:B12 (which are expenses) from "Revenue" (cell B7).

8. In cell B16, create a formula that subtracts both interest and taxes (cells B14:B15) from "Earnings before interest and taxes" (cell B13).

9. Key $ in cell B6 and % in cell C6. Format both cells as bold and centered.

10. In column C, create formulas that divide each item in column B by "Revenue" (B7). (Hint: The first three formulas are **=B7/B7**, **=B8/B7**, and **=B9/B7**.)

11. Format column C in percent style to display one decimal place.

12. Format column B in comma style to display no decimals.

13. Apply bottom borders to cells B12 and B15.

14. Proofread the worksheet.

15. Save the workbook as *[your initials]***u1-4.xls**.

16. Print and close the workbook.

APPLICATION 1-5

Enter data; construct formulas; use AutoSum; format text and numbers; and insert and delete cells, columns, and rows, as needed.

Prepare an income statement for yourself, your household, or another individual.

1. In a new worksheet, enter the income categories and data. Figure U1-3 (on the next page) lists suggested categories to include. (You **must** include categories shown in bold.)

2. Complete the worksheet by including the following information and formatting:

- A title identifying the name of the statement and the period of time it covers.
- Column labels for dollar amounts and for percentage of income.
- Bottom borders on cells before subtotals and totals.
- Numbers and text formatted appropriately.
- Attractive and clear layout.

3. Save your worksheet as *[your initials]***u1-5.xls**.

4. Print and close the worksheet.

FIGURE U1-3

Income (include at least two subcategories)

Job1

Job2

Investments

Interest

Total income

Expenses (include at least three subcategories)

Food

Housing

Utilities

Transportation

Clothing

Insurance

Medical

Loan payments

Entertainment

Total expenses

Earnings before taxes

Taxes

Net income

UNIT

2

Developing a Worksheet

Beautiful Belle Company

Sun Soft Heats Up Skin Care Market

The Beautiful Belle Company, also known as BBC, manufactures a moderately priced line of cosmetics. BBC is currently promoting a product named "Sun Soft." It's a 100%-natural hypo-allergenic lotion that has refined almond and sesame oils as its main ingredients. Although it's not proven, and can't be used in advertising, researchers have recently claimed that these oils are beneficial in protecting against skin cancer.

BBC is test-marketing Sun Soft in its Southwest region. Renata Santo, BBC's Southwest regional-sales manager, has decided to concentrate her efforts in the Phoenix area. However, Phoenix is a challenging market for Soft Sun, because a competing product, Corn Silk Cream, has a significant market share of skin care products there.

For the test marketing, Renata will need the following:

✔ A worksheet to keep track of weekly sales of Sun Soft and the competing product, Corn Silk Cream, over a two-month period. **(Lesson 4)**

✔ Once the test is complete, a worksheet that tracks Sun Soft sales in relation to Corn Silk Cream sales for three months. **(Lesson 5)**

✔ A worksheet that shows sales of selected creams for four quarters, with sales broken down by months and by product. **(Lesson 6)**

✔ A worksheet that compares Sun Soft sales by quarter for the last three years. **(Lesson 7)**

Designing and Printing a Worksheet

LESSON

4

OBJECTIVES

After completing this lesson, you will be able to:

1. Plan a worksheet on paper.
2. Put a worksheet plan on screen.
3. Keep row and column labels in view.
4. Select display options.
5. Create worksheet documentation.
6. Name worksheet tabs.
7. Print workbooks and print areas.
8. Print formulas.

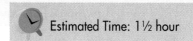

Estimated Time: 1½ hour

Creating a worksheet requires careful planning. A well-designed worksheet is easy to read, the data is arranged in a logical order, and the results are readily apparent. Decide what you need to accomplish with the worksheet before sitting down at the computer to create it. Designing the worksheet with a specific purpose in mind will help you decide what you want Excel to do with the data you enter. You can then choose from a variety of print settings so that the final, printed worksheet has the appearance you intended.

Planning a Worksheet on Paper

To design a worksheet that meets your goals, start your planning using pencil and paper. Even experienced users often create a diagram or sketch of a worksheet before actually keying any data. The plan should include labels that identify the purpose of rows and columns, areas where data will appear, and notes about formulas.

The procedures in this lesson generate a worksheet to help the sales manager of a small manufacturing company analyze the results of a two-month test-marketing program. The purpose of the worksheet is to compare test-market sales with those of a competing product.

EXERCISE   4-1   Sketch the Planned Worksheet

1. Write the worksheet heading **Sun Soft vs. Corn Silk Sales** at the top left-hand corner of a blank piece of paper. The heading of the worksheet must clearly state the purpose of the worksheet and provide a concise overview of its contents. In this case, the heading names the products and promises a competitive analysis based on sales.

2. Write the subtitles **April through May, 1997** and **(Broken down by gender)** on two separate rows underneath the heading.

3. Consider the structure of your worksheet. Its purpose is to store weekly sales information over a two-month period and make calculations that provide some useful competitive information. Although there are no hard-and-fast rules for worksheet design, it is generally a good idea to put consistent terms in columns and repetitive terms in rows.

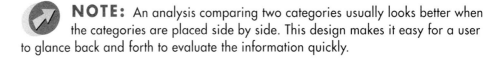 **NOTE:** An analysis comparing two categories usually looks better when the categories are placed side by side. This design makes it easy for a user to glance back and forth to evaluate the information quickly.

4. Define the labels that will identify the rows and columns of the worksheet. They should be as simple and clear as possible. For your worksheet, the weekly time periods can be designated by date, and the gender division can be designated by the labels **Men** and **Women**.

5. Write the following labels in a column along the left side of the page:

   April 5

   April 12

   April 19

   April 26

   Subtotal

   May 3

   May 10

   May 17

   May 24

May 31

Subtotal

Grand total

These weekly time periods are repetitive, so they can form the rows of your worksheet. The labels **Total**, **Subtotal**, and **Grand total** are standard and self-explanatory.

6. Write the labels **Sun Soft Lotion** and **Corn Silk Cream** in a row underneath the worksheet headings. The product categories are consistent, so they can be represented by the columns of the worksheet. You can divide the categories by product first, then by gender.

7. Write the labels **Men**, **Women**, and **Total** twice in the same row—once under each of the product categories, Sun Soft Lotion and Corn Silk Cream. (See Figure 4-1.) The basic design of your worksheet is now complete.

FIGURE 4-1   Preliminary worksheet design

Sun Soft vs. Corn Silk Sales
April through May, 1997
(Broken down by gender)

	Sun Soft Lotion				Corn Silk Cream		
	Men	Women	Total		Men	Women	Total
April 5							
April 12							
April 19							
April 26							
Subtotal							
May 3							
May 10							
May 17							
May 24							
May 31							
Subtotal							
Grand total							

8. Plan the placement of the columns and rows. The first column will hold the date labels. Columns B through D will hold the Sun Soft data. Column E will be blank. Columns F through H will hold the Corn Silk data.

9. Decide which formulas to use and where to put them on the worksheet. Our worksheet calculates monthly subtotals and a grand total of sales for both months. It also calculates total sales to both men and women for both the test product and the competing product. You'll use the SUM function to calculate these values.

FIGURE 4-2   Final worksheet design

Sun Soft vs. Corn Silk Sales
April through May, 1997
(Broken down by gender)

	Sun Soft Lotion				Corn Silk Cream		
	Men	Women	Total		Men	Women	Total
April 5			← =Sum				← =Sum
April 12			← =Sum				← =Sum
April 19			← =Sum				← =Sum
April 26			← =Sum				← =Sum
Subtotal	=Sum ↑	=Sum ↑	=Sum ↑		=Sum ↑	=Sum ↑	=Sum ↑
May 3			← =Sum				← =Sum
May 10			← =Sum				← =Sum
May 17			← =Sum				← =Sum
May 24			← =Sum				← =Sum
May 31			← =Sum				← =Sum
Subtotal	=Sum ↑	=Sum ↑	=Sum ↑		=Sum ↑	=Sum ↑	=Sum ↑
Grand total	=Sum ↑	=Sum ↑	=Sum ↑		=Sum ↑	=Sum ↑	=Sum ↑

Putting the Worksheet Plan on Screen

Once you've sketched the overall plan and know what data and formulas you will include, you are ready to build the worksheet in Excel. The heading, which includes the title and subtitles, is followed by row and column labels that provide structure for the worksheet. These basic design elements describe the purpose of a worksheet and organize its data.

EXERCISE **4-2** **Enter Row and Column Labels**

   1. Open a new Excel workbook.

   2. In cell A1, key **Sun Soft vs. Corn Silk Sales**

   3. In cell A2, key **April through May, 1997**

   4. In cell A3, key **(Broken down by gender)**

   5. In cell B5, key **Sun Soft Lotion**

   6. In cell F5, key **Corn Silk Cream**

   7. In cells B6, C6, and D6, key the following labels:

     Men   **Women**   **Total**

   8. In cells F6, G6, and H6, key the same labels a second time.

   9. In cell A7, key **April 5**. Notice that the date appears in the cell as "05-Apr" and is displayed on the formula bar as "04/05/1997" (or the current year).

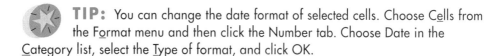

     TIP: You can change the date format of selected cells. Choose C<u>e</u>lls from the <u>F</u>ormat menu and then click the Number tab. Choose Date in the <u>C</u>ategory list, select the <u>T</u>ype of format, and click OK.

 10. In cells A8 through A10, key the following dates:

     April 12

     April 19

     April 26

 11. In cells A13 through A17, key the following dates:

     May 3

     May 10

     May 17

     May 24

     May 31

 12. To complete the worksheet design, key **Subtotal** in cells A11 and A18, and **Grand total** in cell A20. You'll use these rows to summarize the data.

 13. Widen column A to 10 characters to accommodate the row labels.

FIGURE 4-3
Worksheet plan with
labels entered

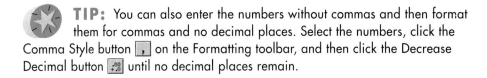

	A	B	C	D	E	F	G	H	I	J	K	L
1	Sun Soft vs. Corn Silk Sales											
2	April through May, 1997											
3	(Broken down by gender)											
4												
5		Sun Soft Lotion				Corn Silk Cream						
6		Men	Women	Total		Men	Women	Total				
7	05-Apr											
8	12-Apr											
9	19-Apr											
10	26-Apr											
11	Subtotal											
12												
13	03-May											
14	10-May											
15	17-May											
16	24-May											
17	31-May											
18	Subtotal											
19												
20	Grand total											

Sheet1 / Sheet2 / Sheet3 / Sheet4 / Sheet5 / Sheet6 /

EXERCISE | **4-3** | **Enter Test Data**

The body of the worksheet will consist of data. Entering test data into the
worksheet allows you to test formula calculations. *Test data* should consist of
numbers that are easy to calculate in your head. You can then tell at a glance
whether your formulas are performing the correct calculations.

1. Key the following test data for Sun Soft in columns B and C and the
appropriate rows as shown below. Start with 500 in cell B7, and include
commas.

TIP: You can also enter the numbers without commas and then format
them for commas and no decimal places. Select the numbers, click the
Comma Style button ⎡,⎤ on the Formatting toolbar, and then click the Decrease
Decimal button ⎡.00⎤ until no decimal places remain.

April 5	**500**	**1,000**
April 12	**600**	**1,200**
April 19	**1,200**	**600**
April 26	**1,000**	**500**
May 3	**1,400**	**1,400**
May 10	**800**	**1,000**
May 17	**900**	**800**
May 24	**1,350**	**1,400**
May 31	**2,000**	**2,200**

2. Key the following test data for Corn Silk in columns F and G and the appropriate rows as shown below. Start with **1,000** in cell F7, and include commas.

April 5	**1,000**	**2,000**
April 12	**1,200**	**2,400**
April 19	**2,400**	**1,200**
April 26	**2,000**	**1,000**
May 3	**2,100**	**2,100**
May 10	**1,800**	**1,600**
May 17	**1,900**	**2,000**
May 24	**1,200**	**1,500**
May 31	**1,150**	**800**

FIGURE 4-4
Worksheet plan with
data entered

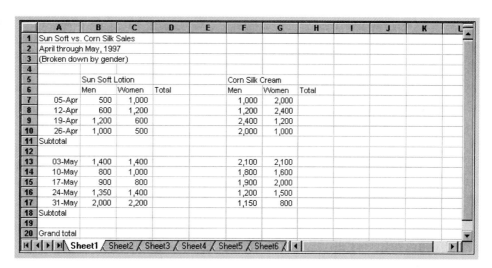

EXERCISE 4-4 Enter Formulas

Once the worksheet data is entered, you can enter formulas to automate the calculations. The AutoSum button Σ totals a range within a row or column. It can also total ranges in several rows and columns at the same time, and can calculate subtotals within rows or columns.

1. Select cells D7 through D10, and click Σ on the Standard toolbar. The SUM function is entered in each cell, and the total values are displayed. If necessary, format these cells in comma style with no decimal places.

2. Select cells B11 through D11, and click Σ. AutoSum totals the three separate ranges in the same step.

3. Select cells B13 through D18 (the data cells and the cells for their totals).

4. Click Σ. Excel automatically sums the rows and columns of selected data.

5. Select cells F7 through H11, hold down Ctrl, and select cells F13 through H18.

6. Release Ctrl.

7. Click Σ to enter the totals for the two cell ranges at the same time. All of the totals and subtotals for Corn Silk are now entered.

8. Move to cell B20, and click Σ. Excel suggests cell B18, the second subtotal.

9. Hold down Ctrl, and click cell B11, the first subtotal.

10. Release Ctrl and press Enter. Excel adds the first subtotal to the formula. The formula =SUM(B18,B11) appears in the formula bar for cell B20.

11. Select cells C7 through C20, and then click Σ. The formula in cell C20 adds the two subtotals.

12. Select cells D7 through D20, and then click Σ.

13. Select cells F7 through H20, and then click Σ. Examine the formula in cell H20, which adds the grand totals of columns F and G instead of summing the subtotals of column H (which would produce the same result).

14. Save the workbook as *[your initials]*4-4.xls.

FIGURE 4-5
Worksheet with formulas

	A	B	C	D	E	F	G	H	I	J	K	L
1	Sun Soft vs. Corn Silk Sales											
2	April through May, 1997											
3	(Broken down by gender)											
4												
5		Sun Soft Lotion				Corn Silk Cream						
6		Men	Women	Total		Men	Women	Total				
7	05-Apr	500	1,000	1,500		1,000	2,000	3,000				
8	12-Apr	600	1,200	1,800		1,200	2,400	3,600				
9	19-Apr	1,200	600	1,800		2,400	1,200	3,600				
10	26-Apr	1,000	500	1,500		2,000	1,000	3,000				
11	Subtotal	3,300	3,300	6,600		6,600	6,600	13,200				
12												
13	03-May	1,400	1,400	2,800		2,100	2,100	4,200				
14	10-May	800	1,000	1,800		1,800	1,600	3,400				
15	17-May	900	800	1,700		1,900	2,000	3,900				
16	24-May	1,350	1,400	2,750		1,200	1,500	2,700				
17	31-May	2,000	2,200	4,200		1,150	800	1,950				
18	Subtotal	6,450	6,800	13,250		8,150	8,000	16,150				
19												
20	Grand total	9,750	10,100	19,850		14,750	14,600	29,350				

Sheet1 / Sheet2 / Sheet3 / Sheet4 / Sheet5 / Sheet6 /

Keeping Row and Column Labels in View

Frequently, the rows and columns of a worksheet extend beyond the display screen. Excel allows you to split the worksheet into multiple *panes* so that you can see row and column labels as you enter data or formulas. Multiple panes also enable you to scroll through data to locate and select cells to be included in calculations. For example, when creating a grand total, you might need to scroll to the top of a large worksheet to include one or more subtotals.

EXERCISE 4-5 Split a Worksheet into Panes

1. Move to cell A7, just under the column labels.

2. In the <u>W</u>indow menu, choose <u>S</u>plit. The screen is split into two horizontal panes by a horizontal double line. Each pane has its own vertical scroll bar, permitting it to be scrolled on its own.

 TIP: You can also split a worksheet vertically by selecting a row first.

3. Click the down vertical scroll arrow for the bottom pane to move row 13 directly under the column labels. Splitting the screen under the column labels makes it easier to enter formulas for the May subtotal and the grand total.

4. Experiment with the scroll buttons of both panes.

FIGURE 4-6
Screen split horizontally

	A	B	C	D	E	F	G	H	I
1	Sun Soft vs. Corn Silk Sales								
2	April through May, 1997								
3	(Broken down by gender)								
4									
5			tion						
6			Women	Total		Men	Women	Total	
13	03-May	1,400	1,400	2,800		2,100	2,100	4,200	
14	10-May	800	1,000	1,800		1,800	1,600	3,400	
15	17-May	900	800	1,700		1,900	2,000	3,900	
16	24-May	1,350	1,400	2,750		1,200	1,500	2,700	
17	31-May	2,000	2,200	4,200		1,150	800	1,950	
18	Subtotal	6,450	6,800	13,250		8,150	8,000	16,150	
19									
20	Grand total	9,750	10,100	19,850		14,750	14,600	29,350	
21									
22									

Split bar / Independent scroll bars

Sheet1 / Sheet2 / Sheet3 / Sheet4 / Sheet5 / Sheet6

5. In the <u>W</u>indow menu, choose Remove <u>S</u>plit. The original view of the worksheet is restored.

NOTE: The <u>S</u>plit option on the <u>W</u>indow menu changes to Remove <u>S</u>plit when a worksheet is split into panes.

6. Move to cell B7.

7. In the <u>W</u>indow menu, choose <u>S</u>plit. The window splits above and to the left of the active cell. In four panes, you can see both row and column labels at the same time.

FIGURE 4-7
Screen split
horizontally and
vertically

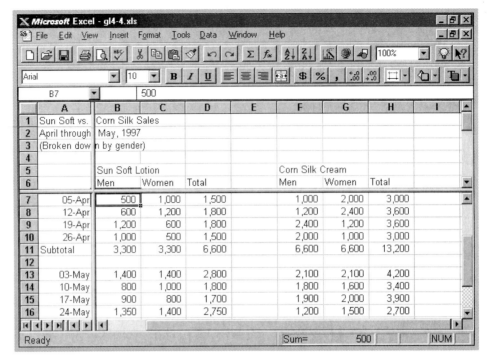

TIP: To create a vertical split only, select a column (or select a cell in row 1) before choosing Split from the Window menu.

EXERCISE **4-6** Freeze Panes

The Freeze Panes command in the Window menu will freeze row labels, column labels, or both. A single set of scroll arrows and buttons moves data only, but leaves labels in place.

1. In the Window menu, choose Remove Split.

2. Move to cell B7, if necessary.

3. In the Window menu, choose Freeze Panes. Single lines divide the worksheet, marking frozen areas.

4. Experiment with the scroll buttons and the arrow keys.

5. In the Window menu, choose Unfreeze Panes to restore the original view of the worksheet.

EXERCISE **4-7** Use Split Boxes and Split Bars

Another way to split a screen into multiple panes is to use the horizontal and vertical *split boxes.* The horizontal split box appears in the upper right-hand corner of the document window; it is the gray, rectangular box located above the vertical scroll arrow. The vertical split box is found at the far right of the horizontal scroll bar at the bottom of the document window.

FIGURE 4-8
Split boxes

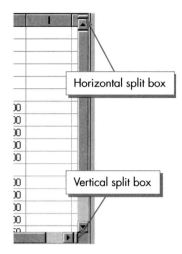

Horizontal split box

Vertical split box

Clicking a split box produces a *split bar,* which can be dragged to the desired position on the worksheet to split the screen. Double-clicking a split box positions the split bar automatically.

1. Move to cell B7, if necessary.

2. Move the mouse pointer to the horizontal split box at the top of the vertical scroll bar. The mouse pointer changes to a split pointer ≑.

3. Double-click the split box. A split bar appears above the active cell.

4. Move the mouse pointer to the vertical split box at the right of the horizontal scroll bar.

5. Hold down the left mouse button, and then drag and drop the split bar between columns A and B.

6. Move the mouse pointer to the intersection of the two split bars. The pointer becomes a four-headed arrow ✛.

7. Double-click the intersection of the two split bars to remove the split.

 TIP: To adjust horizontal or vertical splits, drag the split bar to the new location. You can also change the location of a four-pane split by dragging its intersection.

Selecting Display Options

You can change how a worksheet is displayed on the screen to make it easier to work with. *Zoom* options change the magnification of the display. You can enlarge it to see more detail, or you can reduce it to show more of the worksheet at one time.

You can also choose whether to display gridlines and row and column headings.

EXERCISE **4-8** **Zoom to Magnify and Reduce the Display**

Zoom control acts like a magnifying glass. The size of the characters displayed on the screen is expressed in terms of percentages. Higher percentages mean magnified characters, but show less of the worksheet on the screen. Lower percentages display smaller characters, but show more of the worksheet on the screen. Zoom does not affect the size of the printed worksheet.

Excel provides two ways to use zoom:

- Use the Zoom Control button on the Standard toolbar
- Choose Zoom from the View menu

FIGURE 4-9
Zoom dialog box

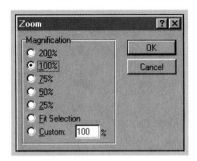

1. Choose Zoom from the View menu.
2. In the Zoom dialog box, click 75%, and then click OK. The displayed text becomes smaller and more of the worksheet can be seen. The Zoom Control box 75% ▼ now displays "75%."
3. Move to cell D7.
4. Choose Zoom from the View menu.
5. Click Custom, key **400**, and click OK. 400% is the largest display type you can specify.
6. Click the Zoom Control button (the arrow at the right of the Zoom Control box) on the Standard toolbar, and click 75% on the drop-down menu.

FIGURE 4-10
Zoom control

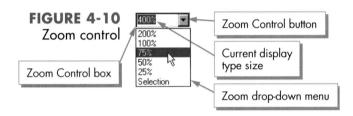

EXERCISE 4-9 **Remove Gridlines and Headers from the Screen**

You can use other Excel options to vary the on-screen appearance of the worksheet. For example, you can choose whether to display cell gridlines or row and column headings.

1. Choose Options from the Tools menu. The Options dialog box appears.
2. Click the View tab, if necessary. See Figure 4-11 on the next page.
3. Under the Window Options, click the Gridlines check box and the Row & Column Headers check box to clear them. Next, click OK. You have now removed gridlines and row and column headings from the worksheet display. Viewing the worksheet without these elements helps you imagine the final printed worksheet's appearance.
4. Move about the worksheet using the Arrow keys. Note that even though the gridlines are not visible, each cell is outlined when active. In addition, although the row and column headers are not visible, the address of the active cell appears in the reference area of the formula bar.

FIGURE 4-11
Options dialog box

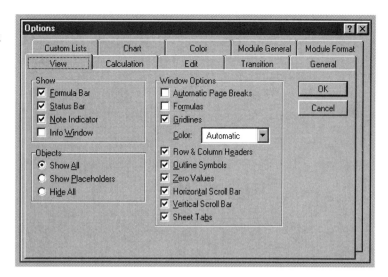

5. Move to cell D20, which contains previously entered formulas. Note that the contents of the cell appear in the entry area of the formula bar. The result of the formula appears in the status bar.

6. Reset the options in the Options dialog box so that both gridlines and row and column headings are displayed on the worksheet.

Creating Worksheet Documentation

Once you've created a worksheet, you may want others to be able to use it. You can provide users with some basic information on a separate worksheet.

EXERCISE 4-10 **Create Worksheet Documentation**

1. Click the Sheet2 tab to move to a new worksheet.

2. In cell A1, key **Worksheet Documentation**

3. Key the following labels in column A, beginning in cell A3:

Name of creator:

Date created:

Date revised:

Revised by:

Purpose and description:

Special instructions:

4. Widen column A to 25 characters to accommodate the row labels.

5. In column B, key the information shown in Figure 4-12.

115

FIGURE 4-12
Worksheet
documentation

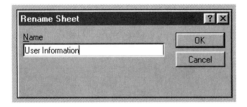

	A	B	C	D	E	F	G	
1	Worksheet Documentation							
2								
3	Name of creator:	Your name						
4	Date created:	06/01/97						
5	Date revised:	06/03/97						
6	Revised by:	Your name						
7	Purpose and description:	To compare weekly sales of Sun Soft and Corn Silk in April and May.						
8	Special instructions:	Do not change "Total," "Subtotal," or "Grand total" formulas.						
9								
10								
11								
12								
13								
14								
15								
16								

Sheet1 \ **Sheet2** / Sheet3 / Sheet4 / Sheet5 / Sheet6 /

6. Save the workbook as *[your initials]***4-10.xls**.

Naming Worksheet Tabs

As you learned in Lesson 1, each new Excel workbook opens with 16 sheets, that are given the name Sheet1 through Sheet16 by default. When you work with more than one worksheet, naming a worksheet tab makes its purpose immediately obvious.

EXERCISE **4-11** **Name Worksheet Tabs**

1. Double-click the Sheet2 tab. Sheet2 becomes active and the Rename Sheet dialog box opens.

2. Key **User Information** in the Name text box, and then click OK.

FIGURE 4-13
The Rename Sheet
dialog box

Rename Sheet	? X
Name	OK
User Information	Cancel

3. Double-click the Sheet1 tab to open the Rename Sheet dialog box.

4. Key **Sales Comparison** in the Name text box.

 NOTE: Sheet names should tell the user exactly what the sheet includes using only a word or two. Sheet names can be up to 31 characters long, including spaces.

Printing

Excel lets you control how your work is printed. You can:

- Preview a worksheet or an entire workbook before printing
- Change page orientation
- Position the print area on the page
- Create headers and footers
- Print with or without gridlines or row and column headings
- Print all or part of a worksheet or workbook

EXERCISE 4-12 Preview the Workbook before Printing

Previewing a worksheet before you print allows you to see the page layout, headers and footers, print formatting, and page breaks. Although it is always a good idea to preview a worksheet, it makes particular sense if it contains graphics, drawings, or charts. After all, it takes less time to preview a complex worksheet than to print it.

1. Make the Sales Comparison worksheet active, if necessary.

2. Choose Print Preview from the File menu, or click the Print Preview button on the Standard toolbar. At the top of the print preview screen, the Next button is dimmed. The current worksheet fits on one page, and the second worksheet is not available.

3. Click the Print button to open the Print dialog box, select Entire Workbook under Print What, and then click the Preview button. Print preview labels the current worksheet "Preview: Page 1 of 2," and the Next button becomes available. See Figure 4-14 on the next page.

4. Click Next. The User Information sheet ("Preview: Page 2 of 2") is displayed.

5. Click Zoom at the top of the preview screen (or click the reduced document). The worksheet is displayed in actual size.

TIP: Click the magnifier pointer ◉ on the full-page document to Zoom to actual size. Click the arrow pointer ⤢ on the enlarged document to Zoom to reduced display.

6. Use the scroll arrows to view other parts of the worksheet in actual size.

7. Click Previous to display page 1 again.

FIGURE 4-14
Print preview
display

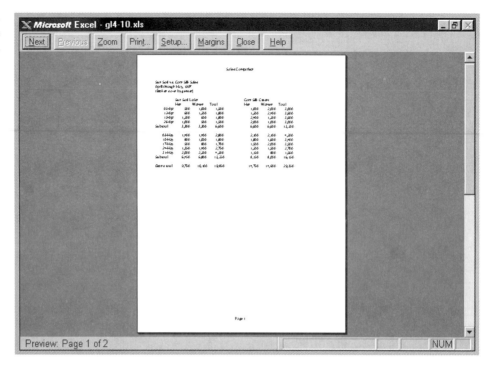

8. Click Zoom (or click the document) again to return the worksheet to full-page size.

9. Click Close to close the preview window.

EXERCISE 4-13 Choose a Page Orientation

One of the most useful print functions offered by Excel is *page orientation*, which allows you to print worksheets in either *portrait* or *landscape* orientation. In portrait orientation, the page is vertical, 8½″ × 11″. In landscape orientation, the page is horizontal, 11″ × 8½″. Worksheets with relatively few columns can be printed in portrait orientation. Wide worksheets will require landscape orientation.

1. Choose Page Setup from the File menu to open the Page Setup dialog box.

 NOTE: The Setup button at the top of the Print Preview screen also opens the Page Setup dialog box.

2. Click the Page tab, if necessary.

3. Click Landscape, and then click OK. (See Figure 4-15 on the next page.)

4. Click the Print Preview button. The worksheet has a better appearance in landscape orientation because its width exceeds its length.

FIGURE 4-15
Choosing page
orientation

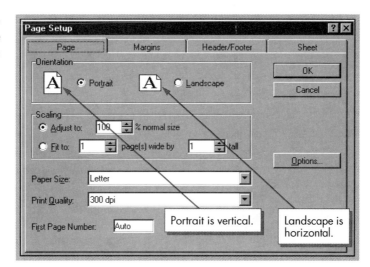

5. Click Next. The second sheet is displayed in portrait orientation. Page Setup options apply only to the current worksheet.

EXERCISE 4-14 Center the Print Area on a Page

You can center worksheets on a page to improve the page layout. This is especially useful when worksheets are relatively small or all of the pages are the same size.

1. While in Print Preview click Previous to display the first worksheet.
2. Click Setup, and then click the Margins tab.
3. Click the Horizontally and Vertically check boxes. The Preview area in the dialog box displays the centered settings.

FIGURE 4-16
Center on Page
options

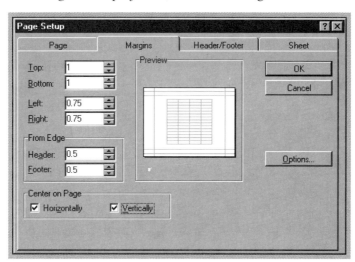

4. Click OK, and then click Close.

EXERCISE 4-15 **Enter a Header and Footer**

Headers and footers provide helpful information about a printed document. You can easily format these features in Excel using the Page Setup dialog box.

1. Choose Page Setup from the File menu.

2. Click the Header/Footer tab.

3. Click Custom Header. The insertion point is automatically positioned in the Left Section box so that you can begin changing the header. Excel uses the sheet name "Sales Comparison" (represented by the code &[Tab]) as the default header.

4. Key your name in the Left Section box. This portion of the header will appear at the upper left-hand corner of the printed page.

5. Press [Tab]. The insertion point moves to the Center Section box.

6. Click the File Name button 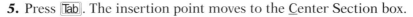 to show the filename in the Center Section header. The ampersand (&) and the word "File" in brackets indicate that the worksheet filename will appear in the header.

7. Click the Date button to include the current date in the Right Section header.

FIGURE 4-17
Creating a custom header

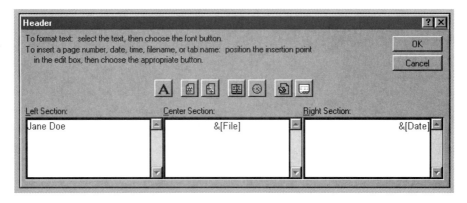

8. Click OK. Your changes appear in the Header text box.

9. Click Custom Footer, and then press [Tab]. The insertion point moves to the Center Section box of the Footer dialog box.

10. Click the Sheet Name button to include the current sheet name in the footer. (See Figure 4-18 on the next page.)

11. Click OK. Your changes appear in the Footer text box.

12. Click OK to close the Page Setup dialog box.

13. Move to the User Information sheet. Use Page Setup to make the same changes to the header and footer of this sheet.

14. Close the Print Preview window.

FIGURE 4-18
New header and
footer

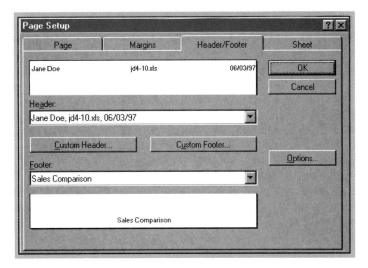

EXERCISE **Print a Workbook**

Now that you've set up the worksheet, it's time to print. Excel enables you to print single sheets or multiple sheets of a workbook.

1. Save the workbook as *[your initials]***4-16.xls**.

TIP: Save a workbook immediately before or after printing to preserve the current print settings.

2. Choose <u>P</u>rint from the <u>F</u>ile menu or press Ctrl+P to open the Print dialog box. The dialog box displays Excel's default settings and identifies your designated printer.

FIGURE 4-19
Print dialog box

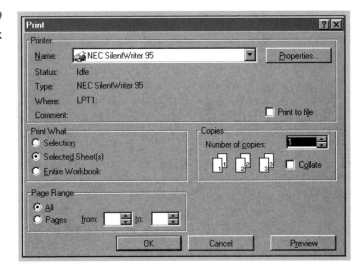

TIP: You can click 🖶 on the Standard Toolbar to print the current worksheet automatically.

3. Click Entire Workbook, and then click OK to print both sheets of your workbook.

4. The Printing dialog box appears as your workbook is sent to the printer. Click Cancel if you want to stop the print job.

EXERCISE 4-17 Change the Print Area

Excel automatically prints the entire worksheet, unless you specify otherwise. Sometimes you may wish to print a specific range of cells—called a *print area*. If you select multiple print areas, each area will begin printing on a separate page. Headers and footers will also appear when you print an area.

1. Move to the Sales Comparison sheet, if necessary.
2. Select cells A5 through D11.
3. Choose Print from the File menu.
4. Click Selection.
5. Click OK. Excel prints the selected portion of the worksheet.

TIP: You can also define a print area by selecting a range of cells, choosing Print Area from the File menu, and then choosing Set Print Area. Clicking 🖶 on the Standard toolbar will print the current print area. To deselect the print area, choose File, Print Area, and then Clear Print Area.

6. Select cells A6 through D11.
7. Hold down the [Ctrl] key, select cells A13 through D18, and release the [Ctrl] key. Two areas are selected.
8. Choose Print from the File menu.
9. Click Selection and click OK. Excel prints the selected portions of the worksheet on two separate pages.

Printing Formulas

You may want to display formulas on-screen or in your printed worksheet for documentation purposes or to find and correct problems. You can either check the Formulas box on the View tab of the Options dialog box or use the keyboard shortcut [Ctrl]+[`].

EXERCISE 4-18 **Set View for Formulas**

1. Choose Options from the Tools menu.

2. Select the View tab, if necessary.

> **NOTE:** View options affect the on-screen appearance of your worksheet. The Formulas option, however, also affects the printed worksheet. Most print options—such as row and column headings and gridlines—must be controlled through the Page Setup dialog box.

FIGURE 4-20
Options dialog box

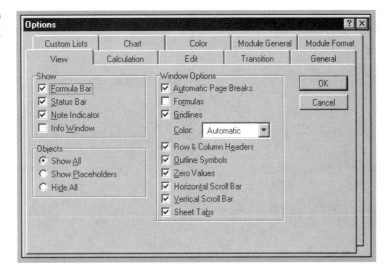

3. Click the Formulas check box, and click OK. Excel displays all formulas entered in their appropriate worksheet cells. Note that the column widths have been changed to accommodate the wider formulas. As a result, only a portion of the worksheet fits on screen. Excel continues to display the sum for each formula in the status bar.

FIGURE 4-21
Formulas displayed
in worksheet

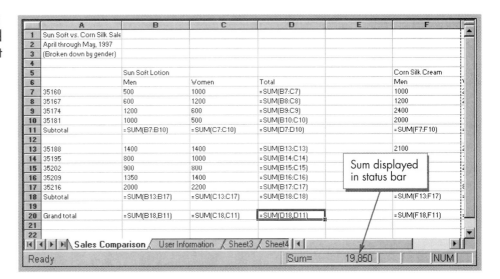

123

4. Press Ctrl+`. The worksheet is displayed normally. (The ` key is found to the left of the 1 key.)

5. Press Ctrl+` to display formulas once again.

EXERCISE 4-19 Print with Grids and Headings

You can add gridlines and row and column headings to your worksheet print-out using Page Setup to help you verify that each formula is in the right place.

1. Choose Page Setup from the File menu, and click the Sheet tab, if necessary.

2. Click Gridlines and Row and Column Headings in the Print area of the dialog box.

3. Move to the Page tab and click Landscape, if necessary.

4. Click Fit to and make sure that the text boxes to the right show 1 page(s) wide by 1 tall.

NOTE: Fit to shrinks the size of printed characters, so the worksheet will fit in the number of pages you indicate.

5. Click the Print Preview button to view the worksheet before printing. Click Zoom if you want to take a closer look.

6. Click the Print button to open the Print dialog box, and then click OK.

7. Close the workbook. Don't save the changes.

TIP: If you save settings that print formulas, you will have to change settings the next time you want to print the normal worksheet.

COMMAND SUMMARY

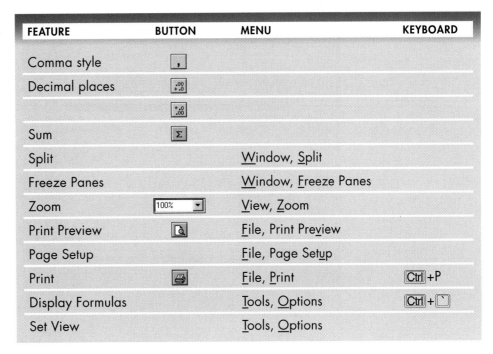

FEATURE	BUTTON	MENU	KEYBOARD
Comma style	,		
Decimal places	.00 →.0		
	←.0 .00		
Sum	Σ		
Split		<u>W</u>indow, <u>S</u>plit	
Freeze Panes		<u>W</u>indow, <u>F</u>reeze Panes	
Zoom	100% ▼	<u>V</u>iew, <u>Z</u>oom	
Print Preview	🔍	<u>F</u>ile, Print Pre<u>v</u>iew	
Page Setup		<u>F</u>ile, Page Set<u>u</u>p	
Print	🖨	<u>F</u>ile, <u>P</u>rint	Ctrl +P
Display Formulas		<u>T</u>ools, <u>O</u>ptions	Ctrl + `
Set View		<u>T</u>ools, <u>O</u>ptions	

USING HELP

Excel offers several ways to display information about a particular Help topic. For example, once you've opened the Help Topics dialog box, you can locate a topic by using the Contents or Index tabs:

- Use the Contents tab in the same way that you would use the table of contents in a book. The Contents tab displays the contents of Help in outline form.

- Use the Index tab in the same way that you would use the index of a book to look up a topic. Simply key a topic, and then scroll through the alphabetical index.

Display a Help screen about the SUM function using the Help Index:

1. Choose <u>M</u>icrosoft Excel Help Topics from the <u>H</u>elp menu or press F1 .

2. Click the Index tab, if necessary.

3. In the first box, key **sum**. As you're keying the word, the box below will scroll within the list of index entries until the entry "sum of power series" is highlighted.

FIGURE 4-22
Using the Help
Index

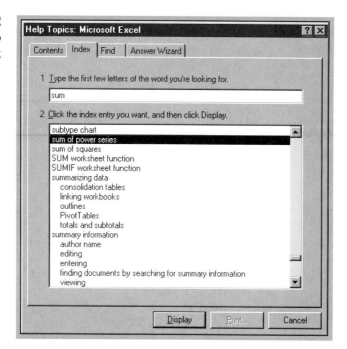

4. In the list of entries, highlight the entry "SUM worksheet function" and click the <u>D</u>isplay button. Two topics appear for the entry.

5. After a few seconds, Excel displays a window about the SUM function.

Concepts Review

TRUE/FALSE QUESTIONS

Each of the following statements is either true or false. Indicate your choice by circling T or F.

T F **1.** It's best to begin entering data in Excel before designing a worksheet with pencil and paper.

T F **2.** Repetitive information should be placed in rows.

T F **3.** The formula bar displays the current cell's contents and address.

T F **4.** Worksheets can be split into either two or four panes.

T F **5.** Zoom is used to speed up the printing process.

T F **6.** You should create worksheet documentation to show how you planned the worksheet.

T F **7.** You select page orientation from the Print Preview dialog box.

T F **8.** You can display gridlines and headings on-screen as well as in a printed worksheet.

SHORT ANSWER QUESTIONS

Write the correct answer in the space provided.

1. What name is given to the simple numbers used to verify the accuracy of formulas?

_____

2. Which function would you use to total a column of numbers?

_____

3. Which command enables you to divide a worksheet into two parts?

_____

4. Which command enables you to keep row and column labels in one place while you scroll data?

_____

5. What do you call a range of cells to be printed?

_____

127

6. Which part of the screen identifies each sheet of an Excel workbook?

_____

7. Which dialog box enables you to enter a custom header and footer?

_____

8. Which page orientation displays the worksheet horizontally?

_____

CRITICAL THINKING

Answer these questions on a separate piece of paper. There are no right or wrong answers. Support your answer with examples from your own experience, if possible.

1. Planning and sketching a worksheet with pencil and paper might seem like a waste of time in the "computer age." What might happen if you skip the planning stage? In what types of situations would it be especially important to plan and sketch the worksheet before entering data in Excel?

2. Describe a project or work situation in which you would have liked to have documentation available. What problem were you trying to solve? How would good documentation of the project have helped you?

3. In this lesson you planned the design of a worksheet, entered data and formulas into the worksheet, and printed it. In your view, which phase of this process is most important? Which phase of the process is least important? Why?

Skills Review

EXERCISE 4-20

Plan a worksheet in pencil, and enter labels, test data, and formulas on-screen.

1. Plan and sketch a worksheet by following these steps:

a. Write the worksheet heading **First Quarter Sales** at the top of a blank page.

b. Write the following labels in a column along the left side of your page:

Sales Rep

Davis

Jackson

Miller

Pierce

Brown

Total

   c. Write the labels **January**, **February**, **March**, and **Total** in a row to the right of the label **Sales Rep**

   d. Label the rows and columns where you will key this information.

   e. Write **=SUM** in the cells that will total rows and columns.

  2. Enter row and column labels on-screen by following these steps:

   b. Open a new Excel workbook.

   c. Key the heading **First Quarter Sales** in cell A1.

   d. Key the row labels from your paper sketch in cells A3 through A9.

   e. Key the column labels from your paper sketch in cells B3 through E3.

  3. Enter the following test data in the worksheet:

FIGURE 4-23

	B	C	D
4	2000	3000	2500
5	2500	3000	2500
6	3000	2500	3000
7	1500	2000	1000
8	2500	2500	3000

  4. Enter formulas on-screen using the following steps:

   a. Select cells E4 through E8 and click Σ.

   b. Select cells B9 through E9 and click Σ.

  5. Save the workbook as *[your initials]***4-20.xls**.

  6. Print and close the workbook.

EXERCISE 4-21

Split a worksheet into panes, freeze panes, use Zoom, and remove gridlines and headers from the screen.

  1. Open the file **Expense1.xls**.

  2. Split the worksheet into panes by following these steps:

   a. Move to cell A10.

    b. Choose <u>S</u>plit from the <u>W</u>indow menu.

    c. Click the down vertical scroll arrow for the bottom pane until the Total row for the Phoenix office becomes visible.

  3. Freeze the worksheet panes by following these steps:

    a. Choose <u>F</u>reeze Panes from the <u>W</u>indow menu.

    b. Click the vertical scroll bar to compare data for the two offices

  4. Change the size of the worksheet on-screen by choosing <u>Z</u>oom from the <u>V</u>iew menu and then selecting 75%.

  5. Remove gridlines from the screen by following these steps:

    a. Choose <u>O</u>ptions from the <u>T</u>ools menu.

    b. When the Options dialog box appears, click the View tab, if necessary.

    c. Clear the <u>G</u>ridlines and Row and Column H<u>e</u>aders check boxes and then click OK.

  6. Save the workbook as *[your initials]***4-21.xls**.

  7. Close the workbook.

EXERCISE 4-22

Create documentation for a worksheet and name worksheet tabs.

  1. Open the file **Expense2.xls**. Look at Sheet1 and Sheet2.

  2. Create documentation for the worksheet by following these steps:

    a. Click Sheet3 and then key **Worksheet Documentation** in cell A1.

    b. Widen column A to 25 characters to accommodate the row labels.

    c. Key the following labels in column A and information in column B:

FIGURE 4-24

	A	B
3	Name of creator:	Renata Santo
4	Date created:	29-Jun-97
5	Date revised:	[today's date]
6	Revised by:	[your name]
7	Purpose and description:	Projected increases in Q1 expenses.
8	Special instructions:	Note formulas in row 10 and column D.

3. Rename the worksheet tabs by following these steps:

    a. Double-click the Sheet3 tab to open the Rename Sheet dialog box.

    b. Key **Documentation** in the <u>N</u>ame text box, and then click OK.

4. Rename Sheet2 as **Phoenix Increase**.

5. Rename Sheet1 as **San Francisco Increase**.

6. Save the document as *[your initials]***4-22.xls**.

7. Print the entire workbook by following these steps:

    a. Press Ctrl+P.

    b. Select <u>E</u>ntire Workbook in the Print dialog box, and then click OK.

8. Close the workbook.

EXERCISE 4-23

Choose page orientation, center the print area, change headers and footers, and print with and without gridlines, headings, and formulas.

1. Open the file **Revenue.xls**.

2. Choose landscape orientation by following these steps:

    a. Choose Page Set<u>u</u>p from the <u>F</u>ile menu.

    b. Click the Page tab, if necessary.

    c. Click <u>L</u>andscape.

    d. Click the Print Previe<u>w</u> button to view the entire worksheet on one page.

3. Center the print area on the page by following these steps:

    a. While still in Print Preview, click <u>S</u>etup.

    b. Click the Margins tab.

    c. Clear the Hori<u>z</u>ontally and <u>V</u>ertically check boxes.

4. Change the headers and footers by following these steps:

    a. Click the Header/Footer tab in the Page Setup dialog box, and then click <u>C</u>ustom Header.

    b. Key your name in the <u>L</u>eft Section box and press Tab.

    c. Click the Filename button in the <u>C</u>enter Section header.

    d. Click the Date button in the <u>R</u>ight Section header, and then click OK.

    e. Click C<u>u</u>stom Footer, and press Tab to select the default footer in the <u>C</u>enter Section box.

    f. Click the Sheet Name button.

5. Print the worksheet without gridlines by following these steps:

    a. Click the Sheet tab in the Page Setup dialog box.

    b. Clear the Gridlines check box, and click OK to view the worksheet in Print Preview.

    c. Click Print to open the Print dialog box, and then click OK to print the worksheet.

6. Change the print area and print the worksheet with headings and formulas by following these steps:

    a. Select columns A through D, choose Print Area from the File Menu, and choose Set Print Area.

    b. Choose Options from the Tools menu, and select the View tab, if necessary.

    c. Check the Formulas box, and then click OK.

    d. Choose Page Setup from the File menu, and then click the Sheet tab, if necessary.

    e. Check the Gridlines and Row and Column Headings boxes.

    f. Click the Page tab and choose Landscape, if necessary.

    g. Click the Print Preview button to view the worksheet before printing. Click Zoom if you want to take a closer look.

    h. Click the Print button to open the Print dialog box, and then click OK to print.

7. Press `Ctrl`+`` ` `` to toggle from formula view to normal view.

8. Choose Print Area from the File Menu, and then choose Clear Print Area.

9. Save the workbook as *[your initials]***4-23.xls** and then close it.

Lesson Applications

Insert a row, enter data, add formulas, apply borders and text attributes, change headers and footers, and print.

Nate Rosario, the controller for the Beautiful Belle company, needs to prepare a forecast of profits (or net income) for the next five years.

1. Open the file **NetInc1.xls**.

2. Insert a row between the "Cost of Goods" and "Marketing" labels.

3. Label the new row **Salaries** and insert the data as shown in Figure 4-23.

FIGURE 4-25

	1997	1998	1999	2000	2001
Sales	$4,586	$5,576	$6,345	$7,125	$7,610
Expenses					
Cost of Goods	$609	$744	$846	$950	$1,015
Salaries	*$1142*	*$1394*	*$1586*	*$1781*	*$1902*
Marketing	$1,218	$1,486	$1,692	$1,900	$2,029
Research	$456	$557	$634	$712	$761
Total Expenses	← —————— *Sum of expenses* —————— →				
Net Income	← ———— *Sales – Total Expenses* ———— →				

4. Insert Total Expense formulas that sum the Cost of Goods, Salary, Marketing, and Research expenses for each year.

5. Insert Net Income formulas for each year. Net income is calculated by subtracting Total Expenses from Sales.

6. Apply a single-line bottom border to the research figures (just above the total expense cells).

7. Format the labels "Sales," "Total Expenses," and "Net Income" in bold italic, and format the net income figures in bold.

8. Center the worksheet on the page and print it without gridlines and headers.

9. Delete the header, and replace the footer in the Center Section with the filename code.

10. Save the workbook as *[your initials]***4-24.xls**, print it, and then close it.

Enter data and labels, create and enter formulas, set up the worksheet to print, and print it.

The executives at Beautiful Belle want to examine third-quarter sales data by comparing the differences in male and female purchasers of Sun Soft and Corn Silk products.

1. Open the file **Totals.xls**.
2. Insert rows and enter the following data for the months of August and September:

		Sun Soft	Corn Silk
Men	July	11,685	9,350
	August	12,550	9,800
	September	7,894	12,810
	Subtotal	11,685	9,350
Women	July	24,030	49,400
	August	22,104	38,465
	September	18,700	24,366
	Subtotal	24,030	49,400

3. Check and correct the subtotal formulas, if necessary.
4. Insert two rows above the Grand Total row and enter the labels **August** and **September** under Total.
5. Create formulas that calculate the August and September totals.
6. Set up the worksheet to print in landscape orientation, with no gridlines or row and column headings.
7. Center the worksheet horizontally and vertically.
8. Delete the header and footer. Create a new footer that includes the filename on the left and the date on the right.
9. Save the workbook as *[your initials]***4-25.xls**, print it, and close it.

Insert rows, freeze panes, enter data and formulas, use Zoom, use set-up options, preview the workbook, and print it.

The Beautiful Belle Company wants to extend the comparative-sales worksheet to include test-marketing data for Sun Soft and Corn Silk through July.

1. Open the file **MktTest.xls**.
2. Edit the title in cell A3 to read **April through July, 1997**.

3. Add new rows to the Sales Comparison worksheet by selecting cells A21 through A32 and choosing Rows from the Insert menu.

4. Freeze panes in cell A8 so that column headings will remain visible.

5. Enter the data shown in Figure 4-26 beginning in row 21.

FIGURE 4-26

	A	B	C	D	E	F	G	H
		Sun Soft				Corn Silk		
		Men	Women	Total		Men	Women	Total
21	07-Jun	2,300	3,400			1,250	1,050	
22	14-Jun	2,200	5,200			1,370	1,100	
23	21-Jun	1,950	4,300			1,290	1,000	
24	28-Jun	2,700	5,800			1,400	950	
25	Subtotal							
26								
27	05-Jul	2,500	4,500			1,500	1,100	
28	12-Jul	2,735	6,900			1,550	1,300	
29	19-Jul	2,800	5,430			1,650	1,550	
30	26-Jul	3,200	5,700			1,780	1,760	
31	Subtotal							

6. Enter or revise formulas to calculate totals, subtotals, and grand totals.

7. Reduce the size of the worksheet to 50%.

8. Click 🔍 to view the worksheet.

9. Set the worksheet to print in landscape orientation without gridlines or row and column headings.

10. Close Print Preview. Change the display to 100% using the Zoom Control box on the toolbar.

11. In the User Information sheet, key today's date for "Date revised" and key your name for "Revised by."

12. Center the Sales Comparison worksheet horizontally and vertically.

13. Save the workbook as *[your initials]***4-26.xls**, print the entire workbook, and close it.

EXERCISE 4-27

Sketch a worksheet plan, enter the plan in a worksheet, keep labels in view, create documentation, name sheet tabs, use print preview and page set-up options, print the workbook, and print formulas.

The Beautiful Belle Company wants a worksheet that calculates the difference between monthly sales of Sun Soft and Corn Silk products to men and women. The worksheet should also calculate the difference in total sales by gender to both groups.

1. Sketch a worksheet with three sections of rows: **Men**, **Women**, and **Total**. Each section should have the following row labels: **April**, **May**, **June**, and **July**. The last row should be **Grand Total**. Data and formulas will go in three columns labeled **Sun Soft**, **Corn Silk**, and **Difference**. Include the title **Sun Soft vs. Corn Silk Sales**.

2. Write formulas in this worksheet plan. You may abbreviate—for example, you might write **=SUM** for subtotals and grand totals, **SS - CS** for differences (Sun Soft minus Corn Silk), and **M + W** for monthly totals (Men plus Women).

3. Label rows and columns in the worksheet plan.

4. Enter the title and labels in a new Excel worksheet.

5. Key the following sales data for men:

		Sun Soft	Corn Silk	Difference
Men	April	3,300	6,600	
	May	6,450	8,150	
	June	9,150	5,310	
	July	11,235	6,480	

6. Key the following sales data for women:

		Sun Soft	Corn Silk	Difference
Women	April	3,300	6,600	
	May	6,800	8,000	
	June	18,700	4,100	
	July	22,530	5,710	

7. Either zoom down to display the whole worksheet, or freeze panes, or split the worksheet so that column labels become visible.

8. Create the formulas to calculate the men's and women's subtotals. (Hint: Use AutoSum.)

9. Create the formulas to calculate differences between Sun Soft and Corn Silk subtotals.

10. Create the formulas to calculate the totals for each month. (Hint: Add men's and women's sales.)

11. Create the formulas for grand totals and the differences between product grand totals.

12. Format in bold the worksheet title, column labels, and the following row labels: Men, Women, Total, Subtotal, and Grand Total.

13. Format the subtotal, grand total, and difference formulas as bold.

14. Rename the Sheet1 tab **Sales by Gender**.

15. Rename the Sheet2 tab **User Information**.

16. Key the following information in the User Information sheet, changing the width of column A as necessary:

Worksheet Documentation

Name of creator:	**Jane Doe**
Date created:	**08/13/97**
Date revised:	*[today's date]*
Revised by:	*[your name]*
Purpose and description:	**Compare Sun Soft vs. Corn Silk sales data by gender.**
Special instructions:	**Note formulas in total, subtotal, and grand total cells.**

17. Center the Sales by Gender sheet horizontally and vertically.

18. Set up both sheets to print in portrait orientation without gridlines or row and column headings.

19. Delete the headers on both sheets. Create footers that show the sheet names on the left, the date in the center, and the filename at the right.

20. Preview the workbook.

21. Print the workbook, and save it as *[your initials]***4-27.xls**.

22. Display the formulas in the Sales by Gender worksheet. Print the sheet in landscape orientation, showing gridlines and row and column headings, on one page.

23. Close the worksheet without saving it. Submit four pages: the plan, the two worksheets, and the formula view.

LESSON

5

Copying Data and Using Toolbars

OBJECTIVES   After completing this lesson, you will be able to:

1. Build a worksheet with copy and paste.
2. Copy using drag and drop.
3. Copy using Fill and AutoFill.
4. Use Excel's toolbars.

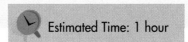

Estimated Time: 1 hour

Designing and developing worksheets in Excel often involves the repetition of many basic elements, including cells, formulas, and formatting. You can copy these elements to build a worksheet quickly and easily. This lesson also demonstrates the versatility of Excel's toolbars and the different ways available to display them.

Building a Worksheet with Copy and Paste

You can cut, copy, and move cell contents in Excel. A copy is an exact duplicate of the element you select that can be pasted or inserted into other locations of a worksheet or the document area of other Windows applications. The data remains in the original location, but also resides on the Clipboard. Unlike cutting or moving, you don't affect the original element when you copy it. Information is erased from the Clipboard upon execution of a new Cut or Copy command.

You can choose the Copy and Paste commands in three different ways:

- Use the <u>E</u>dit menu.
- Use the keyboard shortcuts Ctrl+C for Copy and Ctrl+V for Paste.
- Click the Copy 🗈 and Paste 🖺 buttons on the Standard toolbar.

EXERCISE 5-1 Copy and Paste Using the Edit Menu

In this exercise you will construct a worksheet with both detail and summary comparisons of 1997 second-quarter sales for the test product, Sun Soft Lotion, and its competing product, Corn Silk Cream.

1. Open the file **Compare.xls**.

2. Select cells A6 through B8 as the *source range*. The source range is the area of the worksheet from which you copy or remove data.

3. Choose <u>C</u>opy from the <u>E</u>dit menu. A moving border surrounds the selected cells. The contents of the cells you just copied now appear on the Clipboard.

FIGURE 5-1
Source range with moving border

	A	B	C	D	E
1					
2					
3					
4			Sun Soft	Corn Silk	Difference
5					
6	Men	April	6,540	13,000	
7		May	6,650	9,800	
8		June	9,150	12,810	
9		Subtotal	22,340	35,610	

4. Select cell G6. This cell will be the upper left-hand corner of the *target range*. The target range is the new location for data that you copy or move.

5. Choose <u>P</u>aste from the <u>E</u>dit menu. A copy of the data from the source range now appears in the target range. A copy of the data also remains on the Clipboard. To show this, Excel displays a moving border around the source range.

 TIP: Copy and Paste are available from the shortcut menu. Right-click the selected source or target and choose a command.

6. Select cell G11, and choose <u>P</u>aste from the <u>E</u>dit menu. A second copy of the data from the source range now appears in the new target range.

7. Press Esc to remove the moving border around the source range.

 NOTE: When the moving border is no longer displayed, you cannot paste the data from the Clipboard.

FIGURE 5-2
Source range
copied to two
target ranges

	A	B	C	D	E	F	G	H	I
1									
2									
3									
4			Sun Soft	Corn Silk	Difference				
5									
6	Men	April	6,540	13,000			Men	April	
7		May	6,650	9,800				May	
8		June	9,150	12,810				June	
9		Subtotal	22,340	35,610					
10									
11	Women	April	13,110	20,550			Men	April	
12		May	15,980	13,460				May	
13		June	18,700	16,550				June	
14		Subtotal	47,790	50,560					
15									

EXERCISE **5-2** ## Overwrite and Insert with Copy and Paste

The Copy and Paste commands overwrite existing cell data. Copy can also be used to insert new cells and data between existing cells.

1. Select cell A11, and choose Copy from the Edit menu.

2. Select cell G11, and choose Paste from the Edit menu. The word "Men" in cell G11is replaced by "Women."

3. Press Esc to exit Copy mode.

4. Select cell H4, and key **Percent**.

5. Select cell C4, and choose Copy from the Edit menu.

6. Select cell H4, and choose Copied Cells from the Insert menu.

FIGURE 5-3
Insert Paste
dialog box

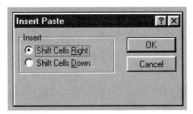

7. Click OK in the Insert Paste dialog box. The copy of "Sun Soft" now appears in cell H4, while the word "Percent" has shifted one cell to the right.

8. Press Esc to exit Copy mode.

EXERCISE **5-3** ## Copy and Paste Using the Toolbar

Like the Copy and Paste commands found on the Edit menu, the Copy and Paste buttons can be used to copy cell values, formulas, and formatting.

1. Enter the formula **=C6/D6** in cell I6. This formula divides Sun Soft sales by Corn Silk sales.

2. Select cell I6, and click the Percent Style button 🔲 on the Formatting toolbar to display the result as 50%.

3. With cell I6 selected, click the Copy button .

4. Select cell I7, and click the Paste button. Excel copies the formula and the formatting; it also adjusts the cell references so that the formula becomes =C7/D7. This change in cells is called a *relative cell reference*. With relative referencing, Excel knows that, if a formula sums a row of numbers, and you copy the formula to a new row, you intend to add the numbers in the new row rather than the numbers in the original row. This type of referencing occurs with any method of copying and pasting that you use.

5. Select cell I8, and click.

6. Select cell I11 and press Enter. Excel pastes the contents and completes the copy action, erasing the Clipboard. Note that all of the copied formulas were adjusted with relative cell references.

7. In cell I11, click.

8. Select cells I12 through I13, and then click.

9. Press Esc to exit the Copy mode.

Copying Using Drag and Drop

You can also copy data and formulas using the drag-and-drop method. This is perhaps the easiest way to copy information using the mouse. Note that you can make only a single copy using this method.

EXERCISE **5-4** **Copy Using Drag and Drop**

1. Select cells A16 through B18.

2. Move the mouse pointer across the border of the selection until it becomes an arrow.

 TIP: Avoid the lower right-hand corner of the selection.

3. Press and hold down the Ctrl key. The pointer becomes the drag-and-drop pointer, with a tiny cross appearing to the right of the arrow. When the cross is present, you're copying data, not moving it.

4. Drag the selected cells to cells G16 through H18. Note the presence of the gray outline in the shape of the source range as you move the mouse.

5. When the selected cells are positioned at the target range, release the mouse button and then the Ctrl key.

UNIT 2 ■ DEVELOPING A WORKSHEET

TIP: The Ctrl key must be depressed to copy while dragging. Notice the + sign that appears to the right of the arrow pointer.

6. Select cell I13.

7. Drag and drop into cell I16. Excel copies both the formula and its formatting, and adjusts the cell references accordingly.

8. Select cells I12 and I13, and drag and drop them into cells I17 and I18. Note that this method can transfer formulas in ranges as well as individual cells.

FIGURE 5-4
Copying using the drag-and-drop method

	A	B	C	D	E	F	G	H	I
5									
6	Men	April	6,540	13,000			Men	April	50%
7		May	6,650	9,800				May	68%
8		June	9,150	12,810				June	71%
9		Subtotal	22,340	35,610					
10									
11	Women	April	13,110	20,550			Women	April	64%
12		May	15,980	13,460				May	119%
13		June	18,700	16,550				June	113%
14		Subtotal	47,790	50,560					
15									
16	Total	April	19,650	33,550			Total	April	59%
17		May	22,630	23,260				May	
18		June	27,850	29,360				June	
19									
20	Grand Total				0				

Drag-and-drop pointer

Sheet 1

9. Verify that both formulas are correct for the new location.

Copying Using Fill and AutoFill

Worksheets frequently contain repetitive formulas. Instead of copying each formula using Copy and Paste, the Fill and AutoFill commands are a quicker technique in many cases.

EXERCISE 5-5 Copy Using the Fill Command

1. To view formulas as you copy them, press Ctrl+` (or choose Options from the Tools menu, click Formulas, and click OK).

2. Enter the formula **=C6-D6** in cell E6.

3. Select cells E6 through E9. Be sure to select the cell that contains the desired formula and all cells to which that formula is to be copied. These cells must be adjacent to one another.

142

4. Choose the Fill command from the Edit menu, and then choose Down from the cascading menu (or press `Ctrl`+`D`). Excel copies the formula to the selected cells and adjusts the cell references.

FIGURE 5-5
Using Fill to copy
formulas (with
formulas displayed)

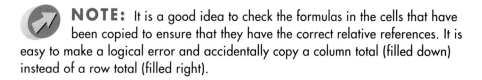

	B	C	D	E	F
5					
6	April	6540	13000	=C6-D6	
7	May	6650	9800	=C7-D7	
8	June	9150	12810	=C8-D8	
9	Subtotal	=SUM(C6:C8)	=SUM(D6:D8)	=C9-D9	
10					
11	April	13110	20550		
12	May	15980	13460		
13	June	18700	16550		
14	Subtotal	=SUM(C11:C13)	=SUM(D11:D13)		
15					
16	April	=C6+C11	=D6+D11		
17	May	=C7+C12	=D7+D12		
18	June	=+C8+C13	=D8+D13		
19					
20				=+C20-D20	

Sheet 1

5. Click outside the selection.

6. Select cell C20, and enter the SUM formula by double-clicking the AutoSum button ⎡Σ⎤.

7. Select cells C20 and D20.

8. Choose Fill from the Edit menu, and then choose Right from the cascading menu (or press `Ctrl`+`R`).

NOTE: It is a good idea to check the formulas in the cells that have been copied to ensure that they have the correct relative references. It is easy to make a logical error and accidentally copy a column total (filled down) instead of a row total (filled right).

9. Select cell E9, and click ⎡📋⎤. Select cell E14, and then click ⎡📋⎤.

10. Select cells E14 through E11.

11. Choose Fill from the Edit menu, and then choose Up from the cascading menu.

12. Click outside the selection.

EXERCISE ▮5-6▮ **Copy Using the AutoFill Command**

Using AutoFill, you can copy a formula in a single cell to multiple cells in a single step. Drag and drop is a good way to copy when the source area and the

143

target area are not adjacent but both are the same size. AutoFill, on the other hand, should be used for copying to adjacent cells.

1. Choose Options from the Tools menu, and click to clear the Formulas checkbox. Click OK. Formulas are no longer displayed on screen.

2. Copy the formula in cell E14 to cell E16.

3. With cell E16 selected, position the mouse pointer on the *fill handle*, which is the small box in the lower right-hand corner of the cell. The mouse pointer changes to a black cross.

FIGURE 5-6
Using AutoFill to
copy formulas

	E16	▼		=C16-D16							
	B	**C**	**D**	**E**	**F**	**G**	**H**	**I**	**J**		
6	April	6,540	13,000	(6,460)		Men	April	50%			
7	May	6,650	9,800	(3,150)			May	68%			
8	June	9,150	12,810	(3,660)			June	71%			
9	Subtotal	22,340	35,610	(13,270)							
10											
11	April	13,110	20,550	(7,440)		Women	April	64%			
12	May	15,980	13,460	2,520			May	119%			
13	June	18,700	16,550	2,150			June	113%			
14	Subtotal	47,790	50,560	(2,770)							
15											
16	April	19,650	33,550	(13,900)		Total	April	59%			
17	May	22,630	23,260				May	97%			
18	June	27,850	29,360				June	95%			
19											
20	al	70,130	86,170	(16,040)	Fill handle						
21											

Ready   Sum=(13,900)   NUM

4. Drag the fill handle, until cells E17 and E18 are both selected. The cells will be bordered in gray.

5. Release the mouse button. Excel copies the formula from cell E16 to cells E17 and E18.

6. Copy the formula in cell I18 to I20.

7. In cells A1 and A2, key the following title:

   Sun Soft Sales as a Percentage of Corn Silk Sales

   April - June 1997

8. Save the workbook as *[your initials]***5-6.xls** and print it.

Using Toolbars in Excel

To this point, you have used Excel's predefined Standard and Formatting toolbars to make your work easier. Excel provides many other predefined toolbars that make chart construction, drawing, and other functions faster and more convenient.

You can control how toolbars appear on the screen and what functions they perform. In addition to the Standard and Formatting toolbars, Excel offers 11 other predefined toolbars.

TABLE 5-1   Predefined Toolbars in Excel

TOOLBAR NAME	FUNCTION
Chart	Used for creating and modifying charts. It automatically displays when you are working on a chart.
Query and Pivot	Used to retrieve and analyze data from databases.
TipWizard	Displays tips while using Excel.
Drawing	Used for creating graphic objects. It contains standard drawing tools such as line, arc, and rectangle.
Auditing	Used for tracing precedents, dependents, and errors within formulas.
Stop Recording	Used to stop the recording of a macro.
Full Screen	Used to return to normal view after displaying the full screen.
Visual Basic	Used when working with macros.
Forms	Used for creating custom forms.
WorkGroup	Used for finding, routing, and sending files.
Microsoft	Used to switch to other Microsoft applications.

FIGURE 5-7
Examples of Excel toolbars

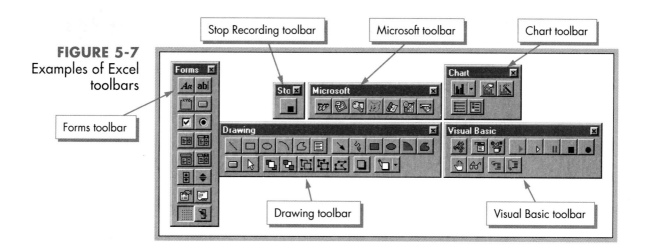

145

EXERCISE 5-7 Display Multiple Toolbars

Sometimes it's useful to display several toolbars simultaneously. For example, you may be working with a worksheet containing multiple formulas and integrated financial analysis that is part of a written report. In that case, the Auditing toolbar would help you trace multiple calculations, while the Microsoft toolbar would be handy for quickly switching to other applications, such as Microsoft Word.

FIGURE 5-8
Toolbars dialog box

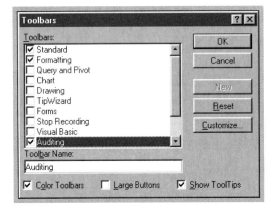

1. Choose <u>T</u>oolbars from the <u>V</u>iew menu. The Toolbars dialog box appears.

2. Scroll down the list of toolbars and choose Auditing.

3. Click OK. The Auditing toolbar appears.

4. Move the pointer across each button on the Auditing toolbar to identify its name and function.

TIP: Remember, to identify a toolbar button, point to the button and pause for a few seconds. A small box containing the name of the button will appear under the button, and a short description of the button's function will appear in the status bar.

5. Select cell C20, and click the Trace Dependents button . An arrow appears on screen tracing the cells that are dependent upon the value in cell C20.

6. With the same cell selected, click the Trace Precedents button . An arrow appears on screen, tracing the precedents for cell C20 (the cells to which the formula in cell C20 refers).

FIGURE 5-9
Using the Auditing toolbar

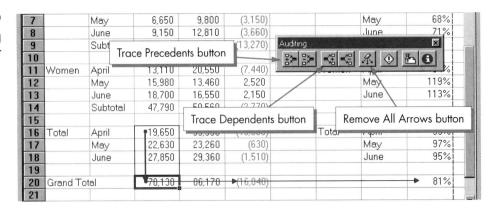

7. Click the Remove All Arrows button .

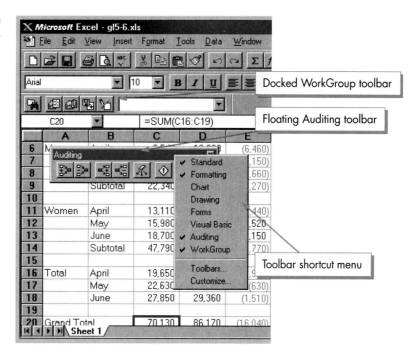

NOTE: Audit arrows are not saved with the file, but you may redisplay them at any time.

8. Click the right mouse button on any visible toolbar. The Toolbar shortcut menu appears.

9. Click WorkGroup. The WorkGroup toolbar appears. Buttons and the drop-down list box are displayed in a row.

EXERCISE 5-8 Move and Reshape Toolbars

Toolbars can appear either "docked" or "floating." A *docked toolbar* appears in a fixed position outside the work area (like the Standard and Formatting toolbars). A *floating toolbar* appears over the work area. You can dock a floating toolbar by dragging it out of the work area, above the Formula bar. You can float a docked toolbar by dragging it into the work area. You can also reshape a floating toolbar.

FIGURE 5-10
Using the Toolbar
shortcut menu

1. Position the pointer on the title bar of the Auditing toolbar (not on a toolbar button), press the left mouse button, and drag the toolbar to a position just above the Formula bar. The Auditing toolbar is docked alongside the WorkGroup toolbar.

2. Position the pointer in any background area of the docked WorkGroup toolbar (not on a button), and hold down the left mouse button. The WorkGroup toolbar is selected, and a light border surrounds it.

3. Drag the toolbar into the work area and release the left mouse button. The WorkGroup toolbar is now floating.

4. Double-click the background area of the docked Auditing toolbar. The docked toolbar becomes a floating toolbar.

NOTE: Double-clicking the background of a toolbar converts it from docked to floating, or from floating to docked. Double-clicking a docking area displays the Toolbar dialog box. If this occurs, click Cancel, and click the background area of the toolbar itself once again.

5. Double-click the background area of the WorkGroup toolbar. The toolbar becomes docked.

6. Drag the Auditing toolbar to the far right-hand side of the screen, until it is vertically positioned over the scroll bar. Excel docks the toolbar on this side of the screen, and the worksheet window is resized to accommodate it.

7. Select and drag the Auditing toolbar back into the work area. Excel resizes the worksheet window.

8. Position the pointer on the left-hand side of the bottom border of the Auditing toolbar so that the pointer changes into a double-headed arrow.

9. Drag the bottom border down about ½ inch, and release the mouse button. The toolbar buttons are grouped in rows.

FIGURE 5-11
Floating, reshaped toolbars

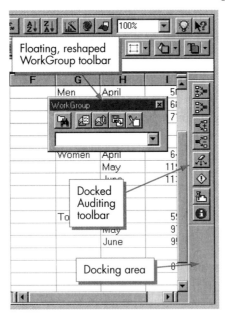

10. Drag the bottom border down even further, until the toolbar becomes a column of buttons. Reshape it again into a more rectangular arrangement.

11. Double-click the Auditing toolbar to dock it.

12. Double-click the background of the WorkGroup toolbar to float it.

13. Drag the bottom border of the WorkGroup toolbar as far down as possible. Note that this toolbar cannot be made any narrower than the drop-down list box it contains.

EXERCISE **5-9** **Close Toolbars**

There's no restriction on the number of toolbars you can display in Excel, but it may be hard to read the worksheet if too many are open.

1. Click the Close button in the upper right-hand corner of the WorkGroup toolbar to close it.
2. Click the right mouse button on any visible toolbar. The Toolbar menu appears. Notice the check mark located next to the open toolbars.
3. Click Auditing to deselect it. Excel closes the Auditing toolbar. Be sure that the Standard and Formatting toolbars remain checked.
4. Close the file.

COMMAND SUMMARY

FEATURE	BUTTON	MENU	KEYBOARD
Copy	📋	Edit, Copy	Ctrl + X
Paste	📋	Edit, Paste	Ctrl + V
Fill right		Edit, Fill	Ctrl + R
Fill down		Edit, Fill	Ctrl + D

USING HELP

This lesson showed you how to use Excel's AutoFill feature to copy data into adjacent cells. AutoFill is a powerful tool you can also use to create a series of data such as numbers, dates, or text.

For example, you can start with the month Jan-97 in a cell and build a series that places Feb-97, Mar-97, and so on in adjacent cells. You can also create custom AutoFill series to build complex worksheets quickly.

To find out how AutoFill can create a series of data, use Excel's Answer Wizard:

1. Choose Answer Wizard from the Help menu.
2. Enter **AutoFill dates** in the Answer Wizard's text box and click Search.
3. Select **Fill in a series of numbers, dates, or other items**.
4. Click Display. The Answer Wizard displays information that shows you how to build a series of data with AutoFill.
5. Review this information and then close the Help screen when you're done.

Concepts Review

Each of the following statements is either true or false. Indicate your choice by circling T or F.

T   F   **1.** Copying a cell moves its data to a new location in the worksheet.

T   F   **2.** You can paste cells using keyboard shortcuts, menu commands, or toolbar buttons.

T   F   **3.** When you copy cells, you must first indicate the source range.

T   F   **4.** The target range is the new location for data that you copy, cut, or move.

T   F   **5.** A relative cell reference is automatically adjusted in any formula you copy.

T   F   **6.** To copy cells using the drag-and-drop method, use the mouse pointer and the Alt key.

T   F   **7.** AutoFill should be used to copy only to adjacent cells.

T   F   **8.** You can dock a floating toolbar by double-clicking its background area.

Write the correct answer in the space provided.

1. Which keyboard command copies the active cell?

_____

2. Which keyboard command pastes the clipboard contents into the active cell?

_____

3. When you copy data, the information remains in the original location and is also copied to what location?

_____

4. What appears around selected cells to highlight them after you choose the Copy command?

_____

5. Which key do you use with the mouse to copy data when using the drag-and-drop method?

_____

6. Which keyboard shortcut copies and fills cells to the right?

_____

7. Which part of the cell do you drag to copy data using AutoFill?

_____

8. Name the two predefined toolbars that appear on screen by default when you first open Excel.

_____

CRITICAL THINKING

Answer these questions on a separate piece of paper. There are no right or wrong answers. Support your answer with examples from your own experience, if possible.

1. What are some of the potential dangers posed by relative cell references when you build a worksheet? What are the advantages? How can you effectively manage this feature?
2. Think of some other ways you might be able to use the Copy, Fill, and AutoFill features. Name at least one new way that you might use these powerful tools.
3. Which of Excel's 13 predefined toolbars do you think you will use most often? Why? What kinds of custom toolbars would you create to make your work easier?

Skills Review

EXERCISE 5-10

Copy and paste using the Edit menu and the toolbar.

1. Open the file **Bonus.xls**.
2. Key the following data in cells B7 through B10:

   1,500

   1,800

   1,800

   1,500

3. Format cell B7 in currency style with no decimal places. Format cells B8 through B10 in comma style with no decimal places.

4. Enter the formula **=B7*C7** in cell D7.

5. Copy the formula in cell D7 using the Copy and Paste commands by following these steps:

   a. Select cell D7.

   b. Choose <u>C</u>opy from the <u>E</u>dit menu.

   c. Select cells D8 and D10, and then choose <u>P</u>aste from the <u>E</u>dit menu.

   d. Press Esc to remove the moving border from the source range.

6. Format cell D7 in currency style with two decimal places. Format cells D8 through D10 in comma style with two decimal places.

7. Select cells B11 and D11, and then click the AutoSum button Σ .

8. Copy and paste data and formulas using the toolbar by following these steps:

   a. Select cells B7 through D7 as the source range.

   b. Click the Copy button .

   c. Select cell B12 as the first cell of the target range.

   d. Click the Paste button .

   e. Press Esc to remove the moving border from the source range.

9. Copy data and formulas by following these steps:

   a. Select cells B8 through D8, and choose <u>C</u>opy from the <u>E</u>dit menu.

   b. Select cell B13, and press Ctrl + V .

   c. Select cell B14, and click .

   d. Select cells B15 through D16, and press Enter .

10. Key the follwoing data in cells B12 through B16, overwriting the data that you previously copied:

   2,800

   1,800

   1,700

   2,750

   4,200

11. Use AutoSum to total the May revenues in cell B17 and the May commissions in cell D17.

12. Key **Total** in cell A18, and use AutoSum to total all revenues in cell B18 and all commissions in cell D18.

13. Format the unlabeled subtotals (cells B11, B17, D11, and D17) as italic.

14. Format the totals (cells B18 and D18) as bold.

15. Save the workbook as *[your initials]***5-10.xls**.

16. Print and close the workbook.

EXERCISE 5-11

Copy and paste using the menus, the toolbar, keyboard shortcuts, and drag and drop.

1. Open the file **SalesUp.xls**.

2. In cell C7, enter the formula **=B7*1.015**.

3. Copy this formula into cells C8 through C16 by following these steps:

    a. Select cell C7 and choose <u>C</u>opy from the <u>E</u>dit menu.

    b. Select cells C8 through C16, and then choose <u>P</u>aste from the <u>E</u>dit menu.

    c. Press Esc to remove the moving border from the source range.

    d. Format cells C8 through C16 in comma style with no decimal places.

4. Copy formulas using drag and drop by following these steps:

    a. Select cells C7 through C16.

    b. Move the mouse pointer across the border of the selection until it becomes an arrow.

    c. Press and hold down the Ctrl key to change the pointer to the drag-and-drop pointer.

    d. Drag the selected cell to the target range, cells D7 through D16.

5. In cell F7, enter the formula **=B7*1.22**.

6. Copy this formula into cells F8 through F16 by following these steps:

    a. Select cell F7, and then press Ctrl+C.

    b. Select cells F8 through F16, and then press Enter.

    c. Format cells F8 through F16 in comma style with no decimal places.

7. Copy formulas using the toolbar by following these steps:

    a. Select cells C7 through D16 as the source range.

    b. Click 🗐.

    c. Select cells G7 through D16 as the target range.

    d. Click 🗐.

    e. Press Esc.

8. Create a "Total" row by following these steps:

    a. Key **Total** in cell A17. Format the text as bold.

    b. Select cells B17, C17, D17, F17, G17, and H17, and then click Σ.

    c. Format the totals as bold and currency style with no decimal places, if necessary.

9. Save the workbook as *[your initials]***5-11.xls**.

10. Print and close the workbook.

EXERCISE 5-12

Copy formulas using the Fill command and AutoFill.

1. Open the file **NetInc2.xls**.
2. Enter the following formulas in cells B9 through B11:

   =B6*0.2

   =B6*0.35

   =B6*0.3

3. Format cells B9 through B11 in comma style with no decimal places.
4. Select cell B12, click ⬚, and then press Enter.
5. Select cells B9 through F12.
6. Choose the Fill command from the Edit menu, and then choose Right from the cascading menu.
7. Enter the formula **=F6-F12** in cell F14 to calculate the net income for the year 2001 ("Sales" - "Total Expenses").
8. Use AutoFill to copy the formula in cell F14 to cells B14 through E14 by following these steps:

   a. With cell F14 selected, position the mouse pointer on the fill handle.

   b. Drag the fill handle to select cells B14 through E14.

   c. Release the mouse button.

9. Check the formulas in your worksheet.
10. Save the workbook as *[your initials]***5-12.xls**.
11. Print and close the workbook.

EXERCISE 5-13

Open multiple toolbars, move and reshape toolbars, and use the Audit toolbar.

1. Open the file **Q4.xls**.
2. Open multiple toolbars using the following steps:

   a. Choose Toolbars from the View menu to open the Toolbars dialog box.

   b. Select the Chart toolbar and the Drawing toolbars, and then click OK.

   c. If necessary, drag one toolbar down to reveal the hidden toolbar.

   d. Right-click the background of the Chart toolbar to open the Toolbar shortcut menu. Select the Forms toolbar from this menu.

   e. Right-click the background of the Forms toolbar to select the Auditing toolbar from the Toolbar shortcut menu.

3. Move and reshape toolbars by following these steps:

   a. If necessary, double-click the background of the Chart toolbar to dock it.

b. Drag the auditing toolbar next to the Chart toolbar to dock it.

   c. Drag the Forms toolbar to the left side of the screen to dock it, if necessary.

   d. Double-click in the background of the Drawing toolbar to make it float, if necessary.

   e. Drag the bottom border of the Drawing border down until it assumes a square shape. The toolbar should contain five rows of buttons.

4. Close the Chart toolbar by right-clicking its background, and then deselecting Chart on the Toolbar shortcut menu.

5. Use the Auditing toolbar to trace formula paths by following these steps:

   a. Select cell D14, and click the Trace Precedents button.

   b. Select cell D6, and then click the Trace Dependents button.

6. Close the Drawing, Forms, and Auditing toolbars.

7. Print the workbook, including the tracing arrows.

8. Save the workbook as *[your initials]***5-13.xls** and then close it.

Lesson Applications

EXERCISE 5-14

Use the Copy and Paste commands, copy using drag and drop, and copy using Fill and AutoFill.

The Beautiful Belle Company needs to break down its revenues by product line and by region. The worksheet must also show product totals and subtotals, regional totals, and the grand total.

1. Open the file **Product.xls.**
2. Create a formula that totals the revenues for the Monterey product line.
3. Copy the formula to cell D16 using the [img] and [img] buttons.
4. Copy the formula from cell D16 to cells D17 through D20 using the Fill, Down command.
5. Select cells D17 through D20. Copy this range to cells D9 through D12 using the drag-and-drop method.
6. Create a formula that finds the subtotal for Creams sold in the Northwest territory.
7. Copy this formula to cells C13 and D13 using AutoFill.
8. Copy cells A13 through D13. Paste them in cells A21 through D21 using Ctrl+C and Ctrl+V.
9. Enter a formula to add the subtotals for Creams and Fragrances in cell B23.
10. Copy this formula to cells C23 and D23 using AutoFill.
11. Print the workbook as *[your initials]***5-14.xls.**
12. Save and close the workbook.

EXERCISE 5-15

Copy using the Fill command, toolbar buttons, drag and drop, and AutoFill.

1. Open the file **Frgrnce.xls.**
2. Copy the labels as shown in Figure 5-13 on the next page. (Copy the labels only. Don't copy the values.)
3. Create a formula that finds the 1997 total revenues for the Santa Barbara product line.
4. Copy this formula to cells D10 through D7 using the Fill, Up command.
5. Enter the formula **=B7*1.1** in cell B16 (Pacifica 1998 sales in the Northwest).
6. Copy and paste this formula to cell C16 using the toolbar buttons.

FIGURE 5-13

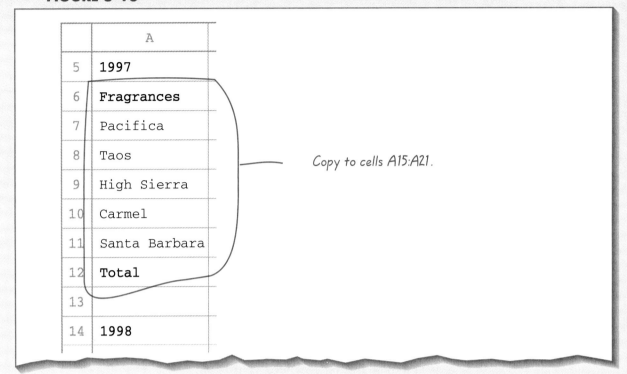

	A
5	1997
6	Fragrances
7	Pacifica
8	Taos
9	High Sierra
10	Carmel
11	Santa Barbara
12	Total
13	
14	1998

Copy to cells A15:A21.

7. Select cells B16 through C20, and then copy the formulas using the Fill, Down command.

8. Copy the formulas from cells D7 through D11 to cells D16 through D20 using drag and drop.

9. Format the numbers in rows 7 and 16 in currency style with no decimals. Format all other numbers in comma style with no decimals.

10. Create a formula in cell B21 that finds the projected total revenues for the Northwest territory in 1998.

11. Copy this formula to cells C21 and D21 using AutoFill.

12. Copy cells A21 through D21 to create a Total line for 1997 using the drag-and-drop method.

13. Format totals in currency style with no decimals, if necessary.

14. Print the workbook as *[your initials]***5-15.xls**.

15. Save and close the workbook.

EXERCISE 5-16

Copy using Fill, AutoFill, and drag and drop.

Build a worksheet to compare sales by quarter for Sun Soft for the years 1996 through 1998. Create formulas that calculate total sales for each year. Include a percentage change for 1996 to 1997 and 1997 to 1998.

1. Open the file **Change%.xls**.

2. Enter the labels and data as shown in Figure 5-14.

FIGURE 5-14

	A	B	C	D
4		1996	1997	1998
5	Qtr 1	64,955	80,530	96,500
6	Qtr 2	70,130	90,130	100,540
7	Qtr 3	110,140	150,350	180,020
8	Qtr 4	95,600	120,040	135,060

3. Create a formula that totals the four quarters for 1998 in cell D10.

4. Copy the formula to total 1996 and 1997 sales using AutoFill.

5. In cell F5, enter a formula that calculates the 1996 to 1997 change in sales as a percentage of 1996 sales. (Hint: Subtract 1996 sales from 1997 sales, and then divide the difference by 1996 sales.)

6. Format the formula in percent style with one decimal place using the Formatting toolbar.

7. Copy the formula to Qtr2 through Qtr4 for 1997 using the Fill, Down command.

8. Copy the Formula to Qtr1 through Qtr 4 for 1998 using the Fill, Right command.

9. Create totals for the 1997 and 1998 percentage changes by copying the Qtr4 formulas to row 10 using drag and drop.

10. Check the cell formats. Format the row labels as bold. Format data and total formulas in comma style with no decimal places. Format Change % formulas in percent style with one decimal place.

11. Change the print settings to no gridlines or row and column headings. Change the page orientation to portrait. Center the page horizontally.

12. Save the worksheet as *[your initials]***5-16.xls**.

13. Print and close the worksheet.

EXERCISE 5-17

Copy and paste formulas, use Fill or AutoFill, copy using drag and drop, and use toolbars.

Construct a worksheet comparing second-quarter sales for Sun Soft and Corn Silk for 1996, 1997, and 1998.

1. Open the file **CmpPcnt.xls**.

2. Key the data as shown in Figure 5-15, beginning in row 6.

FIGURE 5-15

	A	B	C	D	E	F	G	H
4		Sun Soft				Corn Silk		
5		1996	1997	1998		1996	1997	1998
6	April	19,650	24,800	36,540		33,550	28,150	26,540
7	May	22,630	31,300	24,000		23,260	18,440	16,500
8	June	27,850	34,030	31,250		29,360	25,040	21,350

3. Calculate the three-month total for Sun Soft in 1996. Copy that formula to the appropriate cells for Sun Soft and Corn Silk.

4. In cell J6, calculate Sun Soft's sales as a percentage of Corn Silk sales for April 1996. (Hint: Divide Sun Soft sales by Corn Silk sales.)

5. Format that formula in percent style with no decimal places.

6. Use Fill or AutoFill to copy the percentage change formula from cell J6 through cell L8.

7. Use drag and drop to copy the formula to the Total row (cells J10 through L10).

8. After entering the data and formulas, use the Auditing toolbar to trace the precedents for the April 1998 percentage change formula in cell J6.

9. Set up the worksheet to print with gridlines, in landscape orientation, centered vertically and horizontally on one page.

10. Save the workbook as *[your initials]***5-17.xls**.

11. Print the workbook, including the precedent arrows, and then close it.

Range Names

OBJECTIVES   After completing this lesson, you will be able to:

1. **Name ranges and constants.**
2. **Use names in formulas.**
3. **Change and delete range names.**
4. **Navigate in the worksheet using range names.**
5. **Paste names into worksheets.**

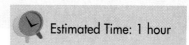

Estimated Time: 1 hour

Instead of trying to remember a particular cell address, such as E17, or a cell range, such as I7:J43, you can use a name to designate a location. For example, you could name a cell that contains a formula "total" and then use the name "total" to refer to the cell when creating other formulas. In addition to naming cells, you can also assign names to constants. For example, you could assign the name "rate" to the constant 0.07. Naming cells also makes it easier to find a particular location in the worksheet.

Naming Ranges and Constants

A *range name*—the name you give to a cell or range of cells—must begin with a letter. Although range names may be from 1 to 255 characters long, it is best to keep them recognizable, but short. Range names must *not*:

- Have the form of a cell reference, such as q1 or A13.
- Be "R" or "C" as a single-letter name.

- Contain spaces.
- Contain hyphens (-) or special characters ($, %, &, #).

To separate parts of a name such as "saleseast," you can use capital letters, a period, or an underline (for example, SalesEast, sales.east, or sales_east).

TABLE 6-1 **Examples of Valid and Invalid Names**

VALID NAMES	INVALID NAMES
Total.Sales	Total Sales
east_sales	east-sales
EntertainPct	Entertain%
qt1	q1
First	1st
X	R

EXERCISE 6-1 Name an Individual Cell

You can name ranges using the Define Name dialog box, or by keying the name in the name box at the left of the formula bar.

1. Open the file **97Sales.xls**.

2. Move to cell E9.

3. Choose <u>N</u>ame from the <u>I</u>nsert menu. A cascading menu appears.

4. Choose <u>D</u>efine. The Define Name dialog box appears.

5. Key **qt1** in the Names in <u>W</u>orkbook text box and click OK. The name appears in the name box at the left of the formula bar.

FIGURE 6-1
Define Name
dialog box

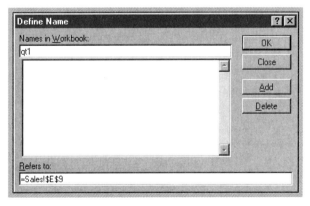

6. Move to cell E18, and then click in the name box at the left of the formula bar. The cell address is selected.

7. Key **qt2** and press Enter. The name appears in the name box.

8. Name cell E27 **qt3** using the Define Name dialog box.

9. Name cell E36 **qt4** by keying this text directly in the name box at the left of the formula bar.

EXERCISE `6-2` **Name a Group of Cells**

You can name any group of cells you like. Excel will suggest a name for the range based on the title of the selected column or row. If you don't want this suggested name, assign the range a different name of your choice.

1. Select all of the totals for "New Century," which appear in cells E5, E14, E23, and E32.

    NOTE: To select nonadjacent cells, press the **Ctrl** key while selecting the cells.

2. Choose Name from the Insert menu.
3. Choose Define.
4. Key **New_Century** in the Names in Workbook text box and click OK.
5. Select cells E6, E15, E24, and E33.
6. Click in the name box at the left of the formula bar.
7. Key **Golden** and press Enter.
8. Name cells E7, E16, E25, and E34 **Monterey**, and name cells E8, E17, E26, and E35 **Herbal**.

EXERCISE `6-3` **Name a Constant**

In addition to assigning names to cells or ranges of cells, you can assign names to *constants*. Constants are unchanging values that are used in formulas. Named constants don't appear in the spreadsheet. For example, if you assign the name "rate" to the constant .075, you could then use the name "rate" in formulas instead of the value. When you change the constant value assigned to "rate," any formula that contains "rate" will automatically change to include the new value.

1. Choose Name from the Insert menu.
2. Choose Define.
3. Key **pro** in the Names in Workbook text box.
4. Edit the text in the Refers to text box to read **=.12**.
5. Click OK. The value 0.12 has been assigned the name "pro." This name will be used to increase the sales figures by 12%.

    NOTE: You cannot name a constant in the formula bar's name box.

Using Names in Formulas

Once you've created names for cell references or constants, you can use these names in formula calculations. Key the formula in the normal way, but key the name instead of the cell reference. To use constants, key the name for the constant wherever you would key the constant in the formula.

EXERCISE **6-4** **Create Formulas Including Names**

---

1. In cell B41, key **=sum(new_century)**, and then press ⌷Enter⌷. Once you enter the formula in the cell, Excel converts the name to include uppercase letters as you created it.

2. In cell B42, enter **=sum(golden)**

3. In cell B43, enter **=sum(monterey)**

4. In cell B44, enter **=sum(herbal)**

5. In cell C41, calculate a 12% projected sales increase for 1998 by keying **=B41*(1+pro)**. (B41 is the 1997 total and "1+pro" equals 1.12, as you earlier defined "pro" to be 0.12.)

6. Copy this formula to cells C42, C43, C44, and C45. (Cell C45 will equal zero for now.)

7. In cell B45, use the cell names you created by keying **=qt1+qt2+qt3+qt4**

FIGURE 6-2
Total projected
1998 sales, so far.

C45 ▼	=B45*(1+pro)		
A	**B**	**C**	**D**
40		1997	1998
41 New Century	474,015	530,897	
42 Golden Gate	328,731	368,179	
43 Monterey	353,950	396,424	
44 Herbal Essence	627,284	702,558	
45 TOTAL:	1,783,980	1,998,058	
46			

8. In cells D32 through D35, enter the data as shown below. When you've finished, the total for 1998 in cell C45 should be 2,199,716.

	Dec
New Century	**79,658**
Golden Gate	**22,457**
Monterey	**32,568**
Herbal Essence	**45,369**

Changing and Deleting Range Names

You can change a name or delete one that is no longer needed. When you change a name, Excel does not replace the old name with the new name in relevant formulas. The old formulas will remain valid, however, unless you delete the old name.

EXERCISE **6-5** **Change and Delete Range Names**

1. Choose Name from the Insert menu, and then choose Define.
2. Choose **New_Century** from the Names in Workbook list box.
3. Delete **New_** from the name. **Century** remains in the Names in Workbook text box.
4. Click OK.
5. Move to cell B41. The name New_Century has not been changed.
6. Choose Name from the Insert menu, and then choose Define.
7. Choose **New_Century** from the Names in Workbook list box.
8. Click Delete and click OK. The formulas that refer to New_Century display the #NAME? error message.

 NOTE: You cannot reverse the deletion of a name by using the Undo command.

9. In cell B41, double-click New_Century in the formula bar to select it and then key **century**
10. Click the check box in the formula bar. Century is converted to a capital C. The #NAME? error message is no longer displayed in cell B41 or cell C41, and the formulas calculate correctly.

 TIP: You can use search and replace to change range names in formulas.

Navigating Using Range Names

Named ranges not only make calculations easier, but also enable you to move around a worksheet more quickly. For example, you can assign a name to a cell and then locate the cell by choosing Go To from the Edit menu (or pressing [F5]). Excel opens the Go To dialog box, which lists all named cells in the worksheet. It also lists the last four cell addresses that the Go To command has located. You can also use the Name box drop-down list to move to named ranges.

EXERCISE 6-6 Move to Named Ranges

1. Select cells A4 through E9.
2. Choose <u>N</u>ame from the <u>I</u>nsert menu, and then choose <u>D</u>efine.
3. Key **one** in the Names in <u>W</u>orkbook text box and click OK.
4. Select cells A13 through E18.
5. Click in the Name box, key **two**, and press Enter.

FIGURE 6-3
Go To dialog box

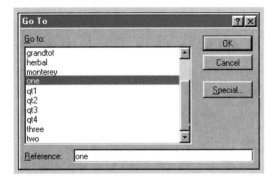

6. Name cells A22 through E27 **three**, cells A31 through E36 **four**, and cells A40 through A45 **grandtot**.
7. Choose <u>G</u>o To from the <u>E</u>dit menu, or press F5, or press Ctrl+G. The Go To dialog box appears.
8. Double-click the named range **one**. Excel moves to the selected range or cell.

FIGURE 6-4
Name box
drop-down list

9. Press Ctrl+Home to move to cell A1. Click the Name box arrow. The drop-down list appears.
10. Click the named range **one**.
11. Practice moving to named ranges using both the Go To command and the Name box drop-down list.

Pasting Names into Worksheets

You can use the Define Name dialog box to display a list of named ranges and constants to see how a worksheet was set up. Using the Paste Name dialog box, a list of range names and references can be pasted into a worksheet as documentation. You can also use this dialog box to paste range names and constants into formulas.

EXERCISE 6-7 Paste Range Names into Worksheets

Before pasting a list of range names, move to a clear area of your worksheet, such as a sheet created to provide worksheet documentation.

1. Move to cell A8 in the sheet named Documentation.

2. Key the label **Range names:** and then press Enter.

3. Move to cell A9.

4. Choose Name from the Insert menu, and then choose Paste. The Paste Name dialog box appears.

FIGURE 6-5
Paste Name
dialog box

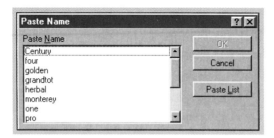

5. Click the Paste List button. The list of named ranges is pasted into the Documentation worksheet. Descriptions of the named ranges can be keyed into the worksheet as necessary.

FIGURE 6-6
Names pasted into
a worksheet

	A	B	C	D	E	F	G	H	I
A1			Worksheet Documentation						
8	Range names:								
9	Century	=Sales!$E$5,Sales!$E$14,Sales!$E$23,Sales!$E$32							
10	four	=Sales!$A$31:$E$36							
11	Golden	=Sales!$E$6,Sales!$E$15,Sales!$E$24,Sales!$E$33							
12	grandtot	=Sales!$A$40:$C$45							
13	Herbal	=Sales!$E$8,Sales!$E$17,Sales!$E$26,Sales!$E$35							
14	Monterey	=Sales!$E$7,Sales!$E$16,Sales!$E$25,Sales!$E$34							
15	one	=Sales!$A$4:$E$9							
16	pro	=0.12							
17	qt1	=Sales!$E$9							
18	qt2	=Sales!$E$18							
19	qt3	=Sales!$E$27							
20	qt4	=Sales!$E$36							
21	three	=Sales!$A$22:$E$27							
22	two	=Sales!$A$13:$E$18							
23									

Sales \ **Documentation**

6. In the documentation worksheet, key today's date for "date revised," and key your name for "Revised by."

7. In cell B44 of the Sales worksheet, key **=sum(**

8. Press F3 to open the Paste Name dialog box.

9. Double-click the name "herbal" in the Paste Name list box, and then press Enter. The formula is complete.

10. In B43, key **=sum(**, click Monterey in the Name box drop-down list, and press Enter. The formula is complete.

11. Save the workbook as *[your initials]***6-7.xls**.

12. Print the entire workbook and close it.

COMMAND SUMMARY

FEATURE	BUTTON	MENU	KEYBOARD
Define Name		Insert, Name, Define	Ctrl + F3
Go To		Edit, Go To	F5 or Ctrl + G
Paste Name		Insert, Name, Paste	F3

USING HELP

Excel allows you to find out the names associated with a particular cell through the use of the Info Window feature. You can open an Info Window next to your worksheet to show a wide variety of information about the cell or range you've selected. You can also use the Info Window to insert notes about cell data or formulas.

To find out how the Info Window feature can show you what names apply to cells, use the Answer Wizard:

1. Choose Answer Wizard from the Help menu. The Answer Wizard appears.
2. Enter **range names** in the text box and click Search.
3. Select **Find out what names apply to cells**.
4. Click Display. The Answer Wizard displays information that shows you how to use the Info Window feature to display names that apply to cells.

FIGURE 6-7
Names displayed in the Info Window

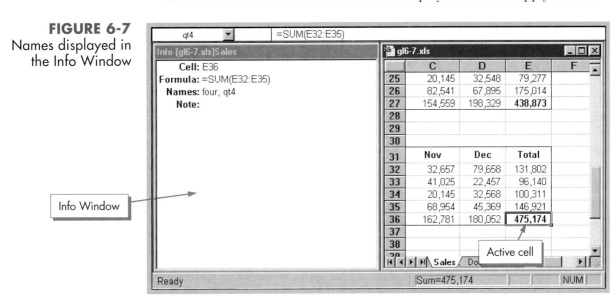

5. Read the information and display the Info Window beside the file *[your initials]***6-7.xls**.
6. Close the Info Window when you're done.

Concepts Review

Each of the following statements is either true or false. Indicate your choice by circling **T** or **F**.

T F **1.** A range name can include spaces and hyphens.

T F **2.** A cell or range name can include as many as 255 characters.

T F **3.** Named cells can contain only formulas.

T F **4.** Range names can include special characters like $, &, and #.

T F **5.** Names applied to constants can later be used in formulas.

T F **6.** Range names can be used to replace cell references in formulas.

T F **7.** When you change a name, Excel automatically replaces the old name with the new name in the appropriate formulas.

T F **8.** The Go To dialog box lists the last three cell addresses located by the Go To command.

SHORT ANSWER QUESTIONS

Write the correct answer in the space provided.

1. Which command enables you to move to the location of a named cell in the worksheet?

_____

2. What do you call an unchanging value in a formula?

_____

3. Which keyboard combination do you use for the Define Name command?

_____

4. Which keyboard combination do you use for the Paste Name command?

_____

5. Which menu commands do you use to name a range?

_____

6. Which dialog box is opened by pressing F5?

_____

7. Which menu commands do you use to paste a range name?

_____

8. With what must the name you give to a cell or range begin?

_____

CRITICAL THINKING

Answer these questions on a separate piece of paper. There are no right or wrong answers. Support your answer with examples from your own experience, if possible.

1. What are some of the possible disadvantages related to using range names and cell names in formulas? How can you avoid these potential drawbacks?

2. Describe some other potential uses for range names in Excel other than those described in this lesson. Explain how you would apply each type of use in a worksheet.

3. List three unacceptable range names, explaining why each name won't work in Excel.

Skills Review

EXERCISE 6-8

Create names for cell ranges and constants, and use names in formulas.

1. Open the file **Lotions.xls**.

2. Create names for cell ranges by following these steps:

a. Select cells B7 through D7.

b. Choose <u>N</u>ame from the <u>I</u>nsert menu, and then choose <u>D</u>efine.

c. Excel suggests the name **Cypress** in the Names in <u>W</u>orkbook text box. Click OK.

d. Select cells B8 through D8.

e. Choose <u>I</u>nsert, <u>N</u>ame, and then choose <u>D</u>efine.

f. Excel suggests the name **Jojoba** in the Names in <u>W</u>orkbook text box. Click OK.

g. Select cells B9 through D9.

h. Choose <u>I</u>nsert, <u>N</u>ame, and then choose <u>D</u>efine.

i. Excel suggests the name **Sesame** in the Names in <u>W</u>orkbook text box. Click OK.

    j. Select cells B10 through D10.

    k. Choose Insert, Name, and then choose Define.

    l. Edit the suggested name **Joshua_Tree** in the Names in Workbook text to **Joshua**, and then click OK.

3. Create names for constants by following these steps:

    a. Choose Insert, Name, and then choose Define.

    b. Key **slow** in the Names in Workbook text box.

    c. Edit the text in the Refers to text box to read **=1.05**. Click the Add button.

    d. Edit the text in the Names in Workbook text box to read **moderate**.

    e. Edit the text in the Refers to text box to read **=1.1**. Click Add.

    f. Edit the text in the Names in Workbook text box to read **fast**.

    g. Edit the text in the Refers to text box to read **=1.15**, Click OK.

4. Use names in formulas by following these steps:

    a. Key **=sum(cypress)** in cell E7.

    b. Key **=sum(jojoba)** in cell E8.

    c. Key **=sum(sesame)** in cell E9.

    d. Key **=sum(joshua)** in cell E10.

5. Build formulas with range names and constant names by following these steps:

    a. Key **=cypress*slow** in cell B17.

    b. Use AutoFill to copy this formula to cells C17 and D17.

    c. Key **=jojoba*moderate** in cell B18.

    d. Use AutoFill to copy this formula to cells C18 and D18.

    e. Key **=sesame*fast** in cell B19.

    f. Use AutoFill to copy this formula to cells C19 and D19.

    g. Key **=joshua*slow** in cell B20.

    h. Key **=joshua*moderate** in cell C20.

    i. Key **=joshua*fast** in cell D20.

    j. Use AutoSum and AutoFill to enter formulas for the totals of each type of lotion in cells E17 through E20.

6. Save the workbook as *[your initials]***6-8.xls**.

7. Print and close the workbook.

EXERCISE 6-9

Use names in formulas, change range names, and delete range names.

1. Open the file **Powders.xls**.

2. Use names in formulas by following these steps:

a. Key **=sum(sahara)** in cell E6.

    b. Key **=sum(marin)** in cell E7.

    c. Key **=sum(mohave)** in cell E8.

    d. Key **=sum(april_fresh)** in cell E9.

    e. Key **=sum(spring_day)** in cell E10.

    f. Key **=april_fresh+spring_day** in cell B12.

3. Use AutoFill to copy the formula from cell B12 to cells C12 and D12.

4. Use AutoSum to enter a formula that totals the new products in cell E12.

5. Change range names by following these steps:

    a. Choose Insert, Name, and then choose Define.

    b. Choose **April_Fresh** from the Names in Workbook list box.

    c. Delete **_Fresh** from the name. Click Add.

    d. Choose **Spring_Day** from the Names in Workbook list box, change the name to **Spring**, and then click OK.

6. Delete range names by following these steps:

    a. Choose Insert, Name, and then choose Define.

    b. Choose **April_Fresh** from the Names in Workbook list box, and then click Delete.

    c. Choose **Spring_Day** from the Names in Workbook list box, click Delete, and then click OK.

7. Use the new range names in formulas by following these steps:

    a. Move to cell E9.

    b. Double-click **April_Fresh** in the formula to select it and key **april**.

    c. Press `Enter`.

    d. In cell E10, change the name **Spring_Day** in the formula to **spring**.

    e. Change the formula in cell B12 to **=april+spring**.

    f. Copy the new formula in cell B12 to cells C12 and D12.

8. In cell A13, key **Grand Total**. In cells B13 through E13, calculate the totals for each month and for the three-month period. Do not include the "New Product Totals" in the "Grand Totals."

9. Save the workbook as *[your initials]***6-9.xls**.

10. Print and close the workbook.

EXERCISE 6-10

Name a range of cells and navigate in the worksheet using range names.

    1. Open the file **Credit.xls**.

    2. Enter the following data into the worksheet:

    Hall, Martha   **$240**   **9%**

Spencer, Jon	$150	10%
May, Violet	$23	7%
Bernard, Frank	$542.21	13%
Brown, JoAnne	$500	11%

3. Name a range of cells by following these steps:

   a. Select cells A24 through C24.

   b. Choose Insert, Name, and then choose Define.

   c. Excel suggests the name **Hall_Martha** in the Names in Workbook text box. Click OK.

4. Use the Go To command with names to navigate in the worksheet by following these steps:

   a. Choose Go To from the Edit menu.

   b. Double-click the range **Ferrara_Joseph**.

   c. Press F5.

   d. Double-click the range **fifteen**. All new customers with credit at the 15% interest rate are selected.

5. Save the workbook as *[your initials]***6-10.xls**.

6. Print and close the workbook.

EXERCISE 6-11

Name constants, paste names into a formula, and paste names into a worksheet.

1. Open the file **Freight1.xls**.

2. Name constants by using the following steps:

   a. Choose Insert, Name, then choose Define.

   b. Key **mileage** in the Names in Workbook text box.

   c. Edit the text in the Refers to text box to read **=4**.

   d. Click Add.

   e. Key **weight** in the Names in Workbook text box.

   f. Edit the text in the Refers to text box to read **=.0015**.

   g. Click OK.

3. Change a formula by inserting the newly named constants using these steps:

   a. Select and delete cell D16.

   b. Key **=(b16/mileage)*(c16*weight)**, and then press Enter.

4. Using AutoFill, copy the new formula in cell D16 to cells D7 through D15.

5. Paste names into a worksheet by following these steps:

   a. Move to cell A8 in the sheet labeled Documentation.

   b. Key the label **Constant names:** and then press Enter.

c. In cell A9, choose <u>N</u>ame from the <u>I</u>nsert menu, and then choose <u>P</u>aste. The Paste Name dialog box appears.

d. Click the Paste <u>L</u>ist button.

e. Change the "Date revised" to today's date, and key your name for "Revised by."

6. Save the workbook as *[your initials]***6-11.xls**.

7. Print the entire workbook and close it.

Lesson Applications

Name constants, use names in formulas, define range names, and change range names.

Complete and revise Beautiful Belle's fuel estimation worksheet, so that managers can better control the costs associated with product shipments.

1. Open the file **Freight2.xls**.

2. Enter the data into the worksheet as shown in Figure 6-8.

FIGURE 6-8

Seattle	827	Van	524
Denver	1270	*Semi* ~~Light Truck~~	1642
Portland	652	Semi	2159
Albuquerque	1127	Van	312
Los Angeles	403	Semi	2493
Phoenix	800	Semi	2200
Dallas	1806	Semi	*3155* ~~3200~~
Salt Lake City	759	Semi	3200
Mexico City	2419	Semi	2047
Topeka	1811	~~Van~~ *Light Truck*	750

3. Name the following constants:

Van = 16

Truck = 10

Semi = 6

4. Substitute the appropriate names (**Van, Truck,** or **Semi**) for the name **mileage** in the Fuel Estimate formulas in column E.

5. Enter the following labels in cells A18 through A21:

Territories

Northwest

Southwest

Midwest

6. Key **Total Fuel** in cell B18.

7. Define the range name **Northwest** to include Fuel Estimates for the following cities: Seattle, Portland, and Salt Lake City.

8. Define the range name **Southwest** to include Fuel Estimates for the following cities: Albuquerque, Los Angeles, Phoenix, and Mexico City.

9. Define the range name **Midwest** to include Fuel Estimates for the following cities: Denver, Dallas, and Topeka.

10. Create a formula using range names to calculate the total estimated fuel for each territory: **Northwest**, **Southwest**, and **Midwest**.

11. Format cells containing these formulas to include only two decimal places.

12. Save the workbook as *[your initials]***6-12.xls**.

13. Print and close the workbook.

EXERCISE 6-13

Define range names, build formulas using range names, change and delete range names, and navigate in a worksheet using range names.

Develop a worksheet that audits selected Beautiful Belle product sales by store.

1. Open the file **Stores.xls**.

2. Define range names for each city in the worksheet by highlighting the corresponding cells in the "Amount" column.

3. In cells A27 through A33, enter the labels shown below. Format the labels in bold.

Store Totals
Dallas
New York
Chicago
San Francisco
Boston
Indianapolis

4. Use these range names to build formulas that calculate the total sales for each store. Enter the formulas in column B beside the appropriate label and format the results in comma style.

5. Change the range name **Dallas** to **Denver**.

6. Delete the range name **Dallas**.

7. Change the name **Dallas** to **Denver** in the formula that calculates the store total.

8. Change the labels in the Store column and Store Totals column from **Dallas** to **Denver**.

9. Use the Go To command to highlight the Denver sales amounts.

10. Save the workbook as *[your initials]***6-13.xls**.

11. Print and close the workbook.

EXERCISE 6-14

Create range names, build formulas using range names, paste names into the worksheet, and use the Go To command to navigate in the worksheet.

Construct a worksheet for the Beautiful Belle Company that calculates the total sales and commissions paid over four quarters.

1. Open the file **Cmsions.xls**.

2. In cell C16, use the AutoSum button to add the column.

3. Use Autofill to copy the SUM formula to cells D16 through J16.

4. Create the name **rt** for the constant **.07** (seven percent).

5. Create formulas using the constant name **rt** in cells D4, F4, H4, and J4 that calculate the commission due for each quarter. Copy the formula using AutoFill to complete the columns.

6. Create the names **sq1**, **sq2**, **sq3**, and **sq4** for the total sales for each quarter.

7. Create a formula in cell B17 that uses names to calculate the total sales for the year.

8. Create the names **com1**, **com2**, **com3**, and **com4** for the total commissions for each quarter.

9. Use the commission range names to create a formula in cell B18 that calculates the total commissions for the year.

10. In cell B21, paste all of the names you've created to the worksheet.

11. Key the following information in cells A21, A25, and A26:

    commission q1

    commsn rate

    sales q1

12. Use the Go To command to locate the cell named **sq4**.

13. If necessary, set up the worksheet to print without gridlines in landscape orientation on a single page.

14. Save the worksheet as *[your initials]***6-14.xls**.

15. Print and close the worksheet.

EXERCISE 6-15

Name cells, and create formulas using named cells.

In an effort to understand its expenses by region, the Beautiful Belle Company needs to calculate quarterly, biannual, and yearly total expenses, based on the 1997 expense information shown in Figure 6-9.

FIGURE 6-9

	Jan	Feb	Mar	Apr	May	Jun
Southeast	32,098	189,074	156,976	82,514	188,365	174,958
Northeast	11,098	294,651	192,634	99,254	201,648	89,254
Northwest	132,098	486,277	326,584	135,698	543,958	142,360
	Jul	Aug	Sept	Oct	Nov	Dec
Southeast	124,725	93,581	54,321	42,587	748,512	154,879
Northeast	124,521	84,516	68,954	859,641	365,894	254,369
Northwest	123,695	99,365	67,987	102,587	411,758	254,879

1. Open a new workbook and create an appropriate title for the worksheet.

2. Set up the worksheet to print in portrait orientation, if necessary.

3. If you need to widen a column, select a cell in that column, choose Column from the Format menu, choose Width, and then key a character width in the Column Width text box.

4. Enter the data from Figure 6-9 in the worksheet. Start a new set of rows for the second half of the year (July through December).

5. Include calculations for monthly total expenses.

6. Name each cell containing a monthly total.

7. Below the monthly data, create labels for four quarterly totals. Use your cell names to calculate quarterly expenses based on the monthly totals for all regions.

8. Below the quarterly totals, create labels for half-year totals. Use cell names to calculate half-year expenses.

9. Format the cells in comma style with no decimal places.

10. Format the cells above monthly totals with bottom borders.

11. Save the workbook as *[your initials]***6-15.xls**.

12. Print and close the workbook.

Spelling, Find/ Replace, and File Management

After completing this lesson, you will be able to:

1. **Check spelling.**
2. **Use AutoCorrect.**
3. **Find and replace data.**
4. **File files.**
5. **Rename, copy, and delete files in Excel.**

 Estimated Time: 1 hour

Creating and building a workbook is only the beginning of effective data management and analysis. You must make your workbooks accurate and easy to use, and Excel can help. Excel provides automated dictionaries to check your spelling. It also provides a Find and Replace function to make global changes and revisions.

Excel's Open dialog box lets you find files easily and offers many other file-management functions.

Checking Spelling

Excel's spell-checker scans the active worksheet and highlights words not found in any of its dictionaries. It also finds repeated words. A Spelling dialog box provides a choice of options for handling the highlighted word, as shown in Table 7-1.

TABLE 7-1   Spell-Checking Options

BUTTON	ACTION
Ignore	Do not take any action; do not change the spelling. If it is a repeated word, do not delete or change it.
Ignore All	Do not take any action for all occurrences of this word in the worksheet.
Change	Change the current spelling of this word to the spelling highlighted in the Change To box.
Delete	Delete a repeated word.
Change All	Change all occurrences of this word to the spelling highlighted in the Change To box.
Add	Add this word to the dictionary. Once added, Excel will no longer highlight this word as "Not in Dictionary."
Suggest	Display a list of proposed suggestions.
Undo Last	Reverse the last action.
Cancel/Close	End spell-checking.
AutoCorrect	Add to the list of corrections that AutoCorrect will make as you key text in a worksheet.

You can customize the spell-checker so that it works smarter for you. Adding words to a dictionary is especially useful for worksheets that contain data from specific fields, such as law, real estate, or science. You can also turn off the Suggestions list box choice and ignore words that contain numbers or all uppercase letters.

EXERCISE   **7-1**   **Spell-Check the Entire Worksheet**

Excel begins spell-checking at the active cell. If you begin spell-checking in the middle of the worksheet, a dialog box will appear when the spell-checker reaches the end. You can then continue spell-checking at the beginning of the worksheet.

1. Open the file **Change%2.xls**.

2. Select cell A1 to begin spell-checking from the beginning of the worksheet.

3. Choose <u>S</u>pelling from the <u>T</u>ools menu, or press F7. Excel highlights the first word not found in its dictionary, "introducsion." The correct spelling appears in both the Suggestio<u>n</u>s drop-down list box and the Change <u>T</u>o text box.

FIGURE 7-1
Spelling dialog box

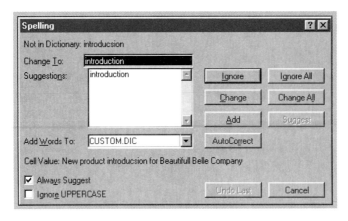

4. Click Change. Excel makes the correction and locates the next word not found in its dictionary.

5. Continue spell-checking until you reach the end of the worksheet. Click Ignore if no change is required. If the correct spelling does not appear in the Suggestions box, key it directly in the Change To box and then click Change.

 TIP: You may want to view a word in the worksheet before you change its spelling. You can move the Spelling dialog box out of the way by dragging its title bar.

6. When the spell-check is completed, click OK in the dialog box that appears.

EXERCISE **7-2** **Spell-Check a Range in the Worksheet**

To spell-check a range in a worksheet, highlight the range to be checked and then choose Spelling from the Tools menu. Excel will check only the highlighted range.

1. Move to the Documentation sheet and select cells A1 through A9.

2. Click the Spelling button ![ABC] on the Standard toolbar. The Spelling dialog box appears. Excel highlights "cretor," the first word in the selected range that is not found in its dictionary.

3. Click Change. Excel replaces the incorrect spelling and locates "Dat," the next word not found in its dictionary.

4. Click **Date** from the Suggestions drop-down list box, and then click Change.

5. Click Change to correct "Revisd" to **Revised**.

6. Key **by** in the Change To text box, and then click Change. A dialog box appears when the spell-check of the range is complete.

7. Click OK.

Using AutoCorrect

The AutoCorrect feature will automatically correct your spelling as you work. You can customize AutoCorrect by adding words that you commonly misspell to the Excel's list. You can also turn off AutoCorrect, if desired.

EXERCISE **7-3** **Use AutoCorrect to Correct Typos**

1. Choose <u>A</u>utoCorrect from the <u>T</u>ools menu. The AutoCorrect dialog box appears.

FIGURE 7-2
AutoCorrect
dialog box

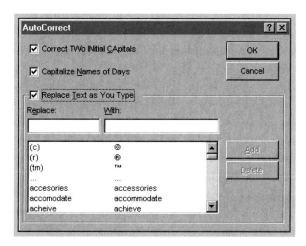

2. Clear the Replace <u>T</u>ext as You Type check box, and then click OK. The AutoCorrect feature is deselected, and Excel will not correct spelling automatically.

3. Key **Purpose adn description:** in cell A12 and press Enter. Remember to type the second word exactly as shown. With AutoCorrect deselected, the spelling error remains in the cell.

4. Choose <u>A</u>utoCorrect from the <u>T</u>ools menu.

5. Click the Replace <u>T</u>ext as You Type check box to select it, and then click OK. AutoCorrect becomes active again.

6. Enter the following text in cell D12 exactly as shown to see AutoCorrect at work:

Analyze teh sale groth of new product line

AutoCorrect changes the word "teh" to "the" as you type. Note, however, that the misspelled word "groth" has not been corrected. In addition, errors in sentence syntax, such as the word "sale" in this entry, will not be corrected by AutoCorrect or the spell-checker.

EXERCISE 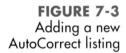 **Train AutoCorrect for Your Common Typos**

You can to train AutoCorrect to automatically correct a word that you misspell often. Simply add the misspelling and its correction to AutoCorrect's list of words.

1. Select cells A12 through D12 in the Documentation worksheet.
2. Click ⟦ᴬᵇᶜ⟧. Excel suggests "Dan" to correct the first word in the range that does not match its dictionary.
3. Double-click **and** from the Suggestions drop-down list box. Excel finds "groth," the next word in the range not found in its dictionary.
4. Click AutoCorrect. Excel changes the spelling of the word and adds this correction to AutoCorrect's list of words to correct as you type. A dialog box appears when the spell-check of the range is complete.
5. Click OK.
6. Move to cell D12 again and change the word "sale" to **sales.**
7. Choose AutoCorrect from the Tools menu.
8. Key the following words in the Replace and With text boxes, and then click Add. Be sure to type the words exactly as shown.

   produtc   product

FIGURE 7-3
Adding a new
AutoCorrect listing

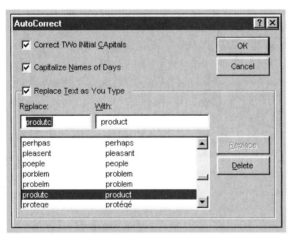

9. Scroll up the Replace With text box to confirm that the word "groth" has been added to the AutoCorrect list.
10. Click OK.

> **TIP:** You can also use AutoCorrect to create abbreviations that speed data entry. For example, assume that you type the phrase "Pending Release" frequently in your worksheets. Just add the abbreviation "pr" to the Replace text box and the full phrase "Pending Release" to the With text box in the AutoCorrect dialog box.

Finding and Replacing Data

Find and Replace are handy tools for updating worksheets. Find locates occurrences of a *character string*—a sequence of characters in a formula or text. You can use Find to return to a particular location in a worksheet, to verify that text is consistent, or to check that a formula appears in all intended locations.

Replace locates occurrences of a character string and replaces them, either one at a time or globally. As a result, it can change a formula that occurs in multiple cells. Replace can also change repeated labels, such as a category or product names.

EXERCISE **7-5** **Find Data in a Worksheet**

The Find command can be used in relatively long worksheets that contain too many formulas and values to check individually. Find is especially useful in locating all instances of a formula or error in a worksheet. Excel uses the asterisk (*) as a *wildcard* symbol, which instructs Excel to allow any combination of letters or numbers to replace it. If, for example, Excel were searching for 7-*, it would locate 7-1, 7-2, 7-A, 7-SOFT, and so on.

All error values begin with # (the number sign), so you can key **#** in the Find What text box to locate any error values in a worksheet. You can also look for specific error values, such as #DIV/0!, the error value produced by division by zero.

1. In the Sun Soft worksheet, choose <u>F</u>ind from the <u>E</u>dit menu (or press Ctrl+F. The Find dialog box appears.

FIGURE 7-4
Find dialog box

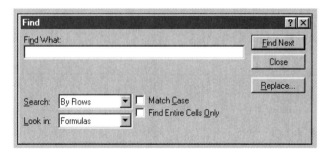

2. Key **=SUM(C7:C10)** in the Fi<u>n</u>d What text box.

3. Choose **Formulas** from the <u>L</u>ook in drop-down list box, if necessary. Make sure the Match <u>C</u>ase box is not checked.

4. Click <u>F</u>ind Next. Excel finds the formula in cell C12, and displays the cell reference and formula in the formula bar.

 TIP: Drag the Find dialog box out of the way, so that you can see the selected cell in the worksheet.

5. Edit the text in the Fi̲nd What text box to read "**=SUM(*7:*10)**", and then click F̲ind Next. Excel selects cell D12.

6. Click F̲ind Next to find the next occurrence of the formula. Excel selects cell E12.

 NOTE: You cannot edit the worksheet when the Find dialog box is open. If you close the Find dialog box, however, you can repeat the last search by pressing F4.

7. Click F̲ind Next. Excel selects cell C12 again.

8. Choose **Values** from the L̲ook in drop-down list box.

9. Key **#** in the Fi̲nd What text box (replacing the formula), and click F̲ind Next. Excel returns cell G7, which contains a formula that attempts to perform division by zero. (The formula "D7/C7" is a division by zero, because cell C7 is empty.)

10. Close the Find dialog box.

11. In cell C7, key **57,809**. The error is corrected.

EXERCISE | **7-6** | **Replace Data in a Worksheet**

You can replace character strings that you find either globally or one at a time.

1. Select cell A6, and choose R̲eplace from the E̲dit menu (or press Ctrl+H). The Replace dialog box appears. The Fi̲nd What text box contains # (the number sign), which is the last entry made in the Find dialog box.

FIGURE 7-5
Replace dialog box

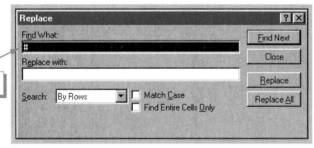

Most recent Find string

2. Key **1995** in the Fi̲nd What text box (replacing #), press the Tab key, and key **Year 1** in the R̲eplace with text box.

3. Click F̲ind Next.

 TIP: Drag the Replace dialog box out of the way, so that you can see the selected cell in the worksheet.

4. Click R̲eplace. The worksheet displays "Year 1" in cell C6.

5. Close the Replace dialog box.

FIGURE 7-6
Worksheet with
new value

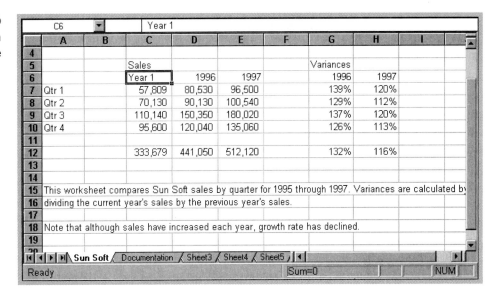

6. Select cell C6, if necessary.

7. Choose Find from the Edit menu, edit the date in the Find What text box to read **1996**, and click Find Next. Cell D6 is selected.

8. Close the Find dialog box.

9. Choose Replace from the Edit menu. Notice that 1996 is already entered in the Find What text box.

 TIP: You can open the Replace dialog box directly from the Find dialog box by clicking Replace.

10. Edit the Replace with text box to read **Year 2** and then choose Replace All. Both occurrences of "1996" are replaced with "Year 2."

11. Choose Replace from the Edit menu. Edit the Find What box to read **1997**, and edit the Replace with box to read **Year 3**.

12. Click Find Next. Excel returns to cell E6.

13. Click Replace.

14. Click Find Next again, and replace **1997** in cell H5 with **Year 3**.

15. Close the Replace dialog box.

16. Save the workbook as *[your initials]***7-6.xls.**

17. Print the entire workbook and then close it.

Finding Files

You can use Excel's Open dialog box to find a file, even if you do not remember its exact name. You can also display different types of details about files to determine which file to open.

TABLE 7-2   **Open Dialog Box Buttons**

BUTTON	BUTTON NAME/ACTION
	Up One Level moves up the file tree shown in the Look in drop-down list.
	Look in Favorites displays a list of folders and files specified as your "favorites."
	Add to Favorites adds the selected item to your Favorites list.
	List displays only folder names and filenames (no details).
	Details displays the filenames and descriptive details like size, type, and date last modified.
	Properties displays filenames and properties of the selected file.
	Preview displays filenames and a window of the contents of the selected file.
	Commands and Settings offers a menu of options.

If you can choose Search Subfolders from the Commands and Settings menu, Excel will look in the current folder and in any subfolders. Excel also allows you to search for files that contain specific words or phrases. To take this approach, you key the text in the Text or property text box before you start your search.

EXERCISE   **7-7**   **Find a Workbook**

Excel can search for specific filenames or for filenames containing a certain pattern. For example, you can search for all filenames with a specific prefix or extension.

1. Click , or choose Open from the File menu, or press Ctrl + O. The Open dialog box appears. (See Figure 7-7 on the next page.)
2. Specify your Student Template Disk in the Look in drop-down list.
3. In the File name text box, key **Frgrnce**.
4. Choose Microsoft Excel Files (*.xl*; *.xls; *.xla;*) in the Files of type drop-down list, if necessary.
5. Click Find Now. The filename, "Frgrnce," is displayed in the list box, and the search results, "1 file(s) found," are displayed in the status bar at the bottom of the dialog box.
6. Key **F*** in the File name text box, and then click Find Now. All Excel files that begin with "F" are displayed.

2. Train AutoCorrect to convert the following abbreviations into complete words:

Abbreviation	Complete word
Qtr	**Quarter**
Tot	**Total**

3. Key the data as shown in Figure 7-12.

FIGURE 7-12

	A	B	C	D	E	F
5		Qtr. 1	Qtr. 2	Qtr. 3	Qtr. 4	Tot
6	1997	26544	25799	30124	35,666	
7	1998	30118	69765	46,552 ~~45625~~	50,217	
8	1999	54339	26001	35612	58,378	

4. Format the worksheet in comma style with no decimal places.

5. Enter formulas to find the annual and quarterly totals.

6. Spell-check the worksheet.

7. Delete the AutoCorrect entries you made in this exercise (**Qtr** and **Tot**).

8. Save the workbook as *[your initials]***7-sales.xls**, and close it.

9. Use the Open dialog box to rename the file *[your initials]***7-sales.xls** as *[your initials]***7-14.xls**.

10. Print the renamed file from the Open dialog box.

EXERCISE 7-15

Find and open a file, find and replace data, spell-check a worksheet, and print a workbook from the Open dialog box.

The Beautiful Belle Company's product sales analysis should be for the year 1997, not 1996. In addition, the company president wants to change the terms "Men" and "Women" in the worksheet to "Males" and "Females."

1. Find and open the file **Compare2.xls**.

2. Replace the column label **Men** with **Males**.

3. Replace the column label **Women** with **Females**.

4. Replace all occurrences of **1996** with **1997**.

5. Spell-check the worksheet.

6. Check the dates in cell A22 to verify the change in year.

7. Save the workbook as *[your initials]***7-15.xls**, and close it.

8. Print the file from the Open dialog box.

Find and open a file, replace labels, spell-check a worksheet, and use the Open dialog box to rename and print a worksheet.

A four-month sales analysis of Sun Soft and Corn Silk sales covers the wrong four months. In addition, the worksheet contains several spelling errors. Make the corrections, and then use the Open dialog box to copy, rename, and print the worksheet.

1. Find and open the file **Brands.xls**.

2. Replace all occurrences of "August," "September," "October," and "November" with **April**, **May**, **June**, and **July**, respectively.

3. Spell-check the worksheet. Make the necessary corrections.

4. Save the workbook as *[your initials]***7-Brands**, and close it.

5. Use the Open dialog box to rename the file *[your initials]***7-16.xls**.

6. Print the file *[your initials]***7-16.xls** from the Open dialog box.

Unit 2 Applications

APPLICATION 2-1

Sketch a worksheet, enter labels in a new Excel worksheet, create and enter formulas, freeze titles, center the worksheet, print it, display formulas, and print in landscape orientation showing column and row labels and gridlines.

The Beautiful Belle Company wants to construct a worksheet that calculates the difference between monthly sales in the first quarter for men and women for two of its products: Pacifica and Taos. The worksheet should also calculate the difference in total sales.

1. Sketch the worksheet giving it a title (**Pacifica vs. Taos Sales**), column labels (**Pacifica Sales**, **Taos Sales**, and **Difference**), and row labels (see Figure U2-1).

2. Open a new worksheet.

3. Enter the title and labels on the worksheet. Include labels for each month for men, each month for women, and each month for men and women combined.

4. Key the data as shown in Figure U2-1 in the appropriate rows and columns.

FIGURE U2-1

		Pacifica Sales	Taos Sales	Difference
Men	January	7,985	16,544	
	February	2,697	9,800	
	March	10,655	9,402	
	Subtotal			
Women	January	9,557	20,550	
	February	10,665	14,675	
	March	9,418	16,550	
	Subtotal			

5. Create a formula that calculates the men's subtotal for "Pacifica Sales."

6. Freeze column titles.

7. Below the "Women" section, create the labels for a "Total" section that includes each month.

8. Create formulas that calculate totals for January, February, and March. Key the actual formulas.

9. Using the AutoSum button on the toolbar, create a formula that calculates the women's subtotal for "Pacifica Sales" and formulas that calculate subtotals for men's and women's "Taos Sales."

10. Calculate the difference between "Pacifica" and "Taos" sales in the "Subtotal" rows.

11. Create a **Grand Total** label and calculate a grand total for "Pacifica Sales," "Taos Sales," and the difference between them.

12. Preview the worksheet.

13. Center the page vertically and horizontally.

14. Save the workbook as *[your initials]*u2-1.xls.

15. Print the workbook.

16. Display formulas, and print the workbook in landscape orientation to fit on one page.

17. Close the workbook without saving it. Submit the worksheet sketch, the normal worksheet, and the worksheet with formulas displayed.

APPLICATION 2-2

Copy using drag and drop, the toolbar, the Fill command, AutoFill, and keyboard shortcuts. Insert data. Open and dock the Auditing toolbar, and trace precedents for a cell.

Complete a worksheet that compares Pacifica and Taos product sales in the second quarter of two consecutive years.

1. Open the file **PacTaos.xls**.

2. Copy cells B8 through B20 to cells G8 through G20 using the drag-and-drop method.

3. Key the 1998 product data as shown in Figure U2-2.

FIGURE U2-2

			H	I
			Pacifica	Taos
8	Men	April	11,600	10,650
9		May	13,500	8,401
10		June	14,877	11,650
13	Women	April	15,400	19,680
14		May	19,102	12,120
15		June	21,241	15,611

4. Copy the formula in cell E8 to cell J8 using the Copy and Paste buttons on the Standard toolbar.

5. Using the Fill command, copy the formula to cells J9 through J11.

6. Use the drag-and-drop method to copy the formulas in cells J8 through J11 to cells J13 through J16.

7. Create a formula that subtotals men's 1998 "Pacifica" sales.

8. Copy the formula in cell H11 to cell I11 using AutoFill.

9. Copy both of these formulas to subtotal women's sales using the Copy and Paste commands.

10. Using drag and drop, copy the formulas for calculating the monthly totals for April 1997 to April 1998.

11. Select cells H18 through J20 and calculate the totals for the remaining months using Fill, Down.

12. Create a grand total for 1998 "Pacifica" sales for the second quarter, and copy it to cell I22 using AutoFill.

13. Copy the difference formula from cell J20 to cell J22 in the "Second-Quarter Total" row using the Cut and Paste buttons.

14. Save the worksheet as *[your initials]***u2-2.xls**.

15. Activate the Auditing toolbar and dock it. Trace the precedents for cell E22.

16. Close the Auditing toolbar using the Toolbar shortcut menu.

17. Print the worksheet, including the tracing arrow.

18. Print the worksheet with formulas and row and column headings displayed.

19. Close the workbook without saving it.

APPLICATION 2-3

Use AutoSum and AutoFill, create range names, build formulas using names, paste names into the worksheet, rename worksheet tabs, create documentation, navigate the worksheet using names, and print formulas.

Create a worksheet that calculates commissions for Beautiful Belle's Southwest region and summarizes yearly sales, commissions, and net sales – that is, gross sales minus commissions.

1. Open the file **SW.xls**.

2. In cell C15, use the AutoSum button to add the column.

3. Use Autofill to copy the SUM formula to cells D15 through J15.

4. Create the name **rt** for the constant **.07** to calculate quarterly commissions due.

5. Create formulas using the constant name in cells D5, F5, H5, and J5 to calculate the commission due for each quarter. To complete the columns, copy the formula using AutoFill.

6. Create the names **sq1**, **sq2**, **sq3**, and **sq4** for the total sales for each quarter.

7. Create a formula in cell B17 that calculates the total sales for the year. Usc names in the formula.

8. Create the names **com1**, **com2**, **com3**, and **com4** for the total commissions for each quarter.

9. Use the commission range names to create a formula in cell B18 that calculates the total commissions for the year.

10. Create a formula in cell B19 that calculates the annual net sales—that is, gross sales minus commissions—for the Southwest territory.

11. Format numbers in columns C through J in comma style with two decimal places. Format the yearly numbers (cells B17:B19) in comma style with no decimal places.

12. Rename the Sheet1 tab **commission**.

13. Rename the Sheet2 tab **user information**.

14. Key the data from Figure U2-3 in the user information sheet, including the corrections.

FIGURE U2-3

```
    Worksheet Documentation
                          a
    Name of cretor:           Jenny Bissell

    Date created:            5/11/97
                                        Today's date
                 e
    Date ryised:             5/12/97

    Revised by:              5/12/97      Your name
 lc
    Description and purpose:  Calculate comission for SW territory
 TR                                     m
                   U/c         based on sales by quarter.    Spell out

 TR Special instructions:     Note range and constant names below.
```

15. After the last line of text entered from Figure U2-3, paste all of the names you created into the worksheet.

16. Spell-check both worksheets.

17. Use the Go To command to locate the cell named "sq4."

18. Save the worksheet as *[your initials]***u2-3.xls**.

19. Print the entire workbook. Display formulas, and then print the commission worksheet with gridlines and row and column headings.

20. Close the workbook without saving it.

APPLICATION 2-4

Find and open a file, replace labels, spell-check the worksheet, train AutoCorrect to recognize typos, use AutoSum and AutoFill to enter formulas, and use the Open dialog box to copy a file and print a worksheet.

Find and adapt a workbook to total fourth quarter cream and fragrance sales for Beautiful Belle.

1. Open the file **Prdcts.xls**.

2. Spell-check the worksheet. Make a list of errors and correct spellings, and then make the necessary corrections in the worksheet.

3. Use the Replace command to replace all occurrences of "July," "August," and "September" with **October**, **November**, and **December**, respectively.

4. Train AutoCorrect to recognize three of the misspelled words you found in the worksheet.

5. Use AutoSum and AutoFill to enter formulas for the "Totals" rows and columns.

6. Replace "Third" with **Fourth**.

7. Save the workbook as *[your initials]*u2-4.xls and close it.

8. Use the Open dialog box to create a copy of *[your initials]*u2-4.xls, and then print that file from the Open dialog box.

9. Delete the copy of your file.

APPLICATION 2-5

Find and open a workbook, check spelling, and copy and paste data and formulas. Create range names, and create formulas using range names. Use AutoSum and AutoFill, find and replace data, paste range names into a worksheet, change print settings, and use the Open dialog box to copy and print a worksheet.

Imagine you are a product manager for the Beautiful Belle Company and are charged with projecting revenue for three new lines of shampoo being launched in the third quarter of the current year. You need to enter product line names in the worksheet, and then change the revenue figures in the worksheet as you see fit.

1. Find and open a workbook whose filename begins with **P** and ends in **3**. The workbook contains the word **shampoo**.

2. Invent three product names for shampoos. Key the names in cells A8 through A10.

3. Spell-check the worksheet and make any necessary corrections.

4. Use AutoSum and AutoFill to create formulas that calculate the monthly totals.

5. Use AutoSum and Autofill to create formulas that calculate the product line totals for the third quarter.

6. In cell E11, create a formula that calculates the total projected sales for the three new products in the third quarter.

7. Copy the range in rows 4 through 11 that contains labels and data, and paste it into the worksheet beneath the third-quarter data, beginning with cell A13.

8. In the pasted text, replace "Third Quarter" with **Fourth Quarter**, and replace "July," "August," and "September," with **October**, **November**, and **December**, respectively.

9. Create the name **rt** for the constant **1.1** to calculate projected sales growth for the fourth quarter.

10. Select cells B8 through D8, and create an appropriate range name for the first product.

11. Select cells B9 through D9, and create an appropriate range name for the second product.

12. Select cells B10 through D10, and create an appropriate range name for the third product.

13. Create a formula in cell B17 that uses the range name for the first product and the name **rt** to calculate projected sales growth for the fourth quarter.

14. Use AutoFill to copy the formula from cell B17 to cells C17 and D17.

15. Create similar formulas for the other two products in cells B18 and B19. Copy the formulas to columns C and D.

16. Rename the worksheet tab **Projections**, and name the Sheet2 tab **User Information**.

17. Create worksheet documentation on the User Information sheet, and include a pasted list of named ranges.

18. Save the workbook *[your initials]***u2-5.xls**, and then print the User Information sheet only.

19. Display formulas in the Projections sheet. Trace the precedents to cell B17 (the first shampoo sales projection for October).

20. Print the worksheet showing formulas, and then turn off the formula display.

21. Use Page Setup to change the print settings to print in portrait orientation, without gridlines and without row and column headings.

22. Save and close the workbook.

23. Use the Open dialog box to create a copy of the file.

24. Print the file **Copy of** *[your initials]***u2-5.xls** from the Open dialog box.

25. Delete the file **Copy of** *[your initials]***u2-5.xls**.

Changing the Appearance of a Worksheet

Short-Camper Gear Stands Tall in Sales

Clearey & Clayton produces camping gear for backpacking, boating, skiing, and other wilderness activities. The business got its start when Bettina Clearey, a former fashion designer, sewed her own backpack to accommodate her petite 5-foot frame. She soon found there was a huge demand for scaled-down camping equipment. John Clayton, an advertising executive, became her partner and Clearey & Clayton was formed.

Clearey & Clayton's products were so well designed that it wasn't long before the company become one of the largest suppliers of camping gear in the country. Their best-selling products are their backpacks, sunglasses, camping chairs, kayaks, duffel bags, and mountaineering tents.

To increase their market share, Clearey & Clayton need to create the following worksheets to use as promotional material.

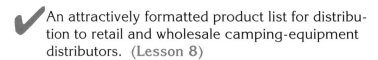 An attractively formatted product list for distribution to retail and wholesale camping-equipment distributors. (Lesson 8)

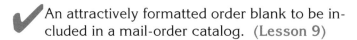 An attractively formatted order blank to be included in a mail-order catalog. (Lesson 9)

Formatting Text and Numbers

OBJECTIVES

After completing this lesson, you will be able to:

1. Format numbers.
2. Suppress the display of zero values.
3. Work with stored numbers.
4. Align text.
5. Change column width and row height.
6. Hide columns and rows.

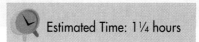
Estimated Time: 1¼ hours

You can change the appearance of a worksheet by formatting numbers and text in different ways. Number formats include commas, dollar signs, and decimal places. Text formats include alignment in a cell, alignment over a group of cells, and text wrap within a cell. You can also change column width and row height.

Formatting Numbers

The default *format*—that is, the attributes of text or numbers, such as font style, underlining, bold, number of decimal places, or alignment—is called the Normal style. For numbers, the General format code is used. With this format, numbers are right-aligned; decimals, commas, and dollar signs are not displayed unless keyed; and the font is 10-point Arial.

NOTE: The default format for text in the Normal style is left-aligned, 10-point Arial.

207

In Lesson 3, you used the Formatting toolbar to perform basic number formatting. In this lesson, you will choose from additional standard formats and create custom formats using the Number options in the Format Cells dialog box. Number formats may be applied to entire columns, rows, worksheets, or individual cells.

EXERCISE **Choose a Number Format**

1. Open the file **TWOut.xls**.

2. Select cells D8 through E10 and cells D13 through E14. (Hint: Press Ctrl to select the second set of cells.)

3. Choose Cells from the Format menu. The Format Cells dialog box appears.

4. Click the Number tab, if necessary, and the Number options appear.

5. Choose Currency from the Category list box.

NOTE: The Currency format is used for general monetary values. The Accounting format will align currency symbols and decimal points in a column.

6. Choose the third format code ($1,234) in the Negative Numbers list.

TIP: The options in the Negative Numbers list indicate how Excel handles negative numbers. For example, if you are "in the red" and want to show a loss in 1997, Quarter 4, the second or last options in red are good choices. (If you don't have a color printer and plan to print the worksheet, avoid all of the red options.)

7. Click the Use $ check box to turn off the dollar sign option. With this option turned off, a dollar sign will not appear beside each number in the selected cells.

8. Key 0 beside Decimal Places to have numbers appear without decimal places.

FIGURE 8-1
Number options in
the Format Cells
dialog box

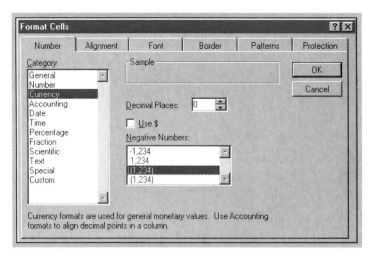

9. Click OK. The numbers in cells E13 and E14 now contain commas that separate thousands from hundreds.

EXERCISE | **8-2** | **Create a Custom Format**

Excel lets you create custom formats to meet any special needs. You can insert dashes within Social Security numbers or parentheses and dashes to indicate area codes and phone numbers. You can even include text in a code by surrounding it with quotation marks.

TABLE 8-1 **Examples of Custom Format Codes**

FORMAT CODE	NUMBER	DISPLAY
000-00-0000	123456789	123-45-6789
(000) 000-0000	2035551234	(203) 555-1234
"Purchase No." 0000	1234	Purchase No. 1234
#.##	0.7	.7
#.##	5211.129	5211.13
#.0#	15	15.0
#.0#	1234.568	1234.57
0.0%	.7889	78.9
00000	06477 (ZIP CODE)	06477
#,##0;#,##0-	-1234	1,234-
#.#0	18.1	18.10

NOTE: A pound sign in a format code represents an integer or whole number, a zero represents leading or trailing zeros that fall immediately before or after the decimal position, and format codes for positive and negative numbers are separated by a semicolon.

In this exercise, we'll insert dashes and create item numbers.

1. Select cells B8 through B10 and cells B13 through B14.

2. Click the right mouse button and choose Format Cells from the shortcut menu. (Make sure the white cross appears in one of the highlighted cells.) The Format Cells dialog box appears.

FIGURE 8-2
Shortcut menu with
Format Cells
highlighted

 TIP: You can also press Ctrl + 1 to open the Format
Cells dialog box.

3. Click the Number tab, if necessary, and choose Custom
from the <u>C</u>ategory list box.

4. Choose the format code 0.00 from the <u>T</u>ype list. The
Type text box appears.

5. Position the insertion point in the <u>T</u>ype text box and delete the period
from the code. After the three zeros, key **0-000**. The new code should read
0000-000.

6. Click OK. Dashes appear in cells B8 through B10 along with the numbers.

7. Key the following data in cells B13 and B14:

5217988

5218088

Notice that the new format now applies to these numbers.

 NOTE: The Custom <u>C</u>ategory list is a good source for format codes. The
original format code that you edited, 0.00, is still available for use in this
workbook, and the new code created is added to the end of the list. If you need the
new code for another workbook, you must recreate it in that workbook.

Suppressing the Display of Zero Values

When a large worksheet contains many zero entries, it can be hard to read.
It's a good idea to suppress the zero values in the worksheet to make it more
readable.

EXERCISE 8-3 **Suppress the Display of Zero Values**

1. Scroll down to rows 17 through 19. Notice the zero values that appear in
columns D and E.

2. To hide these zeros, choose <u>O</u>ptions from the <u>T</u>ools menu. The Options
dialog box appears.

3. Click the View tab, if necessary, and the View options appear.

4. Click the <u>Z</u>ero Values check box to clear it, and then click OK. The zeros
in cells D17 through E19 disappear.

NOTE: The Zero Values setting works for only the active worksheet—not
the entire workbook. You can restore the zeroes by checking the <u>Z</u>ero Values
check box a second time.

FIGURE 8-3
View options in the
Options dialog box

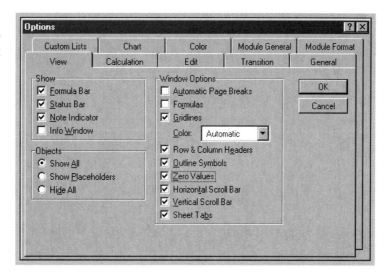

Working with Stored Numbers

When you key a number, Excel rounds it according to the cell's format. For instance, if you key **30** and the cell is formatted for two decimal places, Excel displays 30.00. Similarly, if the cell is formatted for no decimal places, and you key **9.9**, Excel displays 10. Excel internally stores the number that you key (9.9), however, and uses this number in calculations. This characteristic is called *full precision*.

Sometimes if you change numbers in worksheet columns after the column has been totaled and Excel rounds the new numbers up or down, the total may appear to be incorrectly calculated. To avoid this problem, you can store numbers as the rounded values that appear on screen (10). This option is called *Precision as Displayed*.

EXERCISE | 8-4 | **Calculate Using the Precision as Displayed Option**

1. Key the following data to replace the numbers in cells D13 and D14:
   1000.45   2000.35
   Notice that the total for column D is now incorrect. The numbers stored internally in full precision are used in the arithmetic rather than the displayed numbers.

2. Choose Options from the Tools menu.

3. Click the Calculation tab. The Calculation dialog box appears. See Figure 8-4 on the next page.

4. Click the Precision as Displayed check box to turn on this option, and then click OK.

FIGURE 8-4
Calculation options
in the Options
dialog box

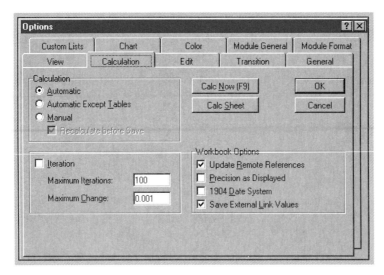

5. Click OK at the prompt that says data will permanently lose accuracy. The sum in Column D is now correct.

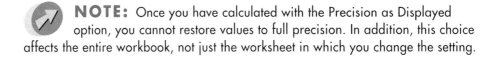

NOTE: Once you have calculated with the Precision as Displayed option, you cannot restore values to full precision. In addition, this choice affects the entire workbook, not just the worksheet in which you change the setting.

6. Delete rows 16 through 21.

Aligning Text

The Normal style for text alignment (left-aligned) can be changed in several ways. You can realign text within a cell or across cells. You can also rotate text or wrap it onto several lines in a cell.

EXERCISE 8-5 Align Text in a Cell

The Alignment command allows you to align text to the left, right, or center of a cell. You can also align text vertically with the top, bottom, or center of the cell. In addition, wrapped text can be justified to fill the entire width of a cell, with even margins appearing on both sides of the cell contents.

1. Select cells A4 through E4 and cells A7 and A12.

2. To center the text horizontally in these cells, click the Center button on the Formatting toolbar.

3. Select cells A8 through A10 and cells A13 through A14.

4. Click the Align Right button 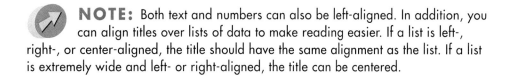 on the Formatting toolbar. All of the text is now right-aligned.

5. To center text vertically in cells A4 through E4, select these cells.

6. Press Ctrl + 1 to open the Format Cells dialog box.

7. Click the Alignment tab, if necessary, and the Alignment options appear.

FIGURE 8-5
Alignment options in
the Format Cells
dialog box

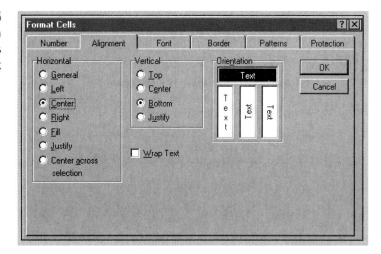

8. Click the Center option button under Vertical. Center under Horizontal is already selected because you previously applied this formatting in step 2.

9. Click OK. Although you cannot see it on the screen, the text is now centered vertically in the cells. (You will see the effects of this alignment in Exercise 8-7.)

NOTE: Both text and numbers can also be left-aligned. In addition, you can align titles over lists of data to make reading easier. If a list is left-, right-, or center-aligned, the title should have the same alignment as the list. If a list is extremely wide and left- or right-aligned, the title can be centered.

EXERCISE ▎8-6▎ **Center Text Over a Range of Columns**

If you want to center the title of a worksheet over all of its columns or other text over a range of columns, you can use the Center Across Columns button on the Formatting toolbar.

NOTE: The title should appear or be entered in the left-most column of the range of columns over which you wish to center it.

1. Position the mouse pointer in cell A1, and key **Clearey & Clayton**

2. In cell A2, key **Product List**

3. Select cells A1 through E2. These selected cells include the range of cells in which you'll center the title.

4. Click and the text becomes a title for the worksheet. Notice that if the screen gridlines are turned on, they do not display between the columns that contain the centered title.

5. To remove the formatting, click ⊞ while the first cell in the range of cells that contains the title is selected. Notice that when the first cell is selected, the title appears in the formula bar.

6. Click ↩ to reapply the formatting.

> **TIP:** You can also access the Alignment dialog box by choosing Format Cells from the shortcut menu after you have selected the text to be aligned. You can then select Center <u>a</u>cross selection to perform the same formatting. (Remember to position the white cross in a highlighted cell when you click the right mouse button.)

EXERCISE | **8-7** | ## Wrap Text on Several Lines Within a Cell

When you key a line of text that is too wide for a column (for example, column A), the text extends into the next column (B), if it's blank. If the next column is not blank, the text to the right in column A is hidden from view. If you don't want to widen the column, you can wrap the text on several lines within the cell.

1. Key the text shown in Figure 8-6 in cell C8. Do not press ⌐Enter⌐ at the end of each line.

FIGURE 8-6

```
This tent is designed for spring, summer, and fall. It has a
separate rain fly and fiberglass poles. Packed size is 18″ x
5.5″. Weight: 4.5 lb.
```

2. Press ⌐Enter⌐. The text is hidden by the next column.

3. To make the text wrap in the cell, select cell C8 and open the Format Cells dialog box.

4. Click the Alignment tab, if necessary.

5. Click the <u>W</u>rap Text check box to select it, and then click OK. The text is now wrapped in the cell and the height of the other cells in the row is adjusted.

NOTE: When you wrap text on several lines within a cell, row height will adjust to accommodate the font size. If you change the font size or column width after wrapping the text, the row height will not change.

EXERCISE **8-8** **Rotate Text Within a Cell**

At some point, you may find it useful to rotate text within a cell. This option highlights the information in that cell and can narrow the column containing the text.

1. Select cell A7.
2. Open the Format Cells dialog box. Click the Alignment tab, if necessary.
3. Under Orientation click the middle box containing the word "Text" tilted upward and click OK. "Tents" becomes rotated upward.
4. Press Ctrl + Z to undo the formatting.

EXERCISE **8-9** **Create Line Breaks Within a Cell**

Text will wrap only to the next line when it reaches the end of the column. If you want it to go to the next line before this point, you must create a *line break*, or a forced movement of the cursor to the next line down within the cell. Line breaks also narrow wide columns.

1. Select cells D4 and E4.
2. Open the Format Cells dialog box using the shortcut menu.
3. Click the Alignment tab, if necessary.
4. Click the Wrap Text check box, and then click OK.
5. Create a line break in cell D4, key **Wholesale** and press Alt + Enter.
6. Key **Price** and press Enter. A line break now appears after "Wholesale."
7. Repeat these steps for cell E4. In this cell, key **Suggested**, press Alt + Enter to create a line break, key **Retail Price**, and press Enter.

Changing Column Width and Row Height

You can increase column width to display text that won't fit in the current column or to make a worksheet more readable. You can also decrease column width to make room for other columns. Additionally, you can adjust row height to create proper spacing between rows or to adjust to a new font size when working with wrapped text.

Excel provides three ways to change column width and row height:

● Using the mouse

● Using the Column Width and Row Height dialog boxes

● Using the AutoFit option to maximize the columns visible on the screen and those that print per page

EXERCISE | **8-10** | **Change Column Width and Row Height with the Mouse**

1. To increase column width, position the pointer along the right border of column C, where it meets with column D in the lettered gray area or column heading.

2. When the pointer becomes a two-headed arrow ✛, drag until the column width increases about 0.5 inch or to approximately 17.00. (The column size displays immediately above column A in the Name box, where the cell address is usually displayed.)

FIGURE 8-7
Changing column width

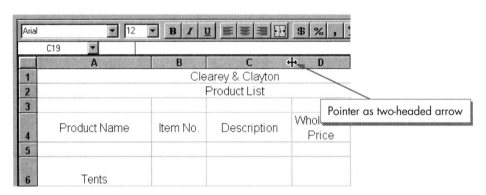

Pointer as two-headed arrow

NOTE: The number in the Name box referes to the average number of characters of the default text font that fit in a cell. Your numbers may vary if your default text font is different from the standard.

3. Change the document view to 75%. Position the pointer along the bottom border of row 8, where it meets with row 9 in the numbered gray area or row heading.

4. When the pointer becomes a two-headed arrow, drag up until the row height decreases to about 147.00 in the Name box.

5. Change the document view back to 100%.

6. Position the pointer along the bottom border of row 4, where it meets with row 5, with the two-headed arrow, drag down until the row height increases about 0.5 inch or to 45.00.

7. To change more than one column at once, select columns C, D, and E.

8. Position the pointer at the top right border of any of the selected columns until the pointer becomes a two-headed arrow. Drag to decrease the column width about 0.5 inch. The width of all selected columns decreases by the same amount.

9. With the columns still selected, increase the width by the same amount. The columns are now all the same width.

EXERCISE 8-11 **Use the Column Width and Row Height Dialog Boxes**

FIGURE 8-8
Column cascading menu

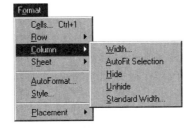

FIGURE 8-9
Column Width dialog box

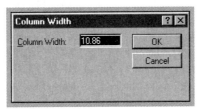

1. Select column B.

2. Choose Column from the Format menu. Notice that the Column cascading menu appears.

3. Choose Width. The Column Width dialog box appears.

4. Key **15** in the Column Width text box and click OK. The column width increases.

5. Select rows 7 and 12.

TIP: If you want to select non-adjacent rows or columns, press Ctrl when selecting subsequent rows or columns.

6. Choose Row from the Format menu. The Row cascading menu appears.

7. Choose Height. The Row Height dialog box appears.

8. Key **30** in the Row Height text box, and then click OK. The row height increases.

EXERCISE 8-12 **Use AutoFit to Change Column Width and Row Height**

The AutoFit option is a fast way to adjust the column width so that the longest item fits exactly in the column. This feature helps maximize the number of columns that you can see on your screen and print on a page. You can also adjust row height using the AutoFit option.

1. Position the pointer on the right border of column B until it turns into a two-headed arrow and then double-click. The column width adjusts to fit the items in the cells.

2. To change the height of row 4 to fit the items in the cells, position the pointer on the bottom border of row 4 until the pointer turns into a two-headed arrow and then double-click. The row height adjusts to fit the items in the cells.

3. To change columns C and D at the same time, select both columns.

4. Choose Columns from the Format menu. The Column cascading menu opens.

5. Choose AutoFit Selection. The column widths of both columns are adjusted.

 NOTE: You can also double-click with the two-headed arrow positioned on the right border of column C or D to change the column widths to fit the items in the cells.

6. Delete row 6.

EXERCISE 8-13 Reset Column Width and Row Height

You may sometimes need to return column widths or row heights to their original settings.

1. To return column B to its standard size, select column B.

2. Choose Column from the Format menu. The Column cascading menu appears.

3. Choose Standard Width. The Standard Width dialog box appears. Notice that a number appears next to Standard Column Width. This value is the default standard width for your computer. (The standard width will vary for different computers.)

4. Click OK. The column is sized down to the standard width.

5. Press Ctrl + Z to undo the column size change.

6. Select rows 6 and 11.

7. Choose Row from the Format menu. The Row cascading menu appears.

8. Choose Height and then key **12.75**, the standard row height, in the Row Height dialog box. (The standard row height may vary depending on your computer. Use 12.75 for the purposes of this exercise.)

9. Click OK. The row height is resized.

10. Press Ctrl + Z to undo the row height size change.

Hiding Columns and Rows

Excel lets you hide rows or columns temporarily so that they do not print or appear on the screen. You may want to hide the salaries column when you print a payroll worksheet, for example, or you may want nonconsecutive rows to appear consecutively when you view them on your screen.

EXERCISE **8-14** **Hide Columns and Rows**

1. Select column D, and then choose <u>C</u>olumn from the F<u>o</u>rmat menu.
2. Click <u>H</u>ide. Column D becomes invisible.
3. Select columns C and E, which appear on either side of the hidden column.
4. Choose <u>C</u>olumn from the F<u>o</u>rmat menu, and then click <u>U</u>nhide. Column D reappears.
5. Select row 4, and then choose <u>R</u>ow from the F<u>o</u>rmat menu
6. Click <u>H</u>ide. The row is hidden from view.
7. Select rows 3 and 5, which are on either side of the hidden row.
8. Choose <u>R</u>ow from the F<u>o</u>rmat menu, and click <u>U</u>nhide. The row becomes visible again.
9. Make sure gridlines are turned on for printing and save the workbook as *[your initials]***8-14.xls**.
10. Print and close the workbook.

COMMAND SUMMARY

FEATURE	BUTTON	MENU	KEYBOARD
Format cells		F<u>o</u>rmat, C<u>e</u>lls	[Ctrl] + [1]
Right-align	🔲	F<u>o</u>rmat, C<u>e</u>lls	
Center	🔲	F<u>o</u>rmat, C<u>e</u>lls	
Left-align	🔲		
Center across columns	🔲	F<u>o</u>rmat, C<u>e</u>lls, Center <u>a</u>cross selection	
Create line breaks			[Alt] + [Enter]
Hide rows		F<u>o</u>rmat, <u>R</u>ow, <u>H</u>ide	[Ctrl] + [9]
Unhide rows		F<u>o</u>rmat, <u>R</u>ow, <u>U</u>nhide	[Ctrl] + [Shift] + [(]
Hide columns		F<u>o</u>rmat, <u>C</u>olumns, <u>H</u>ide	[Ctrl] + [0]
Unhide columns		F<u>o</u>rmat, <u>C</u>olumns, <u>U</u>nhide	[Ctrl] + [Shift] + [)]

219

USING HELP

You've learned how to create custom number formats. Excel can give you more information about their makeup.

Use Excel's Answer Wizard to learn more about custom number formats.

1. Press F1, and the Help Topics dialog box appears.

2. Click the Answer Wizard tab, and the Answer Wizard options appear.

3. In the text box, under number 1, key **Tell me about custom number formats**

4. Click <u>S</u>earch, and a list of topics appears under number 2.

5. Double-click on "Custom number formats" under "Tell Me About." Notice that the Microsoft Excel Help dialog box opens with information about custom number formats.

FIGURE 8-10
Microsoft Excel Help dialog box with information on custom numbers

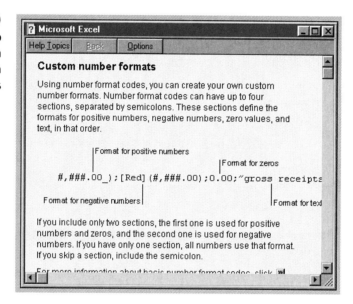

6. Close Help when you're finished learning more about these formats.

Concepts Review

TRUE/FALSE QUESTIONS

Each of the following statements is either true or false. Indicate your choice by circling **T** or **F**.

T F **1.** The default format for numbers is left-aligned, 12-point Palatino.

T F **2.** You cannot insert dashes in custom number formats.

T F **3.** A pound sign in a number format code represents an integer or a whole number.

T F **4.** When you use Suppress the Display of Zeros option, you can see zeros on an on-screen worksheet but cannot print them.

T F **5.** To center a title of a worksheet over all of its columns, you would use ▤.

T F **6.** A forced movement of the cursor to the next line down within the cell is called a line break.

T F **7.** You can use the mouse to increase column width to display text that won't fit in the current column.

T F **8.** Excel lets you hide rows or columns temporarily so that they do not appear on the screen or print.

SHORT ANSWER QUESTIONS

Write the correct answer in the space provided.

1. What are the keystrokes to open the Format Cells dialog box?

_____

2. What do you call Excel's ability to internally store the number that you key in a cell and then use this number in calculations?

_____

3. Under what menu do you access the Columns cascading menu?

_____

4. If you want to align text to the right in a cell, which button would you use?

_____

5. What are the keystrokes to create a line break in a cell?

_____

6. Which check box do you click to suppress the display of zero values?

_____

7. On which toolbar is located?

_____

8. To rotate text in a cell, which dialog box do you open?

_____

CRITICAL THINKING

Answer these questions on a separate piece of paper. There are no right or wrong answers. Support your answer with examples from your own experience, if possible.

1. Imagine that you are the owner of a business with 100 employees and need a spreadsheet that lists your employees and holds valuable information about each of them. What type of information do you think the worksheet should include? To which of these pieces of information could you apply custom number formatting? Would it save the person entering the information time and energy to take this step?

2. If you had to present a projected quarterly report of revenues in 1998, what components would you include? How would you align various components in the report? Why?

3. You can change the column width and row height in Excel in three different ways—using the mouse, with dialog boxes, or using the AutoFit option. Which approach do you prefer? Describe instances of using each option in the same worksheet.

Skills Review

EXERCISE 8-15

Format numbers.

1. Open the file **Employee.xls**.

2. Apply the first currency number format to column D by performing the following steps:

   a. Select column D.

   b. Press [Ctrl] + [1].

   c. Click the Number tab, if necessary.

   d. Select Currency from the Category list.

e. If <u>U</u>se $ is selected, click it to turn this option off.

f. Click OK.

3. Precede the numbers in column B with the abbreviation "No." by completing the following steps:

   a. Select column B.

   b. Press Ctrl + 1 .

   c. Select Custom from the <u>C</u>ategory list.

   d. Click the 0.00 format.

   e. Delete the period in the format code under the <u>T</u>ype list.

   f. Add three zeros to the format code. Key **No.** in quotations marks in front of the six zeros followed by a space.

   g. Click OK.

4. Format the numbers in column C to appear as Social Security numbers.

   a. Select column C.

   b. Open the Format Cells dialog box.

   c. Select Special from the <u>C</u>ategory list.

   d. Select Social Security Number.

   e. Click OK.

5. Delete row 2.

6. Make sure gridlines are turned on for printing and save the workbook as *[your initials]***8-15.xls**.

7. Print and close the workbook.

EXERCISE 8-16

Suppress the display of zero values and work with stored numbers.

1. Open the file **Sales.xls**.

2. Suppress zeros in the worksheet by completing the following steps:

   a. Choose <u>O</u>ptions from the <u>T</u>ools menu.

   b. Click the View tab.

   c. Click <u>Z</u>ero Values to deselect it.

   d. Click OK.

3. Change the total in column C to reflect the correct total for the column. (It is now being calculated using full precision.) Use the Precision as Displayed option by completing the following steps:

   a. Choose <u>O</u>ptions from the <u>T</u>ools menu.

   b. Click the Calculation tab.

   c. Click <u>P</u>recision as Displayed to select it.

   d. Click OK.

223

e. Click OK when the prompt with the information about data losing its accuracy appears.

    4. Save the workbook as *[your initials]***8-16.xls**.

    5. Print and close the workbook.

EXERCISE 8-17

Align text and change column width and row height.

    1. Open the file **States.xls**.

    2. Center "Clearey & Clayton Sales Comparison" over columns A through F by doing the following:

      a. Select cells A1 through F1.

      b. Click ▦.

    3. Key **Please note that this is for the sale of tents only** in cell A12 and make the text wrap in the cell by completing the following steps:

      a. Key the text in cell A12, and then press Enter.

      b. Select cell A12.

      c. Press Ctrl + 1 to open the Format Cells dialog box.

      d. Click the Alignment tab.

      e. Click Wrap Text.

      f. Click OK.

      g. Change the width of column F using the AutoFit option by double-clicking the right border of column F in the column heading with the two-headed arrow.

    4. Change the width of column A using the mouse by completing the following steps:

      a. Drag the right border of column A over with the two-headed arrow just past the "o" in "Mexico."

      b. Release the mouse button.

    5. Change the row height of row 12 by dragging the bottom border of the row up with the two-headed arrow to approximately 60.75.

    6. Save the workbook as *[your initials]***8-17.xls**.

    7. Print and close the workbook.

EXERCISE 8-18

Hide and unhide columns and rows.

    1. Open the file **Clearey.xls**.

    2. Hide column C by performing the following steps:

a. Select column C.

    b. Choose <u>C</u>olumn from the F<u>o</u>rmat menu to open the Column cascading menu.

    c. Choose <u>H</u>ide.

3. Hide row 5 by completing the following steps:

    a. Select row 5.

    b. Choose <u>R</u>ow from the F<u>o</u>rmat menu to open the Row cascading menu.

    c. Choose <u>H</u>ide.

4. Hide row 4.

5. Key the information shown in Figure 8-11 in columns A and B after the entry "Hankle, Michele."

FIGURE 8-11

Jenkins, Ross	125,950
Latham, Mary	256,857
Norton, Marie	301,205
Peters, Joanne	187,500
Ravin, Mike	99,500

6. Hide rows 11 and 12.

7. Unhide rows 4 and 5.

    a. Select rows 3 and 6.

    b. Choose <u>R</u>ow from the F<u>o</u>rmat menu.

    c. Choose <u>U</u>nhide from the Row cascading menu.

8. Save the workbook as *[your initials]***8-18.xls**.

9. Print and close the workbook.

Lesson Applications

Hide a column, format numbers, and change column width and row height.

Clearey & Clayton likes to keep the phone numbers and Social Security numbers of its employees on hand in a separate list. Format the following worksheet for readability, and apply phone number and Social Security formatting.

1. Open the file **Employee.xls**.
2. Hide column B.
3. Clear column D and key the text shown in Figure 8-12, including the corrections, beginning in cell D3.

FIGURE 8-12

Phone

9085515532

9085553474

~~9085551234~~

9085559002

9085556453

9085550984

9085558934

9085559342

~~9085550902~~

9085550221

~~9085555555~~

809555124

908555 6486

4. Format the numbers in column C as Social Security numbers and the numbers in column D as phone numbers with the area code enclosed in parentheses.

5. Use the AutoFit option to change the width of columns C and D as necessary.

6. Increase the height of rows 4 through 13 to 18 points.

7. Save the workbook as *[your initials]***8-19.xls**.

8. Print and close the workbook.

EXERCISE 8-20

Suppress the display of zero values, format numbers, hide rows, work with stored numbers, and align text.

Bettina Clearey would like a printout of sales amounts for tents and kayaks for the first four months of the year. Format the worksheet to remove the excess months listed and have the numbers represent sales amounts with rounded-off column totals.

1. Open the file **Kayaks.xls**.

2. Suppress the zeros found in column E, and hide rows 8 through 17.

3. Format cells A4 through E7 to have no dollar signs.

4. Format the Totals row as currency, with a leading dollar sign but no decimal places.

5. Change the amount in cell B5 to **30,056.95**, the amount in cell B6 to **34,677.55** and the amount in cell B7 to **$458.65**.

6. Correct the total for column B. (Use the Precision as Displayed option.)

7. Right-align the column headings in row 3.

8. Key the title **Tents and Kayaks**, and center it over the worksheet columns.

9. Save the workbook as *[your initials]***8-20.xls**.

10. Print and close the workbook.

EXERCISE 8-21

Align text, format numbers, change column width and row height, suppress the display of zero values, and hide rows.

Clearey & Clayton also sells chairs for camping. Format the worksheet to show the sales figures and totals for January through April for their five best-selling chairs. Resize rows and columns, and add a worksheet title and column headings for readability.

1. Open the file **Monthly.xls**.

2. Create titles over the worksheet columns that include the following text:

Clearey & Clayton

Monthly Sales of Camp Chairs

TIP: Put each line of the title in its own row and align the entire title at the same time.

3. Enter the following data as column headings:
   Ultimate   Rester Chair   Travel Chair   Crazy Chair

4. Format the column headings for word wrap, and center-align them vertically and horizontally.

5. Format the sales figures as currency, without dollar signs or decimals.

6. Use the AutoFit feature to adjust the width of the Totals column.

7. Adjust the height of row 4 to put additional space between the column headings and the data that follows them.

8. Suppress the display of zeros for months that have no data.

9. Hide the rows for months that have no data and the blank row above the totals.

10. Turn gridlines off for printing, and save the workbook as *[your initials]* **8-21.xls**.

11. Print and close the workbook.

EXERCISE 8-22

Change column width and row height, hide columns and rows, format numbers, suppress the display of zero values, and align text.

At the beginning of each quarter, Bettina Clearey likes to see comparisons of the present year's last quarter versus the same quarter for the previous year. The following worksheet needs to be formatted so that all columns are visible, number formats make sense, and the bonus column is filled.

1. Open the file **QDiff.xls**.

2. Key the bonus amounts shown below in cells G6 through G14.

   0

   50

   0

   0

   100

   0

   50

   0

   0

3. Use AutoFit to adjust all of the columns in a single step.

4. Hide column C.

5. Make rows 6 through 14 have a row height of 20.25 points.

6. Adjust row 5 to a row height of 30 points, and center it vertically.

7. Using the mouse, widen each column individually to make it easier to read the screen.

8. The "Difference" column in rows 6, 8, and 12 contains no decimal place. Format columns D, E, and F as numbers with no decimal places displayed and as negative numbers displayed in red within parentheses.

9. Format the "Bonus" column as currency with dollar signs and no decimal places, using the shortcut menu.

10. Suppress the zeros in the worksheet.

11. Key the titles **Clearey & Clayton Sales** in cell A1 and **Quarter-1 1996 v. Quarter-1 1997** in cell A2. Center these titles over the entire worksheet.

12. Widen the "Notes" column by about 0.5 inch, and set it for Wrap Text.

13. Key **Best improvement over last year** in cell H7.

14. Adjust row and column height to have the note wrap to three lines.

15. Set the vertical alignment in cells A6 through H14 to top alignment.

16. Save the workbook as *[your initials]***8-22.xls**.

17. Print and close the workbook.

Changing Fonts, Patterns, Colors, and Formats

O B J E C T I V E S After completing this lesson, you will be able to:

1. Work with fonts.
2. Add borders.
3. Use patterns and colors.
4. Color borders.
5. Copy cell formatting.
6. Work with styles.

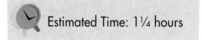

Estimated Time: 1¼ hours

Y ou can enhance the appearance of a worksheet by changing fonts and point size, adding borders and shading, and coloring cell borders. After you make such changes to one cell, you can then copy the format to other cells. You can also create a style and apply it to one or several cells.

Working with Fonts

A *font* is a type design applied to an entire set of characters, including all letters of the alphabet, numerals, punctuation marks, and other keyboard symbols. Fonts can be plain like Arial (Excel's default font) or ornate like Times New Roman.

FIGURE 9-1
Examples of fonts

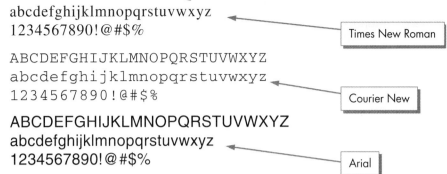

TIP: There are two types of fonts available: TrueType fonts and Postscript fonts. For Postscript fonts to print correctly, you must have a Postscript printer. If you don't have one or are unsure of your printer set-up, select TrueType fonts so that your workbook will print as it appears on your screen. (TrueType fonts have TT beside them in the Font drop-down list that you will use in the first exercise.)

Fonts are also available in a variety of sizes, which are measured in points to give the *point size* of the font. There are 72 points to an inch. Like other character formatting, different fonts and font sizes may be used in the same document.

FIGURE 9-2
Examples of
different point sizes

Excel provides two ways to choose fonts and font size:

- The Formatting toolbar
- The Font dialog box

EXERCISE 9-1
Choose Fonts and Font Size Using the Formatting Toolbar

The easiest way to choose fonts and font sizes is by using the Formatting toolbar. You can also apply bold, italic, and underlining to worksheet data from the Formatting toolbar.

1. Open the file **Order.xls**.

2. Select cells A1 through A2.

3. Click the down arrow in the Font box on the Formatting toolbar to open the drop-down list. Scroll up and choose the font Arial.

FIGURE 9-3
Font drop-down list
on the Formatting
toolbar

4. To apply bold formatting to the worksheet title, click the Bold button **B** on the Formatting toolbar while cells A1 and A2 are still selected. The title becomes boldface Arial.

TIP: You can apply italic with the Italic button *I* and underlining with the Underline button U. The keystrokes for these three formats are Ctrl+B for bold, Ctrl+I for italic, and Ctrl+U for underlining.

5. To change the font size, with cells A1 and A2 still selected, click the down arrow to open the Font Size drop-down list and choose 14 point. The first two rows stand out as worksheet titles.

FIGURE 9-4
Changing font size
from the Font Size
drop-down list

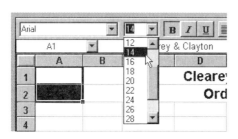

TIP: It's a good idea to use plain fonts such as Arial and Helvetica (if it is available) for all worksheet titles and more ornate fonts such as Times New Roman for the body of a worksheet.

EXERCISE 9-2 **Choose a Font and Font Size Using the Format Cells Dialog Box**

The Font options in the Format Cells dialog box give you a wider variety of options than are available on the Formatting toolbar. They also let you preview the options as you choose them.

1. Select rows 5 through 17.

2. Open the Format Cells dialog box. (Press Ctrl+1 or choose Cells from the Format menu.)

3. Click the Font tab, if necessary.

4. Use the arrow to scroll down under the Font list box.

5. Choose Times New Roman.

6. Choose Regular under the Font Style list box. (The font will appear normal without formatting such as bold or italic.) The Preview box displays the font size and style you select.

NOTE: You can change the font size by selecting a different point size under Size. For this worksheet, we'll leave the font size at 12 points.

FIGURE 9-5
Changing the font
with the Font options
in the Format Cells
dialog box

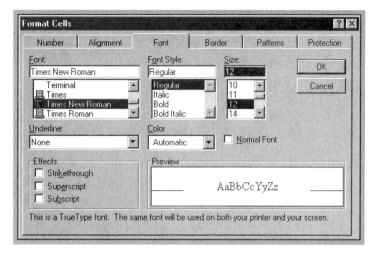

7. Click OK. The rows are formatted for 12-point Times New Roman.

TIP: You can use the Font options in the Format Cells dialog box to underline, color, and create character effects. Choose some of these options and apply them to the text in one of the cells. Make sure you press Ctrl + Z to undo the formatting.

Adding Borders

You can add borders to the right, left, top, or bottom of a cell, to each cell in a range of cells, or around any group of cells for an outline effect. Borders can add emphasis or make a worksheet easier to read or understand. Cells share borders, and adding a border to the bottom of cell A1 has the same effect as adding a border to the top of cell A2.

Excel provides two ways to add borders to a selected cell or cells:

- Use the Format Cells dialog box.
- Use ⊞▾.

You've already learned to apply simple bottom borders using ⊞▾ in Lesson 3. Using the Border options in the Format Cells dialog box, more options become available, such as a wider variety of border line weights and border colors that we will apply in Exercise 9-8.

EXERCISE **9-3** **Add Borders to Cells**

1. Select cells A15 through G15, and choose Cells from the Format menu.

2. Click the Border tab, if necessary. Notice that the Border options appear.

FIGURE 9-6
Border options in
the Format Cells
dialog box

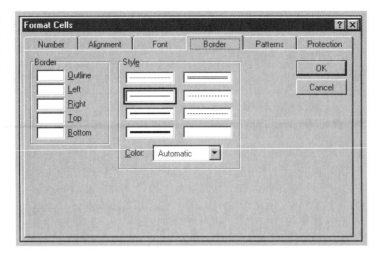

3. Click the second darkest single-line border style, click the <u>T</u>op border box, and then click OK.

4. Click anywhere in the worksheet to deselect the selection. Notice the rule that appears above row 15.

5. To add borders using ⊞▾, select cells A15 through B15.

6. Click the arrow to the right of ⊞▾ on the Formatting toolbar.

7. Click the border in the middle row, second from the left (the darker bottom border).

8. Select cell E15.

9. Click ⊞▾ and select None for borders (the top left choice). Select any other cell and notice that the top border disappears in cell E15. (You can also create this effect by selecting the bottom right box under Style in the Border options of the Format Cells dialog box.)

NOTE: Each border option adds borders to cells. When you select None from the border options, the border tool removes all borders from selected cells. The last border used is displayed in the button. You can select that border by clicking on the button rather than the arrow.

EXERCISE 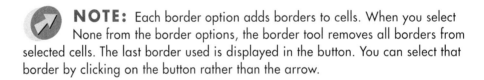 **9-4 Add Gridline Borders to Cells**

Gridlines are lines displayed on every border of a range of cells. The default is for gridlines to be displayed on the entire worksheet and to print. We will turn this option off and display borders for a range of selected cells. (Turning off gridlines in the entire worksheet is not required to apply borders to cells.) By removing gridlines around every cell and using them on only cells that need them, the worksheet looks cleaner and is easier to read.

1. Choose Options from the Tools menu.

2. Click the View tab, if necessary. The View options in the Options dialog box appears.

3. Click Gridlines to turn gridlines off.

4. Click OK. No gridlines appear in the worksheet.

5. Select cells A5 through G13.

6. Press Ctrl+1 to open the Format Cells dialog box.

7. Click the Border tab, if necessary.

8. To apply gridline borders to the cells, click the Left, Right, Top, and Bottom border boxes and click OK. Gridline borders appear around the selected cells.

FIGURE 9-7
Cells with gridlines

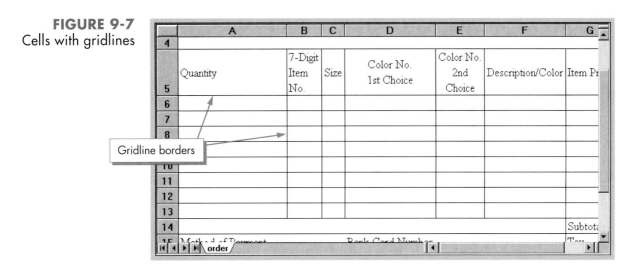

9. Select cells F14 through G17.

10. Click the arrow to the right of ⊞▾.

11. Click the gridline border (last row, second from the left). Gridline borders are added to the cells.

EXERCISE 9-5 Outline Cells

You can outline any group of selected cells, placing a border on the outer edges of these cells.

1. Select cells A15 through B17.

2. Open the Format Cells dialog box.

3. Click the Border tab, if necessary.

4. Click the Outline border box under Border, and then click OK. The cells are outlined.

Using Patterns and Colors

You can shade cells with a variety of gray or colored patterns. You can also give cells a solid color. Patterns and colors can improve the appearance of a worksheet and make the data easier to read. It can also give the worksheet a more interesting appearance.

EXERCISE 9-6 Add a Shading Pattern

1. Select cells A5 through G5.
2. Press Ctrl + 1 to open the Format Cells dialog box.
3. Click the Patterns tab, if necessary. The Patterns options appear.
4. Click the arrow in the Pattern box. A palette of patterns and colors appears.

FIGURE 9-8
Patterns options in the Format Cells dialog box

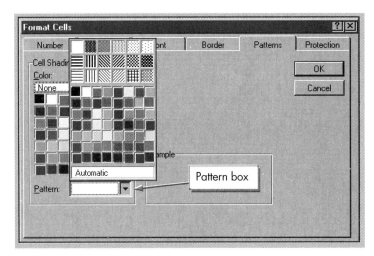

5. Choose the dotted pattern in the top row, second cell from the right, and then click OK. The cells now contain a dotted pattern.
6. Open the Pattern options again. Click the arrow in the Pattern box to apply a color to the dotted pattern. (Cells A5 through G5 should still be selected.)
7. Choose light green (top row of colors, fourth cell from the left), and then click OK. The pattern is now made up of green dots.

EXERCISE 9-7 Add Background Colors

You can choose background colors for plain cells or cells with patterns. If you choose colors for cells with patterns, the color will appear behind the pattern.

NOTE: Background colors and colored patterns will print if you have a color printer; they will print as different shades of gray if your printer doesn't have a color option. If you do not want them to print this way, choose the Sheet options in the Page Setup dialog box, and click the Black and White check box.

1. Select cells A1 through G2.

2. Click the arrow next to the Color button on the Formatting toolbar.

3. Choose turquoise (fourth row, fourth cell from the left). Select any other cell to see that the cells have a solid turquoise background.

4. Select cells F17 through G17.

5. Open the Format Cells dialog box.

6. Click the Patterns tab, if necessary.

7. Choose yellow (fourth row, third cell from the left) from the Color box, and then click OK. Select any other cell to see that these cells are yellow.

TIP: When you use dark colors or heavy shading patterns in cells, it can be hard to read the text. Either increase the font size, make text bold, or change the font color to a light color or white with the Font Color button on the Formatting toolbar. Click the arrow next it to see the available font colors. Note, however, that some printers have trouble printing white text on black backgrounds.

Coloring Borders

Borders can also be colored. Colored gridlines draw attention to important areas of a worksheet.

EXERCISE 9-8 **Color Cell Borders**

1. Select cells C15 through D15.

2. Open the Format Cells dialog box.

3. Click the Border tab, if necessary.

4. Click the arrow beside the Color box. The color palette opens.

5. Choose red from the color palette.

6. Click the Outline border box to apply an outline around the cells.

7. Click the thickest border style and click OK. Select any other cell to see that the cells have a thick red outline.

Copying Cell Formatting

You can copy the formatting of a cell, like its shading or color. Excel provides two ways to copy these characteristics:

- Use the Format Painter button on the Standard toolbar.
- Use the Copy and Paste Special options from the Edit menu.

EXERCISE 9-9 **Use the Format Painter Button**

---

1. Select cells C15 through D15.
2. Click ✍.
3. Select cells C16 through D16. Select any other cell and notice that the red outline appears around cells C16 and D16.
4. Repeat the process for cells C17 through D17.

> **TIP:** You can double-click ✍ to repaint repeatedly in cells you select. When you've finished painting, either click on ✍ again or press Esc.

EXERCISE 9-10 **Use Copy and Paste Special**

---

1. Select cells C15 through D17.
2. Choose Copy from the Edit menu or press Ctrl + C.
3. Select cells A15 through B17.
4. Choose Paste Special from the Edit menu. The Paste Special dialog box opens.
5. Click the Formats option button and click OK. Press Esc to turn off Paste Special. Select any other cell, and notice that the cells A15 through B17 have a thick red outline around them.

> **TIP:** You can also use Paste Special to copy formulas, values, notes, everything in the cell, or everything except the borders, as well as the formatting of a selected cell or cells.

EXERCISE 9-11 **Use the Repeat Command**

Once a cell is formatted, you can use the Repeat button 🗘 on the Standard toolbar to apply the same format to another cell or range of cells. This command can also be used to repeat other procedures.

1. Select cells F14 through G14.

2. Apply the same yellow background color to these cells as the color found in cell F17. (Use [icon] on the Formatting toolbar, and select the yellow in the fourth row.)

3. Select cells F15 through G16.

4. Click [icon] to repeat the formatting. Select any other cell, and notice that cells F15 through G16 have a yellow background.

> **TIP:** The AutoFormat feature applies formatting automatically. When you click AutoFormat under Format, Excel applies a built-in set of formats to a selected range of cells. You can choose from 16 preset formats as well as options that can be turned off and on. It's a quick, easy, and fun feature to apply.

Working with Styles

A *style* is a set of formatting instructions that can be applied to the cells of a worksheet. Styles make it easier to apply formatting and ensure consistency of formatting throughout the worksheet.

In every workbook, Excel maintains a list of style names and their formatting specifications. Every workbook contains six predefined styles for numbers and text: Comma, Comma [0], Currency, Currency [0], Normal, and Percent. The first four styles are used for accounting formatting. You can apply these styles as they are, modify them, or create your own styles.

EXERCISE 9-12 **Work with Styles**

The default style for a workbook is called *Normal style*. Unless you have changed your system's default, Normal contains these formatting specifications: general Number format, 10-point Arial, general bottom-alignment, no borders, no shading, and no protection.

1. Key the items shown in Figure 9-9 in rows 6 through 8.

FIGURE 9-9

2	34521	Blue	Red	Sierra backpack	25
1	24375	Green	Brown	Round top	250
2	12432	Black	Blue	Kiowe	400

2. Select cells A6 through E6.

3. Choose <u>S</u>tyle from the F<u>o</u>rmat menu. The Style dialog box opens.

FIGURE 9-10
Style dialog box

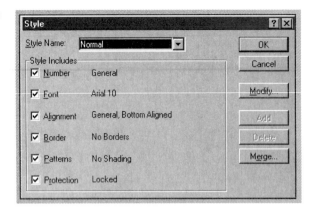

4. Key **INVOICE** in all caps in the <u>S</u>tyle Name text box. The settings change to reflect the formatting of selected cells.

5. Click <u>M</u>odify, and the Format Cells dialog box opens.

6. Click the Font tab, and change the Font to regular, 12-point Arial. Do not click OK yet.

7. Click the Alignment tab, and then choose <u>L</u>eft horizontal alignment.

8. Click OK. The settings beside the check boxes are changed.

9. Click <u>A</u>dd to add the style to the style list, and click OK. Notice that the cells are now left-aligned, 12-point Arial.

TIP: To create a style based on an example cell, select the cell that has the formatting you want in the style, open the Style dialog box, and type in a new style name. You don't have to add it to the list. Just close the dialog box by clicking OK, and the style will become available for use in the workbook.

10. To apply the INVOICE style, select cells A7 through E8.

11. Open the Style dialog box.

12. Choose INVOICE from the <u>S</u>tyle Name drop-down list.

13. Click OK. The style is applied to these cells.

14. You can also delete unnecessary styles from the style list. Open the Style dialog box and choose Comma from the list of styles.

15. Click <u>D</u>elete and the style is removed from the list. Repeat this process for Comma [0], Currency, Currency [0], and Percent. Only the Normal and INVOICE styles remain in the list.

16. Turn off gridlines for printing and save the workbook as *[your initials]* **9-12.xls**.

17. Print and close the workbook.

COMMAND SUMMARY

FEATURE	BUTTON	MENU	KEYBOARD
Bold	**B**	F<u>o</u>rmat, C<u>e</u>lls	Ctrl + B
Italic	*I*	F<u>o</u>rmat, C<u>e</u>lls	Ctrl + I
Underline	<u>u</u>	F<u>o</u>rmat, C<u>e</u>lls	Ctrl + U
Add borders	⊡·	F<u>o</u>rmat, C<u>e</u>lls	
Add outline border	⊡·	F<u>o</u>rmat, C<u>e</u>lls	Ctrl + Shift + &
Remove all borders	⊡·	F<u>o</u>rmat, C<u>e</u>lls	Ctrl + Shift + ＿
Add background color	▱·	F<u>o</u>rmat, C<u>e</u>lls,	
Copy cell formatting	▨	<u>E</u>dit, <u>C</u>opy, <u>P</u>aste Special	
Repeat formatting	↻	<u>E</u>dit, <u>R</u>epeat	Ctrl + Y

Concepts Review

TRUE/FALSE QUESTIONS

Each of the following statements is either true or false. Indicate your choice by circling **T** or **F**.

T F **1.** A font is a type design applied to an entire set of characters, excluding punctuation marks.

T F **2.** The easiest way to choose fonts is by using the Formatting toolbar.

T F **3.** You can add borders to only the right and left sides of a cell.

T F **4.** You can copy cell formatting using Copy and Paste Special options.

T F **5.** You cannot outline any group of selected cells.

T F **6.** You cannot choose colors for cells with patterns.

T F **7.** Borders can also be colored.

T F **8.** A style is a set of formatting instructions that can be applied to text.

SHORT ANSWER QUESTIONS

Write the correct answer in the space provided.

1. What do you call a list of style names and their formatting specifications?

_____

2. Which button do you use to repeat a command?

_____

3. Where are Font options located?

_____

4. What do you call lines on every border of a range of cells?

_____

5. Where is 🖋 located?

_____

6. What is the default font in Excel?

_____

7. How many points are there in one inch?

_____

8. Which button do you use to apply bold formatting to items in cells?

_____

CRITICAL THINKING

Answer these questions on a separate piece of paper. There are no right or wrong answers. Support your answer with examples from your own experience, if possible.

1. You have been asked to modify a quarterly report for the president of the company for which you work. The report is quite long and includes a variety of fonts, font sizes, and borders. Which methods will you use to make the formatting of the worksheet consistent? Will you use styles to apply consistent formatting? Why or why not?

2. You have just been given a spreadsheet that lists sales of all products made by the water ski company for which you work. You need to make certain areas of the worksheet stand out. The list needs to be printed, and you do not have a color printer. How might you enhance these areas of the worksheet?

3. Excel provides many ways to use color in worksheets. Do you find that using color is more helpful in drawing attention to a specific area? What colors look best to you? When do they become overwhelming?

Skills Review

EXERCISE 9-13

Work with fonts.

1. Open the file **Market.xls**.

2. Change the title in cells A1 through A3 to 16-point, bold Arial using the Formatting toolbar:

    a. Select cells A1 through A3.

    b. Click the arrow beside the Font box on the Formatting toolbar.

    c. Choose Arial from the drop-down list.

    d. Click the arrow beside the Font Size box.

    e. Choose 16.

    f. Click **B**.

3. Change the column titles to 14-point, italic Times New Roman using the Format Cells dialog box:

   a. Select cells A5 through C5.

   b. Open the Format Cells dialog box. (Press Ctrl+1.)

   c. Click the Font tab, if necessary.

   d. Choose Times New Roman under Font, Italic under Font Style, and 14 under Size.

   e. Click OK.

4. Change the font in rows 6 through 14 to Times New Roman.

5. Save the workbook as *[your initials]*9-13.xls.

EXERCISE 9-14

Add borders and use patterns.

1. Open the file **Market2.xls**.

2. Turn off the display of gridlines. (Open the Options dialog box under the Tools menu and click the View tab. Then deselect Gridlines.)

3. Add gridline borders to cells A5 through C14 using ⊟▾:

   a. Select cells A5 through C14.

   b. Click the arrow beside ⊟▾.

   c. Choose gridline borders (third row, second from left).

4. Outline the worksheet title with a double-line border using the Format Cells dialog box:

   a. Select cells A1 through C3.

   b. Open the Format Cells dialog box. (Press Ctrl+1.)

   c. Click the Border tab, if necessary.

   d. Choose Outline.

   e. Choose the double-line border.

   f. Click OK.

5. Add a dotted yellow pattern to the title box:

   a. Select cells A1 through C3, if necessary.

   b. Open the Format Cells dialog box.

   c. Click the Patterns tab.

   d. Click the arrow beside the Pattern box to open the Pattern palette.

   e. Choose the fourth dotted pattern from the right in the top row.

   f. Click the arrow beside the Pattern box to open the Pattern palette again.

   g. Choose green in the top row of colors.

   h. Click OK.

6. Save the workbook as *[your initials]*9-14.xls.

7. Print and close the workbook.

EXERCISE 9-15

Color borders and copy cell formatting.

1. Open the file **Clearey2.xls**.

2. Color the border around the worksheet title blue:

   a. Select cells A1 through C1.

   b. Open the Format Cells dialog box.

   c. Click the Border tab, if necessary.

   d. Select the third thickest single-line border.

   e. Click the arrow beside the Color box.

   f. Choose the royal blue in the top row.

   g. Choose Outline and click OK.

3. Copy the outline border color from the title to the column headings using 🖌:

   a. Select cells A1 through C1.

   b. Click 🖌.

   c. Select cells A3 through C3. (All formatting is copied, including center-alignment.)

4. Copy the outline border coloring to the rest of the worksheet using Copy and Paste Special:

   a. Select cells A1 through C1.

   b. Click 📋.

   c. Select the remainder of the cells with uncolored borders.

   d. Choose Paste Special from the Edit menu.

   e. Select Formats, and then click OK.

5. Format the worksheet, except for the title, as left-aligned.

6. Save the workbook as *[your initials]*9-15.xls.

7. Print and close the workbook.

EXERCISE 9-16

Work with styles.

1. Open the file **Months.xls**.

2. Key the text shown in Figure 9-11 in rows 13 through 15.

FIGURE 9-11

```
Oct    745   456    677

Nov    345   7465   3532

Dec    2456  5678   867
```

3. Create a style named "months" that is 12-point Times New Roman, center-aligned vertically, with a currency number format containing no "$" and no decimals:

   a. Open the Style dialog box under the Format menu.

   b. Key **months** for Style Name.

   c. Click Modify, and then click the Number tab.

   d. Choose Currency. Deselect $, and key **0** for Decimals.

   e. Click the Alignment tab.

   f. Select General under Horizontal, if necessary, and Center under Vertical.

   g. Click the Font tab.

   h. Choose Times New Roman, Regular, 12 point, and then click OK.

   i. Click Add and click OK.

4. Apply the style to rows 4 through 15:

   a. Select rows 4 through 15.

   b. Open the Style dialog box.

   c. Choose months from under Style Name.

   d. Click OK.

5. Delete rows 1 and 2.

6. Center-align the column headings.

7. Save the workbook as *[your initials]***9-16.xls**.

8. Print and close the workbook.

Lesson Applications

Work with fonts, add borders, and color borders.

A worksheet that gives a sales comparison for the years 1995, 1996, and 1997 in seven of Clearey & Clayton's biggest states is needed for a sales meeting next week. Format the worksheet so that the printout of this comparison is attractive and easy to follow.

1. Open the file **States.xls**.
2. Use the Formatting toolbar to make the title 16-point, bold italic Arial.
3. Center the title over the columns, and place a blue outline around it.
4. Increase column F using AutoFit, so that the text fits in the column.
5. Apply a gridline border around cells A3 through F10 using ▦▾.
6. Delete column B, and increase the size of column A using Best Fit.
7. Turn off the default display of gridlines. Save the workbook as *[your initials]*__9-17.xls__.
8. Print and close the workbook.

Work with fonts, add borders, and use patterns and colors.

Nine of the top performers at Clearey & Clayton are monitored based on sales. Format this comparison of 1996 and 1997 sales in an easy-to-read worksheet for the Board of Directors meeting next month.

1. Open the file **Perform.xls**.
2. Change the title in the first row to 14-point, bold Arial.
3. Make the rest of the worksheet title 12-point, bold Arial.
4. Change the text in cells A5 through F14 to 12-point Times New Roman.
5. Turn off the default display of gridlines. Place borders on the left, right, top, and bottom sides of cells A5 through F5.
6. Apply a gray pattern to these same cells. (Make sure that the pattern is light enough that you can see the text. Do not add a color background.)
7. Do the same for the worksheet title, but use green as the color. (Apply this pattern to cells C1 through E3.)
8. Give the column headings a yellow background using ⬛▾. (The colored pattern should remain in place.)
9. Increase the height of row 5, and then center the text vertically.

10. Increase the width of column C so that the worksheet title appears more evenly centered in the patterned area. Make sure that the "Difference" column fits on page 1.

11. Save the workbook as *[your initials]*9-18.xls.

12. Print and close the workbook.

EXERCISE 9-19

Work with fonts, add borders, copy cell formatting, and use patterns and colors.

The New York and San Diego store locations of Clearey & Clayton are the company's two largest. For this reason, the head office maintains a worksheet for each quarter's budget for these two stores. In the past, the format of the spreadsheet has been dreary and hard to review. Change this worksheet and make the information easy to pick out.

1. Open the file **Budget.xls**.

2. Turn off the display of gridlines on the screen.

3. Change the font for the entire worksheet to 12-point Times New Roman.

4. Change the font in cells A1 and A2 to Arial.

5. Add top and bottom borders to rows C4 through G4 and cells C6 through G6.

6. Copy the formatting of these rows using ▧ or <u>C</u>opy and <u>P</u>aste Special to the rows for "Equipment and Advertising" under the "New York, NY" section only.

7. Add a light shading pattern to cells C6 through G6, C8 through G8, and C10 through G10.

8. Enclose cells C4 through G18 in an outline.

9. Copy the format of cells C5 through G10 to cells C12 through G17.

10. Change cells C4 through G4 to bold, Arial with a turquoise background.

11. Widen the "Totals" column to 12.00.

12. Make the worksheet titles bold, left-aligned.

13. Delete row 11 and make the new row 11 have a height of 27.75 points.

14. Save the workbook as *[your initial]*9-19.xls.

15. Print and close the workbook.

EXERCISE 9-20

Work with fonts, use patterns and colors, add borders, and work with styles.

One very important item to track is employee birthdays, especially since the company owners at Clearey & Clayton love to surprise employees with their favorite cake on or around the big day. Format the following worksheet so that the birthdays are easier to read.

1. Open the file **Birth.xls**.

2. Turn off the default display of gridlines. Change the font of the worksheet title, making it bold.

3. Give the titles a simple patterned background and a light background color. (Do not create a colored pattern.)

4. Insert a blank row after the title. Make sure you clear the pattern and colors from the inserted row.

5. Place a left, right, and top border around cells A4 and B4.

6. Create a style called "employee." Choose whatever font you'd like, but keep it 12-point, Regular. Make the text left-aligned with borders on the left, right, top, and bottom. The birth dates should have the format of a date with slashes between the month, day, and year. (Use the Custom number format to create the date; just add slashes in parentheses to separate the month, day, and year that should be represented by zeros.)

7. Left-align the column heads.

8. Apply the "employee" style to the cells containing the employee names and their birth dates.

9. Turn off gridlines for printing and save the workbook as *[your initials]* **9-20.xls**.

10. Print and close the workbook.

Unit 3 Applications

APPLICATION 3-1

Format numbers, suppress the display of zero values, align text, change column width, and add a border.

John Clayton needs to construct worksheet for the bank showing employee bonuses. He's asked you to make the worksheet attractive.

1. Open the file **C&CBon.xls**.
2. Choose a currency format for columns B through E that includes no dollar signs, but has decimal places.
3. Suppress zeros in the worksheet.
4. Left-align the text in cells A4 through A13, and center the worksheet title over the columns.
5. Change the font for the column headings, make the headings bold, and right-align the headings in columns B through E.
6. Use AutoFit to adjust all columns that need widening at the same time.
7. Delete row 2 and add a gridline border around the cells that contain data in the worksheet, including the title.
8. Turn off the default display of gridlines.
9. Save the workbook as *[your initials]***u3-1.xls**.
10. Print and close the workbook.

APPLICATION 3-2

Hide a column, color borders, use patterns and colors, change row height, and work with fonts.

John Clayton must include the first-quarter budget in a report he is making to the Board of Directors. He would like you to make the worksheet attractive.

1. Open the file **Budget2.xls**.
2. Hide column G.
3. Add a background color to the title of the worksheet. Make sure the title text is readable.
4. Add thick red top and bottom borders to the column heading row (cells A4 through H4).
5. Make the cell background a shaded blue pattern in the same row.
6. Make the background color in cells A5 through H18 the lightest green you can find.
7. Change the font size for the entire worksheet to 12 point.

8. Make row 4's height 17.25 and row 12's height 16.50.

9. Turn off default gridlines for viewing.

10. Save the workbook as *[your initials]***u3-2.xls**.

11. Print and close the workbook.

APPLICATION 3-3

Work with fonts, add borders, color borders, format numbers, change column width and row height, and change alignment.

Bettina Clearey is meeting with an insurance salesperson. She wants to provide the agent with an attractive list of employee insurance plans.

1. Open the file **Insure.xls**.

2. Create a worksheet title that is centered over the columns. Make it 16-point, bold, italic Arial.

3. Add a blue outline around the title.

4. Format the policy numbers to have dashes after the first two numbers and after the next three numbers.

5. Make the row height 24.00 for the rows containing the employee names and insurance information.

6. Make the column titles wrap to the next line if you cannot read them now.

7. Left-align the employee names.

8. Increase the width of column D so that the column heading fits, and left-align the text in the column.

9. Change the column headings from bold to italic, and use Best Fit to increase row height.

10. Make sure a blank row appears between the title and the body of the worksheet.

11. Turn off gridlines for viewing.

12. Save the workbook as *[your initials]***u3-3.xls**.

13. Print and close the workbook.

APPLICATION 3-4

Work with fonts, copy cell formatting, work with styles, hide rows, and work with stored numbers.

John Clayton wants to show the sales force the monthly sales totals in an attractive format.

1. Open the file **Monthly2.xls**.

2. Create a worksheet title in 14-point, bold Arial, and center it over the columns.

3. Copy the formatting in cell A5 to the rest of the month cells in column A.

4. Create a style based on cell B5. Change the number format to currency with no dollar signs and no decimal places. Change the alignment to right-aligned, and create a green border similar to the one in cell A5.

5. Apply the style to cells B5 through F16.

6. Hide rows 9 through 16.

7. Turn on the Precision as Displayed option to correct the total in column B.

8. Delete row 17. Copy the formatting in row 4 to the totals row.

9. Delete row 2. Turn off the default display of gridlines.

10. Save the workbook as *[your initials]***u3-4.xls**.

11. Print and close the workbook.

APPLICATION 3-5

Create a worksheet title; create column heads; choose fonts, font size, and font style; and use color backgrounds, borders, and shading.

Bettina Clearey needs to see the projections for 1998 for Clearey and Clayton's top-nine selling tents. Key the data in Figure U3-1 with corrections, in order from 1 to 9, as the body of the worksheet (do not key the numbers before the tent). The number columns are for years 1996, 1997, and 1998.

Create an appropriate worksheet title and worksheet column headings. Be creative in your use of fonts, colors, borders, and cell backgrounds. Make the worksheet as colorful and attractive as possible. Be sure to use colors that do not hide text. Save the workbook as *[your initials]***u3-5.xls**.

FIGURE U3-1

1. Boston (blue) ROM	25380	37870	(02500
3. Yuelow rover	16920	14320	15000
9. (locker Zip) Gray	58760	48760	550000
4. Purple ptite	7870	15130	49500
7. (brown) baskin ROM	8320	9380	10000
6. Small round	9960	178870	12000
2. Green moun tain	108920 5	78560	85000
8. Hikers night	55850	77420	65000
5. Snow bound	78520	65900	60000

Formula and Template Construction

Dunkirk Canvas Company

Custom Boat Covers Keep Business Afloat

For over 40 years, the Dunkirk Canvas Company manufactured sails for boats. Facing increased competition, the company recently began making boat covers. They make covers to fit almost any boat manufactured in the U.S. Each boat cover is custom made, using a special computerized cloth-cutting machine that stores patterns and data about the amount of cloth used in a particular customer's boat cover.

Dunkirk was founded by Frank Bouchard and Mickey Finnegan. The company spent a considerable amount of money buying the cutting machine and is just beginning to see a profit on its boat cover operation. Sales volume has increased so much, however, that the company needs to use independent contractors to make some of its sails. This has caused the company to focus on automating some of its everyday business tasks.

In order to start automating the business records, the Dunkirk Canvas Company needs to produce:

✔ A worksheet that shows the hours worked by independent contractors, and calculates the average, maximum, and minimum number of hours worked per month. (Lesson 10)

✔ Worksheets calculating commissions and markup for canvas goods, bonuses for sales reps, and the costs and prices of some of Dunkirk's products. (Lesson 11)

✔ Worksheets maintaining employee information and analyzing the present value of a business loan. (Lesson 12)

✔ A balance sheet template and a template for invoices. (Lesson 13)

Using Functions

OBJECTIVES   After completing this lesson, you will be able to:

1. Enter functions.
2. Use the AVERAGE function.
3. Use the MIN and MAX functions.
4. Use the COUNT function.
5. Use the COUNTA function.
6. Use the INT and ROUND functions.
7. Use nested functions.

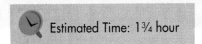
Estimated Time: 1¾ hour

Functions are built-in formulas. Excel provides many functions besides the SUM function introduced in Lesson 2. The SUM function is an example of a mathematical function. This lesson covers the statistical functions AVERAGE, MIN, MAX, COUNT, and COUNTA, as well as two additional mathematical functions, INT and ROUND.

Entering Functions

You have previously seen that using the SUM function is easier than typing a long formula for adding numbers.

The values that a function operates on are called *arguments,* which are placed inside parentheses after the function name. A function's arguments can consist of:

- Constants (a number keyed directly in a formula)
- Cell references (such as A10 or A1:A10)
- Additional functions

To use a cell range as an argument, separate the beginning and ending cell references with a colon. If the function takes more than one argument, the arguments are separated by commas. The value that the function returns is called the *result*.

 NOTE: Functions used as arguments are discussed later in this lesson.

You have two ways to enter functions in your worksheets. You can key the formulas yourself or use the Function Wizard to paste in the function. Using the Function Wizard is easier, but keying the formulas helps you learn formula construction.

Using the AVERAGE Function

The AVERAGE function calculates a mean. The arguments for this function can be cell references or constants. For example, in the Dunkirk1 workbook, you will be tracking the hours contractors work for the Dunkirk Canvas Company. You could use the AVERAGE function to calculate the average hours worked per month by all contractors.

Use the format =AVERAGE(arguments). The arguments can be one or more cell ranges or constants for which you want to find the average. The AVERAGE function ignores:

- Text
- Blank cells (but not zeros)
- Error values
- Logical values (*logical values* are the values TRUE and FALSE, which are the results of formulas that use comparison operators such as = or >)

TABLE 10-1   Examples of the AVERAGE Function

FUNCTION	CELL DATA	RESULT
=AVERAGE(A1:A3)	A1=10, A2=20, A3=30	20
=AVERAGE(50,60)	(none)	55
=AVERAGE(A1,100)	A1=50	75

EXERCISE **10-1** **Use the AVERAGE Function**

1. Open the file **Dunkirk1.xls**.

2. Select cell A15, and key **Average Hours:**

3. Select cell C15, and enter **=AVERAGE(C4:C13)**. Excel displays the error value #DIV/0!. Error values always start with the # symbol and indicate that the formula contains some sort of problem. This error indicates that there is no data in the specified range to calculate, or that division by zero has been attempted.

 TIP: You can key formulas in lowercase letters for convenience. Excel will convert the text to uppercase in the formula bar automatically.

4. Key the following data in column C, starting with cell C4:

10
N/A
20
10
10
20
20
0
0
0

The result, 10, is displayed in cell C15. The cells with zeros are counted in the Average, while the cell containing "N/A" does not affect the average.

5. Compare your result to that found with AutoCalculate by highlighting the range C4:C13. If the AutoCalculate area at the bottom of the screen does not show Average, click on the AutoCalculate area with the right mouse button and select Average. The AutoCalculate value and the number in C15 should both be 10.

6. Copy the formula in cell C15 to cells D15 through F15.

Using the MIN and MAX Functions

The MIN and MAX functions return the minimum and maximum value in a range of values, respectively. For example, in the Dunkirk1 worksheet, you can use the MIN and MAX functions to return the lowest and highest number of hours worked.

The MIN and MAX functions ignore:

- Text
- Blank cells (but not zeros)
- Error values
- Logical values (such as TRUE and FALSE)

Use the format =MIN(arguments) or =MAX(arguments). The arguments represents the values for which you want to find a minimum or maximum.

TABLE 10-2   Examples of the MIN and MAX Functions

FUNCTION	CELL DATA	RESULT
=MAX(A1:A3)	A1=10, A2=20, A3=30	30
=MIN(A1:A3)	A1=2, A2=20, A3=30	2
=MIN(-50,60)	(none)	-50
=MIN(A1,0)	A1=50	0

EXERCISE 10-2 Use the MIN Function

1. Select cell A16, and key **Least Hours Worked:**
2. Select C16, and key **=MIN(C4:C13)**.
3. Copy the formula in cell C16 to cells D16 through F16.
4. Key the following data in column D, starting with cell D4 and leaving the second-to-last cell blank, as indicated:

   22
   19
   20
   N/A
   21
   20
   15
   30
   (blank)
   10

   The results, 0 and 10, are displayed in cells C16 and D16, respectively. The MIN function ignores the blank cell, D12, and the cells with text, C5 and D7.
5. Select cell D12 and key **0**. That zero is now counted as the minimum value in the column, and the result becomes 0.

EXERCISE 10-3 Use the MAX Function with the Function Wizard

In the previous exercises, you keyed the specified formulas. Now you'll use the Function Wizard to write the function for you.

1. Select cell A17, and key **Most Hours Worked:**
2. Select cell C17.

3. Click the Function Wizard button `fx` or press the keys `Shift` + `F3`. The Function Wizard - Step 1 of 2 dialog box appears.

FIGURE 10-1
Function Wizard -
Step 1 of 2
dialog box

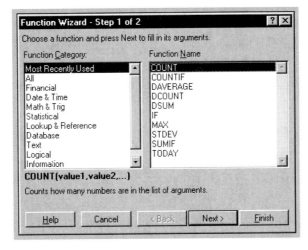

4. Choose Statistical from the Function Category list box.

5. Choose MAX from the Function Name list box. The Function Wizard displays the function in the formula bar. If the formula bar is covered by the dialog box, drag the dialog box by its title bar to move it down.

6. Click the Next button to go to step 2. The Function Wizard - Step 2 of 2 dialog box appears. It provides text boxes for each of the function's arguments. You can key the cell reference, constant, or nested function desired in each of these boxes.

FIGURE 10-2
Function Wizard -
Step 2 of 2
dialog box

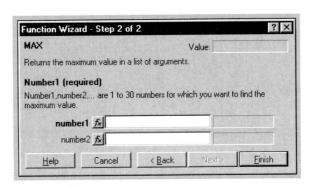

7. Key **C4:C13** in the number1 argument box. As you key the arguments, the Function Wizard enters the cell range in the formula bar, displays the values of the cells in the text box to the right of the argument box, and shows the result of the function in the Value box in the upper right-hand corner of the dialog box.

 TIP: Instead of keying the cell range, you can move the pointer out of the dialog box and select the cell range in the worksheet by clicking and/or dragging.

8. Click the Finish button.

9. Copy the formula in cell C17 to cells D17 through F17.

10. Key the following data in column E, starting with cell E4 and leaving the second-to-last cell blank, as indicated:

N/A
18
20
N/A
21
23
19
10
(blank)
10

The results are displayed in cells C17, D17, and E17. The MAX function ignores the blank cell and the cells that contain text.

Using the COUNT Function

The COUNT function counts how many cells contain numbers within a specified range of cells. For example, you can use the COUNT function in the Dunkirk1 worksheet to count how many cells in C4 through C13 contain numbers.

The COUNT function ignores:

- Text
- Blank cells (but not zeros)
- Error values
- Logical values (such as TRUE and FALSE)

Use the format =COUNT(arguments), where the arguments refer to the values you want to count.

TABLE 10-3 Examples of the COUNT Function

FUNCTION	CELL DATA	RESULT
=COUNT(A1:A3)	A1 is blank, A2=40, A3=30	2
=COUNT(A1:A3)	A1=31, A2 is blank, A3=N/A	1
=COUNT(A1:A3)	A1=0, A2 is blank, A3=N/A	1
=COUNT(13,21,111)	(none)	3

EXERCISE **10-4** Use the COUNT Function with the Function Wizard

1. Select cell A18, and key **Available Contractors:**

2. Select cell C18.

3. Click [*f*] or choose Function from the Insert menu. The first Function Wizard dialog box appears.

4. Choose Statistical from the Function Category list box.

5. Choose COUNT from the Function Name list box.

6. Click the Next button to go to step 2.

7. Key **C4:C13** in the number1 argument box. The Function Wizard enters the cell range in the formula bar and displays the values of the cells and the result of the function in the dialog box.

8. Click the Finish button.

9. Copy the formula in cell C18 to cells D18 through F18.

10. Key the following data in column F, starting with cell F4 and leaving the second-to-last cell blank, as indicated:

20
15
15
20
N/A
22
N/A
10
(blank)
N/A

The result, 6, is displayed in cell F18. The COUNT function does not count the blank cell and the cells that contain text.

11. Highlight the range F4:F13 and use AutoCalculate, selecting Count Nums. The result should agree with the value in F18.

Using the COUNTA Function

The COUNTA function counts how many items are found in a range of cells. Unlike the COUNT function, COUNTA counts cells that contain text as well as cells that contain numbers.

The COUNTA function ignores:

● Blank cells (but not zeros)

● Error values

● Logical values (such as TRUE and FALSE)

Use the format =COUNTA(arguments), where the arguments refer to the values you want to count.

TABLE 10-4 Examples of the COUNTA Function

FUNCTION	CELL DATA	RESULT
=COUNTA(A1:A3)	A1 is blank, A2=40, A3=30	2
=COUNTA(A1:A3)	A1=31, A2=40, A3=N/A	3
=COUNTA(A1:A3)	A1=0, A2 is blank, A3=N/A	2

EXERCISE 10-5 Use the COUNTA Function

1. Select cell A19, and key **Total Contractors:**
2. Widen column A to accommodate row headings in rows 15 through 19. Do not use Best Fit.
3. Select cell B19, and enter **=COUNTA(B4:B13)**. The COUNTA function counts all of the cells that contain text. The result is 10.
4. Copy the formula in cell B19 to cells C19 through F19. The COUNTA function counts text and numbers, but not blank cells.
5. Right-align the text in columns C through F.
6. Save the workbook as *[your initials]***10-5.xls**.
7. Print and close the workbook.

FIGURE 10-3
Worksheet with functions entered

	A	B	C	D	E	F	G	H
	F19		=COUNTA(F4:F13)					
6	Callahan	Linda	20.00	20.00	20.00	15.00		
7	Kramer	Paul	10.00	N/A	N/A	20.00		
8	Ledder	Sam	10.00	21.00	21.00	N/A		
9	Michals	Mark	20.00	20.00	23.00	22.00		
10	Michals	Bruce	20.00	15.00	19.00	N/A		
11	Openheimer	James	0.00	30.00	10.00	10.00		
12	Smith	Tina	0.00	0.00				
13	Wallace	Michael	0.00	10.00	10.00	N/A		
14								
15	Average Hours:		10.00	17.44	17.29	17.00		
16	Least Hours Worked:		0.00	0.00	10.00	10.00		
17	Most Hours Worked:		20.00	30.00	23.00	22.00		
18	Available Contractors:		9	9	7	6		
19	Total Contractors:	10	10	10	9	9		

Dunkirk1

Ready | Count Nums=1 | CAPS

Using the INT and ROUND Functions

Sometimes the numbers that Excel uses in its calculations do not match the numbers displayed. This discrepency occurs because Excel stores the full number of decimals keyed or calculated for a cell, even if the cell is formatted for rounded values. For example, if you key 3.569 in a cell formatted for two decimal places, the cell displays 3.57. In calculations, however, Excel uses the full precision, 3.569. You can use the INT (integer) and ROUND functions to control the amount of precision that Excel uses in your calculations.

The INT function rounds a number down to the nearest integer. For example, the INT function would round 2.99 to 2. Use the format =INT(number), where number is the number you want to round down to the nearest integer.

TABLE 10-5   **Examples of the INT Function**

FUNCTION	RESULT
=INT(9.7)	9
=INT(-9.7)	-10
=INT(100.55)	100

The ROUND function rounds a number to a specified number of decimal places.

Use the format =ROUND(number, num_digits), where number is the number you want to round and num_digits is the number of decimal places to which you want to round the number.

- If num_digits is greater than 0, the number will round to the specified number of decimal places.
- If num_digits is 0, the number will round to the nearest integer.
- If num_digits is less than 0, the number will round the specified number of places to the left of the decimal point.

TABLE 10-6   **Examples of the ROUND Function**

FUNCTION	RESULT
=ROUND(1.55,1)	1.6
=ROUND(1.55,0)	2
=ROUND(100.55,-1)	100
=ROUND(-1.555,-2)	0

EXERCISE 10-6 Use the INT Function

1. Open the file **Dunkirk2.xls**.

2. Select cell E4, and enter **=INT(B4)**. The result is 0.

3. Go to the formula bar, and enter ***D4** at the end of the formula. The result is still 0.

4. Key the following data in column B, beginning in cell B4:

   5.22
   5.52
   6.23
   6.42
   6.86

5. Copy the formula in cell E4 to cells E5 through E8. The INT function in the formula rounds down the column B values to the nearest integer, providing a whole number in column E. The result in E4 is 135.

EXERCISE 10-7 Use the ROUND Function

1. Select cell F4, and enter **=ROUND(C4*D4,0)**. The result is 0.

 TIP: A quick way to ensure that you include all required arguments and parentheses when you enter a function manually is to press Ctrl + Shift + A after you type the equal sign and function name. These keystrokes automatically insert the argument names and parentheses.

2. Key the following data in column C, beginning with cell C4:

   5.09
   5.45
   6.14
   6.23
   6.51

   Excel rounds the total to the nearest integer.

3. Copy the formula in cell F4 to cells F5 through F8. (See Figure 10-4 on the next page.)

4. Save the workbook as *[your initials]***10-7.xls**.

5. Print and close the workbook.

FIGURE 10-4
Results of the
ROUND function

	A	B	C	D	E	F
	F8		=ROUND(C8*D8,0)			
1	Dunkirk Canvas Co. - Material Order List					
2						
3	Material	Weight in Lbs. Per Yard	Cost Per Yard	Quantity	Total Lbs.	Total Cost
4	Canvas 101	5.22	5.09	27	135	137
5	Canvas 102	5.52	5.45	120	600	654
6	Canvas 103	6.23	6.14	320	1920	1965
7	Canvas 104	6.42	6.23	220	1320	1371
8	Canvas 105	6.86	$ 6.51	550	3300	3581
9						
10						
11						
12						
13						
14						
15						

Dunkirk2

Ready   Count Nums=1

Using Nested Functions

A function used as an argument inside another function is called a *nested function*. The Function Wizard is especially useful for inserting nested functions. In the following exercise, you will use nested functions to sum separate groups of items, and then take an average of the two sums.

EXERCISE 10-8 Use Nested Functions

1. Open the file **Dunkirk3.xls**.
2. Select cell C8, and then click 𝑓𝑥.
3. Choose Most Recently Used from the Function Category list box.

FIGURE 10-5
Function Wizard
dialog box for
nested functions

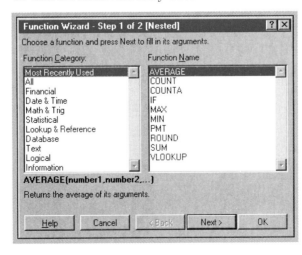

4. Choose AVERAGE from the Function Name list box.
5. Click the Next button to go to step 2.
6. Click 𝑓𝑥 next to the number1 argument box to insert a function as an argument. A new Function Wizard dialog box appears, with the word "Nested" in its title bar.

265

7. Choose Math & Trig from the Function Category list box.

8. Choose SUM from the Function Name list box.

9. Click the Next button to go to step 2.

10. Key **B4:B6** in the number1 argument box, and then click OK. The original Function Wizard dialog box appears.

 NOTE: Always click OK—and not Next—to finish adding a nested function (unless you want another level of nesting).

11. Click [fx] next to the number2 argument box to insert a function as an argument. A new Function Wizard dialog box appears and "Nested" is displayed in the title bar.

12. Choose Math & Trig from the Function Category list box.

13. Choose SUM from the Function Name list box.

14. Click the Next button to go to step 2.

15. Key **C4:C6** in the number1 argument box, and then click OK.

16. Click the Finish button.

FIGURE 10-6
Worksheet with nested functions

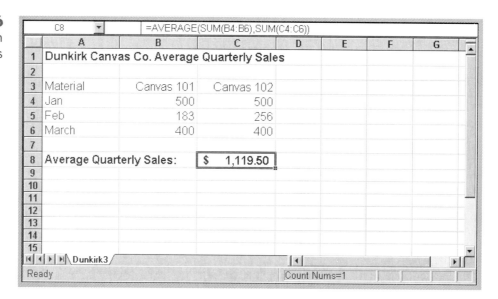

17. Save the workbook as *[your initials]***10-8.xls**.

18. Print and close the workbook.

TIP: Function Wizard can be used to both create and edit formulas that contain functions. To edit an existing formula containing a function, select the desired cell, and click [fx]. Excel opens the Editing Function dialog box for the first function in the formula. You can make any necessary changes to the arguments. Click Next to enter your changes and to display the next function in the formula. Click the Finish button to enter any additional changes and to close the dialog box.

COMMAND
SUMMARY

FEATURE	BUTTON	MENU	KEYBOARD
Function Wizard	f_*	Insert, Function	Shift + F3

USING HELP

This lesson introduced you to seven of Excel's built-in functions and the Function Wizard, which assists you in entering them. You can use Excel's on-line Help feature to learn more about specific functions and how they are used.

To view detailed information about an individual function, use on-line Help from the Function Wizard dialog box.

1. Click ⬜ to open a new workbook.

2. Click f_*. The first Function Wizard dialog box appears.

3. Choose Statistical from the Function Category list box.

4. Choose COUNT from the Function Name list box.

5. Click the Help button in the dialog box.

6. Scroll through the Help information provided, which includes an explanation of the function, its syntax, and examples of its use.

FIGURE 10-7
COUNT function
Help screen

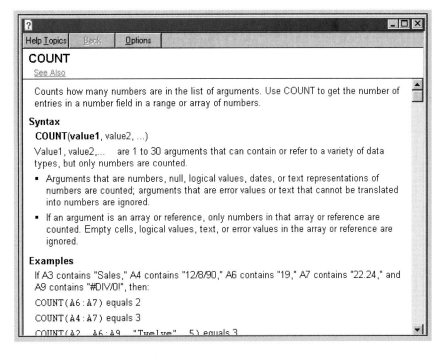

7. Close the Help window.

8. Click the Cancel button to close the Function Wizard dialog box.

Concepts Review

Each of the following statements is either true or false. Indicate your choice by circling T or F.

T F **1.** Functions can be entered in a worksheet in only one way—through the Function Wizard.

T F **2.** The arguments for an Excel function are enclosed in parentheses following the function name.

T F **3.** The arguments for an Excel function can consist of only constants or cell references.

T F **4.** All arguments shown in text boxes in the Function Wizard - Step 2 of 2 dialog box must be completed.

T F **5.** The value returned by a function is called the result.

T F **6.** The MAX function can be found in the Function Wizard's Math & Trig function category.

T F **7.** The COUNTA function counts cells containing text and cells containing numbers.

T F **8.** The AVERAGE function ignores blank cells and zeros.

Write the correct answer in the space provided.

1. Which menu command is used to access the Function Wizard?

_____

2. What is the value operated on by a function called?

_____

3. If a function takes more than one argument, which keyboard character is used to separate the arguments?

_____

4. What name is given to a function which is itself the argument of another function?

_____

5. Which category of functions in the Function Wizard contains the AVERAGE, MIN, and MAX functions?

_____

6. Which function is used to calculate a mean?

_____

7. Which function is used to round a number down to the nearest integer?

_____

8. Which function is used to round a number to a specific number of decimal places?

_____

CRITICAL THINKING

Answer these questions on a separate piece of paper. There are no right or wrong answers. Support your answers with examples from your own experience, if possible.

1. What advantages and disadvantages do you see in using Excel's Function Wizard when developing formulas in your worksheets?

2. Can you think of another method previously covered in this book for specifying cell ranges? Why is it advantageous to use this method when creating functions?

3. Discuss the use of nested functions. When can they be especially useful?

Skills Review

EXERCISE 10-9

Enter formulas using the AVERAGE, MIN, and MAX functions.

1. Open the file **Dunkirk4.xls**.

2. Enter a formula that calculates the average price per yard by following these steps:

   a. Select cell B16.

   b. Key **=AVERAGE(B4:B14)**

3. Enter a formula that calculates the minimum stock by following these steps:

   a. Select cell F17, and then click _fx_.

   b. Choose Statistical from the Function Category list box.

   c. Choose MIN from the Function Category list box.

   d. Click the Next button to go to step 2.

   e. Key **F4:F14** in the number1 argument box.

    f. Click the Finish button.

  4. Enter a formula that calculates the maximum stock by following these steps:

    a. Select cell F18, and then click [fx].

    b. Choose Statistical from the Function Category list box.

    c. Choose MAX from the Function Category list box.

    d. Click the Next button to go to step 2.

    e. Key **F4:F14** in the number1 argument box.

    f. Click the Finish button.

  5. Save the workbook as *[your initials]***10-9.xls**.

  6. Print and close the workbook.

EXERCISE 10-10

Enter formulas using the COUNT and COUNTA functions.

  1. Open the file **Dunkirk5.xls**. Key the data shown in Figure 10-8 beginning in cell C4 (leave cells blank where indicated.)

FIGURE 10-8

	C	D
4	yes	1
5		n/a
6	yes	3
7	yes	2
8		n/a

  2. Enter a formula that counts the number of employees whose insurance covers dependents by following these steps:

    a. Select cell D10, and then click [fx].

    b. Choose Statistical from the Function Category list box.

    c. Choose COUNT from the Function Name list box.

    d. Click the Next button to go to step 2.

    e. Key **D4:D8** in the number1 argument box.

    f. Click the Finish button.

  3. Enter a formula that counts the employees with hospitalization coverage by following these steps:

   a. Select cell C11.

   b. Key the COUNTA function, specifying the range for the argument as C4:C8.

  4. Save the workbook as *[your initials]***10-10.xls**.

  5. Print and close the workbook.

EXERCISE 10-11

Create a formula using the INT and ROUND functions.

  1. Open the file **Dunkirk6.xls**.

  2. Enter a formula that rounds the product of the price and cost by following these steps:

   a. Select cell E4, and then click f_x .

   b. Choose Math & Trig from the Function Category list box.

   c. Choose ROUND from the Function Name list box.

   d. Click the Next button to go to step 2.

   e. Key **B4*.10+B4** in the number argument box.

   f. Key **2** in the num_digits argument box.

   g. Click the Finish button.

  3. Copy this formula from cell E4 to cells E5 through E8.

  4. Enter a formula that totals the sales and round the total down to the nearest integer by following these steps:

   a. Select cell F4.

   b. Key **=INT(C4*E4)**

  5. Copy this formula from cell F4 to cells F5 through F8.

  6. Save the workbook as *[your initials]***10-11.xls**.

  7. Print and close the workbook.

EXERCISE 10-12

Create a formula using nested functions.

  1. Open the file **Dunkirk7.xls**.

  2. Select cell B8, and then key **5126**

  3. Select cell C8, and then key **6295**

  4. Enter a formula using a nested function that finds average annual sales by following these steps:

   a. Select cell B10, and then click f_x .

   b. Choose Statistical from the Function Category list box.

c. Choose AVERAGE from the Function Name list box.

   d. Click the Next button to go to step 2.

   e. Click [fx] next to the number1 argument box.

   f. Choose Math & Trig from the Function Category list box.

   g. Choose SUM from the Function Name list box.

   h. Click the Next button to go to Step 2 of 2 - Nested.

   i. Key **B5:B8** in the number1 argument box.

   j. Click OK.

   k. Click [fx] next to the number2 argument box.

   l. Choose Math & Trig from the Function Category list box.

   m. Choose SUM from the Function Name list box.

   n. Click the Next button to go to Step 2 of 2 - Nested.

   o. Key **C5:C8** in the number1 argument box.

   p. Click OK.

   q. Click Finish.

5. Format all values in currency style with two decimal places.

6. Save the workbook as *[your initials]***10-12.xls**.

7. Print and close the workbook.

Lesson Applications

Create a worksheet that includes formulas using the AVERAGE, MIN, MAX, COUNT, and COUNTA functions.

Create a worksheet that calculates weekly commissions for salespeople. It should also include average sales earned, the minimum and maximum sales earned, the number of salespeople selling that week, and the total number of salespeople on the regular sales force.

1. Open the file **Dunkirk8.xls**.
2. Key the data shown in Figure 10-9, beginning in cell B4.

FIGURE 10-9

Callahan	23,098.00	.045
Davis	32,427.00	.055
Jefferson	vacation	.040
Lerner	12,835.44	.056
Matthews	10,098.53	.060
Nicholson	42,098.65	.030
Peters	56,987.54	.050
Stuart	vacation	.065
Vaughn	5,098.87	.133

3. To calculate the commissions, rounding the number to two decimal places, select cell D4 and then key **=ROUND(B4*C4,2)**
4. Copy the formula in cell D4 to cells D5 through D12.
5. Key **0** in cells D6 and D11.
6. Select cell A14, and key **AVERAGE:**
7. To calculate the weekly average, select cell B14 and then key **=AVERAGE(B4:B12)**
8. Select cell A15, and key **MAX:**
9. To calculate the maximum sales earned by a salesperson, select cell B15 and key **=MAX(B4:B12)**
10. Select cell A16, and key **MIN:**

11. To calculate the minimum sales earned by a salesperson, select cell B19 and key **=MIN(B4:B12)**

12. Select cell A18, and key **Active Salespersons:**

13. To calculate the number of salespersons working that week, select cell B18 and key **=COUNT(B4:B12)**

14. Select cell A19, and key **Total Salespersons:**

15. To calculate the number of salespeople on the regular sales force, select cell B19 and key **=COUNTA(B4:B12)**

16. Format cells B18 and B19 with no decimal places.

17. Select cell A20, and key **% Active:**

18. To calculate the percentage of salespeople working this week, select cell B20 and key **=B18/B19**

19. Format cell B20 for percent with no decimal places.

20. Format the range D4:D12 in currency style with two decimal places.

21. Save the workbook as *[your initials]***10-13.xls**.

22. Print and close the workbook.

EXERCISE 10-14

Construct a worksheet that includes formulas using nested AVERAGE, MIN, MAX, INT, or ROUND functions.

Construct a worksheet that analyzes monthly sales by product. For each product, calculate the most units sold and the least units sold by any region. In addition, calculate the average revenue and the total revenue for all regions, rounded to the nearest dollar.

1. Open the file **Dunkirk9.xls**. Key the data shown below, beginning in cell C5:

   Units Sold
   320
   254
   634
   300
   720
   310
   540
   230

2. Center the region text in the range B4:B12.

3. In cell A16, key **Most Units**

4. In cell B16, calculate the most units sold for Cover C-9087.

5. In cell C16, calculate the most units sold for Cover C-9088.

6. In cell A17, key **Least Units**

7. In cell B17, calculate the least units sold for Cover C-9087.

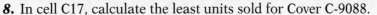

8. In cell C17, calculate the least units sold for Cover C-9088.

9. In cell A18, key **Average Units**

10. In cell B18, calculate the average number sold for Cover C-9087.

11. In cell C18, calculate the average number sold for Cover C-9088.

12. In cell A19, key **Total Revenue**

13. In cell B19, calculate the total revenue rounded to the nearest dollar for Cover C-9087. Use 11.5 as the price of each unit.

14. In cell C19, calculate the total revenue rounded to the nearest dollar for Cover C-9088. Use 13.11 as the price of each unit.

15. Format cells B19 and C19 for currency with no decimal places.

16. Save the workbook as *[your initials]***10-14.xls**.

17. Print and close the workbook.

EXERCISE 10-15

Create a worksheet that includes formulas using the AVERAGE, MIN, MAX, and COUNT functions.

Create a worksheet that shows employees, their salaries, and job performance ratings.

1. Open the file **Dunk10.xls**. Key the data shown in Figure 10-10.

FIGURE 10-10

Name	Full-time	Part-time Hourly	Performance Rating
Anderson	50,000		3
Boyd		18.00	4
Carlson	35,000		3
Dugan	28,000		4
Evans	45,000		4
Jenkins		10.00	2

2. In cell A11, key **Count:**

3. In cell B11, enter a function that counts the number of full-time employees.

4. In cell C11, enter a function that counts the number of part-time employees.

5. In cell A12, key **Max:**

6. In cell A13, key **Min:**

7. In cells B12 and C12, enter functions that show the highest salary for full-time employees and the highest hourly rate for part-time employees, respectively.

8. In cells B13 and C13, enter functions that show the lowest salary for full-time employees and the lowest hourly rate for part-time employees, respectively.

9. Format column B in accounting style, with dollar signs and no decimal places.

10. Format column C in accounting style, with dollar signs and two decimal places.

11. Format cells B11 and C11 in number style with no decimal places.

12. Save the workbook as *[your initials]***10-15.xls**.

13. Print and close the workbook.

EXERCISE 10-16

Construct a worksheet using the AVERAGE, INT, and ROUND functions.

Construct a worksheet for the Dunkirk Canvas Company that shows transportation charges for the month of May, using the data provided. Include a column that calculates the total charge for each carrier, rounded to the nearest dollar.

1. Open a new workbook and key the following data:

Carrier	Miles	Charge Per Mile
Allied Trans.	5736.5	0.75
United Freight	4397.6	0.47
Eastern Trans.	5107.1	0.95
Coastal Trans.	7130.4	0.49

2. In the worksheet, include the total number of carriers and the total mileage and average mileage for all carriers, rounded down to the nearest mile.

3. Show the total transportation charge for the month, rounded to the nearest dollar. Use the Function Wizard to create formulas with nested functions.

4. Use the ROUND function to round the total for each carrier.

5. Use the INT function to round the total mileage and the average mileage.

6. Format all cells that show the number of miles to have commas and one decimal place.

7. Format all dollar amounts in the currency style with no decimal places, except for the "Charge Per Mile" cells, which should have two decimal places.

8. Save the workbook as *[your initials]***10-16.xls**.

9. Add the filename to the header.

10. Print and close the workbook.

Advanced Formulas

OBJECTIVES

After completing this lesson, you will be able to:

1. Use absolute and mixed cell references.
2. Create an IF function.
3. Create an IF function with multiple conditions.
4. Insert text comments with the IF function.
5. Use the VLOOKUP and HLOOKUP functions.
6. Use notes to annotate a formula.
7. Correct circular references.

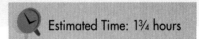
Estimated Time: 1¾ hours

Understanding differences in the types of cell references is the key to making the most of Excel's formula capabilities. As this lesson demonstrates, using the right type of cell reference is important when you copy formulas between cells. This lesson also explains how to use the IF function to create more powerful formulas, how to create lookup tables to automate data-entry tasks, and how to document complicated formulas by attaching notes to cells. Finally, circular cell references—a common error in creating formulas—are explained.

Using Absolute and Mixed Cell References

So far, you have been working primarily with *relative cell references* in formulas. In relative cell references, the cell's address is relative to the address of the cell containing the formula. Excel automatically adjusts relative cell addresses when you copy a formula from one cell to another.

Sometimes, you will want Excel not to adjust the cell references when you copy a formula. In those instances, use *absolute cell references* or *mixed cell references*. In absolute cell references, the addresses of cells remain unchanged when a formula is copied from one cell to another. With mixed cell references, either the row or the column portion of the address is absolute, and the other portion of the address is relative.

 NOTE: Cell references of named cells are absolute.

EXERCISE **Use an Absolute Cell Reference in a Formula**

Absolute cell references are created by placing dollar signs in front of the column letter and row number (for example, $A$3, $A$4).

 TIP: With the insertion point within a cell reference in the formula bar, pressing F4 provides a shortcut method for cycling among relative, absolute and mixed cell references.

1. Open the file **Rates.xls**.
2. Select cell C6.
3. Key **=B6+(B6*G4)**. This formula calculates a 50% markup price for the first yardage item—the markup amount is in cell G4.
4. Use AutoFill to copy the formula to cells C7 and C8. The formulas in cells C7 and C8 are incorrect because of the relative reference to cell G4.
5. Double-click cell C6, move the insertion point after the "G" in the formula, and then press F4. Dollar signs appear before the "G" and the "4," indicating that both column G and row 4 are absolute references.

 NOTE: Pressing F4 doesn't work if the insertion point is positioned in front of the equals sign in the formula. Always move the insertion point within the cell reference that requires the $ signs.

FIGURE 11-1
Copying a formula with absolute cell references

B	C
Cost	Price
25	=B6+(B6*$G$4)
50	=B7+(B7*$G$4)
75	=B8+(B8*$G$4)

6. Enter the formula, and then use AutoFill to copy it to cells C7 and C8. The results are 75.00 and 112.50, respectively. The formulas are now correct, because the absolute cell reference $G$4 does not adjust in its copied locations.

EXERCISE **11-2** ## View a Named Cell as an Absolute Reference in a Formula

When you use named cells in formulas, Excel makes the reference to the named cell absolute.

1. Select cell G5.
2. Give this cell a name by choosing Insert, Name, Define. The Define Name dialog box is displayed.
3. Key **sixty**. At the bottom of the box, the cell reference is absolute: $G$5.
4. Click OK.
5. Select cell C6, and change the formula to =**B6+(B6*sixty)**
6. Copy the formula to cells C7 and C8. The name "sixty," which always refers to cell $G$5, is copied to each cell, as references to named cells are absolute.

FIGURE 11-2
Copying a
named cell

B	C
Cost	Price
25	=B6+(B6*sixty)
50	=B7+(B7*sixty)
75	=B8+(B8*sixty)

TIP: It is good practice to use named cells for constant values in formulas whenever possible. Names make formulas easier to understand, and changing the value of the constant doesn't necessitate changing the formula.

EXERCISE **11-3** ## Use a Mixed Cell Reference

To create a mixed cell reference, place a dollar sign ($) in front of the part of the cell reference (the row number or column letter) that you want to be absolute.

1. Select cell D6, and key =**C6*D4**. This formula is intended to multiply the price in column C by the commission rate in row 4. The result should be 4.
2. Copy this formula to cells D6 through F8.
3. Select cell F8. The cell references in the formula are incorrect. The formula should refer to column C, the "Price" column, but now it refers to column E. Similarly, the formula should refer to row 4, which contains the commission rates. Instead, it refers to row 6.
4. Double-click cell D6.
5. Position the insertion point in the cell reference C6 (after the equals sign).
6. Press F4 three times to make the reference to column C absolute. The cell reference changes to $C6.
7. Position the insertion point in the cell reference D4.
8. Press F4 twice to change the cell reference to D$4, making row 4 absolute.

9. Enter the formula, and then copy it to cells D6 through F8.

10. Compare the formula in D6 (=$C6*D$4) with the formula in cell F8 (=$C8*F$4).

FIGURE 11-3
Copying a formula
with mixed cell
references

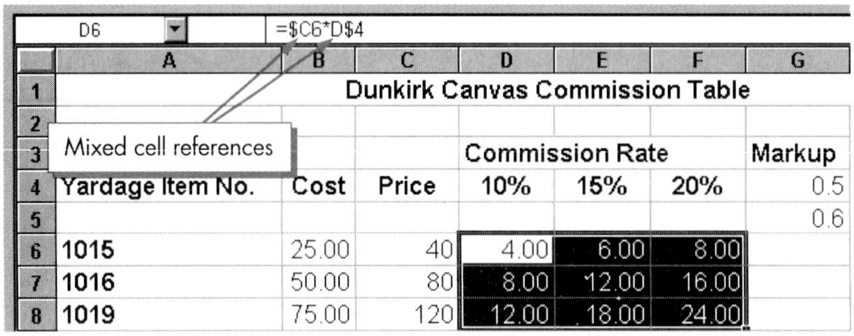

	A	B	C	D	E	F	G
	D6	▼	=$C6*D$4				
1			Dunkirk Canvas Commission Table				
2							
3	Mixed cell references			Commission Rate			Markup
4	Yardage Item No.	Cost	Price	10%	15%	20%	0.5
5							0.6
6	1015	25.00	40	4.00	6.00	8.00	
7	1016	50.00	80	8.00	12.00	16.00	
8	1019	75.00	120	12.00	18.00	24.00	

11. Save the workbook as *[your initials]***11-3.xls** and then print it.

12. Close the workbook.

Creating an IF Function

The IF function is used to create conditional expressions—that is, formulas of the form "If X, then Y." For example, "If the bill is past 30 days late, then you will pay a late fee of 2%."

The IF function in Excel takes the form, "If X, then Y, otherwise Z." The IF function evaluates whether X is true or false; it returns the value Y if the conditional expression is true, and the value Z if it is false. An example is "If cell C5 is greater than 50, then charge a late fee; otherwise, state 'Thank you for your payment.'"

The IF function takes three arguments in this format:

=IF(logical_test, value_if_true, value_if_false)

- Logical_test is the expression that evaluates to true or false. For example, the expression C5>50 is either true or false.

- Value_if_true is the value that is returned if logical_test is true. Value_if_true can be a constant, a formula, text, or a cell reference.

- Value_if_false is the value that is returned if logical_test is false. Value_if_false can be a constant, a formula, text, or a cell reference.

Table 11-1, on the next page, shows the operators you can use to construct the logical_test portion of the function.

EXERCISE **11-4** **Use the IF Function in a Formula**

1. Open the file **DunBon.xls**.

TABLE 11-1   Operators to Use in Functions

OPERATOR	MEANING
=	Equals
<>	Not equal to
>	Greater than
<	Less than
>=	Greater than or equal to
<=	Less than or equal to

2. Select cell D4, and then key **=IF(B4>20000,500,0)**. The formula returns a bonus of $500 if the value in B4 is greater than $20,000; otherwise, it returns a zero. Since Jack Bell's sales are greater than $20,000, he receives a $500 bonus.

3. Copy the formula in cell D4 to cells D5 through D8.

 NOTE: No commas or dollar punctuation are allowed for numbers inside the IF function.

FIGURE 11-4
IF function determining who receives bonuses

D4	▼	=IF(B4>20000,500,0)				
	A	**B**	**C**	**D**	**E**	**F**	**G**

	A	B	C	D	E	F	G
1	Dunkirk Canvas Bonus Table						
2	Formula using IF function						
3	Name	Sales	Rate	Bonus 1	Bonus 2	Bonus 3	Bonus 4
4	Bell, Jack	21,000	10%	500			
5	Brandeis, Sue	0	15%				
6	Caulder, Liz	18,000	10%				
7	Edwards, Tom	20,000	20%				
8	Summers, Lynn	21,305	20%				

IF Functions with Multiple Conditions

You can use logical functions such as AND, OR, and NOT for the logical_test part of the conditional. When you use functions for the logical_test argument, the functions are enclosed in parentheses. Excel then evaluates the conditional formula, starting with the innermost parentheses that enclose the nested arguments.

The AND expression can be summed up as "All conditions must be met." It returns true if all of its conditions test true, and false if one or more of its conditions tests false. Use the format AND(logical_1,logical_2,...), where as many as 30 conditions, beginning with logical_1, can be tested.

TABLE 11-2 Examples of the AND Function

EXPRESSION	EXCEL RETURNS
AND(1+2=3, 3+3=6)	TRUE
AND(2+2=4, 1+1=3)	FALSE
AND(1<C2, C2<100)	TRUE if cell C2 contains a number greater than 1 and less than 100; otherwise FALSE

The OR expression can be summed up as "At least one condition must be met." Use the format OR(logical_1,logical_2,...), where as many as 30 conditions, beginning with logical_1, can be true or false.

TABLE 11-3 Examples of the OR Function

EXPRESSION	EXCEL RETURNS
OR(1+1=3, 3+3=6)	TRUE
OR(2+0=4, 1+1=1)	FALSE
OR(A1:A3)	TRUE only if the cells in A1:A3 contain at least one formula or expression that evaluates true; otherwise FALSE

When using the AND and OR functions, the following restrictions apply:

- AND and OR ignore empty cells and cells with text.
- If the references in AND or OR contain no logical values, Excel returns the #VALUE! error message.

The NOT expression can be summed up as "reverse the result of testing a logical condition." Use the format NOT(logical), where logical is an expression or value that can be true or false.

TABLE 11-4 Examples of the NOT Expression

EXPRESSION	EXCEL RETURNS
NOT(A3=0)	TRUE if cell A3 contains any number other than 0; FALSE if cell A3 contains 0
NOT(2+2=4)	FALSE

EXERCISE 11-5 Use AND in a Formula

1. Select cell E4.

2. Click ⨍ₓ or choose <u>F</u>unction from the <u>I</u>nsert menu. The Function Wizard - Step 1 of 2 dialog box appears.

3. Choose Logical from the Function <u>C</u>ategory list box.

4. Choose IF from the Function <u>N</u>ame list box.

5. Click the Next button to go to step 2.

6. Click the Function Wizard button next to the logical_test box to insert the AND function as a nested argument. The Function Wizard dialog box for nested functions appears.

FIGURE 11-5
Function Wizard
dialog box for a
nested argument

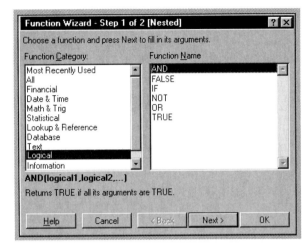

7. With the function category Logical and the function name AND selected, click the Next button. The Step 2 of 2 dialog box allows you to key the arguments for the nested AND function.

8. Key **B4>20000** in the logical1 box.

9. Key **C4=.2** in the logical2 box, and then click OK. The original Function Wizard dialog box appears. The AND function has been inserted as the "X" part of the "If X, then Y, otherwise Z" conditional.

10. Key **500** in the value_if_true box. It becomes the "Y" part of the conditional.

11. Key **0** in the value_if_false box. It becomes the "Z" part of the conditional.

> **NOTE:** If you forgot to key 0 in the value_if_false box, Excel displays the value FALSE in the worksheet instead of the value 0. To complete the formula, you can edit it manually in the formula bar. Key **0** preceded by a comma where the value_if_false argument belongs.

12. Click the <u>F</u>inish button. Because cell B4 is greater than 20,000, but cell C4 is not 20%, the formula calculates 0 (no bonus).

13. Copy the formula to cells E5 through E8.

EXERCISE 11-6 Use OR in a Formula

1. Select cell F4, and then click ⨍ₓ.

2. In the Step 1 of 2 dialog box, choose Logical from the Function Category list box and IF from the Function Name list box.

3. Click the Next button to go to step 2.

4. Click ⨍ₓ next to the logical_test box to insert the OR function as a nested argument.

5. Choose Logical from the Function Category list box and OR from the Function Name list box.

6. Click the Next button to key the arguments.

7. Key **B4>20000** in the logical1 box.

8. Key **C4=.2** in the logical2 box, and then click OK.

9. Key **500** in the value_if_true box.

10. Key **0** in the value_if_false argument box, and then click the Finish button. Because one condition was met, the formula calculates a $500 bonus.

11. Copy the formula to cells F5 through F8. Notice the difference in bonus amounts using OR versus AND.

EXERCISE **11-7** **Use NOT in a Formula**

1. Select cell G4.

2. Key **=IF(NOT(B4=0),500,0)**

3. Copy the formula to cells G5 through G8. Using NOT in the IF formula, all salespeople receive $500 commissions under Bonus Plan 4, unless they have zero sales.

FIGURE 11-6
Using the NOT expression in an IF formula

G4		=IF(NOT(B4=0),500,0)					
	A	B	C	D	E	F	G
3	Name	Sales	Rate	Bonus 1	Bonus 2	Bonus 3	Bonus 4
4	Bell, Jack	21,000	10%	500	0	500	500
5	Brandeis, Sue	0	15%	0	0	0	0
	NOT expression lder, Liz	18,086	10%	0	0	0	500
	Edwards, Tom	20,000	20%	0	0	500	500
8	Summers, Lynn	21,305	20%	500	500	500	500

4. Save the workbook as *[your initials]***11-7.xls** and then print it.

5. Close the workbook.

Using IF Functions to Insert Text Comments

You can create a formula using the IF function that displays variable or conditional comments based on whether a condition is true or false. For example, you could display the text "Delinquent Account" if the value in the "Days Overdue" column of a worksheet is greater than 30. To add variable comments in an IF function, surround the comments with quotes. For example, you could use the following IF statement to display "Current Account" if an account is less than or equal to 30 days late, and "Past Due" if the account is more than 30 days late: IF(G3<=30,"Current Account","Past Due")

You also can use conditional comments to replace Excel's error messages with easier-to-understand messages. For example, if a cell contains a formula for division, and the number is divided by zero, the #DIV/0! error message appears. To replace this error message, you can create a formula with a conditional comment, such as IF(B2=0,"You cannot divide by zero.",B1/B2). If a user keys 0, the text you defined appears; otherwise, Excel performs the division.

EXERCISE **11-8** **Insert Text Comments in an IF Function**

1. Open the file **Costs.xls**.

2. In cell E4, enter the formula **=IF(D4>40,"Yes","No")**. Because the value in cell D4 is greater than 40, Excel displays "Yes."

FIGURE 11-7
Using variable comments in an IF formula

=IF(D4>40,"Yes","No")

D	E	F	G
Hours	OT	Yardage Cost	Labor Cost
42	Yes	0.00	0.00
39	No	0.0	
40	No	0.0	Variable comments
44	Yes	0.00	0.00
50	Yes	0.00	0.00
20	No	0.00	0.00
41	Yes	0.00	0.00

3. Copy the formula to cells E5 through E10.

TIP: You can insert a blank as either the true or false statement by using double quotation marks ("") with no space in between.

Using *VLOOKUP and HLOOKUP*

You can create a table in one area of a worksheet that is used to retrieve values for another area of the worksheet. This operation involves using the VLOOKUP and HLOOKUP functions. For example, you could create a table that lists item numbers and prices in one area of an invoice worksheet. When you key the item number in the item column of the worksheet, Excel looks up the price for the item in the table and automatically places it in the price column. Besides saving work, these functions help prevent data-entry errors.

Use this format:

=VLOOKUP(lookup_value,table_array,col_index_num,range_lookup)

- Lookup_value is the value for which VLOOKUP searches. It can be a value, text string, or cell reference.
- Table_array is the range of cells through which Excel searches for lookup_value. It is a good idea to use a range name for the table. VLOOKUP searches down the left-most column in the table for a match

to the lookup_value; HLOOKUP searches the top row in the table. Table_array can contain numbers, text, or logical values. The values in the first column must appear in ascending order (1,2,3...A-Z...FALSE, TRUE) unless an exact match is desired.

- Col_index_num is the column number in the table_array from which the matching value should be returned. A col_index_num of 1 will return the value in the first column in table_array; a col_index_num of 2 returns the value in the second column in table_array; and so on.

- Range_lookup is an optional argument. It is a logical value (TRUE or FALSE) that specifies whether you want VLOOKUP to find an exact match or an approximate match. When it is TRUE or omitted, VLOOKUP finds the largest value that is less than the lookup_value. If you want VLOOKUP to find an exact match for the lookup_value, the range_lookup should be FALSE.

HLOOKUP works just like VLOOKUP, except that it searches the top row of the table for the lookup_value, and it uses a row_index_num to indicate the row number in the table from which the matching value is returned. Use the following format:

=HLOOKUP(lookup_value,table_array,row_index_num,range_lookup)

Note the following restrictions to VLOOKUP and HLOOKUP:

- IF VLOOKUP and HLOOKUP cannot find lookup_value, and range_lookup is TRUE, they use the largest value that is less than the lookup_value.

- If lookup_value is less than the least value in the first column of the table_array, VLOOKUP returns the #N/A error value. The same applies to HLOOKUP and the first row of the table_array.

EXERCISE **Use the VLOOKUP Function**

1. Select cell B4, and key **=VLOOKUP(A4,A14:B20,2)**

 TIP: Give range names to your tables and use these names in your VLOOKUP and HLOOKUP functions instead of the cell addresses.

2. Select cell B4 again, and position the pointer in the formula bar.

3. Highlight the A14:B20 portion of the function's argument text.

4. Press F4 to make the reference absolute. The reference changes to $A$14:$B$20.

5. Press Enter. The formula can now be copied, keeping the table_array reference absolute.

6. Copy the formula in cell B4 to cells B5 through B10. Because lookup_value is relative, Excel adjusts the formula and looks up all of the corresponding yardage items in the table.

FIGURE 11-8
VLOOKUP function
used in the
worksheet

	B4	▼		=VLOOKUP(A4,$A$14:$B$20,2)						
	A	B	C	D	E	F	G	H	I	J
3	No.	Yards	Cost/Yard	Hours	OT	Yardage Cost	Labor Cost	Total Cost	Price	
4	106	35	7.00	42	Yes	245.00	350.00	595.00	892.50	
5	107	44	9.50	39	No	418.00	440.00	858.00	1,287.00	
6	105	72	7.00	40	No	504.00	720.00	1,224.00	1,836.00	
7	101	50	6.00	44	Yes	300.00	500.00	800.00	1,200.00	
8	101	50	5.25	50	Yes	262.50	500.00	762.50	1,143.75	
9	107	44	3.99	20	No	175.56	440.00	615.56	923.34	
10	101	50	6.22	41	Yes	311.00	500.00	811.00	1,216.50	
11										
12										
13	Yardage Lookup								Markup	
14	101	50							-66.67%	
15	102	95								
16	103	48								
17	104	60								

Costs

Ready   Sum=35   NUM

Using Notes to Annotate Formulas

Excel allows you to attach a note to a cell that contains descriptive text. This approach is helpful for explaining complicated formulas or warning other users not to key data in a cell containing a formula.

To create and view the notes in a worksheet, use the No<u>t</u>e option on the <u>I</u>nsert menu. You can also use the Attach Note button 🔖 and the Show Info button 🛈. In addition, the keyboard shortcut Shift + F2 allows you to create and view notes. Pressing Ctrl + Shift + ? highlights all cells in a worksheet to which notes are attached.

Cells with notes have a small, red dot in their upper right-hand corner. You can print the notes when you print the worksheet by selecting <u>F</u>ile, Page Set<u>u</u>p, and selecting <u>N</u>otes from the Sheet tab.

EXERCISE **11-10** **Use a Note to Annotate a Formula**

1. Select cell B4.

2. Choose No<u>t</u>e from the <u>I</u>nsert menu, or press Shift + F2. The Cell Note dialog box appears. (See Figure 11-9 on the next page.)

3. Key the following text in the Text Note text box:

Do not key data in this column. Change data only in the Yardage Lookup Table.

4. Click OK. A red marker appears in cell B4 to indicate the presence of a note.

FIGURE 11-9
Cell Note
dialog box

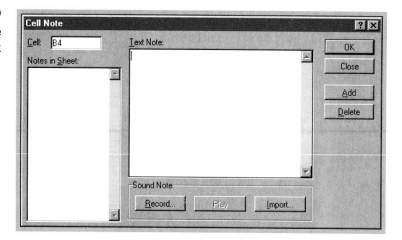

EXERCISE **11-11** **View and Edit the Contents of a Note**

1. Select cell B4, if necessary.
2. Choose Note from the Insert menu, or press Shift + F2. The Cell Note dialog box appears, along with the contents of the note.
3. Select the beginning of the Note and key **IMPORTANT!**
4. Click OK.

Correcting Circular References

A formula cannot contain a reference to its own cell address. For example, the formula =A1+A2+A3 is incorrect if it appears in cell A3. Cell A3 cannot be operated on by a formula and contain the formula simultaneously. Such a reference in a formula, called a *circular reference*, is a fairly common mistake. If you try to enter a formula with a circular reference, Excel produces an error message to let you know that you need to correct the formula.

EXERCISE **Enter and Correct a Circular Reference and Print Notes on a Sheet**

1. Select cell E4.
2. In the formula bar, change "D4" to **E4** and enter the formula. Excel displays the error message, "Cannot resolve circular references."
3. Click OK.
4. Change "E4" back to **D4** to correct the formula.

5. Select <u>F</u>ile, Page Set<u>u</u>p from the menu. Click the Sheet tab if it is not already displayed, and select <u>N</u>otes. The notes will now be printed on a separate page after the worksheet.

6. Save the workbook as *[your initials]***11-12.xls** and then print it.

7. Close the workbook.

COMMAND SUMMARY

FEATURE	BUTTON	MENU	KEYBOARD
Create or show a cell note	🔖		Shift + F2
Show all cells in a worksheet that have attached notes	ⓘ		Ctrl + Shift + ?
Switch between displaying formulas and displaying values		<u>T</u>ools, <u>O</u>ptions, View	Ctrl + ` (left single quote)

Concepts Review

Each of the following statements is either true or false. Indicate your choice by circling **T** or **F**.

T F   **1.** Excel automatically adjusts relative cell references in a formula when the formula is copied from one cell to another.

T F   **2.** $A$3 is an example of a relative cell address.

T F   **3.** Two types of cell references exist in Excel: relative and absolute.

T F   **4.** When creating or editing a formula, the F4 function key is pressed to move through the cell reference types.

T F   **5.** Cell references of named cells are considered absolute.

T F   **6.** An IF function takes two arguments.

T F   **7.** An IF function can use logical functions such as AND, OR, and NOT for the logical_test part of the conditional.

T F   **8.** Excel will automatically display an error message when a circular reference is used in a formula.

Write the correct answer in the space provided.

1. Which type of cell reference combines absolute and relative cell addresses?

_____

2. Which keyboard character is added to a cell address in a formula when the F4 key is pressed?

_____

3. Which type of cell reference is used in a formula when you want to copy a formula but do not want the cell reference to change?

_____

4. Which function evaluates a condition and provides one answer if the condition is true and another answer if the condition is false?

_____

5. Which keyboard character is used to surround a variable comment in an IF function?

_____

6. Which functions retrieve a value from a table on another area of the worksheet and places it in the formula cell?

_____

7. Which command from the <u>I</u>nsert menu is used to annotate a worksheet cell?

_____

8. What type of marker is displayed in a cell that contains a note?

_____

CRITICAL THINKING

Answer these questions on a separate piece of paper. There are no right or wrong answers. Support your answers with examples from your own experience, if possible.

1. Think about how you can set up your checkbook in Excel using the following columns: "No.", "Date," "Check Issued To," "Amount of Check," "Amount of Deposit," and "Balance." How can you write a formula in the "Balance" column to add a deposit and subtract a check from the previous balance? When the formula is copied down the worksheet, the previous balance becomes displayed in all cells in the "Balance" column. How can you revise your original formula using an IF function with an OR expression and a variable comment so that the "Balance" column cells will be blank until a deposit or a check is entered in the checkbook?

2. Think about how the VLOOKUP function was used in this lesson. Could a table be set up in a separate workbook and then be referenced in a VLOOKUP function? How might this option prove useful in a company?

3. When someone sets up a worksheet for another person, are the purpose of the worksheet and how the formulas work always clear? Which Excel command is useful for adding annotations in a worksheet cell? How might this feature be beneficial to you as an employee taking over someone else's work?

Skills Review

EXERCISE 11-13

Use relative, mixed, and absolute cell references.

1. Open the file **DunRev.xls**.
2. Select cell C7.

UNIT 4 ■ FORMULA AND TEMPLATE CONSTRUCTION

3. Key **=$B7*C$4+$B7**. This formula contains mixed cell addresses. Each quarterly projection is based on the percentage indicated in row 4 multiplied by the fourth quarter's actual numbers in column B. The fourth-quarter number is then added to the increase.

4. Copy the formula to cells C7 through F8. Because mixed cell references were used, the formula can be keyed once and copied to the cell range.

5. Copy the formula from cell B10 to cells C10 through F10.

6. Select cell C15.

7. Key **=B15*F13+B15**. The projections for expenses for each quarter are based on the percentage in cell F13 multiplied by the previous quarter's expenses.

8. Edit the formula in cell C15. Use F4 to make cell reference F13 the absolute cell address, $F$13. The formula should now be: =B15*$F$13+B15.

9. Copy the formula from cell C15 to cells D15 through F15.

10. Copy the formula from cell B18 to cells C18 through F18.

11. In cell F4, key **7%**

12. In cell F13, key **4%**. Changes appear in affected worksheet cells.

13. Save the workbook as *[your initials]***11-13.xls**.

14. Print the worksheet and close the workbook.

EXERCISE 11-14

Use relative, absolute, and mixed cell references with an IF function with a single condition.

1. Open the file **Salaries.xls**.

2. In cell F5, key **4%**

3. In cell F6, key **5%**

4. Select cell D5.

5. Key **=IF(C5>3,$F$6,$F$5)**

6. Copy the formula from cell D5 to cells D6 through D8.

7. Format column D in percentage style with no decimal places.

8. Select cell E5.

9. Key **=$B5*D5+$B5**

10. Copy the formula from cell E5 to cells E6 through E8.

11. Format column E in accounting style, with dollar signs and no decimal places.

12. Save the workbook as *[your initials]***11-14.xls**.

13. Print the worksheet and close the workbook.

EXERCISE 11-15

Create an IF function with multiple conditions, one of which inserts text comments.

1. Open the file **Reorder.xls**.

2. Select cell G4, and then click f_x.

3. Choose Logical from the Function Category list box, choose IF from the Function Name list box, and then click the Next button.

4. Click f_x next to the logical_test text box.

5. Choose Logical from the Function Category list box, choose OR from the Function Name list box, and then click the Next button.

6. Key **F4<=D4*.10** in the logical1 text box.

7. Key **F4<5** in the logical2 text box, and then click OK.

8. Key **YES** in the value_if_true text box.

9. Key **""** (double quotation marks) in the value_if_false text box. The cell will be left blank if the answer is false.

10. Click the Finish button. Copy the formula from cell G4 to cells G5 through G8. The cells in column G that meet either condition contain the answer YES; otherwise, they are left blank.

11. Change the value in cell E4 to **23**. Cell G4 is updated with the answer YES.

12. Save the workbook as *[your initials]***11-15.xls**.

13. Print the worksheet and close the workbook.

EXERCISE 11-16

Use relative, absolute, and mixed cell references with the VLOOKUP function; use notes to annotate the formula; and correct a circular reference.

1. Open the file **Vacation.xls**.

2. Key the data by following these steps:

    a. In cell B5, key **8/10/94**

    b. In cell B6, key **2/3/95**

    c. In cell B7, key **5/5/95**

    d. In cell B8, key **6/1/96**

    e. In cell B9, key **10/10/90**

    f. In cell B10, key **4/2/93**

3. Select cell C5 and key **=($F$1-B5)/365.25**. This formula subtracts the employment date in cell B5 from the current date in cell F1; it then divides by 365.25 to convert the days to years.

4. Copy the formula from cell C5 to cells C6 through C10.

5. Format column C in number style, with one decimal place.

6. Key the table as shown in Figure 11-10, beginning in cell A12.

FIGURE 11-10

	A	B
12	Years of Service	Vacation Days Due
13	1	5
14	2	5
15	3	5
16	4	5
17	5	10
18	6	10
19	7	10
20	8	10
21	9	10
22	10	15

7. Make the titles in row 12 bold, and format cell A12 so that the text wraps.

8. Select cell D5, and then key **=VLOOKUP(C5,$A$13:$B$22,2)**

9. Copy the formula from cell D5 to cells D6 through D10.

10. Select cell D4, and then choose Note from the Insert menu.

11. Key **Maximum vacation is 15 days.** in the Text Note text box and then click OK. A red marker appears in cell D4.

12. Select cell B11, and key **Employees with vacation due:**

13. Select cell D11, key **=COUNT(D5:D11)**, and then press Enter.

14. Click OK to remove the Alert message, "Cannot resolve circular references."

15. Edit the formula in cell D11. Change "D11" to **D10**.

16. Save the workbook as *[your initials]***11-16.xls**.

17. Print the worksheet and note, and close the workbook.

Lesson Applications

Use relative, absolute, and mixed cell references, and use notes to annotate a formula.

Create a worksheet that determines quantity-based discounts received from a supplier. Create formulas with relative and absolute cell addresses that calculate the discount prices.

1. Open a new workbook.
2. Construct the worksheet as shown in Figure 11-11.

FIGURE 11-11

	A	B	C	D	E	F
1	Dunkirk Canvas Company					
2	Material Order List					
3			2%	3%	4%	5%
4	Part No.	Cost Per Yard		Quantity Ordered		
5			50	100	200	Over 200
6	Canvas 101	5.09				
7	Canvas 102	5.45				
8	Canvas 103	6.14				
9	Canvas 104	6.23				
10	Canvas 105	6.51				

3. Format the range B6:F10 in number style, with two decimal places and right alignment.
4. Right-align the headings in the ranges C3:F3 and C5:F5.
5. Center the "Quantity Ordered" heading over the four columns below it.
6. Select cell C6, and then key **=B6*C3+B6**. The formula calculates the new price for a quantity of 50, based on a 2% discount.
7. Edit the formula in cell C6. Change cell reference C3 to the mixed cell reference that will adjust the column, but not the row, when the formula is copied.
8. Change both B6 cell references in the formula to the mixed cell reference that will adjust the row, but not the column, when the formula is copied.

295

9. Copy the formula from cell C6 to cells C7 through F10.
10. Widen columns to display the values, if necessary.
11. Create a note in cell A1. Key the following:
    Call supplier on a monthly basis to review discounts received.
12. Rename the sheet tab **Discounts**.
13. Save the workbook as *[your initials]***11-17.xls**.
14. Add the filename to the header.
15. Print the worksheet and note, and close the workbook.

EXERCISE 11-18

Create an IF function with a single condition, and correct a circular reference

Construct a worksheet for analyzing overtime. Use formulas that include IF functions that track hours worked and overtime pay.

1. Open a new workbook.
2. Key the worksheet as shown in Figure 11-12.

FIGURE 11-12 The worksheet to be keyed.

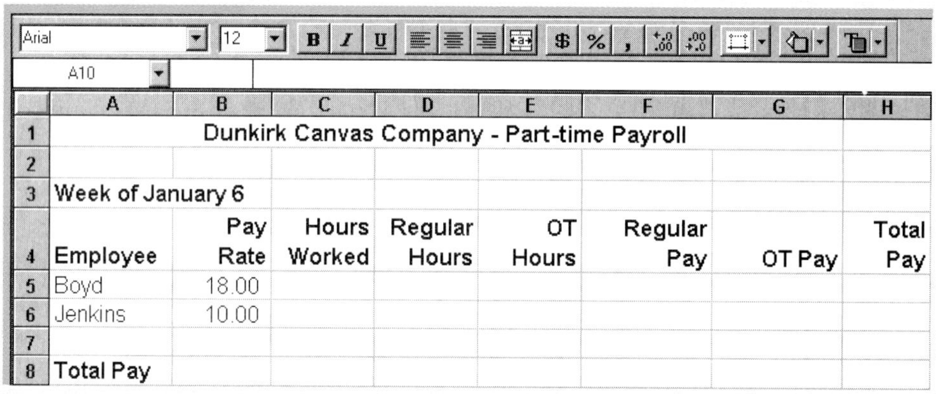

	A	B	C	D	E	F	G	H
1	Dunkirk Canvas Company - Part-time Payroll							
2								
3	Week of January 6							
4	Employee	Pay Rate	Hours Worked	Regular Hours	OT Hours	Regular Pay	OT Pay	Total Pay
5	Boyd	18.00						
6	Jenkins	10.00						
7								
8	Total Pay							

3. Make sure that the text in cells B4 through F4 wraps, and make the necessary cell format and column format changes as shown in the figure.
4. Select cell D5.
5. Key **=IF(C5>=40,40,C5)**. This formula tests the value in cell C5. If the value is greater than or equal to 40, the number 40 is entered in cell D5 as regular hours worked. If the value is less than 40, the value in cell C5 is entered in cell D5 as regular hours.
6. Copy the formula in cell D5 to cell D6.
7. Select cell E5, and then enter a subtraction formula that determines the overtime hours. Copy the formula from cell E5 to cell E6.
8. Select cell F5, and then enter a multiplication formula that determines the regular pay.
9. Copy the formula from cell F5 to cell F6.

10. Select cell G5, and then enter a multiplication formula that determines the overtime pay. Overtime hours are paid at 1.5 times the regular pay rate.

11. Copy the formula in cell G5 to cell G6.

12. Select cell H5, and then enter a formula that adds regular pay to overtime pay. Copy the formula to cell H6.

13. To test the formulas, select cell C5 and key **43**

14. In cell C6, key **50**

15. Select cell F8 and key **=SUM(F5:F8)**. When the error message, "Cannot resolve circular references," is displayed, click OK.

16. Correct the circular reference error in cell F8. Copy the corrected formula to cell G8.

17. Format the ranges F5:H6 and F8:G8 in accounting style with dollar signs and two decimal places.

18. Rename the sheet1 tab to **part-time payroll**.

19. Save the workbook as *[your initials]***11-18.xls**.

20. Add the filename to the header.

21. Print the worksheet and close the workbook.

EXERCISE 11-19

Create an IF function that inserts text comments, and use the VLOOKUP function.

Construct a worksheet that shows the status of delinquent accounts and calculates a 2% late fee using the IF function. Use a lookup table to insert the company name next to the corresponding company number.

1. Open the file **Accounts.xls**.

2. Use the information shown in Figure 11-13 for the following steps.

FIGURE 11-13

Co. No.	Invoice Date	Amount
1014	6/28/97	24,369.00
1011	5/30/97	13,254.21
1015	8/20/97	34,547.33
1013	4/22/97	6,241.01
1016	9/14/97	27,362.00
1012	7/9/97	14,925.08

3. Enter the first row of data in cells A4, C4, and D4.

4. Select cell E4. This cell contains a formula that calculates the number of days late. Create a better formula that hides the numbers appearing in the "Days Late" column if the invoice date is blank and that calculates days late when an invoice date exists.

5. Key **=IF(C4=0,0,TODAY()-C4)**. The value_if_false argument calculates the days late when an invoice date exists.

6. Copy the formula in cell E4 to cells E5 through E9.

7. Enter the rest of the data from Figure 11-13.

8. Select cell F4.

9. Click ☐ to begin entering a formula that displays "Over 30" for accounts 30 days past due, "Over 60" for accounts 60 days past due, and "Collection" for accounts 90 days past due.

10. Choose Logical from the Function Category list box.

11. Choose IF from the Function Name list box.

12. Click the Next button to key the arguments for the IF function.

13. Key **E4>90** in the logical_test box.

14. Key **"Collection"** in the value_if_true box.

15. Click ☐ next to the value_if_false box.

16. Choose Most Recently Used from the Function Category list box.

17. Choose IF from the Function Name list box, and click the Next button to key the arguments for the nested IF function.

18. Key **E4>60** in the logical_test box.

19. Key **"Over 60"** in the value_if_true box.

20. Click ☐ next to the value_if_false box to insert another IF function as a nested argument.

21. Choose Most Recently Used from the Function Category list box.

22. Choose IF from the Function Name list box.

23. Click the Next button to key the arguments for the twice-nested IF function.

24. Key **E4>30** in the logical_test box.

25. Key **"Over 30"** in the value_if_true box.

26. Key **0** in the value_if_false box.

27. Click OK twice, and then click the Finish button.

28. Copy the formula in cell F4 to cells F5 through F9.

29. Place a note in cell F4 explaining how the formula works. Select cell F4, and choose Note from the Insert menu.

30. Key the following in the Text Note text box:

    Logical tests are for 90, 60, and 30 days past due.

31. Click OK.

32. Create a name for the constant .02 called **late_fee**.

33. Select cell G4.

34. Create a formula that charges a 2% late fee for accounts more than 60 days past due by keying **=IF(E4>60,D4*late_fee,0)**

35. Copy the formula in cell G4 to cells G5 through G9.

36. Select cells J4 through K9, and name this range **table**. It will serve as the table_array in a VLOOKUP function.

37. Select cell B4.

38. To create a formula that inserts the company name next to the corresponding company number, key **=VLOOKUP(A4,table,2)**

39. Copy the formula in cell B4 to cells B5 through B9.

40. Delete column I (the blank column), and change the text in rows 3 through 9 to 10-point type. Adjust the column widths so that all text shows and the worksheet can print on one page.

41. Save the workbook as *[your initials]***11-19.xls**

42. Print the worksheet and its notes. Print a second version in landscape orientation with formulas displayed, using gridlines and row and column headings. Be sure to widen the columns so that all of the formulas are displayed; it will require three pages to show all columns with formulas.

43. Close the workbook.

EXERCISE 11-20

Creat an IF function with multiple conditions, one of which inserts text comments, and use the VLOOKUP function.

Create a worksheet that lists debits and credits against specific accounts.

1. Open a new workbook.

2. Select cell A1 and key **Dunkirk Canvas Co. Monthly Journal**

3. Create a worksheet using the information shown in Figure 11-14. This is the monthly journal portion of the worksheet.

FIGURE 11-14

Acc#	Description	Category	Debit	Credit
100			100	85
201			300	325
101			142	

4. Below this information, create a lookup table using the information shown in Figure 11-15.

FIGURE 11-15

Acc#	Description	Category
100	Cash	Asset
101	Securities	Asset
102	Notes Receivable	Asset
200	Notes Payable	Liability
201	Taxes Payable	Liability
202	Wages Payable	Liability

5. In the "Description" column of the monthly journal (top) portion of the worksheet, create a formula to enter the description automatically when the account number is keyed. Construct the formula so that no #N/A messages appear if the "Account Number" column is blank.

6. In the "Category" column, create another formula to enter the category automatically when the account number is keyed. Construct the formula so that no #N/A messages appear if the "Account Number" column is blank.

7. Assume that nine additional rows of data will be entered. Extend the formulas through these rows.

8. Add a row to total the debits and credits.

9. Below the total, enter a formula that displays the message, "Debits do not equal credits," when the total debits do not match the total credits.

10. Enhance the worksheet by adding formatting such as bold and borders.

11. Save the workbook as *[your initials]***11-20.xls**

12. Add the filename to the header.

13. Print the worksheet in landscape orientation. Print a second version showing formulas, gridlines, and row and column headings. Make sure all columns are widened to display the formulas.

14. Close the workbook.

Working with Dates, Times, and Financial Functions

OBJECTIVES After completing this lesson, you will be able to:

1. Use automatic date formats.
2. Work with date functions.
3. Use date math.
4. Work with time functions.
5. Work with financial functions.

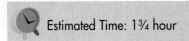
Estimated Time: 1¾ hour

This lesson covers several of Excel's date and time functions and introduces you to calculations involving dates and times. In addition, you will see how the financial functions can assist you in evaluating and analyzing loan and investment terms. You can calculate present and future values of investments, interest rates and amounts, the number of payment periods in an annuity, and payment amounts. Once you become familiar with Excel's financial functions, you will be able to evaluate an investment and even choose the best loan terms.

Working with Dates

In Excel, dates are stored as numbers. Excel uses the 1900 Date System, which uses *serial numbers* from 1 to 65,380 to store dates in cells having the date format. Each serial number represents a date: 1 stands for the date January 1, 1900, while the last number, 65,380, represents December 31, 2078. Storing dates as numbers enables Excel to perform calculations with dates.

You can key dates in a variety of ways. As with numbers, Excel will assign the closest matching date format to the date you key. The date displayed on the screen may not exactly match the date that you keyed, depending on whether your date format matches one of Excel's built-in date formats.

TABLE 12-1   Excel's Date Formats

KEYED CHARACTERS	DATE CODE	SCREEN DISPLAY
12-1-97	m/d/yy	12/1/97
12/1/97	m/d/yy	12/1/97
1-Jan-97	d-mmm-yy	1-Jan-97
1-January-1997	d-mmm-yy	1-Jan-97
March-97	mmm-yy	Mar-97
3-97	mmm-yy	Mar-97

EXERCISE **12-1** **Use Automatic Date Formats**

Excel formats the cells for dates when you enter them. The date that you key is sometimes displayed differently on the screen.

1. Open a new workbook.

2. In cells A6:F6, key the following data:

12/1/97   **12-1-97**   **1 Dec 97**   **1 December 1997**   **12/97**

3. Select cell D6, and choose Cells from the Format menu. In the Format Cells dialog box, Excel chooses the date format code that most closely matches the date you keyed.

4. Click Cancel.

NOTE: When you see a number in a cell where you keyed a date, the cell is formatted for a number and the date's serial number is displayed. Conversely, when you see a date in a cell where you keyed a number, the cell is formatted for the date. When this type of formatting error occurs, change the cell's format to the appropriate option.

Working with Date Functions

Excel's built-in date functions make it possible to use dates in calculations. You can enter functions into your worksheet in the following ways:

- Key the function call directly
- Use the <u>F</u>unction command on the <u>I</u>nsert menu
- Use f_* to select from several types of date and time functions.

TABLE 12-2   **Excel's Date Functions**

FUNCTION	DESCRIPTION OF FUNCTION
=DATE()	Returns the serial number of a specified date
=NOW()	Returns the current date and time
=TODAY()	Returns the current date
=YEAR()	Returns the year, given a serial number or a date enclosed within quotes
=MONTH()	Returns the month number (e.g., 3 for March), given a serial number or a date
=DAY()	Returns the day number of the month, given a serial number or a date
=WEEKDAY()	Returns the day of the week (e.g., 2 for Monday), given a serial number or a date

EXERCISE   12-2   View the Serial Number of a Date

The DATE function returns the serial number of a particular date. The arguments of the DATE function must be entered in the order of year, month, day.

1. In cell A1, enter **=DATE(97,8,27)**

2. Select cell A1, and then choose C<u>e</u>lls from the F<u>o</u>rmat menu. Click the Number tab, if necessary, and choose Number in the <u>C</u>ategory list box. Choose 0 from the <u>D</u>ecimal Places option box. The Sample box displays the serial number for the date.

3. Click OK. The serial number appears on the screen.

4. To display the date again, choose C<u>e</u>lls from the F<u>o</u>rmat menu.

5. Choose the Date category and the format 3/4/95, and click OK. The date is displayed.

> **TIP:** You can also click the right mouse button and choose Format Cells from the shortcut menu to open the Format Cells dialog box. One date format can be generated with a keyboard shortcut: Ctrl + Shift + # produces the d-mmm-yy format.

6. Add the filename as a header.

7. Save the workbook as *[your initials]***12-2.xls** and then print it.

EXERCISE 12-3 **Enter the Current Date**

The TODAY function displays the current date stored in your computer. This date is updated each time you recalculate your worksheet. TODAY uses the format TODAY().

1. Open the file **Employ1.xls**.

2. In cell F1, enter **=TODAY()**

 TIP: You can also generate the current day by pressing Ctrl + ; .

Using Date Math

You can use addition and subtraction to perform calculations with dates. For example, the formula =TODAY()+30 displays the date 30 days from today. To calculate with a cell formatted for date, simply key the cell reference in the formula. To enter a date directly in a formula, key quotation marks around the date. This format instructs Excel to use the serial number for the date. For example, to calculate the number of days between April 15, 1995 and March 1, 1997, you could use the formula ="3-1-97"-"4-15-95".

When you calculate dates, make sure that the dates in the cell are formatted appropriately for a date. Excel uses the stored serial number to calculate no matter how the date is formatted on the screen.

EXERCISE 12-4 **Calculate Elapsed Days**

---

1. Select cell E5, and key **=TODAY()-D5**

2. Copy the formula from cell E5 to cells E6 through E10. The results display as dates rather then numbers, so the format needs to be changed.

FIGURE 12-1
Calculating
differences in dates

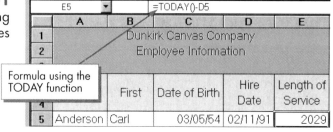

3. Format the cells in column E in the general format. The values in cells E5 through E10 show the length of service in days.

EXERCISE 12-5 **Convert Days to Years**

After the length of service is calculated, the result will become more meaningful if you convert the days to years.

1. Double-click cell E5 to edit its contents.

2. Enclose the existing formula in parentheses by placing a left parenthesis before the "T" in "Today" and a right parenthesis at the end of the formula.

3. At the end of the formula, key **/365.25**

 NOTE: 365.25 is the average number of days in a year, taking into account leap years.

FIGURE 12-2
Converting number of days into years

	A	B	C	D	E
	E5		=(TODAY()-D5)/365.25		
1			Dunkirk Canvas Company		
2			Employee Information		
3					
4	Last	First	Date of Birth	Hire Date	Length of Service
5	Anderson	Carl	03/05/54	02/11/91	5.5551

4. Press Enter.

5. Copy the formula from cell E5 to cells E6 through E10.

EXERCISE 12-6 **Use the Integer Part of a Year**

You may want to show only the whole number of years elapsed. Use the INT(Number) function to round down to the integer.

1. Select cell E5. The result of the formula is displayed in the general format.

2. Double-click cell E5 to edit the contents of the cell.

3. Position the insertion point after the = symbol and key **INT(**

4. Position the insertion point at the end of the formula and key a closed parenthesis, **)**

5. Press Enter. The number of years elapsed is rounded down to the integer.

6. Copy the formula from cell E5 to cells E6 through E10.

FIGURE 12-3
Rounding down number of years to an integer

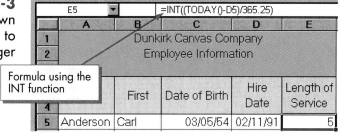

7. Save the workbook as *[your initials]* **12-6.xls** and then print it.

8. Close the workbook.

EXERCISE **12-7** **Calculate a Future Date**

You may need to use the serial number of a specific date in a calculation. You can use the DATE function to calculate the serial number for a given date. The function uses the format DATE(year,month,day).

1. Open a new workbook. You will use Excel to calculate the maturity date of a loan based on the issue date of June 6, 1994, and a term of 20 years.

2. Select cell A1, and key **Dunkirk Canvas Company**

3. Select cell A3, and key **Loan**

4. Select cell B3, and key **Maturity Date**

5. Select cell A4, and key **No.100**

6. Widen column B to accommodate the heading.

7. Select cell B4, and then key **=DATE(94,6,6)+20*365.25**

8. Format cell B4 in the date format of March 4, 1995. The calculation determines that the loan will mature on June 6, 2014.

EXERCISE **12-8** **Calculate the Day of the Week**

The WEEKDAY function returns a date's day number of the week. Sunday is 1, Monday is 2, and so on. The function uses the form WEEKDAY(serial_number,return_type), where the serial_number is a date or the cell address of a date.

1. Select cell C3, and then key **Weekday**

2. Widen the column to accommodate the heading, and right align the heading.

3. Select cell C4, and then enter **=WEEKDAY(B4)**. The result is 6, which represents Friday.

NOTE: The return_type text box is optional. Enter a value to change the day of the week start number. With a return_type of 2, number 1 represents Monday and number 7 represents Sunday.

4. Save the workbook as *[your initials]***12-8.xls**.

5. Add a header with the filename.

6. Print the worksheet and close the workbook.

Working with Time Functions

Excel's time functions operate much like its date functions. Time is stored as a number and is displayed according to the format you select. A time number is stored as a decimal number. For example, the time number for 12:00 noon is 0.5, because it is half of the day (12 hours divided by 24 hours).

You can calculate with time numbers, and Excel provides several useful time functions.

TABLE 12-3   Excel's TIME Functions

FUNCTION	DESCRIPTION OF FUNCTION
=NOW()	Returns the current date and time
=TIME()	Returns the serial number of the specified time
=TIMEVALUE()	Returns the serial number of a time written as text and enclosed in quotation marks
=HOUR()	Returns the hour portion of a given serial number
=MINUTE()	Returns the minute portion of a given serial number
=SECOND()	Returns the second portion of a given serial number

EXERCISE   12-9   Use Automatic Time Formats

The TIME function returns the serial number of a particular time. It uses the format TIME(hour,minute,second).

1. Open the file **Employ2.xls**.
2. Select cell E1, and then key **=TIME(7,30,25)**
3. Format cell E1 in number format with two decimal places.

FIGURE 12-4
Time in number
format, displaying
as a decimal

	D	E	F	
		=TIME(7,30,25)		Formula using the TIME function
1		0.31		
2				

4. Format cell E1 in time format, using the 13:30:55 format. The time displays as 7:30:25.

 TIP: One time format can be generated with a keyboard shortcut: Ctrl + Shift + @ generates the h:mm AM/PM format.

EXERCISE 12-10 **Use Time Math**

You can calculate with time numbers as well as date numbers. Remember to multiply a time number by 24 to convert it to hours.

1. In the range A6:F6, key the following data:

1/7/97   7:00 am   11:30 am   12:00 pm   4:00 pm

 NOTE: You can key "am" or "pm" in lowercase letters, and Excel will automatically convert them to uppercase.

2. In cells A7:F7, key the following data:

1/8/97   7:30 am   12:00 pm   12:45 pm   5:00 pm

 TIP: You can generate the current time from the computer's clock by pressing Ctrl+Shift+;.

3. Select cell E6, and then key **=(D6-C6)*24**

4. Format cell E6 in number format with two decimal places. The date is replaced by the time number.

5. Copy the formula from cell E6 to cell E7.

6. Select cell G6, and then key **=(F6-B6)*24**

7. Format cell G6 in number format with two decimal places.

8. Double-click cell G6 to edit the formula so that it subtracts the lunch time.

9. Position the insertion point at the end of the formula. Key **-E6** and press Enter.

10. Copy the formula from cell G6 to cell G7.

11. Save the workbook as *[your initials]***12-10.xls** and then print it.

12. Close the workbook.

FIGURE 12-5
Completed worksheet with formula converting time number into hours

	A	B	C	D	E	F	G
1	Dunkirk Canvas Company				7:30:25		
2	Part-time Employees - Weekly hours						
3							
4	Jennifer Boyd						
5	Date	Start Time	Lunch Out	Lunch In	Lunch Time	Out Time	Hours Worked
6	1/7/97	7:00 AM	11:30 AM	12:00 PM	0.50	4:00 PM	8.50
7	1/8/97	7:30 AM	12:00 PM	12:45 PM	0.75	5:00 PM	8.75

G7 =(F7-B7)*24-E7

Employ2   Ready   Sum=8.75

Working with Financial Functions

Excel's financial functions are used to evaluate and analyze various loan and investment terms. This lesson focuses on the financial functions PMT, PV, RATE, NPER, FV, IPMT, and PPMT. In all financial functions, amounts of payments are represented by negative values if the payments are to be paid out and by positive values if they are to be received.

Many of these functions take the same arguments. Note that some of the argument names are the same as the function names themselves. For clarity, argument names are shown here in lowercase letters within parentheses, and function names are in uppercase letters:

- (rate)
  The interest rate per period. To reflect the rate period in which the payments are made, the annual rate must be entered as a fraction that indicates how many payments per year are made. For example, a loan at an 8% annual rate for which the payments are made monthly would be shown as 8%/12.

- (nper)
  The number of payment periods in an annuity. For a five-year loan with monthly payments, nper is shown as 5*12.

- (pv)
  The present value of an annuity. It is the total current value of the future payments.

- (fv)
  The future value of an annuity, or the balance remaining after the last payment is made. In the case of loans, the future value should be 0 (and, in that instance, it is omitted).

- (type)
  Specifies whether payments are to be made at the beginning of the period (type 1) or at the end of the period (type 0, or omitted from function).

EXERCISE 12-11 Use the PMT Function

The PMT function calculates the amount of each payment for an *annuity*, which is a constant periodic payment paid over a fixed time period. The PMT function uses the format PMT(rate,nper,pv,fv,type).

1. Open the file **Finance.xls** and display the PMT worksheet.

2. In cell B4, key **10**

3. To calculate the (nper), select cell B5 and key **=B4*12**

4. In cell B6, key **150000** for the present value of the loan.

5. In cell B7, key **13%**

6. In cell B9, enter **=PMT(B7/12,B5,B6)**

7. Adjust the column width, if necessary. The result ($2,239.66) is negative because it represents a value that is owed, and negative numbers in this format are displayed in red. When the type argument is omitted, Excel makes the calculation based on a monthly payment made at the end of each month.

FIGURE 12-6
Using the
PMT function

	A	B	C
	B10	=PMT(B7/12,B5,B6,0,1)	
1	Dunkirk Canvas Company		
2	Business Loan Payments		
3			
4	Length of loan in years	10	
5	Number of periods	120	
6	Present value	150000	
7	Annual rate	13%	
8			
9	Type 0 payment	($2,239.66)	
10	Type 1 payment	($2,215.66)	
11			
12			

8. In cell B10, enter **=PMT(B7/12,B5,B6,0,1)**. The inclusion of the type argument shows the monthly payment of ($2,215.66) when payment is made at the beginning of each month. It is clear from the two formulas that payments are lower when they are made at the beginning of the month.

9. Save the workbook as *[your initials]***12-11.xls**.

EXERCISE **12-12** **Use the PV Function**

The PV function is used to determine the value of an annuity at the present time. It uses the format PV(rate,nper,pmt,fv,type). The pmt argument is the payment made each period. It must be entered as a negative value. If both fv and type are 0, they may be omitted.

1. Display the PV worksheet in **Finance.xls**.

2. Select cell B4, and key **9.7%**

3. Select cell B5, and key **10**

FIGURE 12-7
Using the
PV function

	A	B	C
	B9	=PV(B4/2,B6,B7)	
1	Dunkirk Canvas Company		
2	10 Year Bond		
3			
4	Annual rate	9.70%	
5	Years	10	
6	Number of payments (nper)	20	
7	Amount of payments (pmt)	(7,900.00)	
8	Cost	100,000.00	
9	Present value (pv)	$99,715.76	
10			
11	Difference	($284.24)	
12			

4. Select cell B6. The formula in this cell will calculate the nper argument.

5. Because the bond will pay semi-annually, key **=B5*2**

6. In cell B7, key **-7900**

7. In cell B8, key **100000**

8. Format cells B7 and B8 in number format with commas and no decimal places. Adjust the column width, if necessary.

9. In cell B9, enter **=PV(B4/2,B6,B7)**. The result returned is $99,715.76.

10. In cell B11, enter **=B9-B8**. The difference between the cost and the actual value of the bond is ($284.24). Because the asking price is higher than the present value of the bond, it is not a good investment.

11. Save the workbook as *[your initials]***12-12.xls**.

EXERCISE 12-13 Use the RATE Function

Excel's RATE function calculates the interest rate per period of an annuity. It uses the format RATE(nper,pmt,pv,fv,type,guess). The guess argument is your estimate of what the rate will be. If you omit it, Excel will assume that the rate is 10% annually. If the result is not at least 0.0000001 (or 0.00001%), RATE does not find a result, and the #NUM error value is displayed. You can then try entering different values as a guess.

1. Display the RATE worksheet in **Finance.xls**.

2. Beginning in cell B4, key the following data in column B:

4
=B4*12
-100
3500
350

3. Format the range B4:B8 in comma style with two decimal places.

4. In cell B9, enter the formula with the "guess" argument omitted: **=RATE(B5,B6,B7,B8)**

5. Change the format to show the percentage with two decimal places.

6. In cell B11, enter **=B9*12**

7. Format the cell in percent style with two decimal places.

8. Save the workbook as *[your initials]***12-13.xls**.

FIGURE 12-8
Using the RATE
function

	B9	▼		=RATE(B5,B6,B7,B8)	
		A		B	C
1	Dunkirk Canvas Company				
2	Equipment Lease				
3					
4	Length of lease in years			4	
5	Number of payment periods			48	
6	Amount of payments			-100	
7	Present value			3500	
8	Future value of balance			350	
9	Monthly rate of lease			1.11%	
10					
11	Yearly rate of lease			13.31%	
12					

EXERCISE **12-14** **Use the NPER Function**

The NPER function is used to calculate the number of periodic, constant payments for an annuity at an unchanging interest rate. It uses the format NPER(rate,pmt,pv,fv,type). The pv and fv arguments may be omitted if they are both zero.

1. Display the NPER worksheet in **Finance.xls**.

2. Beginning in cell B4, key the following data in column B:

3%

210

3000

FIGURE 12-9
Using the
NPER function

B7		=NPER(B4/12,B5,B6,0,1)
	A	**B**	**C**
1	Dunkirk Canvas Company		
2	Company Loan		
3			
4	Rate	3%	
5	Payment amount	210	
6	Present value	3000	
7	Number of payments	-14	
8			

3. In cell B7, enter **=NPER(B4/12,B5,B6,0,1)**. The result is a negative 14 because payments paid out are represented as negative values, and payments received are shown as positive values.

4. Format the cell to have no decimal places.

5. Save the workbook as *[your initials]***12-14.xls**.

EXERCISE **12-15** **Use the FV Function**

The FV function calculates the future value of an annuity. It provides the value of an investment or loan after all payments are made over a given period of time at a given interest rate. The FV function uses the format FV(rate,nper,pmt,pv,type).

The pmt argument is the amount of each periodic payment for the annuity and is represented by a negative number because it is paid to the lender.

1. Display the FV worksheet in **Finance.xls**.

2. Beginning in cell B4, key the following data:

4.5%

12

-250

-500

3. In cell B9, enter **=FV(B4/12,B5,B6,B7,1)**

4. Increase the column width to display the future value of $3,597.11.

FIGURE 12-10
Using the
FV function

B9	▼	=FV(B4/12,B5,B6,B7,1)		
	A		**B**	**C**
1	Dunkirk Canvas Company			
2	One-Year Savings Plan			
3				
4	Rate		4.50%	
5	Number of payments		12	
6	Amount of payment		-250	
7	Present value		-500	
8				
9	Future value		$3,597.11	
10				

5. Save the worksheet as *[your initials]*__12-15.xls__.

EXERCISE **12-16** **Use the IPMT Function**

When payments are made to reduce a loan, each payment includes both an interest amount and a portion of the principal. The *principal* is the amount borrowed, or the present value. *Interest* is the amount paid to the lender as the lender's profit; it accrues at a set rate.

The IPMT function calculates the amount of the interest payment for a period of an annuity. It uses the format IPMT(rate,per,nper,pv,fv,type).

The per argument is the period for which you want to calculate the interest amount. It must be a whole number ranging from 1 to the number of payments (nper).

1. Display the PMT worksheet in **Finance.xls**.

2. Beginning in cell A12, key the following data:

Type 0 Payments

Interest for the first month

Principal payment for the first month

3. Increase the width of column A.

4. In cell B13, enter **=IPMT(B7/12,1,B5,B6)**. The result is $1,625.00, which is the amount of the interest payment for the first month.

EXERCISE **12-17** **Use the PPMT function**

The PPMT function calculates the amount of the principal payment for a period of an annuity. It uses the format PPMT(rate,per,nper,pv,fv,type).

1. In cell B14, enter **=PPMT(B7/12,1,B5,B6)**. The result is $614.66, which is the principal payment for the first month. The result from cell B13 and the result from cell B14 add together to make up the periodic payment.

FIGURE 12-11
Using the IPMT and
PPMT functions

	A	B	C
	B13 ▼	=IPMT(B7/12,1,B5,B6)	
4	Length of loan in years	10	
5	Number of periods	120	
6	Present value	150000	
7	Annual rate	13%	
8			
9	**Type 0 payment**	($2,239.66)	
10	**Type 1 payment**	($2,215.66)	
11			
12	Type 0 payments		
13	Interest for the first month	($1,625.00)	
14	Principal payment for the first month	($614.66)	
15			

2. Save the workbook as *[your initials]***12-17.xls**, and print the entire workbook.

3. Close the workbook.

COMMAND SUMMARY

FEATURE	BUTTON	MENU	KEYBOARD
Current date			Ctrl + ;
Current time			Ctrl + Shift + :
d-mmm-yy date format		Format, Cells	Ctrl + Shift + #
h:mm AM/PM time format		Format, Cells	Ctrl + Shift + @

Concepts Review

Each of the following statements is either true or false. Indicate your choice by circling T or F.

T   F   **1.** When you key a date in a cell, it is sometimes displayed differently on the screen.

T   F   **2.** The TODAY function displays the current date and time.

T   F   **3.** Because Excel stores dates as numbers, date calculations are possible.

T   F   **4.** In all financial functions, amounts of payments are represented by positive values if the payments are to be paid out.

T   F   **5.** The function TIMEVALUE() returns the current date and time.

T   F   **6.** When using the PV(rate,nper,pmt,fv,type) function, the fv and type arguments may be omitted if their values are both 0.

T   F   **7.** When you type a time in a cell, it is stored as a time number and is displayed according to the format you select.

T   F   **8.** The RATE function, which is used to calculate the interest rate per period of an annuity, always returns a result.

Write the correct answer in the space provided.

1. Which function would you use to determine the serial number of a specific date?

_____

2. Which function would you use to calculate the amount of each payment for an annuity over a certain period of time at a given interest rate?

_____

3. Dates are stored as what type of number so that they can be used in calculations?

_____

4. Given a serial number or a date, which function would you use to calculate the day of the week?

_____

5. If you want to enter a date directly in a formula, you would surround the date with which keyboard symbol?

_____

6. How is a time number recorded in a cell?

_____

7. When payments are to be made at the beginning of the period, is the type argument in a financial function specified as 1 or 0?

_____

8. The PPMT function is used to calculate the amount of which type of payment for a period of an annuity?

_____

CRITICAL THINKING

Answer these questions on a separate piece of paper. There are no right or wrong answers. Support your answers with examples from your own experience, if possible.

1. What are some examples of when a business may need to determine elapsed days but needs to calculate only the workdays? Is there a date and time function that will perform this calculation?

2. Loans are not the only way to finance a business expansion. Can you think of other alternatives? Which financial functions can assist you in calculating interest and principal payments?

3. Can you use financial functions to evaluate an adjustable rate mortgage? Why or why not?

Skills Review

EXERCISE 12-18

Use date and time functions and date math.

1. Open the file **Employ3.xls**.

2. Select cell F1, and then key the formula for the current date: **=TODAY()**

3. Select cell E5, and then key the formula to calculate the years to retirement based on age 65: **=65-INT((TODAY()-C5)/365.25)**

4. Copy the formula from cell E5 to the range E6:E8.

5. Save the workbook as *[your initials]***12-18.xls** and then print it.

6. Close the workbook.

EXERCISE 12-19

Use functions that calculate the day of the week, and create formulas that place the day of the week in worksheet cells.

1. Open the file **Schedule.xls**.

2. Select cell G5, and then key the formula **=WEEKDAY(F5)**.

3. Copy the formula from cell G5 to the range G6:G12.

4. Select cell H5, and enter a formula using a VLOOKUP function to look up the number of the weekday in the table provided and return the day of the week to the formula cell. (Think about where to use absolute cell references in this formula.)

5. Copy the formula from cell H5 to the range H6:H12.

6. Save the workbook as *[your initials]***12-19.xls** and print it.

7. Close the workbook.

EXERCISE 12-20

Use automatic time formats and time math to compute the total number of hours worked in a day.

1. Open the file **Contract.xls**.

2. Select cell A8, and then key **Wallace, M.**

3. In cells D8 and E8, key the following data:

   6:00 am   6:00 pm

4. Select cell L5, and then key the formula:
   =SUM((C5-B5),(E5-D5),(G5-F5),(I5-H5),(K5-J5))

5. Copy the formula from cell L5 to the range L6:L8.

6. Save the workbook as *[your initials]***12-20.xls** and then print it.

7. Close the workbook.

EXERCISE 12-21

Use financial functions to analyze different payment plans for a loan, and calculate the future value of the loan amount.

1. Open the file **Analysis.xls**.

2. In cells B5:B8, key the following data:

   1   =B5*12   10,000   10%

3. Select cell B10, and then key **=PMT(B8/12,B6,B7)**

4. Select cell B11, and then key **=PMT(B8/12,B6,B7,0,1)**

5. In the range E5:E8, key the following data:

    6%   12   1,000   1,000

6. Select cell E10, and then key **=FV(E5/12,E6,E7,E8,1)**

7. Save the workbook as *[your initials]***12-21.xls** and then print it.

8. Close the workbook.

Lesson Applications

EXERCISE 12-22

Use automatic date formats, and use date functions to compute the days late based on the current date.

One of Dunkirk Canvas Company's largest clients is overdue on its accounts. Set up an accounts receivable worksheet for overdue accounts.

1. Open the file **Smith1.xls**.
2. Key the following data in columns B and C, beginning in cell B3:

$1,009.65	6/10/97
$2,376.23	6/10/97
$34,987.22	6/12/97
$203,979.00	6/19/97
$542.18	7/12/97
$1,409.67	7/14/97
$311.98	7/18/97
$2,906.12	8/14/97
$4,032.86	8/15/97
$22,091.48	8/18/97

3. To calculate the "Due Date" column, key **=C3+30** in cell D3.
4. Copy the formula through cell D12 by dragging the fill handle.
5. To calculate the numbers of days late in column E, key **=TODAY()-D3** in cell E3.
6. Copy the formula to cells E4 through E12.
7. In the range F3:F12, use the IF function to enter a formula that will display "Yes" if the invoice is more than thirty days late and "No" if it is not.
8. Save the workbook as *[your initials]***12-22.xls**.
9. Print the workbook and then print a second version showing formulas. Make sure columns are wide enough to display all of the formulas.
10. Close the workbook.

EXERCISE 12-23

Use automatic date formats and date math to compute the number of days between dates.

In an effort to improve customer service, Dunkirk Canvas Company is researching the number of days it took to ship a product after it was ordered.

1. Open the file **DunShip.xls**.

2. Beginning in cell C5, key the following data:

   9/5/96

   9/5/96

   9/6/96

   9/6/96

   9/6/96

   9/9/96

   9/9/96

   9/10/96

   9/11/96

   9/11/96

   9/11/96

3. Select cell D5, and then key a formula that subtracts the date that the order was received from the date that the order was shipped.

4. Copy the formula from cell D5 to the range D6:D15.

5. Select cell A17, and then key **Average**

6. Select cell D17, and then key a formula using the AVERAGE function to calculate the average turnaround days. Format the cell to display one decimal place.

7. Save the document as *[your initials]***12-23.xls.**

8. Print and close the workbook.

EXERCISE 12-24

Use automatic date and time format, and date and time math, to compute elapsed times.

Dunkirk Canvas Company needs a worksheet to track customer inquiries received by phone. It wants to know when the phone call was returned and whether the problem was resolved, using sample phone data collected by the Customer Service Department.

1. Open the file **Customer.xls**.

2. Key the following data in columns C and D, beginning in cell C6:

9-16 3:00 pm	Yes
9-17 9:00 am	Yes
9-17 12:30 pm	No
9-18 9:30 am	Yes
9-18 10:00 am	No
9-19 8:00 am	Yes

3. In cell E6, key a formula to determine the turnaround time. The first part of the formula should subtract the dates and times of the two phone calls (make sure to place parentheses around this part of the formula); the second part should multiply this value by 24.

4. Format the range A5:E11 with an outline border, choosing the third line in the Style list box.

5. Format column E to display one decimal place. Copy the formula from cell E6 to the range E7:E11.

6. Add a border (second line in the Style list box) between each of the columns and rows in the A5:E11 range.

7. Save the document as *[your initials]***12-24.xls**.

8. Print and close the workbook.

EXERCISE 12-25

Use a financial function to calculate mortgage payments at different interest rates.

Dunkirk Canvas Company is in the process of choosing a mortgage loan to finance its expansion. Information has been obtained from four banks about their interest rates. Calculate the monthly payments based on the following: All loans are 15-year mortgages with payments due at the end of each month, and all have a present value of $200,000.

1. Open the file **Mortgage.xls**.

2. Beginning in cell B5, key the following data in column B:

15

=B5*12

200,000

3. In the range C4:F4, key the following data:

11.00%   10.50%   9.7%   11.30%

4. Select cell C10, and then key the formula using mixed and absolute cell addresses: **=PMT(C$4/12,$B$6,$B$7)**

5. Copy the formula from cell C10 to the range D10:F10.

6. Save the document as *[your initials]***12-25.xls**.

7. Print and close the workbook.

LESSON

13

Templates

After completing this lesson, you will be able to:

1. Create a template.
2. Use a template.
3. Work with Excel's built-in templates.
4. Use the Template Wizard.

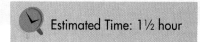

Estimated Time: 1½ hour

emplates are models for worksheets. They include style elements such as fonts, font style, font size, alignment, and borders. They can also include boilerplate text or formulas, such as comments on data included in specific reports. Two basic differences exist between template files and workbook files:

- When you open a template, you open a copy of the template instead of the actual file.
- Template files are assigned an .xlt extension while workbook files are assigned an .xls extension.

You can create your own templates or use the built-in templates provided by Excel. In a Typical installation of Microsoft Excel, the following templates are available from the Spreadsheet Solutions tab when you choose New from the File menu: Invoice, Loan Manager, Purchase Order, and Village Software.

Creating Templates

You create templates by example or by definition, which is similar to how you create styles, as described in Lesson 9. Any worksheet can become a template. To create a template:

- Create a new workbook or complete any formatting changes to an existing workbook.
- Choose Save As from the File menu.
- Key the template name in the File name text box, and select the folder from the Save in text box.
- From the Save as type list, choose the Template format (.xlt extension).
- Click the Save button.

EXERCISE 13-1 Create a Template by Example

1. Open the file **Balance.xls**.
2. Choose Page Setup from the File menu.
3. Click the Page tab, if necessary, and then click Landscape.
4. Click the Margins tab. Key **.65** in both the Left and Right margin text boxes, and then click OK.
5. Select cells C6 through D6, and change the font size to 12 points.
6. Select cell C6, and edit it to read 1996.
7. Select to cell D6, and edit to to read 1997.
8. Clear cells C7 through D11 and cells C14 through D16.
9. Choose Save As from the File menu.
10. Key *[your initials]***13-1** in the File name text box.
11. Click the arrow to open the Save as type drop-down box, and click Template. The filename extension changes to .xlt, and the Save in: drop-down box displays the Templates folder. See Figure 13-1 on the next page.

 NOTE: Excel stores its built-in template files in a folder called Templates in the MSOffice folder. You can access these templates by choosing File, New. If you save templates to the Templates folder, they will be displayed in the New dialog box. A template can be opened from any folder, but only the templates saved to the Templates folder appear in the New dialog box.

12. Click the arrow to open the Save in: drop-down text box, and then click 3½ Floppy (A:). For classroom purposes, student files will be saved to the A: drive.

FIGURE 13-1
Saving a file as
a template

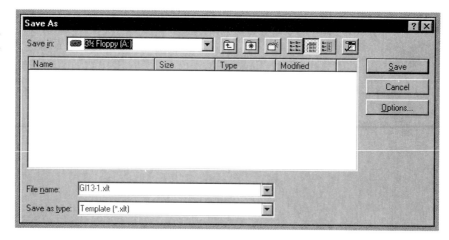

13. Click the Save button. When the file is saved as a template, Excel changes the file extension from .xls to .xlt.

14. Print the template and then close it.

Using Templates

Templates are similar to regular worksheets in most ways. The difference is that when you open a template under the Template file folder, Excel makes a copy of it. Excel appends a number to the template name to make it unique and changes the template extension to the worksheet extension. For example, when qtr.xlt is opened, qtr.xlt becomes qtr1.xls.

EXERCISE **13-2** **Use a Template**

1. Choose Open from the File menu. This action opens the actual template file.

 NOTE: When the template is saved to the Templates folder on the hard drive, you can access a copy of the template file through the File, New command.

2. Open the template file *[your initials]***13-1.xlt**.

3. In the range C7:D11, key the following data:

186,425	190,200
52,949	60,110
22,324	20,211
695,356	809,113
388,385	355,423

4. In the range C14:D16, key the following data:

578,325	**555,313**
310,440	**313,445**
456,674	**453,111**

5. Choose Save <u>A</u>s from the <u>F</u>ile menu. Because you are working in the actual template—not a copy of it—you will want to save the file as a workbook file.

NOTE: In a typical situation, when you use the template copy and want to save it, just choose <u>S</u>ave from the <u>F</u>ile menu. The Save As dialog box is automatically displayed with the file type already specified as a Microsoft Excel Workbook.

6. In the File <u>n</u>ame box, key *[your initials]***13-2**

7. Choose Microsoft Exel Workbook from the Save as <u>t</u>ype box. The file extension changes from .xlt to .xls.

8. Click <u>S</u>ave. The file is now saved as a workbook file.

9. Print the workbook and close it.

Working with Built-In Templates

Excel provides several built-in template files that can assist you in running your business, handling finances, and providing consistency in your documentation. These templates may already include text, formatting, formulas, cell notes, and even toolbars. Before you create new templates, try using the ones provided to see whether they meet your needs. The built-in templates can also be customized to reflect information about your company. For example, your company logo, name and address can be added to a template.

EXERCISE **13-3** **Open a Copy of the Invoice Template**

1. Choose <u>N</u>ew from the <u>F</u>ile menu or press Ctrl + N.

NOTE: The New button ▯ on the Standard toolbar is used to open a new, blank workbook. This button is the shortcut for accessing a copy of the Workbook template. To view a list of available built-in templates, the New dialog box must be displayed.

2. Click the Spreadsheet Solutions tab.

FIGURE 13-2
Available templates
in the New dialog
box, Spreadsheet
Solutions tab

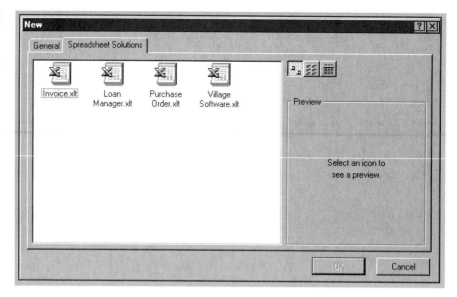

3. Click the Invoice template, and then click OK. A copy of the Invoice template is displayed. The title bar shows the filename as Invoice1, which is a copy of Excel's built-in invoice template. All templates accessed via File, New open a copy of the template, rather than the actual template itself.

EXERCISE **13-4** **Customize the Invoice Template**

If you plan to use a built-in template repeatedly, you can customize it. In addition to adding your company information, you can change fonts, add default information, and even include your corporate logo. To customize a template and save it for future use, follow these steps:

- Choose New from the File menu, click the Spreadsheet Solutions tab and click the template you want to use.
- Click the Customize button found in the upper right corner of the template and complete the information on the Customize worksheet.
- To permanently save the changes, click the Lock/Save Sheet button on the form. Under Locking Options, click Lock and Save Template.
- Key a name for your customized template in the File name box in the Save Template dialog box; then click the Save button. Click Close.

1. Click the Customize button in the upper right corner of Invoice1. The Customize Your Invoice worksheet is displayed. See Figure 13-3 on the next page.

2. Point to the red marker at the top, center of the worksheet to display the cell note. It is one of many cell notes that can assist you in customizing the template. See Figure 13-4 on the next page.

FIGURE 13-3
The Customize Your
Invoice worksheet

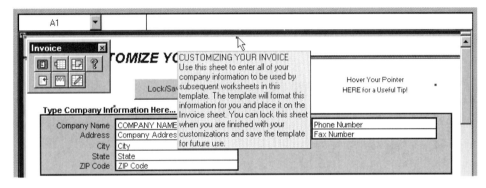

Assign a Number button
on Invoice toolbar

FIGURE 13-4
Cell note explaining
how to use
worksheet

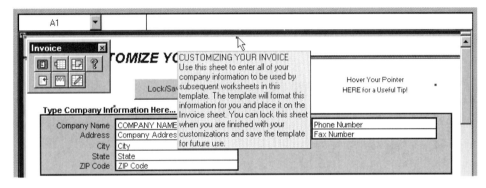

3. Scroll through the invoice template to view the areas available for customization.

4. Click the arrow on the Name box (next to the formula bar), scroll down to the cell named vital1, and select it. This cell is labeled COMPANY NAME and is in the "Type Company Information Here" section of the invoice. All input cells in this section of the invoice are named vital1, vital2, and so on; the Name box shows you the name of the current cell.

 TIP: You can also place the pointer in a named cell by typing the name of the cell in the Name box and pressing Enter.

5. Key the following information in the cells located in the "Type Company Information Here" section of the invoice, starting with the named cell vital1. Drag the toolbar to another location on the screen if it obstructs your view of the template.

vital1   **Dunkirk Canvas Company**

vital2   **14 River Street**

vital4   **Boston**

vital5   **MA**

vital6   **02205**

vital8   **617-555-4410**

vital9   **617-555-4411**

6. Click the Change Plate Font button at the bottom of the worksheet and choose Times New Roman from the Font list box. Click OK.

7. Click the Assign a Number button 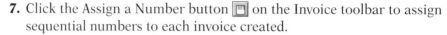 on the Invoice toolbar to assign sequential numbers to each invoice created.

FIGURE 13-5
Message describing how a unique number will be assigned to the form

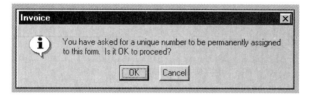

 NOTE: If you prefer, you can type your own number in the designated cell on the worksheet.

8. Click OK to continue.

9. Click the Lock/Save Sheet button on the form. Select the Lock and Save Template option from the dialog box, and then click OK. The Save Template dialog box appears.

10. Click the arrow to open the Save in box, and click the 3½ Floppy (A:) disk drive.

11. In the File name text box, key *[your initials]***13-4**. The Save as type text box displays Templates. Click the Save button. A message appears with instructions on how to access your customized template.

 NOTE: Remember that you are saving templates to the 3½ Floppy (A:) disk drive for classroom purposes only.

FIGURE 13-6
Message describing how to access a customized template

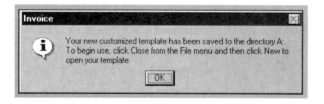

12. Click OK.

13. Add your initials as a header, and then print the template.

EXERCISE **13-5** **Enter Data into the Invoice Template**

With the template displayed, you can key in the necessary information just as you would complete a worksheet, moving from cell to cell using the mouse or pressing the arrow keys, Tab , or Enter .

1. Close the Invoice toolbar.

2. Click the arrow in the Name box and select the named cell data1, which is the cell adjacent to the "Date" label. The current date is automatically displayed in the cell named data1.

3. Select the cell named data2, which is adjacent to the "Order No." label.

4. Key the following customer information in cells named data2 through data10:

data2   **1350**

data3   **Davis**

data5   **Atlanta Yacht Club**

data6   **12 Lakeview Road**

data7   **Atlanta**

data8   **GA**

data9   **30358**

data10 **404-555-5555**

The customer information is complete.

5. Select the cell named data11 to key the following order information:

data11 **25**

data12 **Cover C-9087**

data13 **150**

A formula is included in cell L18. After keying the unit price in cell data13, the "TOTAL" cost is automatically calculated.

6. Scroll to the bottom of the invoice. The "Shipping & Handling" cell is already filled in, and the "SubTotal" and "TOTAL" cells contain formulas based on the invoice information. Data entry for the invoice is complete.

7. Click the Fine Print box at the bottom of the form. Delete the text, and click OK.

8. Click the Farewell Statement box at the bottom of the form. Delete the text, and click OK.

9. Print the invoice worksheet. If a company logo has not been inserted on the invoice form, the logo box will not print.

10. Close the template file without saving the changes. You do not want the newly created Atlanta Yacht Club invoice to become part of the template or to be saved as a workbook.

Using the Template Wizard

Excel provides a Template Wizard with a Data Tracking *add-in* that enables you to create a data entry template from a worksheet. The template is linked to a database file that copies data from worksheet cells into specified fields in the database. A *database* is a file containing an organized list of related data. It can be used for information tracking and analysis. To add data to the database, you open the template, key in data, and save the workbook. In addition to using the Excel worksheet as a database, you can work with Access, dBase, and FoxPro database file formats.

Because the Template Wizard is add-in software, it must be loaded in Excel before it can be used. If it is loaded, the Template Wizard command appears on the Data menu. If it is not displayed on the menu, try loading the software by choosing Add-Ins from the Tools menu and selecting the Template Wizard with Data Tracking from the Add-Ins dialog box.

EXERCISE **13-6** **Use the Template Wizard**

1. Open the file *[your initials]***13-4.xlt**.

2. Close the Template toolbar.

3. Choose Template Wizard from the Data menu. The Template Wizard - Step 1 of 5 dialog box appears. The template file *[your initials]***13-4.xlt** will be used to create a database template.

FIGURE 13-7
Template Wizard -
Step 1 of 5
dialog box

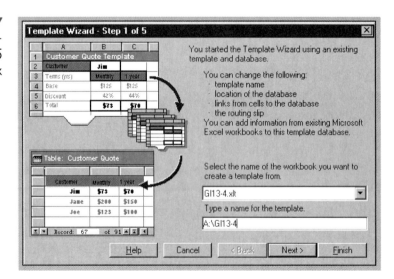

4. Key **A:\\[***your initials]***13-7t** in the Type a name for the template text box; click the Next button. The Template Wizard - Step 2 of 5 dialog box appears.

5. Key **A:[***your initials]***13-7d.xls** in the Type the location and name of the database text box; click the Next button. The Template Wizard - Step 3 of 5 dialog box appears. Because this database is new, the default name "Table1" in the Sheet text box will be used. The "No." heading represents the column that will receive the data when it is copied.

FIGURE 13-8
Worksheet cells and their corresponding fields in the database

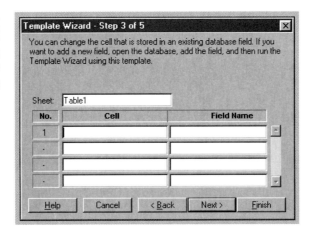

6. Click the first blank text box below the heading "Cell." Click the cell named data5 on the Invoice worksheet (the cell is next to the title "Name" on the worksheet). $E$12 is displayed in the text box.

7. Click the first blank text box below the heading "Field Name." Data5 is entered in the text box automatically because it is the cell name assigned to cell E12 on the worksheet.

8. Delete the data5 field name, and key **Customer**.

 NOTE: You can change this field name because the database is new; if you are using an existing database, however, you will not be allowed to change the field name.

9. Click the next blank text box below the heading "Cell" next to "No 2." Now click the cell named data11 on the Invoice worksheet (the cell is below the title "Qty" on the worksheet). $D$18 is displayed in the text box.

10. Click the next blank text box below the heading "Field Name." Data11 is entered in the text box automatically.

11. Delete the data11 field name, and key **Quantity**.

12. Click the next blank text box below the heading "Cell" next to "No 3." Click the cell named data12 on the Invoice worksheet (the cell is below the title "Description" on the worksheet). $E$18 is displayed in the text box.

13. Click the next blank text box below the heading "Field Name." Data12 is entered in the text box automatically.

14. Delete the data12 field name, and key **Description**.

15. Click the next blank text box below the heading "Cell" next to "No 4." Click the cell named data13 on the Invoice worksheet (the cell is below the title "Unit Price" on the worksheet). $K$18 is displayed in the text box.

16. Click the next blank text box below the heading "Field Name." Data13 is entered in the text box automatically.

17. Delete the data13 field name, and key **Price**. Click the Next button to display the Template Wizard - Step 4 of 5 dialog box.

18. Select the option "No, Skip It" as you do not want to add information from existing workbooks.

19. Click the Next button. The Template Wizard - Step 5 of 5 dialog box confirms that the template and database files have been created.

20. Click the Finish button as the data entry form is complete. The files are saved to their designated location.

21. Close the workbook without saving the changes.

EXERCISE | **13-7** | **Use the Template Form and Update the Database**

1. Open the template file *[your initials]***13-7t.xlt**.

2. Key the following customer information, beginning in named cell data2:

data2 **1351**
data3 **Callahan**
data5 **Mariner's Supplies**
data6 **40 Oceanway Drive**
data7 **West Palm Beach**
data8 **FL**
data9 **33405**
data10 **407-123-1234**

3. Select named cell data11, and key the following order information:

data11 **10**
data12 **Cover C-9087**
data13 **150**

4. Delete the text in the Fine Print and Farewell Statement text boxes.

5. Add your initials as a header, and then print the invoice.

6. Choose Save As from the File menu. Because you are saving data with this workbook for the first time, The Template File - Save to Database dialog box prompts you to either create a new record in the database or continue without updating the database.

FIGURE 13-9
Adding the just-entered record to the database

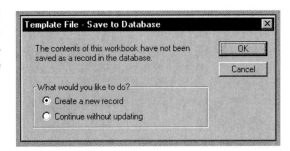

7. The option "Create a new record?" is already selected. Click OK. The Save As dialog box is displayed. Click Cancel, as you do not want to save each invoice you create.

NOTE: If you have already saved records from the worksheet (template form) to the database, the Template File - Save to Database dialog box presents a third option: update the existing record.

8. Close the workbook without saving the changes.
9. Open the file *[your initials]***13-7d.xls**. The data from the invoice you just created has been copied to the database in the designated fields.
10. Add your initials as a header, print the workbook, and then close it.

TIP: Once an Excel database file is created, you can use Excel's list management (database) features, such as sorting and filtering data, to analyze the information in the database. These features are covered in Unit 7: "Using Excel's Database Features."

COMMAND SUMMARY

FEATURE	BUTTON	MENU	KEYBOARD
Templates		File, New	Ctrl + N
Template Wizard		Data, Template Wizard	

Concepts Review

Each of the following statements is either true or false. Indicate your choice by circling **T** or **F**.

T F **1.** Any worksheet can become a template.

T F **2.** Templates can contain style elements, formatting, and boilerplate text, but not formulas.

T F **3.** Only two built-in templates are provided with the Excel software.

T F **4.** When you open a template file, only a copy of the file is opened to protect the original template.

T F **5.** When you create a template, it can be saved to any folder.

T F **6.** You can view a list of available built-in templates by clicking 🗋 on the Standard toolbar.

T F **7.** Built-in templates can be customized with your personal or company information.

T F **8.** When any of Excel's built-in templates is used, an automatic link to a database file is created.

Write the correct answer in the space provided.

1. Which Excel command displays a list of built-in templates?

_____

2. Which file extension is assigned to Excel template files?

_____

3. Which feature does Excel use in its built-in templates to provide you with information and assistance?

_____

4. Templates should be saved to which folder if they are to be accessed from the New dialog box?

_____

5. Which Excel command creates a template form from a worksheet and links cells to a database file?

_____

6. Which button on the Invoice toolbar is used to assign sequential numbering to the invoice number cell?

_____

7. When a template is customized, which button is used to save changes to a template?

_____

8. Which file extension does the database file normally have when you create a database linked to a template?

_____

CRITICAL THINKING

Answer these questions on a separate piece of paper. There are no right or wrong answers. Support your answers with examples from your own experience, if possible.

1. Give some examples of how a company could use Excel's built-in templates. In what ways would it be beneficial if the worksheet cells in the template were linked to a database file?

2. A company creates many worksheets for business and financial analysis. Can you think of any examples of worksheets, other than Excel's built-in templates, that can be converted to templates to assist in running a business and to help ensure documentation is consistent?

3. Excel's built-in templates are stored in the Spreadsheet Solutions sub-folder in the Templates folder. As you can set up your own filing system for customized template files, what folders would you create to store the template files? Does it make a difference where the folders are stored?

Skills Review

EXERCISE 13-8

Create a template from an existing workbook file.

1. Open the file **DunBud.xls**.
2. Clear cells B5 and B7, and cells B9 through D11.
3. Choose Save As from the File menu.
4. Key *[your initials]***13-8** in the File name text box.
5. Click the arrow to open the Save as type drop-down list box, and then click Template. The Save in text box displays the Templates folder.

6. Click the arrow to open the Save in drop-down list box, and then click 3½ Floppy (A:). For classroom purposes, student files are saved to the A: drive.

7. Click the Save button. When the file is saved as a template, Excel changes the file extension from .xls to .xlt.

8. Print and close the template file.

EXERCISE 13-9

Use a template to create a workbook file; enter data in the worksheet and save the data without changing the template file.

1. Open the file **DunBudT.xlt**.

2. In columns B, C, and D, key the following data:

B5	**Apr**	C4	**5%**	D4	**5.5%**
B6	**78,375**	C5	**May**	D5	**Jun**
B8	**52,250**	C10	**1,300**	D10	**1,200**
B10	**1,400**	C11	**300**	D11	**350**
B11	**250**	C12	**700**	D12	**700**
B12	**700**				

3. Choose File, Save As to save the worksheet as *[your initials]***13-9.xls**. Remember to change the Save As type to Microsoft Excel Workbook.

4. Close the workbook.

EXERCISE 13-10

Use a built-in template, customize it, and save it under a different filename.

1. Choose New from the File menu. Click the Spreadsheet Solutions Tab.

2. Open the Invoice template.

3. Click the Customize button.

4. Using the Name box (next to the formula bar) to locate cells, key the following data in the named cells shown below:

vital1	**DUNKIRK CANVAS CO.**
vital2	**12 RIVER ST.**
vital4	**BOSTON**
vital5	**MA**
vital6	**02205**
vital8	**(617) 555-4410**
vital9	**(617) 555-4411**

5. Click the Lock/Save Sheet button on the form.

6. Select the Lock and Save Template option in the dialog box.

7. Click the arrow to open the Save in box, and then click the 3½ Floppy (A:) disk drive.

8. In the File name box, key *[your initials]***13-10.xlt**. If the Save as type box does not show Templates, select Templates.

9. Click Save, and then click OK when the message appears describing how to access your new template.

10. Click the Invoice tab at the bottom of the form.

11. Add your name as a header, and then print the template.

12. Close the Invoice template file without saving the changes.

EXERCISE 13-11

Use the Template Wizard to create a template form from a worksheet and link it to a database file.

1. Open the file **Timecard.xls**.

2. Choose Template Wizard from the Data menu.

3. Key **A:***[your initials]***13-12t.xlt** in the Type a name for the template text box. Click the Next button.

4. Key **A:***[your initials]***13-12d.xls** in the Type the location and name of the database text box. Click the Next button.

5. In the Template Wizard - Step 3 of 5 dialog box, click the first blank text box below the "Cell" title. Click cell B4 on the worksheet; Timecard!$B$4 is displayed. Click the corresponding blank text box below the title "Field Name;" Date: is displayed.

6. Complete the next two cells and corresponding field names:

   Cell 2   **$A$6**   Field Name 2   **Name**
   Cell 3   **$G$6**   Field Name 2   **Hours Worked**

7. Click the Next button. In the Step 4 dialog box, choose No, skip it, and click the Next button.

8. Click the Finish button.

9. The template and database are set up for future use. Close the workbook.

10. Open the template file *[your initials]***13-11t.xlt** and key the following data in the cells indicated:

    B4   **1/7/97**
    A6   **Boyd**
    B6   **7:00 am**
    C6   **11:30 am**
    D6   **12:00 pm**
    F6   **4:00 pm**

11. Choose <u>S</u>ave As from the <u>F</u>ile menu. Click OK to create a new record in the database.

12. Choose the Cancel button. Print the worksheet, and then close the file without saving the changes.

13. Open the database file *[your initials]***13-11d.xls**. Jennifer Boyd's record has been added to the database. Add the filename as a header, and then print the workbook.

14. Close the workbook.

Lesson Applications

EXERCISE 13-12

Create a template from an existing worksheet file.

Dunkirk Canvas Company needs a template created from its current income statement worksheet.

1. Open the file **Income.xls** to display the workbook containing Dunkirk's current income statement.
2. Clear the contents of cells B4 through B10, cells C12 through C13, and cell C15. The formulas will remain intact.
3. Choose Save As from the File menu.
4. Key *[your initials]* **13-12** in the File name text box.
5. Choose Template from the Save file as type drop-down list box, and then choose the 3½ Floppy (A:) drive from the Save in list.
6. Click Save.
7. Print and close the template.

EXERCISE 13-13

Create a template from an existing worksheet and save it as a template file; enter data into the new template and save it as a worksheet file.

Dunkirk Canvas Company needs to create a new financial template from the model for the "Asset & Liability" report.

1. Open the file **Assets.xls**.
2. Copy the contents of the range D7:D11 to the range C7:C11. Copy the contents of the range D14:D16 to the range C14:C16.
3. Delete the contents of the ranges D7:D11 and D14:D16.
4. In cell C6, key **1997**
5. In cell D6, key **1998**
6. Save the file as a template with the name *[your initials]* **13-13.xlt**.
7. In the range D7:D11, key the following data:

   200,500

   40,220

   10,000

   900,400

   375,500

8. In cells D14:D16, key the following data:

500,000

300,500

475,254

9. Save the file as a workbook with the name *[your initials]***13-13.xls**.

10. Print and close the workbook.

EXERCISE 13-14

Create a customized template from a built-in Excel template.

Dunkirk Canvas Company would like to customize the Purchase Order template.

1. Choose New from the File menu. Click the Spreadsheet Solutions tab.

2. Click the Purchase Order template, and then click OK.

3. Click the Customize button at the upper right-hand corner of the form.

4. Using the Name box to locate cells, key the following information in the named cells located in the "Type Company Information Here" section of the purchase order:

vital1	**Dunkirk Canvas Company**
vital2	**14 River Street**
vital4	**Boston**
vital5	**MA**
vital6	**02205**
vital8	**617-555-4410**
vital9	**617-555-4411**

5. Scroll to the "Specify Default Purchase Order Information Here" section.

6. Click the *Click here if company information is same as "Ship to" information* check box to select it.

7. Key **VISA** in the Credit Card #1 text box.

8. Choose File, Save As, choose the "Continue without updating" option, and click OK.

9. Key *[your initials]***13-14** in the File name text box. Click the arrow to open the Save file as type list and choose Template.

10. Click the arrow to open the Save in list, and then choose 3½ Floppy (A:) drive. Click the Save button.

11. Click the Purchase Order tab.

12. Add your name to the header, print the template, and then close the file.

EXERCISE 13-15

Use the Template Wizard to create a database from an existing template; enter data in the new, database-linked template, and update the database file.

Dunkirk Canvas Company wants to use its existing Invoice template to create a new database-linked template that records customer names and addresses.

1. Open the file **Invoice2.xlt**.

2. Delete the 10 in the named cell NO in the upper right-hand corner of the form.

3. Choose Te*m*plate Wizard from the *D*ata menu.

4. At step 1, key **A:\[*your initials*]13-15t** for the template name.

5. At step 2, key **A:\[*your initials*]13-15d** for the database name.

6. At step 3, in the "No. 1 Cell" field, key **data5**. For the "No. 1 Field Name," key **Name**

7. In the "No.2 Cell" field, key **data6**. For the "No.2 Field Name," key **Address**

8. In the "No. 3 Cell" field, key **data7**. For the "No. 3 Field Name," key **City**

9. In the "No 4 Cell" field, key **data8**. For the "No. 4 Field Name," key **State**

10. In the "No. 5 Cell" field, key **data9**. For the "No. 5 Field Name," key **Zip**

11. At step 4, choose *N*o, skip it, and click *F*inish at step 5. The template is displayed once again.

12. Close the **Invoice2.xlt** file without saving.

13. Open your just-created template, *[your initials]***13-15t.xlt**.

14. Key the following customer information in the named cells:

    data2 **1352**

    data3 **Callahan**

    data5 **Jensen's Sailboats**

    data6 **Marina Drive**

    data7 **Myrtle Beach**

    data8 **SC**

    data9 **29577**

    data10 **803-555-6612**

15. Key the following order information in the named cells:

    data11 **20**

    data12 **Cover C-9088**

    data13 **100**

16. Delete the text in the Fine Print and Farewell Statement text boxes at the bottom of the invoice.

17. Choose Save <u>A</u>s from the <u>F</u>ile menu. Click OK. The record will be saved to the linked database **A:**[*your initials*]**13-15d.xls**.

18. Click <u>C</u>ancel when the Save As screen returns so as to not overwrite the new template with the just-entered data.

19. Add the filename as a header, print the template, and then close the workbook.

20. Open the new database file [*your initials*]**13-15d.xls**. The data from the invoice you entered should be displayed.

21. Widen the columns appropriately, add the filename as a header, and then print the worksheet.

22. Save the changes and close the workbook.

Unit 4 Applications

Create a worksheet using the functions IF, VLOOKUP, and TODAY; use text comments and date math in the formulas.

The owners of Dunkirk Canvas Company want to make sure that their employees receive an annual performance review. They need a worksheet that shows each employee's last review date and whether he or she is due for a review now.

1. Open the file **Reviews.xls**.

2. Select cell B5. Use the Function Wizard to write a formula using a VLOOKUP function. The function should look up the employee name in the table and return the review date. Remember to use absolute cell references in the formula where required so that it can be copied.

3. Copy the formula from cell B5 to cells B6 through B10. Format the cells in the Date format - m/d/yy.

4. Select cell C5. Write a formula using an IF function that determines whether the difference between =TODAY() and the date in cell B5 is greater than or equal to 365. If the answer is true, return the text comment "Yes" to cell C5. If the answer is false, return the text comment "No" to cell C5.

5. Copy the formula from cell C5 to cells C6 through C10. Note the review date answer in column C.

6. Save the workbook as *[your initials]***u4-1.xls**.

7. Print the worksheet.

8. Print a second version of the worksheet showing cell formulas. Make sure that the columns are wide enough to display the whole formula.

9. Close the workbook.

Use statistical functions COUNT, COUNTA, MIN, and MAX to analyze worksheet data; use logical functions with multiple conditions, text comments, and nesting.

The Dunkirk Canvas Company has sent out an employee survey regarding company benefits. Surveys have been returned and are now being reviewed. A worksheet is needed to analyze the survey results to determine the correct benefits plan for each employee.

1. Open the file **Survey.xls**.

2. Select cell F5, and then key the following information in cells F5 through I10 (some cells will be left blank):

FIGURE U4-1

	F	G	H	I
5	X	X	X	X
6		X		
7		X		X
8	X	X	X	X
9		X	X	X
10		X		

3. Select cell A12, and key **Count**. Apply bold formatting to cell A12.

4. Select cell E12, and write a formula using the COUNT function that counts the number of employees needing dependent coverage.

5. Select cell F12, and write a formula using the COUNTA function that counts the number of employees with co-insurance. Copy this formula to cells G12 through I12 to count the employees needing insurance in those categories.

6. Select cell J5. Write a formula using a nested IF function and multiple conditions to determine whether Plan A, B, C, or D would be appropriate for the employee. If cells G5 and H5 and I5 equal "X," then "Plan A" should be assigned; if not, create another IF statement. If cells G5 and H5 equal "X", then "Plan B" should be assigned; if not, create another IF statement. If cells G5 and I5 equal "X," then "Plan C" should be assigned; if not, "Plan D" should be assigned.

7. Copy the formula from cell J5 to cells J6 through J10.

8. Select cell A13, and key **Maximum**. Apply bold formatting to cell A13.

9. Select cell D13, and write a formula using the MAX function that determines the maximum life insurance policy written.

10. Select cell A14, and key **Minimum**. Apply bold formatting to cell A14.

11. Select cell D14, and write a formula using the MIN function that determines the minimum life insurance policy written.

12. Save the workbook as *[your initials]***u4-2.xls**.

13. Print and close the workbook.

APPLICATION 4-3

Create a worksheet with a lookup function that uses date math to compute discounts; include a cell note that describes appropriate data entry.

Dunkirk Canvas Company wants to use a worksheet to keep track of its accounts payable. Bills paid within 25 days of receipt receive a discount. The bills are date-stamped in the worksheet, and a VLOOKUP function determines the appropriate discount. Calculations determine the date that the invoice should be paid and the amount to be paid based on the discount.

1. Open the file **Payable.xls**.

2. Select cell C4. Create a cell note that provides information about the dates to be entered in column C. Key the following text for the cell note:

   Type the current date. Do not use the TODAY function.

    NOTE: A red marker appears in cell C4, indicating that a note is attached to the cell.

3. Point to cell C4 and display the cell note.

4. Select cell A5, and key the following data (as the cell note indicates, "current date" means to type in today's date in the format m/d/yy.):

FIGURE U4-2

	A	B	C	D	E
5	1250	Office, Inc.	*Current date*		250
6	1100	Materials, Inc.	*Current date*		575
7	1305	Regional Supply	*Current date*		990

5. Format the numbers in column E in Accounting format, with two decimal places.

6. Select cell D5. Write a formula that displays the due date for the invoice by adding 25 days to the date in cell C5. Copy the formula from cell D5 to cells D6 through D7.

7. Select cell F5 and determine the appropriate discount. Write a formula using the VLOOKUP function; the Lookup table is found in cells A23 through B26 of this worksheet. (Make sure to use absolute cell references when identifying the table_array so that the formula can be copied.)

8. Copy the formula from cell F5 to cells F6 through F7.

345

9. Format the numbers in column F in Percent format, with no zero decimal places.

10. Select cell G5. Write a formula that calculates the dollar amount of the discount and subtracts it from "Amount of Invoice." The dollar amount due should be displayed in cell G5.

11. Copy the formula from cell G5 to cells G6 through G7. Format the numbers in column G in Accounting format with two decimal places.

12. Left-align the invoice numbers in column A.

13. Select cell A3. Key a formula that will use the computer clock to display the current date and time. Each time the worksheet is accessed, the current date and time should be updated.

14. Save the workbook as *[your initials]*u4-3.xls.

15. Print the workbook, including the Note. Print a second version showing formulas. Exclude the Note from the second printout.

16. Close the workbook.

APPLICATION 4-4

Create worksheets using the NPER, PMT, and ROUND functions for analysis of a loan repayment schedule. Use a built-in template to create an amortization schedule; create a worksheet that calculates the number of payment periods for a savings schedule.

Dunkirk Canvas Company needs to buy several company cars, and a local bank has quoted an interest rate of 7% for a $20,000 loan for three years or an interest rate of 8% for a $20,000 loan for five years. The PMT financial function will be used to calculate the monthly payments and make a decision between the two loans. The built-in template Loan Manager will be used to create an amortization schedule showing each monthly payment. The company also needs to know whether $200 per month, placed in an investment account starting today and earning a specific interest rate, will enable it to save enough money to buy a car in a certain amount of time.

1. Open the file **Carloan.xls**.

2. In the PMT worksheet, key the following data:

B5	3	D5	5
B6	=B5*12	D6	=D5*12
B7	20,000	D7	20,000
B8	7%	D8	8%

3. Select cell B10. Use the PMT function to determine the monthly payment due at the end of the month.

4. Select cell B11. Use the PMT function to determine the monthly payment due at the beginning of the month.

5. Select cell D10. Use the PMT function to determine the monthly payment due at the end of the month.

6. Select cell D11. Use the PMT function to determine the monthly payment due at the beginning of the month.

7. Edit the formulas in cells D10 and D11 only, adding the ROUND function so that the answers are rounded to zero decimal places.

8. Save the workbook as *[your initials]***u4-4a.xls.** Print the worksheet.

9. Choose New from the File menu. Click the Spreadsheet Solutions tab. Open the Loan Manager template.

10. Using the Name box next to the formula bar, select the cell named "data1." Key the following data into the named cells indicated:

data1	**Home Bank**
data2	**20,000**
data3	**7%**
data4	**01/01/97**
data5	**3**
data6	**12**

11. Compare the Loan Manager payment of $617.54 to the result shown in cell B10 of the worksheet you created in step 1. The Loan Manager Summary information indicates that in three years you will pay out $22,231.51, with a total interest of $2,231.51.

12. Print the Loan Amortization Table.

13. Choose Save As from the File menu and save the workbook with the filename *[your initials]***u4-4b.xls**. Close the workbook.

14. In the NPER worksheet, key the following data:

B3 **6%**

B4 **$200**

B5 **$20,000**

15. Select cell B6 and write a formula using the NPER function that determines the number of periods it will take to save enough money to reach the $20,000 goal. The answer is displayed as a negative number.

16. Edit the formula in cell B6 to round the number to zero decimal places.

17. Key a new rate in cell B3, **7%,** and key a new payment amount in cell B4, **$500**.

18. Print the worksheet.

19. Save the workbook, and then close it.

APPLICATION 4-5

Create a worksheet that uses formulas with logical and statistical functions to compute operating expenses; convert the worksheet to a template; enter data in the new template.

Dunkirk Canvas Company needs a worksheet to track its actual annual operating expenses for use in budget analysis and planning. Formulas using the SUM, IF with multiple conditions, and AVERAGE functions should be used in the worksheet. Once the worksheet is set up, including the formulas, you will create a template. You will then use the template to start the 1997 operating expenses worksheet, entering January's data into the form.

The expense categories for the company are shown in Figure U4-3.

FIGURE U4-3

Expense Categories	January Expenses
Advertising	245
Depreciation - Equipment	800
Lease - Building	900
Insurance	500
Office Supplies	375
Salaries	45,250
Travel	400
Utilities	1,350

You can now create an operating expenses worksheet for Dunkirk Canvas Company. The months of the year and the individual expense categories should be the worksheet headings. You should total the expenses for each month. In addition, you need to calculate the average spent for the year for each expense category. Make sure error messages are not displayed in the formulas cells because data has not been filled in. (Hint: Have one of your conditions in your nested function test for the presence of 0.) Be creative in formatting the headings and numbers in the worksheet. You may need to use a smaller font and landscape orientation to fit all the information on one printed sheet. After completing the formulas, save the worksheet as a template with the filename *[your initials]***u4-5.xlt**. Print the template, using the filename as the header.

Once the template is developed, you can use it to enter the data for the January expenses as shown in Figure U4-3. Save the workbook with a new filename, *[your initials]***u4-5.xls,** so that you do not save the changes in the template file. Print the worksheet, and then close the workbook.

Multiple Worksheets and Advanced Printing

Feestone
Electronics

Electronic Company Goes High-Tech

Feestone Electronics is a nationwide distributor of business machines. Its main products are cellular phones, fax machines, copy machines, and postage meters.

Feestone has four regional offices. Each office writes its own invoices and keeps track of its own sales and inventory. The regional offices send reports to the main office each quarter. Craig Herman, the company's bookkeeper, has requested that the information be delivered as Excel files via e-mail so that he can easily consolidate the figures.

Craig has discussed this project at length with the regional managers. They're enthusiastic, but a little unsure of the process, so Craig needs to make the transition as easy as possible. He needs to receive the sales information in a specific form for the consolidation reports.

Craig needs to create the following worksheets for both the regional managers and for his own use:

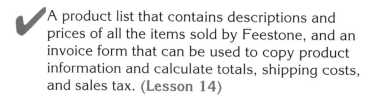

A product list that contains descriptions and prices of all the items sold by Feestone, and an invoice form that can be used to copy product information and calculate totals, shipping costs, and sales tax. **(Lesson 14)**

A worksheet for each region that is easy to use, and a consolidation sheet for the main office. **(Lesson 15)**

A national sales report that is attractively formatted and can be printed in convenient sections. **(Lesson 16)**

Working with Multiple Worksheets and Files

O B J E C T I V E S   After completing this lesson, you will be able to:

1. Manage worksheets.
2. Open multiple workbooks.
3. Arrange workbook windows.
4. Switch between open workbooks.
5. Copy and paste between open workbooks.

 Estimated Time: 1½ hours

As you know, Excel worksheets are contained in files called workbooks. A workbook can consist of 1 to 255 worksheets. Frequently, you may need to copy data from one worksheet to another in the same file. You may also need to work with information in multiple files. You already know how to navigate between worksheets. Now you will learn how to manage worksheets and navigate between workbooks.

Managing Worksheets

You can add and delete worksheets, change the sequence of worksheets, copy data between worksheets, edit multiple worksheets, and print a range of worksheets.

EXERCISE 14-1 Add and Delete Worksheets

Each new workbook opens with 16 worksheets named Sheet1 through Sheet16. You can add and delete worksheets by using the standard menu or the sheet tab shortcut menu.

1. Open the file **Emplist.xls**. This workbook contains data on five worksheets.

FIGURE 14-1
Sheet tab
shortcut menu

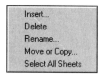

2. Right-click the Sheet3 worksheet tab. The sheet tab shortcut menu appears.

3. Choose the Insert command on the sheet tab shortcut menu. The Insert dialog box appears.

FIGURE 14-2
Insert dialog box

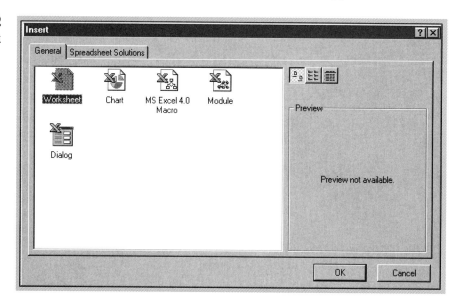

4. If necessary, click the General tab, click the Worksheet icon, and then click OK. A new worksheet called Sheet17 is inserted to the left of Sheet3.

5. Choose Worksheet from the Insert menu. A new worksheet called Sheet18 is inserted to the left of Sheet17.

6. Right-click the Sheet18 tab. The sheet tab shortcut menu appears.

7. Click Delete. An Excel Warning box appears, informing you that the selected sheets will be permanently deleted.

8. Click OK. Sheet18 is deleted.

9. With Sheet17 selected, choose Delete Sheet from the Edit menu, and click OK in the warning box. Sheet17 is deleted.

14-2 Move a Worksheet

Worksheets can be rearranged in a workbook by dragging the sheet tabs. Giving descriptive names to worksheets also helps you manage the information in them.

1. Double-click the Sheet5 tab, and then key **Total Staff** in the Rename Sheet dialog box.

2. Rename sheets 1 through 4 **NE**, **NW**, **SE**, and **SW**, respectively.

 TIP: Using short names for worksheet tabs lets you see more tabs at one time. Be sure your worksheet names are clear, however.

3. Position the mouse pointer on top of the tab named "Total Staff." Press and hold the mouse button. When you click a sheet tab, a worksheet icon appears attached to the pointer, and a black triangle indicates where the sheet will be inserted.

4. Drag it to the left until the pointer is positioned on top of the NE tab—the first tab in the workbook—and the small triangle is in front of that tab.

5. Release the mouse button. The sheet that will contain the employee list for all four offices is moved to the beginning of the workbook.

14-3 Copy and Paste Data Between Worksheets

You can use the Copy and Paste commands to build a worksheets without rekeying information. For instance, you can copy the lists of sales staff in each region into the Total Staff sheet.

1. Click the NE tab.

2. Select cells A6 through C9.

3. Click the Copy button on the Standard toolbar. A moving border surrounds the selected range.

4. Click the tab named "Total Staff." The worksheet's full title is "Total Sales Staff."

5. Click cell A6, and click the Paste button on the Standard toolbar to paste the Northeast data into the Total Sales Staff worksheet.

6. Click the NW tab, and select cells A6 through C9.

7. Right-click the selected range.

8. Click Copy on the shortcut menu.

9. Click the Total Staff tab, right-click cell A10, and click the Paste command on the shortcut menu. The data is copied to the Total Sales Staff worksheet.

 TIP: You can press [Enter] instead of choosing Paste. You can also use the Copy and Paste commands on the Edit menu and the shortcut key combinations [Ctrl]+[C] and [Ctrl]+[V].

10. Copy the names from the SE sheet to cell A14 in the Total Staff sheet, and from the SW sheet to cell A18 in the Total Staff sheet.

FIGURE 14-3
Total Staff worksheet
after pasting data

	A18	▼	LaConte				
	A	**B**	**C**	**D**	**E**	**F**	
4	Last Name	First Name	Employee ID Number				
5							
6	Abbott	Martha	27641				
7	Conrad	Leon	48962				
8	Garcia	Ramone	88976				
9	Winkler	Brian	63947				
10	Santos	Julia	61577				
11	Tellman	Lowell	55409				
12	Underwood	Marc	84692				
13	Zimmer	Joseph	33448				
14	Edwards	Victor	33284				
15	O'Connor	Patrick	62390				
16	Wang	Thomas	22546				
17	Young	Emma	47899				
18	LaConte	Danielle	65347				
19	Northridge	Leroy	44739				
20	Panzer	Max	87642				
21	Williams	Celeste	59833				
22							

Total Staff / NE / NW / SE / SW / Sheet6 / Sheet7 / Sheet

Ready   Sum=257561   NUM

EXERCISE **14-4** **Edit Multiple Worksheets**

You can select several worksheets, and then edit and format them all at once. This technique produces a uniform look. However, if you delete a row or column, it is deleted from all of the selected worksheets.

1. Click the Total Staff tab, hold down [Shift], and then click the SW tab. The five worksheets are selected. The word "[Group]" appears in the title bar.

 TIP: To select nonadjacent worksheets, click the first worksheet tab, hold down [Ctrl], and click the other worksheet tabs.

2. In the Total Staff sheet, make the column labels in row 4 bold and italic.

3. Resize column C to be nine characters wide.

4. Click the tabs for the rest of the selected worksheets to view the formatting changes, which are reflected in all selected worksheets.

5. Right-click the Total Staff tab, and choose Ungroup Sheets on the shortcut menu. Only the current sheet is selected now.

 TIP: You can also click any unselected sheet in the workbook to deselect the selected sheets.

EXERCISE 14-5 **Print a Range of Worksheets**

You may print all of the worksheets in a workbook or only selected worksheets.

1. Click the Total Staff tab, hold down Ctrl, and click the SW tab.

2. Press Ctrl + P. The Print dialog box appears.

3. In the Print What section, make sure the Selecte<u>d</u> Sheet(s) button is selected. If you wanted to print all five worksheets in the workbook, you would click the <u>E</u>ntire Workbook radio button in the Print What section.

4. Click OK. The Total Staff sheet and the SW worksheet are printed.

 TIP: To print selected worksheets, you can also click the Print button on the Standard toolbar.

5. Click the NE tab to deselect the selected worksheets.

6. Click the Total Staff tab, and save the workbook as *[your initials]***14-5.xls**.

7. Close the workbook.

Opening Multiple Workbooks

When you open a new or existing workbook, Excel opens a new workbook window. The new window covers the other windows, but they all remain open. As a result, you can easily move among them. You can also open multiple windows for one workbook if you need to view two different worksheets at the same time.

You can move to other windows by choosing them from the <u>W</u>indow menu. You can also display the next window by pressing Ctrl + F6 or the previous window by pressing Ctrl + Shift + F6.

EXERCISE 14-6 **Open Multiple Windows**

1. Close any open workbooks, and then open the file **Invoice.xls**.

355

2. Choose <u>N</u>ew Window from the <u>W</u>indow menu. A new window is opened and covers the first window. The title bar displays **Invoice.xls:2**, indicating that it is a second window containing that workbook.

FIGURE 14-4
Window menu listing open windows

Window
<u>N</u>ew Window
<u>A</u>rrange...
Hide
U̶n̶h̶i̶d̶e̶...
<u>S</u>plit
<u>F</u>reeze Panes
<u>1</u> Invoice.xls:1
✓ <u>2</u> Invoice.xls:2

All open windows are listed.

3. Choose <u>W</u>indow on the menu bar. The two open windows are listed at the bottom of the drop-down menu. The checkmark indicates the active window.

NOTE: Windows of the same workbook are just images of the same file. If you edit **Invoice.xls:1**, your changes will appear in **Invoice.xls:2** simultaneously.

4. Close the <u>W</u>indow drop-down menu.

5. With **Invoice.xls:2** still displayed, open the file **Custlist.xls**.

6. Choose <u>W</u>indow on the menu bar. The three open windows are listed at the bottom of the drop-down menu. The checkmark indicates that **Custlist.xls** is the active window.

7. Choose **Invoice.xls:1** from the <u>W</u>indow menu. The window containing the first version of **Invoice.xls** appears on top.

8. Open the <u>W</u>indow menu again. The checkmark appears next to **Invoice.xls:1**.

9. Close the <u>W</u>indow menu.

Arranging Workbook Windows

You will usually work with three or fewer windows at a time. The number of windows that you can open, however, is limited only by your computer's memory.

You can arrange windows as Tiled, Horizontal, Vertical, or Cascade. The best arrangement depends on the type of data and the layout of the worksheets. For example, if columns of data are being copied from one worksheet to another, use the vertical arrangement. If rows are being copied, use the horizontal arrangement.

EXERCISE **14-7** **Arrange Windows Using the Arrange Command**

1. Open the file **Shipping.xls**.

2. Choose <u>A</u>rrange from the <u>W</u>indow menu. The Arrange Windows dialog box appears.

3. Click <u>C</u>ascade, and then click OK. The windows are arranged diagonally so that you can see the workspace of the **Shipping.xls** workbook, but only the title bars and row selector buttons of the other windows behind it.

FIGURE 14-5
Cascading windows

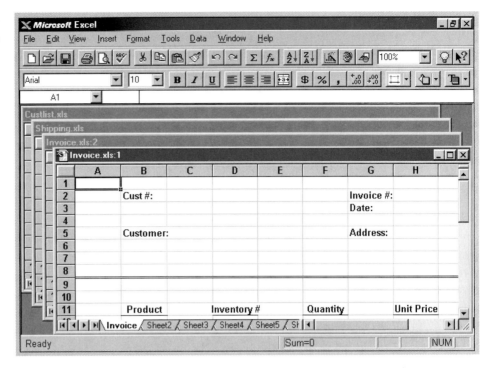

4. Click the title bar of the **Custlist.xls** window. The workbook moves to the front of the display, like a card pulled from the bottom of the deck and placed on top. It also covers the other title bars.

5. Click the title bar of the window containing **Invoice.xls:2**. Only one window can be active at any time.

6. Choose <u>W</u>indow from the menu bar, and then choose <u>A</u>rrange.

7. Click the <u>W</u>indows of Active Workbook check box, click <u>V</u>ertical, and click OK. The two windows containing **Invoice.xls** are arranged side by side.

8. Click the Sheet2 tab in **Invoice.xls:2**. The Invoice sheet is still displayed in the window containing **Invoice.xls:1**.

9. Choose <u>A</u>rrange from the <u>W</u>indow menu.

10. Clear the <u>W</u>indows of Active Workbook check box, click <u>T</u>iled, and click OK. All windows are tiled. Notice that only the active workbook displays control buttons in its title bar. (See Figure 14-6 on the next page.)

EXERCISE | **14-8** | **Maximize, Restore, and Minimize Windows**

You can expand an active workbook to its full size by double-clicking the title bar, or clicking the workbook Maximize button ▢. The Maximize button then becomes a Restore button ▣. Clicking ▣ displays the workbook in its previous, arranged size.

FIGURE 14-6
Tiled windows

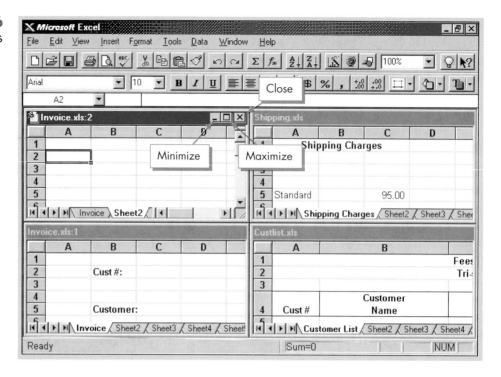

The Minimize button ▬ reduces a workbook to a title bar in the lower part of the Excel window. You may need to drag windows out of the way to find and restore a minimized workbook it. You also can choose a minimized workbook from the Window menu to restore it.

1. Click anywhere in the **Custlist.xls** window to activate it.

2. Click the worksheet Maximize button ▢. The window is displayed at full size. The Restore button replaces the Maximize button.

FIGURE 14-7
Maximized window

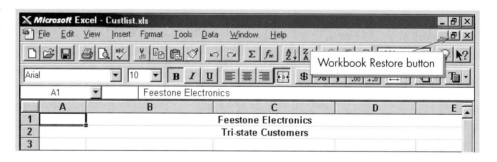
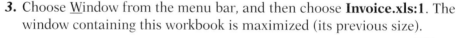

3. Choose Window from the menu bar, and then choose **Invoice.xls:1**. The window containing this workbook is maximized (its previous size).

4. To restore all windows to their tiled size, click the Restore button ⧉ in the workbook window.

5. Click anywhere in the window containing **Shipping.xls**, and then click the worksheet Minimize button ▬. The worksheet changes to a title bar and moves to the lower left corner of the Excel window behind another window.

6. Drag the window in the lower left corner over to the right. The minimized title bar for the workbook **Shipping.xls** becomes visible.

7. Minimize the window containing **Custlist.xls** (see step 5).

8. To restore the **Shipping.xls** icon to its previous size, click it and choose <u>R</u>estore from the shortcut menu.

FIGURE 14-8
Restoring a mini-
mized workbook

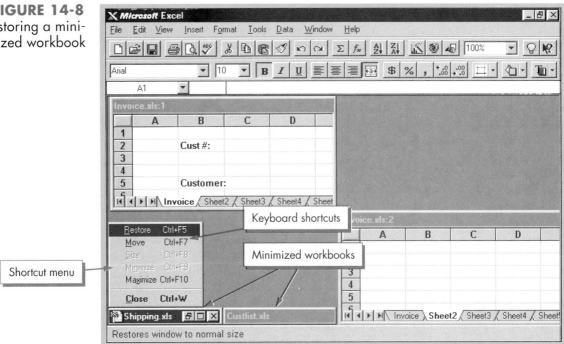

NOTE: In the active workbook, you can use the keyboard shortcuts Ctrl+F5 to restore, Ctrl+F10 to maximize, and Ctrl+W to close the window.

9. Restore the **Custlist.xls** window.

10. Arrange all windows horizontally.

Switching Between Open Workbooks

As you've seen, you can click a window to switch to it. You can also choose a window from the <u>W</u>indow menu or use keyboard shortcuts. Ctrl+Tab or Ctrl+F6 moves to the next open window. Shift+Ctrl+Tab or Shift+Ctrl+F6 moves to the previous open window.

EXERCISE 14-9 **Switch Between Open Windows**

1. Double-click the title bar of the **Shipping.xls** window. The window becomes active and is maximized to fill the screen.

2. Choose **Custlist.xls** from the <u>W</u>indow menu. The **Custlist.xls** window moves to the front.

3. Press Ctrl + Tab . The **Shipping.xls** window moves to the front.

4. Press Ctrl + Tab three more times to cycle through all open windows.

5. Choose **Invoice.xls:2** from the <u>W</u>indow menu.

6. Press Ctrl + W to close the **Invoice.xls:2** window.

Copying and Pasting Between Workbooks

You can copy and paste between workbooks, just as you can between worksheets. The same commands are used to transfer data to another workbook window. After you cut or copy a section to the Clipboard, switch documents, position the pointer where you want the copied data to go, and paste it.

EXERCISE 14-10 **Copy and Paste Between Workbooks**

1. Choose **Shipping.xls** from the <u>W</u>indow menu, and click the Minimize button.

2. Choose <u>A</u>rrange from the <u>W</u>indow menu, and then choose <u>V</u>ertical. **Custlist.xls** and **Invoice.xls** are arranged vertically.

3. Right-click cell A14 in **Custlist.xls**, and choose Copy from the shortcut menu.

4. Click anywhere in the **Invoice.xls** window to activate it.

5. Right-click cell D2 in **Invoice.xls**, choose Paste from the Shortcut menu, and press Esc to clear the moving border from the source cell.

6. Using the same method, copy cell B14 from **Custlist.xls** to cell D5 in **Invoice.xls**.

7. Select cells C14 and D14 in **Custlist.xls**, and then click 📋 on the Standard toolbar.

8. Click cell I5 in **Invoice.xls**, and then click 📋.

9. Move cell J5 in **Invoice.xls** to cell I6 by dragging it.

10. Close **Custlist.xls**, and open the file **Products.xls**.

11. Arrange the windows vertically.

12. Select cells A8 through E10 in **Products.xls**. Press Ctrl + C to copy them to the Clipboard.

13. Activate **Invoice.xls**, click cell B13, and then click 📋 or press Enter.

14. In **Invoice.xls**, select the Unit Prices in cells F13 through F15 and drag them to cells H13 through H15.

15. Close the **Products.xls** workbook.

16. Restore the file **Shipping.xls**, and then arrange the windows vertically.

17. Scroll to make cell J12 visible in **Invoice.xls**.

18. Using the drag-and-drop method, copy the charge for standard shipping from **Shipping.xls** to cell J28 in **Invoice.xls**.

19. Save **Invoice.xls** as *[your initials]***14-10.xls**.

EXERCISE **14-11** **Complete the Invoice**

1. Complete the invoice by entering the following data in the cells indicated:

I2	**20460**
I3	*[today's date]*
F13	**10**
F14	**2**
F15	**1**

2. Enter the formula **F13*H13** in cell J13, and then copy the formula down two cells.

3. Enter the SUM function in cells J26 and J29.

4. Format numbers in the Total column in comma style with no decimal places.

5. Set up the workbook to print without gridlines or row headings, and centered horizontally on the page.

6. Press Ctrl + Home, save the workbook as *[your initials]***14-11.xls**, and print the Invoice worksheet.

7. Close all workbooks.

 TIP: To close all workbooks with one menu command, press Shift, and then choose <u>C</u>lose All from the <u>F</u>ile menu.

COMMAND SUMMARY

FEATURE	BUTTON	MENU	KEYBOARD
Arrange windows		Window, Arrange	
Close all workbooks		Shift+File, Close	
Delete a worksheet		Edit, Delete Sheet	
Insert a worksheet		Insert, Worksheet	
Maximize window	▫		Ctrl + F10
Minimize window	_		Ctrl + F9
Open second workbook window		Window, New	
Restore a window	▣		Ctrl + F5
Switch to next window		Window, name	Ctrl + Tab or Ctrl + F6
Switch to previous window		Window, name	Shift + Ctrl + Tab or Shift + Ctrl + F6

USING HELP

If you often had to work with several windows open, you might become tired of constantly opening and arranging them. In Excel, you can save a workspace.

To find out more about workspaces, follow these steps to look up topics in Excel's Help:

1. Choose Answer Wizard from the Help menu.

2. Key **workspace** in the Type your request text box, and click Search.

3. In the "Tell Me About" section in the Select a topic text box, display the topic "What is a workspace file?"

4. After reading the definition, click Help Topics at the top of the Help window to return to the Answer Wizard.

5. Click Search. In the "How Do I" section, display the topic "Create and save a workspace file."

6. When you're finished reading the steps, close the Help window.

Concepts Review

Each of the following statements is either true or false. Indicate your choice by circling **T** or **F**.

T   F   **1.** To delete a worksheet, you must first move it so that it becomes the last worksheet in the workbook.

T   F   **2.** To edit multiple worksheets, you select the worksheets to be modified and then make your changes to one of the selected sheets.

T   F   **3.** You can print only selected sheets in a workbook, but they must be next to one another.

T   F   **4.** If you are copying columns of data from one workbook window to another, the best window arrangement is horizontal.

T   F   **5.** Tiling windows is a good option when you have many workbooks open and you need to see all of them at the same time.

T   F   **6.** To minimize a workbook, click the Minimize button in the workbook window.

T   F   **7.** After switching to an open window using the keyboard or menu commands, you must click in it to make the window active.

T   F   **8.** You can use the same techniques to copy data between workbooks as you do to copy data between worksheets.

Write the correct answer in the space provided.

1. What indicates the position of a worksheet tab while you are moving it?

_____

2. Which key do you hold down while clicking worksheet tabs to select nonadjacent worksheets?

_____

3. Which window arrangement displays open windows in a grid, both horizontally and vertically?

_____

4. Which window arrangement displays the open windows diagonally, showing only the title bars and row selector buttons of the nonactive windows?

_____

5. Which is the keyboard combination to switch to the next open workbook?

_____

6. Which command do you choose to arrange open workbooks on the screen?

_____

7. How many workbooks can you open at the same time?

_____

8. When two workbooks are open, which window arrangement has the same effect as the tiling option?

_____

CRITICAL THINKING

Answer these questions on a separate piece of paper. There are no right or wrong answers. Support your answers with examples from your own experience, if possible.

1. Excel provides several ways to arrange open workbook windows, including minimizing them. Discuss the advantage of each method. Why would you prefer one arrangement to another? Would you ever resize the windows manually? Why?

2. In Excel, you can rename worksheets and workbooks. In Windows, you can create folders to contain workbooks. Name and discuss situations in which good file management could be important.

3. Copying data from one worksheet to another and from one workbook to another is easy to do. People generally understand that plagiarizing words from a published book directly into something you are writing is wrong, both morally and legally. What about copying spreadsheet structures, formatting, and formulas from someone else's worksheet into your own? Is it the same as copying words? Consider that some worksheets are standard in business and existed long before electronic spreadsheets were used.

Skills Review

EXERCISE 14-12

Add and delete worksheets, rename a worksheet, move a worksheet, copy and paste data between worksheets, edit multiple worksheets, and print a range of worksheets.

1. Open the file **Invoice2.xls**.

2. Add and delete worksheets by following these steps:

    a. Click the Shipping worksheet tab.

    b. Choose Worksheet from the Insert menu.

    c. Right-click the Sheet1 worksheet tab.

    d. Choose the Insert command on the sheet tab shortcut menu.

    e. If necessary, click the General tab, click the Worksheet icon, and click OK.

    f. Click the Sheet1 tab, and choose Delete Sheet, from the Edit menu.

    g. Click OK in the Warning box.

    h. Right-click on the Sheet2 tab, choose the Delete command on the sheet tab shortcut menu, and then click OK.

3. Rename Sheet3 as **Invoice1**, Sheet4 as **Invoice2**, and Sheet5 as **Invoice3**.

4. Drag the Invoice3 sheet to the right of the Shipping sheet.

5. Copy data from the Customer List worksheet to the Invoice3 worksheet by following these steps:

    a. Click the Customer List sheet tab.

    b. Select cells A11 and B11, and then click 🗐.

    c. Click the Invoice3 sheet.

    d. Click cell D2, and then click 🗐.

    e. Drag cell E2 to cell D5.

    f. Copy cells C11 through D11 on the Customer List sheet to the Clipboard.

    g. Paste the contents of the Clipboard to cell I5 in the Invoice3 sheet.

    h. In the Invoice3 sheet, drag cell H5 to cell I6.

6. Copy the standard shipping charge from cell C4 in the Shipping worksheet to cell J28 in the Invoice3 sheet.

7. In the Invoice3 sheet, enter **20478** in cell I2 and enter today's date in cell I3.

8. Edit a group of worksheets by following these steps:

    a. With the sheet named Invoice3 selected, press and hold [Shift], and then click the sheet tab of the Invoice2 worksheet.

    b. Format cell J29 in currency style with two decimal places.

    c. Widen column J to display the number.

    d. Click the Invoice2 and Invoice1 sheet tabs to make sure that column J is wide enough to accommodate the formatting in cell J29.

9. Click the Customer List tab to deselect the worksheets. Save the workbook as *[your initials]***14-12.xls**.

10. Select the three Invoice sheets again, and choose Print from the File menu.

11. With the Selecte<u>d</u> Sheets option button selected, click OK.

12. Close the workbook.

EXERCISE 14-13

Open multiple workbooks, arrange workbook windows, arrange multiple windows of the same workbook, maximize a window, and restore a window.

1. Open the following files: **Westcott.xls**, **Automatn.xls**, **Allcity.xls**, and **Stageup.xls**.

 TIP: In the Open dialog box, you can Ctrl+click to select multiple filenames, and then click Open to open them all.

2. Choose <u>A</u>rrange from the <u>W</u>indow menu, click the <u>H</u>orizontal option button, and click OK.

3. Arrange the windows using the <u>C</u>ascade option.

4. Arrange multiple windows of the same workbook by following these steps:

    a. Click the **Automatn.xls** title bar.

    b. Choose <u>N</u>ew Window from the <u>W</u>indow menu.

    c. With **Automatn.xls:2** active, choose <u>N</u>ew Window from the <u>W</u>indow menu again.

    d. Choose <u>A</u>rrange from the <u>W</u>indow menu, and check the <u>W</u>indows of Active Workbook box.

    e. Click the <u>T</u>iled option button, and then click OK.

5. Maximize a worksheet and enter data by following these steps:

    a. Click the **Automatn.xls:3** window, and then click the worksheet Close button.

    b. Click the **Automatn.xls:2** window, and then click the worksheet Close button.

    c. Choose <u>A</u>rrange from the <u>W</u>indow menu, and clear the <u>W</u>indows of Active Workbook check box.

    d. Make sure the <u>T</u>iled option button is still selected, and click OK.

    e. Click the Maximize button in the **Automatn.xls** worksheet.

    f. Key **Feestone Electronics** in cell A1.

    g. Click cell A2, and choose <u>I</u>nsert, <u>R</u>ows on the menu bar.

    h. Key **Invoice** in cell A2.

    i. Click cell A3, and choose <u>I</u>nsert, <u>R</u>ows on the menu bar.

6. Click the **Automatn.xls** worksheet Restore button to display the tiled arrangement.

7. Copy data between open workbooks by following these steps:

a. Click in the **Allcity.xls** window to activate it, click cell A2, and insert two rows.

    b. Insert two rows above row 2 in the **Stageup.xls** and **Westcott.xls** windows.

    c. Select cells A1 and A2 in the **Automatn.xls** window, and click 📋.

    d. Click in the **Allcity.xls** window to activate it, click cell A1, and click 📋.

    e. Click in the **Stageup.xls** window to activate it, click cell A1, and click 📋.

    f. Paste the contents of the Clipboard to cell A1 in **Westcott.xls**.

8. Save and print the workbooks by following these steps:

    a. Save **Westcott.xls** as *[your initials]***14-13a.xls**, and then click 🖨.

    b. Click in the **Stageup.xls** window, save it as *[your initials]***14-13b.xls**, and then click 🖨.

    c. Click in the **Allcity.xls** window, save it as *[your initials]***14-13c.xls**, and then click 🖨.

    d. Click in the **Automatn.xls** window, save it as *[your initials]***14-13d.xls**, and then click 🖨.

9. Close all open workbooks.

EXERCISE 14-14

Switch between open workbooks.

1. Open the following files: **Westcot2.xls**, **Automat2.xls**, **Allcity2.xls**, and **Stageup2.xls**.

2. Choose **Allcity2.xls** from the <u>W</u>indow menu.

3. Press Ctrl + Tab three times to make **Westcot2.xls** active.

4. Format cells A1 and A2 by following these steps:

    a. In the **Westcot2.xls** window, format cells A1 and A2 as 12-point bold and center them across columns A through K.

    b. Press Ctrl + Tab.

    c. In the **Allcity2.xls** window, format cells A1 and A2 as 12-point bold and center them across columns A through K.

    d. Repeat steps b and c to activate the **Stageup2.xls** and **Automat2.xls** windows and format cells A1 and A2 in those workbooks.

5. Save and print the workbooks by following these steps:

    a. Choose <u>A</u>rrange from the <u>W</u>indow menu, click the <u>C</u>ascade option button, and click OK.

    b. Save **Automat2.xls** as *[your initials]***14-14a.xls**, click 🖨, and click the worksheet Close button.

c. Click in the **Westcot2.xls** window, save it as *[your initials]***14-14b.xls**, click 🖨, and click the worksheet Close button.

    d. Click in the **Allcity2.xls** window, save it as *[your initials]***14-14c.xls**, click 🖨, and click the worksheet Close button.

    e. Click in the **Stageup2.xls** window, save it as *[your initials]***14-14d.xls**, click 🖨, and click the worksheet Close button.

EXERCISE 14-15

Arrange windows, and copy and paste between open workbooks.

    1. Open the files **Stageup3.xls** and **Allcity3.xls**.

    2. In the **Allcity3.xls** worksheet, insert a row above row 31.

    3. In cell H31, key **1 year service contract**.

    4. In cell J31, key **150**. Format it in comma style with two decimal places, if necessary.

    5. Choose <u>W</u>indow, <u>A</u>rrange from the menu bar, click the <u>V</u>ertical option button, and click OK.

    6. Click in the **Stageup3.xls** window to activate it.

    7. Insert a row above row 31 in the **Stageup3.xls** worksheet.

    8. Click in the **Allcity3.xls** window to activate it.

    9. Copy data from one workbook to another by following these steps:

        a. Copy cells H31 through J31 in the **Allcity3.xls** worksheet.

        b. Click the **Stageup3.xls** window to activate it.

        c. Right-click cell H31 in **Stageup3.xls**.

        d. Choose Paste from the shortcut menu that appears.

    10. Save **Stageup3.xls** as *[your initials]***14-15a.xls**, click 🖨, and close the workbook.

    11. Save **Allcity3.xls** as *[your initials]***14-15b.xls**, click 🖨, and close the workbook.

Lesson Applications

Arrange windows, switch between windows, copy data from one worksheet to an-other, and format and print a group of worksheets.

Complete the invoice for Electronic Discount using information in several worksheets.

1. Open the file **Invoice3.xls**.

2. Open a second window of this workbook.

3. Arrange the two workbooks vertically.

4. In the Invoice sheet, complete the customer information for Electronic Discount by copying from Figure 14-9 and the Customer List sheet.

FIGURE 14-9

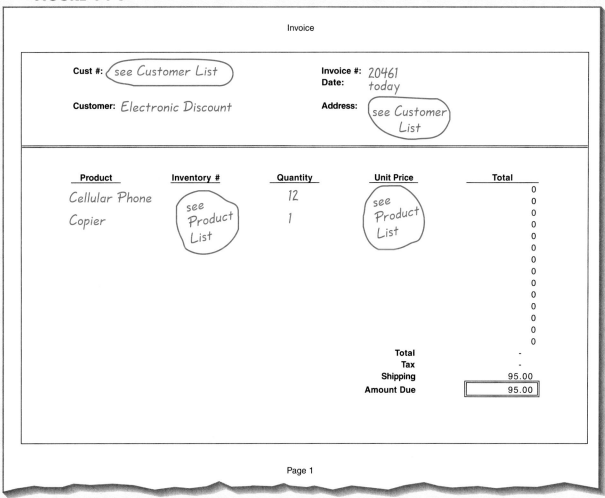

Invoice

Cust #:	see Customer List		Invoice #:	20461
Customer:	Electronic Discount		Date:	today
			Address:	see Customer List

Product	Inventory #	Quantity	Unit Price	Total
Cellular Phone	see Product List	12	see Product List	0
Copier		1		0
				0
				0
				0
				0
				0
				0
				0
				0
				0
				0
				0

Total	-
Tax	-
Shipping	95.00
Amount Due	95.00

Page 1

5. Complete the order information by copying from Figure 14-9 and the Product List sheet.

   6. Delete the unnecessary formulas in the "Total" column.

   7. Check the formulas to verify "Amount Due."

   8. Select the Invoice and Product List sheets. Print them in landscape orientation, centered both vertically and horizontally.

   9. Save the workbook as *[your initials]***14-16.xls**.

  10. Select the Invoice and the Product List sheets, and print them only.

  11. Close all open windows.

EXERCISE 14-17

Open multiple workbooks, arrange windows, switch between windows, copy and paste data between workbooks, and maximize a window.

Complete a worksheet that totals product sales by copying data from several workbooks.

   1. Open the following files: **Totprods.xls**, **Automatn.xls**, **Allcity.xls**, and **Westcott.xls**.

   2. Tile the windows.

   3. Copy the quantities from the three invoice worksheets to the appropriate cells in the **Totprods.xls** workbook. For instance, copy cells F13 and F14 in **Allcity.xls** to cells B4 and B5 in **Totprods.xls**.

   4. Maximize the **Totprods.xls** window.

   5. Use Σ in cells E4 through E7 to sum the data in the four columns to the left of each cell.

   6. Key **Total** in cell A9, and format it as bold and right-aligned.

   7. Use Σ in cell E9 to sum the subtotals in rows 4 through 7.

   8. Format cells B4 through D7 as 12-point type.

   9. Save the workbook as *[your initials]***14-17.xls**, and print it.

  10. Close all workbooks.

EXERCISE 14-18

Open multiple workbooks, arrange workbook windows, switch between open workbooks, and copy data from one workbook to another.

Feestone Electronics does not think that its analysis of total products is as useful as possible. Create a worksheet that lists not only the quantity of each product, but also the total sales for each product.

1. Open the files **Totprod2.xls** and **Products.xls**.

2. In **Totprod2.xls**, copy the three rows that are below "Cell phones" and insert them below each of the other products. Each product should be followed by a blank row, a "Quantity" row, and a "Total Dollars" row.

3. Format the worksheet to print centered horizontally with gridlines.

4. Move the quantities to the correct rows.

5. Enter 0 in every cell in the "Quantity" rows that does not contain a quantity for a product.

6. Copy the unit prices from **Products.xls** to the first cell directly below each product name (like cell A5) in **Totprods.xls**.

 TIP: Arrange windows vertically, and freeze panes in **Products.xls** to display column A beside column E.

7. Format the cells containing the unit prices in **Totprods.xls** as 12-point type in currency style.

 TIP: Use the Format Painter button 🖋 to copy styles.

8. In the "Total Dollars," rows enter formulas to multiply the quantity of each product by its unit price.

 TIP: Use an absolute or mixed reference for the unit price.

9. Format the "Total Dollars" rows in comma style.

10. Sum the values in the "Total Dollars" rows by using the AutoSum function in the appropriate cells in column E.

11. Check the formula in cell E21, and edit it to sum only the dollar values in column E.

12. Format cell E21 in currency style with a box border.

13. Save the workbook as *[your initials]***14-18.xls**, and then print it.

14. Close all workbooks.

Insert a new worksheet, rename a worksheet, open a new workbook, switch between open workbooks, and copy and paste data between workbooks.

For the month of December, Feestone Electronics hires extra sales staff to help meet the increased demand for its products. The payroll for the temporary staff has to be entered and calculated separately.

1. Open the file **Emplist2.xls**.

2. Insert a new worksheet to the left of the Northeast worksheet.

3. Copy the worksheet title and column heads from one of the other sheets to the new worksheet. Resize the columns in the new worksheet to be the same size as in the other worksheets.

4. Edit the title in row 2 to **December Temporary Sales Staff**

5. Enter the following names and ID numbers into the new worksheet. Use the same format as the names in the other worksheets in the file.

Last Name	First Name	Employee ID Number
Adams	**Julia**	**90123**
Bronfman	**Harvey**	**90124**
Castleman	**Leonard**	**90125**
Daly	**Maureen**	**90126**
Johns	**Lisa**	**90127**
Franks	**Waldo**	**90128**
Meth	**Zena**	**90129**
O'Reilly	**Mcgan**	**90130**
Petersen	**Irene**	**90131**
Wagner	**Charlotte**	**90132**

6. Rename the worksheet tab **Temp Staff**

7. Save this file as *[your initials]***14-19a.xls**.

8. Open a new workbook.

9. Create a worksheet that lists each temporary staff member's name, number of hours worked, and wages due. All temporary staff are paid at the rate of $9.50 per hour. Everyone except Maureen Daly and Waldo Franks worked 82 hours. Maureen Daly and Waldo Franks each worked 105 hours.

10. Calculate the wages due for each individual.

11. Calculate the total payroll for the temporary staff.

12. Give this worksheet the title **Temporary Sales Staff Payroll**

13. Format the entire worksheet attractively.

14. Save this workbook as *[your initials]***14-19b.xls**.

15. Print the Temp Staff worksheet in *[your initials]***14-19a.xls** and the *[your initials]***14-19b.xls** workbook, and then close the files.

Consolidating Worksheets and Exchanging Data

OBJECTIVES

After completing this lesson, you will be able to:

1. Link multiple files through formulas.
2. Design worksheets for consolidation.
3. Create the consolidated worksheet.
4. Protect files.

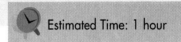

Estimated Time: 1 hour

In Excel, you can link worksheets and workbooks, so that changes in one place are reflected in another place automatically. You can also create a consolidated worksheet—one that automatically summarizes data from other sources.

Linking Multiple Files through Formulas

You can include ranges from other worksheets or workbooks in a formula. References to such cells are called *dynamic links* (or "hot links"). Excel keeps track of the references for you. An *external reference* points to a different workbook. An *internal reference* points to different worksheet within the same workbook.

A *dependent worksheet* uses data from another worksheet, known as the *source worksheet*. Source workbooks do not have to be opened after the links are created.

External references begin with the filename in brackets([]). Their cell references are absolute by default:

[external filename]worksheet name!absolute cell reference
[INVOICES.XLS]AUTOMATION!$A$1

Internal references begin with the worksheet name in single quotation marks. Notice that the exclamation point separates the worksheet name from the cell reference:

'internal worksheet name'!cell reference
'AUTOMATION'!A1

EXERCISE 15-1 Use Paste Link

Feestone Electronics wants an Invoice Analysis that shows the average unit price for each invoice. To perform this analysis, you must first link the customer names from the Invoices to the Invoice Analysis.

1. Open the files **Invoices.xls** and **Average.xls**, and arrange them horizontally.

2. In **Invoices.xls**, select cell D5 in the Automation worksheet and copy it.

 TIP: To select a cell in another window quickly, double-click it. The first click activates the window, and the second click selects the cell.

3. In **Average.xls**, select cell A4. Choose Paste Special from the Edit menu. The Paste Special dialog box appears.

4. Click the Paste Link button. The formula bar displays the external reference to cell D5 in the Automation worksheet of **Invoices.xls**.

FIGURE 15-1
Linking data between worksheets

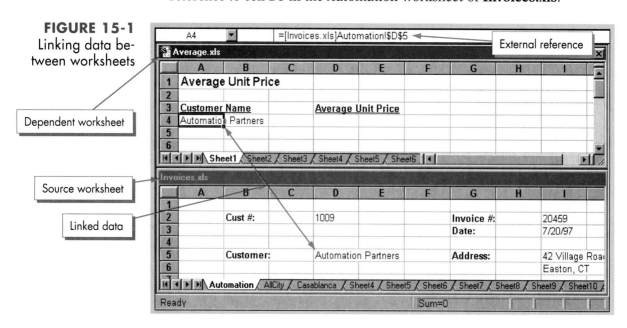

5. Press [Esc] to remove the moving border that surrounds cell D5.

6. In **Invoices.xls**, key **Westcott** in cell D5 and press [Enter]. Cell A4 in **Average.xls** is updated automatically.

7. Click the AllCity worksheet tab, and copy the contents of cell D5 to the Clipboard.

8. In **Average.xls**, select cell A5, choose Paste Special from the Edit menu, and click Paste Link. The contents of cell D5 in the AllCity worksheet are linked to the **Average.xls** workbook.

9. Paste Link the contents of cell D5 in the Casablanca worksheet in the **Invoices.xls** workbook to cell A6 in the **Average.xls** workbook.

 TIP: You can right-click the target cell and choose Paste Special from the shortcut menu.

EXERCISE | 15-2 | **Create a Link with Formulas**

A dynamic link can refer to a single label or to a range of cells within a formula. In this exercise, you will average the unit prices for each invoice and then average the invoice totals.

1. In **Average.xls**, key **=average(** in cell D4.

2. In the Automation worksheet in the **Invoices.xls** workbook, select cells H13 through H15, and press [Enter]. Cell D4 is updated with the average unit price from the Automation invoice. Notice that the formula contains brackets that identify the workbook name and an exclamation point that separates the worksheet name from the range address.

FIGURE 15-2
Linking worksheets with an external reference formula

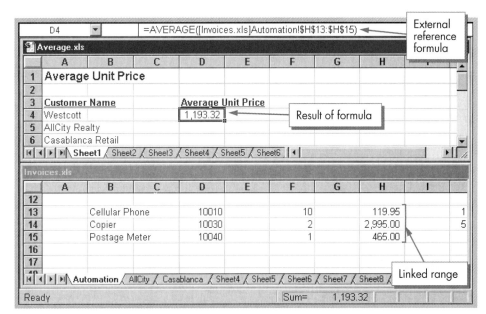

375

3. In **Average.xls**, key **=average(** in cell D5.

4. In **Invoices.xls** in the AllCity worksheet, select cells H13 through H14, and press Enter.

5. In **Average.xls**, use the same steps to enter the following formula in cell D6: **=AVERAGE([Invoices.xls]Casablanca!$H$13:$H$15)**

6. In **Average.xls**, key **Total Average Invoice** in cell A8. Make the text bold.

7. In **Invoices.xls**, open a second and third window of the workbook (choose New Window from the Window menu twice).

8. Choose Arrange from the Window menu, select the Tiled option, and click OK. The three windows containing **Invoices.xls** and the window containing **Average.xls** appear tiled on the screen.

9. In the first **Invoices.xls** window, click the Automation tab, and scroll until you can see cell J29.

TIP: To move to another worksheet, use the worksheet tab scroll buttons at the bottom left corner of the worksheet, if necessary. You can also choose a worksheet from the shortcut menu by right-clicking a worksheet tab scroll button.

10. In the second **Invoices.xls** window, click the AllCity tab and scroll until you can see cell J29.

11. In the third **Invoices.xls** window, scroll until you can see cell J29 of the Casablanca worksheet.

12. In **Average.xls**, key **=average(** in cell D8.

13. Double-click cell J29 in the Automation worksheet.

14. Key a comma in the formula, and then double-click cell J29 in the AllCity worksheet.

15. Key a comma, double-click cell J29 in the Casablanca worksheet, and press Enter. The formula with references to three different worksheets is complete.

16. Maximize the **Average.xls** workbook window, press Ctrl + Home, and resize column D to accommodate the data in cell D8. The finished Invoice Analysis contains four formulas with external references.

17. Save the **Average.xls** workbook as *[your initials]***15-2.xls**, and print it.

18. Close all workbooks. Do not save changes to **Invoices.xls**.

Designing Worksheets for Consolidation

You can design worksheets so that people in different departments can record data in the same way. The worksheets can then be consolidated as long as common data items appear in the same positions or if they have common row or column labels.

EXERCISE 15-3 **Copy the Base Form with Fill Across Worksheets**

In general, the source worksheets and the consolidated worksheet should resemble one another. The F<u>i</u>ll Across Worksheets command from the <u>E</u>dit menu can help keep content and formats consistent.

1. Open the file **Secndqtr.xls**.

2. Rename sheets 2, 3, 4, and 5 **Northwest**, **Southeast**, **Southwest**, and **Consolidated Report**, respectively.

3. Group all five sheets. (Hint: Activate the first sheet and Shift+click the last sheet tab.)

4. Select cells A1:E12 on the Northeast sheet.

FIGURE 15-3
Fill Across
Worksheets
dialog box

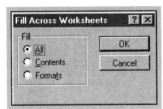

5. Choose F<u>i</u>ll from the <u>E</u>dit menu, and choose <u>A</u>cross Worksheets from the cascading menu. The Fill Across Worksheets dialog box appears.

6. Make sure that the <u>A</u>ll option button is selected, and then click OK.

7. Examine the worksheets to review the copied material.

8. With the five sheets still selected, widen column A to fit the labels.

9. Format all five sheets to print centered horizontally. (Hint: Select Set<u>u</u>p from the <u>F</u>ile menu.)

10. Ungroup the sheets. (Hint: Right-click a tab to use the shortcut menu.)

11. Change the title in cell A1 in the Northwest sheet to **Northwest** and change the name in cell A3 to **Adrian Needlehoffen**. The copied sheets still have the same data as the Northeast sheet.

12. Change the title in the Southeast sheet to **Southeast** and the name to **John Frisbee**.

13. Change the title in the Southwest sheet to **Southwest** and the name to **Jamaica Martin**.

14. Change the title in the Consolidated Report sheet to **Consolidated Report**, and delete the name Holly Maplethorpe.

15. Save the file as *[your initials]***15-3.xls**.

Creating the Consolidated Worksheet

A *consolidation table* summarizes the data from one or more source ranges. Placing your table in a separate worksheet—a *consolidated worksheet*—makes it easy to find. Source ranges can be on the same worksheet as the consolidation table or in different workbooks. When you consolidate the source data, you apply a summary function, such as Sum, to create the summary data.

Data can be consolidated as long as common data items appear in identical positions or have common row or column labels.

EXERCISE 15-4 Consolidate Data Using Labels

In the last exercise, you created four regional worksheets and one worksheet for consolidating them. Because the row labels are identical, you can use these worksheets to create the consolidation table. The area for the consolidation table, however, must be blank.

1. Delete the row labels and data in the Consolidated Report worksheet. (Select cells A7 through D11, and press Delete to clear the cells.)

2. Choose Consolidate from the Data menu. The Consolidate dialog box appears, with Sum being the default function for the Consolidate command.

3. Drag the Consolidate dialog box out of the way (to the top right of the screen).

4. With the insertion point in the Reference text box, click the Northeast tab, select the row labels and the data (cells A7 to D11), and click Add in the dialog box. The absolute reference Northeast!$A$7:$D$11 is added to the All References text box.

FIGURE 15-4
Consolidate
dialog box

Consolidate	? X
Function:	OK
Sum ▼	Close
Reference:	
Northeast!$A$7:$D$11	Browse...
All References:	
Northeast!$A$7:$D$11	Add
	Delete
Use Labels In	
☐ Top Row	
☐ Left Column ☐ Create Links to Source Data	

5. Add the same range for the Northwest, Southeast, and Southwest worksheets. Excel assumes that you wish to select the same range as in the Northeast worksheet and surrounds it with a moving border.

6. Check the Left Column box in the Consolidate dialog box, and then click OK. Excel consolidates the data. The Consolidate command has correctly incorporated labels and data.

7. Click anywhere on the Consolidated Report worksheet to deselect the cells.

EXERCISE 15-5 Consolidate Data by Position

Because the data elements in each worksheet appear in identical locations, you can also consolidate by position. You don't have to select labels, allowing you to protect those labels later. The consolidation range must be blank, as before.

1. In the Consolidated Report worksheet, select cells B7 through D11. Press Delete to clear the consolidation range.

2. Choose Consolidate from the Data menu.

3. To define a new consolidation, select each of the previous cell references in the All References text box and click Delete.

 NOTE: The Consolidate command uses previously defined references, so you must delete old references if your ranges change.

4. Click the Reference text box, so you can select a range in a worksheet.

5. Click the Northeast tab, select cells B7 through D11, and then click Add in the Consolidate dialog box.

6. Add the same range for the Northwest, Southeast, and Southwest worksheets.

FIGURE 15-5
Consolidated data

	A	B	C	D	E
	B7	▼	1160		
1	Consolidated Report				
2	2nd Quarter				
3					
4					
5	Products	April	May	June	Total
6					
7	Cellular Phones	1160	1240	1220	3620
8	Fax Machines	520	840	420	1780
9	Copy Machines	160	112	140	412
10	Postage Meters	268	100	224	592
11	Laser Printers				0
12	Total	2108	2292	2004	6404
13					
14					
15					
16					

Consolidation table

◄◄ ► ►►\ Southeast / Southwest \ Consolidated Report / Sheet6 ◄

7. Clear the Left Column check box, if necessary, and click OK. The data from the four source worksheets are summed in the destination range of the Consolidated Report worksheet.

8. Select cell B7 in the Consolidated Report sheet. By default, Excel places values—not formulas—in the consolidation table.

9. Save the workbook as *[your initials]***15-5.xls**.

 NOTE: When your source data changes, you can consolidate again quickly. First, clear the consolidation table. Next, choose Consolidate from the Tools menu, and then click OK. Your last consolidation will be repeated with the new data.

Protecting Files

Workbooks often include formats and formulas that you don't want changed. You can protect a file, so users can key in only the areas you leave unlocked. Protecting the file is a two-step process:

- Unlocking areas for data entry
- Protecting the file

EXERCISE | **15-6** | **Unlock Data Entry Areas**

1. Select all five worksheets. Because the data entry areas and the consolidation table occupy the same positions, you can unlock them together.

2. Select the data entry area in the Northeast sheet (cells B7 through D11).

3. Choose C*e*lls from the F*o*rmat menu, and click the Protection tab in the Format Cells dialog box.

FIGURE 15-6
Protection tab of the Format Cells dialog box

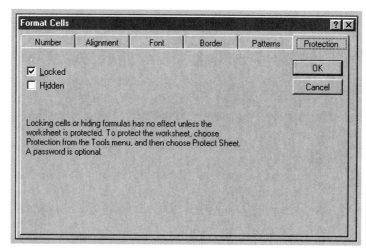

4. Clear the *L*ocked check box, and click OK. The selected cells are now unlocked. When you protect the workbook, they will remain available to users.

 NOTE: By default, all cells are locked in a workbook. Locked cells become inaccessible only after the worksheet has been protected.

EXERCISE | **15-7** | **Protect a Worksheet**

The *P*rotection command on the *T*ools menu offers two options:

- Protect *W*orkbook prevents a user from adding, deleting, renaming, or moving worksheets or from resizing or moving windows.

• Protect Sheet prevents a user from changing data in a worksheet.

FIGURE 15-7
Protect Sheet
dialog box

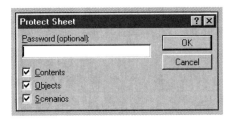

1. Right-click the Northeast tab, and choose Ungroup. Worksheets must be protected individually.

2. Point to Protection on the Tools menu, and choose Protect Sheet. The Protect Sheet dialog box appears.

3. In the Password text box, key *[your initials]*. The text box displays asterisks instead of the characters you key to ensure the secrecy of your password. A password can be up to 255 characters long and can include any combination of letters, numerals, and symbols. Passwords are case-sensitive, so your must remember whether you use upper- or lowercase characters.

4. Click OK. The Confirm Password dialog box appears.

5. Rekey *[your initials]* in this dialog box and click OK.

6. Repeat steps 1 through 5 for each of the other four worksheets in the workbook.

7. Click the Northwest tab, and then click cell A1.

8. Key **A**. A Microsoft Excel message box appears, indicating that locked cells cannot be changed.

9. Click OK to close the message box.

10. Key new data for the Northwest region in cells B7 through D10, as shown in Figure 15-8. This region had no laser printer sales.

FIGURE 15-8

Northwest

	A	B	C	D
6		April	May	June
7	Cellular Phones	208	321	280
8	Fax Machines	205	310	400
9	Copy Machines	56	84	78
10	Postage Meters	24	32	27

11. Click the Southeast tab, and enter the data shown in Figure 15-9 in cells B7 through D10. This region had no laser printer sales.

FIGURE 15-9

Southeast

	A	B	C	D
6		April	May	June
7	Cellular Phones	132	154	108
8	Fax Machines	165	236	191
9	Copy Machines	30	23	18
10	Postage Meters	36	83	40

12. Click the Southwest tab, and enter the data shown in Figures 15-10 in cells B7 through D11.

FIGURE 15-10

Southwest

	A	B	C	D
6		April	May	June
7	Cellular Phones	310	405	135
8	Fax Machines	100	45	92
9	Copy Machines	34	67	46
10	Postage Meters	80	54	65
10	Laser Printers	456	287	675

13. Click the Consolidated Report tab.

14. Select the consolidation table area (cells B7:D11). Press ⎡Delete⎤ to clear these cells.

15. Choose Consolidate from the Tools menu, and then click OK. Excel uses your last consolidation definition to summarize the updated data.

16. Save the workbook as *[your initials]***15-7.xls**.

17. Choose Print from the File menu, click Entire Workbook, and click OK.

18. Close the workbook.

Concepts Review

Each of the following statements is either true or false. Indicate your choice by circling **T** or **F**.

T F **1.** When cells are linked, changing the value in the source cell causes the value in the dependent cell to change as well.

T F **2.** Dependent worksheets can be linked only to other worksheets or workbooks that are currently open.

T F **3.** Individual cells can be linked together, unlike cell ranges.

T F **4.** You must clear the cells in a consolidation table before consolidating data.

T F **5.** If you plan to consolidate worksheets, it's a good idea to plan them so that common data items appear in identical locations.

T F **6.** If data elements do not appear in exactly the same location on each worksheet to be consolidated, then you cannot use the Data Consolidate feature.

T F **7.** You can protect a file so that unauthorized users cannot change data.

T F **8.** Protecting a worksheet and protecting a workbook are the same thing.

Write the correct answer in the space provided.

1. When cells in another worksheet or workbook are referenced, what are the references called?

_____

2. In an external reference, which symbol separates the name of a worksheet from the referenced cell range?

_____

3. Which command duplicates a format to several worksheets?

_____

4. When values from related worksheets in a workbook are linked in formulas in a summary worksheet, what is the summary worksheet called?

_____

5. When rows and column headings are the same in source worksheet, but the headings are not in the same location and the data elements are not identical, how does Excel consolidate?

_____

6. What should you do to ensure that unauthorized users cannot accidentally erase or change data or formulas?

_____

7. To prevent a user from renaming, moving, adding, or deleting worksheets or moving or resizing windows, which command should you use?

_____

8. To allow a user to enter data in a worksheet, what must you do before applying protection?

_____

CRITICAL THINKING

Answer these questions on a separate piece of paper. There are no right or wrong answers. Support your answer with examples from your own experience, if possible.

1. Would linking values be the best choice when creating a quarterly or annual report? Why or why not?

2. Preventing unauthorized users from changing your worksheet and workbook is one reason to use protection. How might you protect your worksheets from inadvertent changes that you make? Discuss a situation when it would be a good idea to protect your own worksheets.

3. In what types of situations might you need to consolidate data from different workbooks?

Skills Review

EXERCISE 15-8

Link multiple files.

1. Open the files **Invoices.xls** and **Totdollr.xls**, and arrange the workbooks horizontally.

2. Link the number of units of cellular phones sold on the three invoices in **Invoices.xls** to the **Totdollr.xls** workbook by following these steps:

   a. Scroll **Totdollr.xls** until you can see rows 4 through 7.

b. Click cell D4, and then click the AutoSum button $\boxed{\Sigma}$.

c. Click cell F13 in the Automation worksheet in the **Invoices.xls** workbook, and then key a comma.

d. Click the AllCity tab, click cell F14, and then key a comma.

e. Click the Casablanca tab, click cell F13, and press $\boxed{\text{Enter}}$.

3. Link the number of units of fax machines sold by following these steps:

a. Click cell D5 in **Totdollr.xls**, and then click $\boxed{\Sigma}$.

b. Click cell F13 in the AllCity sheet in **Invoices.xls**, and then key a comma.

c. Click cell F14 in the Casablanca sheet, and then press $\boxed{\text{Enter}}$.

4. Link the number of copiers sold by following these steps:

a. Click cell D6 in **Totdollr.xls**, and click $\boxed{\Sigma}$.

b. Click cell F14 in the Automation worksheet in **Invoices.xls**, and then key a comma.

c. Click cell F15 in the Casablanca worksheet in **Invoices.xls**, and then press $\boxed{\text{Enter}}$.

5. Link the number of postage meters sold by following these steps:

a. Click cell F15 in the Automation worksheet of **Invoices.xls**.

b. Copy the cell's contents to the Clipboard.

c. Click cell D7 in **Totdollr.xls**, and then choose Edit, Paste Special.

d. Click Paste Link, and then press $\boxed{\text{Esc}}$.

6. Maximize **Totdollr.xls**, and then press $\boxed{\text{Ctrl}}$+$\boxed{\text{Home}}$.

7. Save the **Totdollr.xls** workbook as *[your initials]***15-8.xls**, and print it.

8. Close all workbooks.

EXERCISE 15-9

Copy a base form, style worksheets, and copy formulas across worksheets.

1. Open the file **Regnpay.xls**.

2. Rename sheets 1 through 4 as **NE**, **NW**, **SE**, and **SW**, respectively.

3. Copy the base form on the NE sheet to the other worksheets by following these steps:

a. Click the NE tab, and copy the cell range A1:F7 to the Clipboard.

b. Click the NW tab, press and hold $\boxed{\text{Shift}}$, and click the SW tab.

c. Click cell A1 in the NW tab, and paste the contents of the Clipboard to this location.

d. Adjust columns A and B to accommodate 15 characters. Adjust columns C, D, and E to accommodate 10 characters.

e. Right-click the NW tab, and choose Ungroup Sheets from the shortcut menu.

4. Change the title in cell A1 of the NW tab to **Northwest Region**

5. Change the titles in cell A1 of the SE and SW worksheets.

6. Edit the style of the worksheets by following these steps:

     a. Click the NE tab, press and hold down [Shift], and then click the SW tab.

     b. Center the titles in cells A1 and A2 across columns A through F.

     c. Add light shading to the titles in cells A1 through F7.

     d. Make the labels in cells A6 through F7 bold, and then add a border below row 7.

     e. Format cells D8 through D12 and cells F8 through F12 in comma style with two decimal places.

     f. Set the worksheets to print centered horizontally on the page.

     g. Edit the header to include the filename instead of the worksheet tab name.

7. Copy formulas across the worksheets by following these steps:

     a. With all four worksheets selected, select cells F8 through F12 in the Northeast worksheet.

     b. Choose F̲ill from the E̲dit menu, and choose A̲cross Worksheets from the cascading menu.

     c. Ensure that the A̲ll option button is selected, and then click OK.

     d. Right-click the Northeast tab, and choose Ungroup Sheets. Click each tab to view the changes.

8. Save the workbook as *[your initials]***15-9.xls**.

9. Print and close the workbook.

Fill data across worksheets, and consolidate data by location and by labels.

1. Open the workbook **Dllrsals.xls**.

2. Rename Sheet5 as **Consolidated Report**

3. Copy labels to the Consolidated Report worksheet by following these steps:

     a. Click the Northeast tab, press and hold [Ctrl], and click the Consolidated Report tab.

     b. Select cells A1 through E1 in the Northeast worksheet.

     c. Choose F̲ill from the E̲dit menu, and choose A̲cross Worksheets from the cascading menu.

     d. Click the Forma̲ts option button, and then click OK.

     e. Select cells A2 through E2, and choose E̲dit, F̲ill, A̲cross Worksheets. Click the A̲ll option button, and then click OK.

f. Right-click the Consolidated Report tab, and choose Ungroup Sheets from the shortcut menu.

      g. Key **Feestone Electronics** in cell A1 in the consolidated report.

4. Consolidate data by position by following these steps:

      a. In the Consolidated Report worksheet, select cells B8 through D11.

      b. Choose Consolidate from the Data menu.

      c. Click the Northeast tab, select cells B8 through D11, and click Add in the Consolidate dialog box.

      d. Repeat the previous step for the Northwest and Southeast worksheets, and then click OK.

      e. Resize columns B through D to accommodate the values.

5. Consolidate data using labels by following these steps:

      a. Select cells B8 through D11 in the Consolidated Report worksheet, and then choose Edit, Clear, All.

      b. Click cell A8, and choose Consolidate from the Data menu.

      c. Delete the previous cell references from the Consolidate dialog box, and then click in the Reference text box.

      d. Click the Northeast tab, select cells A8 through D11, and click Add.

      e. Repeat the previous step for the Northwest and Southeast worksheets.

      f. In the Southwest worksheet, select cells A8 through D12, and then click Add.

      g. Click the Left Column check box to select it, and click OK.

6. Format the consolidated worksheet by following these steps:

      a. Click the Southwest tab, press and hold `Shift`, and then click the Consolidated Report tab.

      b. Select cells A13 through E13, and choose Edit, Fill, Across Worksheets.

      c. Click the All option button, and then click OK.

      d. Repeat steps b and c for cells A5 through E6.

      e. Select cells E8 through E12, and then choose Edit, Fill, Across Worksheets.

      f. Click the Contents option button, and then click OK.

      g. Right-click the Consolidated Report tab, and choose Ungroup Sheets from the shortcut menu.

      h. Resize columns A through E to accommodate the values.

      i. Format cells E8 through E12 in comma style with two decimal places.

      j. Add a border below cells A12 through E12.

      k. Format all worksheets to print centered horizontally on the page.

7. Save the workbook as *[your initials]***15-10.xls**.

8. Print the Consolidated Report worksheet, and close the workbok.

EXERCISE 15-11

Unlock data entry areas and protect a worksheet.

   1. Open the file **Hourly.xls**.

   2. Unprotect areas of entry by following these steps:

   a. Select the cell range E8:E12.

   b. Choose F_ormat, C_ells, and then click the Protection tab.

   c. Clear the L_ocked check box to deselect it. Click OK.

   d. Click anywhere in the worksheet to deselect the cells.

   3. Protect the worksheet by following these steps:

   a. Choose P_rotection from the T_ools menu, and then choose P_rotect Sheet on the cascading menu.

   b. Key *[your initials]* in the P_assword text box, and click OK.

   c. Rekey *[your initials]* in the Confirm Password dialog box, and click OK.

   4. Key the following data in the "Hours Worked" column:

Williams	**38**
Carroway	**35**
Bassett	**39**
Artis	**40**
Curtis	**40**

   5. Save the workbook as *[your initials]***15-11.xls**.

   6. Print and close the workbook.

Lesson Applications

Paste link values from one workbook to another, and protect the worksheet.

Feestone Electronics does not think that the analysis of average unit price is as useful as it might be. Create a worksheet that calculates averages that include not only the average unit price for each invoice, but also the average quantity ordered for each item.

1. Open the file **Average2.xls.** Click Yes to reestablish the links. If necessary, use the File Not Found dialog box to locate the file.

2. Make the changes indicated in Figure 15-11. When you've finished, "Average Unit Price" appears in column G, and column B is blank.

FIGURE 15-11

Average ~~Unit Price~~ *Invoice* ← (center across columns)

Customer Name	Average Unit Price
Automation Partners	1,193.32
AllCity Realty	342.48
Casablanca Retail	2,893.32
~~Total~~ Average Invoice	$ 9,755.49

add 4 columns: Cell Phones, Fax Machines, Copiers, Postage Meters

3. Format the headings in columns C through G as centered and aligned to wrap text, and make the column widths 10.

4. Open the file **Invoices.xls**, arrange the windows horizontally, and display the Automation sheet in the **Invoices.xls** window.

5. Paste Link the quantity ordered of each item from column F in each invoice in the **Invoices.xls** workbook to columns C, D, E, and F, respectively, in the Average Invoices worksheet. If an item was not ordered, key **0** in the cell.

6. Maximize the **Average2.xls** window.

7. Calculate the average quantity ordered of each item. If necessary, format the averages in normal type (not bold).

8. Delete the blank column B.

9. Change the header to display the filename instead of the sheet tab. Set up the worksheet to print in portrait orientation, centered horizontally on the page.

10. Protect the worksheet from changes using *[your initials]* as a password.

11. Save the workbook as *[your initials]***15-12.xls** and print it.

12. Close all workbooks. Do not save changes to **Invoices.xls**.

Design worksheets for consolidation, rename worksheets, consolidate worksheets, format worksheets, and save and print a workbook.

Feestone Electronics needs to add unit prices and dollar-value sales revenues to its regional sales reports and to produce a consolidated report.

1. Open the file **Slsreprt.xls**.

2. In sheets 1 through 4, key **Unit Price** in cell H7, and key the following unit prices in cells H8:H12. (Hint: Select the sheets and work in sheet 4.)

Cellular phones	**119.95**
Fax machines	**565.00**
Copy machines	**7,995.00**
Postage meters	**465.00**
Laser printers	**1899.00**

3. In all four sheets, copy the labels in cell A8:A13 to cells A18:A23. Key **Revenue** in cell A15, centered over columns A through F.

4. In all four sheets, calculate revenues based on unit sales and unit price. (In cell C18, enter the formula **=$H8*C8** and then copy this formula through cell E22.)

5. In all four sheets, calculate totals for the "Revenue" section (columns and rows).

6. In all four sheets, format the unit prices in currency style, the individual product revenues in comma style with no decimal places, and the revenue totals in currency style with no decimal places.

7. Adjust column widths to accommodate values. Rename the worksheets as follows:

Sheet1	**Northeast**
Sheet2	**Northwest**
Sheet3	**Southeast**
Sheet4	**Southwest**
Sheet5	**Consolidated Report**

8. Copy the Southwest sheet to the Consolidated Report sheet, rename the sheet as **Consolidated Report**, and delete the regional manager's name.

9. In the Consolidated Report, delete the contents of the unit sales data (cells C18:E12), and consolidate the unit sales of the four regions by position.

10. Delete columns B and G.

11. Adjust column widths to accommodate data, check formulas, and make formats consistent across all worksheets.

12. Format all sheets to print centered horizontally on the page, and view the sheets in print preview.

13. Save the workbook as *[your initials]***15-13.xls** and print all worksheets.

14. Close the workbook.

Paste Link data from one workbook to another, and protect a workbook.

Feestone Electronics includes current prices in its product list. Recently, the vendor prices increased, and the company decided to link its product list and its vendor price list, so that the product list would automatically be updated.

1. Open the files **Prodlist.xls** and **Vendpric.xls**, and arrange the workbooks vertically.

2. Clear the prices in **Prodlist.xls** (cells B5:B8).

3. Paste Link the vendor prices in column B of **Vendpric.xls** to the appropriate cells in column B of **Prodlist.xls**.

4. Maximize **Prodlist.xls**, and examine the newly inserted references.

5. Format the prices in 12-point type.

6. In case someone else needs to use the worksheet, key in cell A10 **The vendor prices are linked to the workbook Vendpric.xls.**

7. Protect the worksheet from changes. No cells should be unlocked.

8. Set the worksheet to print centered horizontally on the page.

9. Save the **Prodlist.xls** workbook as *[your initials]***15-14.xls** and print it.

10. Display formulas, and set the worksheet to print in landscape orientation, fitting on one page, with gridlines and row and column headings.

11. Print *[your initials]***15-14.xls**.

12. Close all open workbooks without saving.

Design worksheets for consolidation, consolidate worksheets, and Paste Link the consolidated worksheet into a word-processing document.

To decide how much inventory to keep on hand this year, Feestone Electronics is analyzing the quantity of product sold in 1995 and 1996 by quarter and on an annual basis. Construct a workbook containing a 1995 worksheet, a 1996 worksheet, and a consolidated worksheet averaging quantity of product sold by quarter and for each year. Paste Link the averaged data into your word-processing application.

1. Open a new workbook to create the three worksheets. Create two worksheets using the data in Figure 15-12.

FIGURE 15-12

	Qtr 1	Qtr 2	Qtr 3	Qtr 4
1995				
Cellular Phones	2,576	2,958	3,213	3,364
Fax Machines	2,287	2,189	2,608	2,367
Copy Machines	516	539	1,004	777
Postage Meters	536	589	1,323	656
Laser Printers		1,418	3,828	4,719
1996				
Cellular Phones	3,439	3,426	3,429	3,948
Fax Machines	2,904	1,986	2,578	3,255
Copy Machines	679	457	895	980
Postage Meters	543	498	783	486
Laser Printers	6,457	7,896	7,498	8,302

2. Create the consolidated worksheet, and format all three worksheets using group edit. Remember to use the Average function for consolidation. The consolidation worksheet should not contain any decimal places.

3. Save the workbook as *[your initials]***15-15a.xls** and print it.

4. Create the memo shown in Figure 15-13 using your word-processing application. Paste Link the average sales data into the document.

FIGURE 15-13

```
To:         Regional Sales Managers/Feestone Electronics
From:       Craig Herman
Date:       [today's date]
Subject:    1995-1996 Average Sales

After consolidating 1995 and 1996, we have created the
following average sales analysis:
```

5. Save the memo as *[your initials]***15-15b.***[your word processor's three-letter extension]*.

6. Print the memo and the workbook.

7. Close the document and the workbook.

Advanced Printing

OBJECTIVES After completing this lesson, you will be able to:

1. Insert and remove page breaks.
2. Scale a worksheet.
3. Add print titles.
4. Change margins in Print Preview.
5. Change column widths in Print Preview.
6. Modify preset headers and footers.
7. Change page order and print page ranges.
8. Print named ranges.

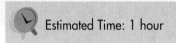 Estimated Time: 1 hour

Excel provides many features that can make the printed worksheet more readable. You can create a logical, attractive layout and automate repetitive data-entry tasks.

Inserting and Removing Page Breaks

You can insert page breaks to control what appears on each printed page. On-screen, inserted page breaks appear as long dashed lines. Automatic page breaks appear as short dashed lines.

In Lesson 4, you learned to split windows. Page breaks are inserted and removed in much the same way—above and to the left of the active cell.

You choose Page Break (or Remove Page Break) from the Insert menu.

EXERCISE 16-1 **Insert and Remove Page Breaks**

1. Open the file **Salesyr.xls**, and zoom to 50% to see more of the worksheet.

2. Choose Options from the Tools menu, click the View tab, check Automatic Page Breaks in the Windows Options group, and click OK. An automatic page break is displayed between columns G and H.

3. View the worksheet in Print Preview, click Next or the scroll bar to see all three pages, and then close Print Preview.

 TIP: To navigate in Print Preview, you can also use PgUp, PgDn, ↑, ↓, Ctrl+↑, and Ctrl+↓.

4. Select cell F1, and choose Page Break from the Insert menu. Excel inserts a vertical page break to the left of the active cell. A new automatic page break appears between columns K and L. First quarter (Q1) information will now appear on a separate page.

FIGURE 16-1
Page breaks

	A	B	C	D	E	F	G	H	I	J	K	L	M
1	NATIONAL SALES												
2	Full Year												
3	CONSOLIDATED REPORT												
4													
5	Unit Sales												
6	Produ	Jan	Feb	Mar	Q1	Apr	May	Jun	Q2	Jul	Aug	Sep	Q
7													
8	Cellular	980	978	988	2946	898	960	1100	2958	1056	1020	1102	31
9	Fax Ma	765	763	771	2299	701	749	858	2308	824	796	860	24
10	Copy M	229	229	231	689	210	225	258	693	247	239	258	7
11	Postag	251	251	253	755	230	246	282	758	271	261	282	8
12	Laser Pr	851	849	858	2558	780	833	955	2568	917	885	957	27
13	Total	3076	3070	3101	9247	2819	3013	3453	9285	3315	3201	3459	997
14													
15	Dollar Sales												
16	Produ	Jan	Feb	Mar	Q1	Apr	May	Jun	Q2	Jul	Aug	Sep	Q
17													
18	Cellular	117,551	117,311	118,511	353,373	107,715	115,152	131,945	354,812	126,667	122,349	132,185	381,20
19	Fax Ma	432,225	431,095	435,615	1,298,935	396,065	423,185	484,770	1,304,020	465,560	449,740	485,900	1,401,20
20	Copy M	1,830,855	1,830,855	1,846,845	5,508,555	1,678,950	1,798,875	2,062,710	5,540,535	1,974,765	1,910,805	2,062,710	5,948,28
21	Postag	116,715	116,715	117,645	351,075	106,950	114,390	131,130	352,470	126,015	121,365	131,130	378,51
22	Laser Pr	1,616,049	1,612,251	1,629,342	4,857,642	1,481,220	1,581,867	1,813,545	4,876,632	1,741,383	1,680,615	1,817,343	5,239,34
23	Total	#####	#####	#####	#####	#####	#####	#####	######	#####	#####	#####	#####
24													
25													
26	Manual page break				→			Automatic page break					→
27													

Year Sales / Sheet2 / Sheet3 / Sheet4 / Sheet5 / Shee
Ready   Sum=0   NUM

5. Select cell J1, and choose Page Break from the Insert menu. Second quarter (Q2) information will now appear on a separate page.

6. Insert a page break between columns M and N, and between columns R and S.

7. Select cell A15, and insert a page break. This page break appears above the active cell.

8. View the worksheet in Print Preview. It now stretches over ten pages.

9. Close Print Preview.

10. Select cell F15. This cell is below one page break and to the right of another.

11. Choose Insert, Remove Page Break from the menu bar. The page breaks between columns E and F and above row 15 are removed.

12. Remove the page break between columns M and N.

Scaling a Worksheet

Scaling is enlarging or reducing the size of a worksheet's contents. As you learned in Lesson 4, you can fit a worksheet onto the number of pages you want. You can also enlarge or reduce worksheet contents by a specified percentage. The Page tab of the Page Setup dialog box offers scaling options.

EXERCISE **16-2** **Scale a Worksheet by a Percentage**

1. Click Setup at the top of the Print Preview window.

2. Click the Page tab.

FIGURE 16-2
Page tab of the
Page Setup
dialog box

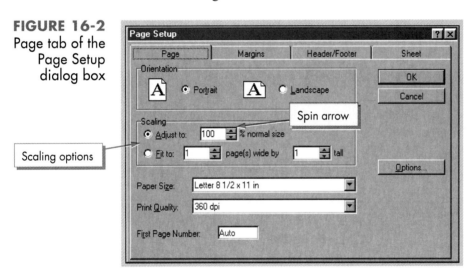

3. Click the Landscape option button.

4. Select the Adjust to option, if necessary, and key **80** in the % normal size box (or click the down spin arrow to change the value to 80).

5. Click OK. The worksheet now spans three pages.

6. Move to page 2 in Print Preview. The data on page 2 almost fills the landscape page.

7. Click Previous. The data on page 1 does not fill the page.

Adding Print Titles

You can generate consistent titles and column or row headings across multiple pages. You specify which rows or columns to use in the Print Titles section of the Sheet tab in the Page Setup dialog box. Print titles may be in multiple rows or columns, but they must be adjacent.

EXERCISE 16-3 **Set Print Titles for Each Printed Page**

1. Switch to Print Preview. Only page 1 of the worksheet has the print title beginning "National Sales" and the labels in column A.
2. Close Print Preview.
3. Choose Page Setup from the File menu.

 NOTE: You *cannot* set print titles by clicking Setup from the Print Preview window.

4. Click the Sheet tab.

FIGURE 16-3
Sheet tab of the
Page Setup
dialog box

Print Area section

Print Titles section

Page Order section

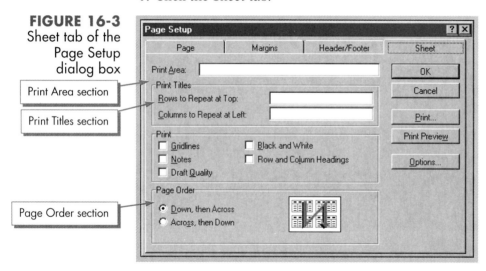

5. Key **A:A** in the Columns to Repeat at Left text box. You must key a range of columns (like A:A or B:D), even if you want to print titles from only one column.
6. Click Print Preview, and page through the worksheet. All the pages now have the titles and labels from column A on page 1.

Changing Margins in Print Preview

You can change margins in the Page Setup dialog box or in Print Preview. To change margins in Print Preview, drag margin lines to the desired position. An advantage of changing margins in Print Preview is that you see the results immediately.

EXERCISE 16-4 Change Margins in Print Preview

1. If margin lines do not appear in Print Preview, click <u>M</u>argins at the top of the Print Preview window. Dotted lines delineate the header and footer areas and the margins, and column handles appear at the top of the page.

FIGURE 16-4
Changing margins
in Print Preview

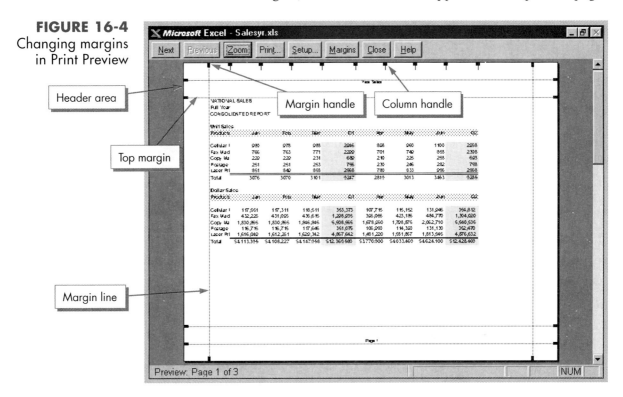

2. Click <u>S</u>etup, and click the Margins tab.
3. Double-click in the <u>T</u>op text box and key **2** to set the top margin to 2 inches.
4. Click OK. Print Preview displays the new margin setting.
5. Position the pointer on the top margin, either on the margin handle or on the dotted line itself. The pointer changes to the sizing pointer ✛, like the one used in sizing rows in a worksheet.
6. Drag the line up to the one-inch point. Watch the indicator in the status bar.

 NOTE: You may not be able to move a margin to an exact position by dragging.

Changing Column Widths in Print Preview

You can change column widths in Print Preview by dragging the column handles (the square boxes at the top of the page).

EXERCISE | **16-5** | **Change Column Widths in Print Preview**

1. In Print Preview, with the Margins showing, display page 2.

2. Position the pointer on the first column handle. This is the Print title column, A. The pointer changes to the sizing pointer ↔.

3. Drag the first column handle to the right until you see all the titles. The status bar will show a measurement of about 27.

4. Move to page 1, and notice that column A is widened there, too. Adjust the remaining column widths on page 1, so that the data fills the page and columns B through I are evenly spaced (each about 15 characters wide).

FIGURE 16-5
Page 1 in Print Preview after resizing columns

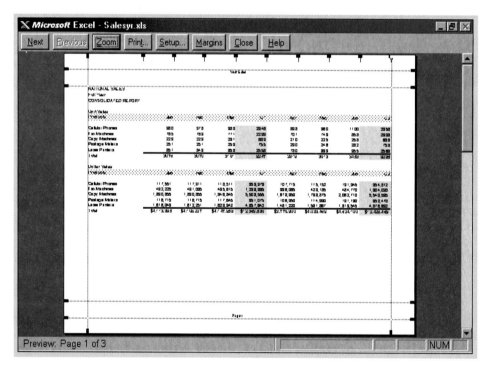

5. Click <u>N</u>ext. The columns on page 2 already fill the page, and need no adjustment.

6. Click <u>N</u>ext. Only the Print titles and current prices appear on page 3.

7. Move to page 1.

Modifying Preset Headers and Footers

Headers print repetitive information about the worksheet across the top of the page. *Footers* print repetitive information across the bottom of the page. Headers and footers are positioned above and below the margins on the printed page.

You can key information in a header or footer; insert codes for the page number, total number of pages, date, time, filename, or sheet name; and format header and footer text. Excel also offers several preset headers and footers that you can use or edit.

FIGURE 16-6
Buttons in the
Header dialog box

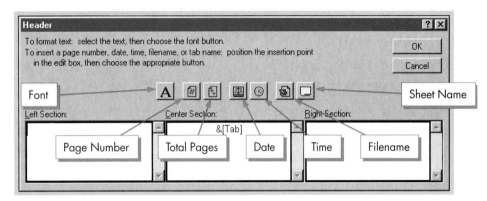

EXERCISE **16-6** ## Use and Customize Preset Headers and Footers

1. Click <u>S</u>etup in Print Preview, and then click the Header/Footer tab.

2. Click the He<u>a</u>der drop-down arrow. The Header drop-down list displays preset headers.

FIGURE 16-7
Header/Footer tab
in Page Setup
dialog box

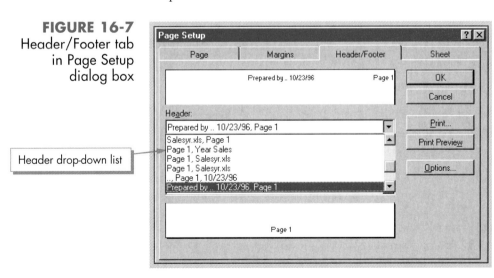

Header drop-down list

3. Choose the preset header: Prepared by.. *[today's date]*, Page 1. The list closes.

4. Click Custom Header to edit the header.

5. In the Header dialog box, delete the two periods (..) after "Prepared by," and key *[Your Name]*.

6. Select the text in the Left Section (Prepared by *[Your Name]*), and click the Font button [A].

7. In the Font dialog box, choose Bold from the Font Style list, and then click OK.

8. Click OK to close the Header dialog box.

9. In the Header/Footer tab, click the Footer drop-down arrow and choose the preset footer: Year Sales, *[a name]* Confidential, Page 1.

10. Click Custom Footer to edit the footer.

11. Replace the name before Confidential with **Feestone Electronics**, and replace Page [&Page] with [&File]. (Hint: Click the Filename button [S].)

12. Click OK to close the Footer dialog box, and then click OK to close Page Setup. Examine the headers and footers in Print Preview.

13. Close Print Preview.

14. Press [Ctrl]+[Home].

15. Save the workbook as *[your initials]***16-6.xls**.

16. Print and close the workbook.

Changing Page Order and Printing

When data is on more than one page, Excel prints by default from the first page down, and then across. If you want the pages to print across, and then down, you specify this in the Page Setup dialog box.

You can also print a specified range of pages. In the Print dialog box, choose Pages in the Page Range section, and then specify the beginning and ending pages in the from and to boxes.

EXERCISE | 16-7 | **Print a Range of Pages Across and Then Down**

1. Open the file **Salesyr2.xls**.

2. Move around the worksheet. The data for the first quarter is in the top, left-hand portion of the worksheet, the data for the second quarter is to the right of the first-quarter data, and the data for the third and fourth quarters is below the first and second quarters. It is clear that this worksheet is meant to be read across and then down, rather than down and then across.

3. Press `Ctrl`+`Home` to move to the top of the worksheet, and open Print Preview. The data on page 1 is the first-quarter data.

4. Click <u>N</u>ext to move to page 2. The third-quarter data is on page 2.

5. Click <u>N</u>ext. Page 3 contains the prices used in the formulas calculating Dollar Sales.

6. Page through the rest of the worksheet. The second-quarter data is on page 4 and the fourth quarter data is on page 5. Excel is reading down the worksheet, then across, which is not the order intended.

 NOTE: Page 6 is blank because there is no data in the area to the right of the price data and below the fourth-quarter data.

7. Click the <u>P</u>revious button until you return to page 1.

8. Click the <u>S</u>etup button, and then click the Sheet tab.

9. In the Page Order section, choose Acro<u>s</u>s, and then Down, and click OK.

10. Page through the worksheet in Print Preview to see the corrected page order. The second-quarter data is on page 2, the third-quarter data is on page 3, and the fourth-quarter data is on page 4.

11. Close Print Preview.

12. Save the workbook as *[your initials]****16-7.xls**.

13. Press `Ctrl`+`P`, choose Pages in the Print dialog box, key **1** in the <u>f</u>rom box and **2** in the <u>t</u>o box, and click OK.

Printing Named Ranges

As you know, you can select an area and print it, or you can define the print area for a worksheet. You can also name ranges that you expect to print frequently. You can then quickly select the named range and print it.

EXERCISE 16-8 Print a Named Range

1. Select cells A1 through G24.

2. Click in the Name box, key **Qtr1**, and then press `Enter`.

 TIP: To name a range, you can also choose <u>N</u>ame from the <u>I</u>nsert menu, and click <u>D</u>efine.

3. Assign the name **Qtr2** to the range I1:O24, **Qtr3** to the range A26:G49, and **Qtr4** to the range I26:O49.

4. Save the workbook as *[your initials]***16-8.xls**.

5. Select Qtr2 from the Name drop-down list or the Go To dialog box.

6. Choose <u>P</u>rint from the <u>F</u>ile menu, choose the Selectio<u>n</u> option, and click OK. Excel prints the selected cells.

 TIP: You can also specify a named range to print in the Page Setup dialog box. Key the named range in the Print <u>A</u>rea text box.

7. Close the workbook without saving it.

Concepts Review

TRUE/FALSE QUESTIONS

Each of the following statements is either true or false. Indicate your choice by circling **T** or **F**.

T F **1.** You can delete manual and automatic page breaks.

T F **2.** When you scale a worksheet, you change the size of the worksheet contents.

T F **3.** An advantage of changing the margins and column widths in Print Preview is that you can see the results immediately.

T F **4.** To change column widths in Print Preview, you double-click on the column handles.

T F **5.** Although Excel has many preset headers and footers you can apply to your worksheets, you cannot change or add to any of the preset information.

T F **6.** Excel can only print going down the worksheet first, then across.

T F **7.** You must use the mouse to move around in Print Preview.

T F **8.** Printing a named range is like printing a selection.

SHORT ANSWER QUESTIONS

Write the correct answer in the space provided.

1. What do you call enlarging or reducing the size of data on a physical page?

_____

2. Which option on the Page tab of the Page Setup dialog box do you use to make the worksheet automatically fit on a specific number of pages?

_____

3. Which area on the Sheet tab of the Page Setup dialog box do you use to generate identical titles on each printed page?

_____

4. What do you drag to adjust column widths in Print Preview?

_____

5. What is the information positioned at the top of the page above the margin called?

_____

6. If the preset headers and footers do not provide the information you need, what option can you use to modify them?

_____

7. In what default direction does Excel begin to read a multiple page worksheet?

_____

8. Which print option must you select to print a selected named range?

_____

CRITICAL THINKING

Answer these questions on a separate piece of paper. There are no right or wrong answers. Support your answers with examples from your own experience, if possible.

1. Excel offers several ways to adjust the layout of the data before you print your worksheet, including inserting page breaks, adjusting column widths and margins, and two ways of scaling. What are the advantages of each method? Which methods do you prefer, and why?

2. You know how to adjust column widths in several ways, in both the worksheet and in Print Preview. Which would you recommend to an inexperienced user? Why?

3. People are growing more conscious of the environmental impact of trash. The "paperless office" has long been a goal of the corporate world. Many people think, however, that the use of computers has actually caused people to use *more* paper than ever. Can you think of any alternatives to printing worksheets? What are some other ways to share relevant information without using paper?

Skills Review

EXERCISE 16-9

Add manual page breaks and scale the worksheet.

1. Open the file **Halfyrl.xls**.
2. Key the second-quarter information in the range F8:I13 as shown in Figure 16-8, entering SUM formulas in the "Q2" column and "Total" row.

FIGURE 16-8

Products	April	May	June	Q2
Cellular phones	341	365	418	
Fax Machines	266	285	326	
Copy Machines	80	86	98	
Postage Meters	87	93	107	
Laser Printers	296	317	363	
Total				

2. Add and remove page breaks in the worksheet by following these steps:

   a. Select cell F15.

   b. Choose Page Break from the Insert menu.

   c. Select cell A15.

   d. Choose Remove Page Break from the Insert menu.

3. Scale the data to fill the page by following these steps:

   a. Click [icon].

   b. Click Setup, and then choose the Page tab.

   c. Choose Adjust to and key **125** in the % normal size box (or use the spin arrow).

   d. Click the Landscape option button.

   e. Click the Margins tab and center the pages horizontally. Click OK.

   f. Page through the worksheet, and then close Print Preview.

4. Save the workbook as *[your initials]***16-9.xls**.

5. Print and close the workbook.

EXERCISE 16-10

Add print titles and change margins in Print Preview.

1. Open the file **Halfyr2.xls**.

2. Add print titles as indicated by following these steps:

   a. Choose Page Setup from the File menu.

   b. Click the Sheet tab.

   c. Key **A:A** in the Columns to Repeat at Left text box.

TIP: Instead of keying a range, you can click in the <u>C</u>olumns to Repeat at Left text box, and then select columns in the worksheet.

   d. Click Print Previe<u>w</u>.

3. If margin lines are not displayed, click <u>M</u>argins.

4. Drag the left margin line to the right, to the 1.5-inch mark.

5. Drag the right margin line to the left, to the 1.75-inch mark.

6. Close Print Preview.

7. Save the workbook as *[your initials]***16-10.xls**.

8. Print and close the workbook.

EXERCISE 16-11

Change column widths in Print Preview and create headers and footers.

   1. Open the file **Halfyr3.xls**.

   2. Open Print Preview. If margin lines are not displayed, click <u>M</u>argins.

   3. Adjust the column widths by following these steps:

   a. Drag the first column handle to the right until column A is about 22 characters wide.

   b. Drag the rest of the column handles to the right so that each column is between 12 and 13 characters wide and the data fills the page.

   c. Click <u>N</u>ext.

   d. Starting with the second column handle, drag each column handle to the right so that each column is between 12 and 13 characters wide and the last column moves onto page 3.

   4. Choose a preset header and modify it by following these steps:

   a. Click <u>S</u>etup, and click the Header/Footer tab.

   b. Open the He<u>a</u>der drop-down list and choose *[a name]* Confidential, Northeast, Page 1.

   c. Replace *[a name]* with **Feestone Electronics**.

   d. Select all the text in the <u>L</u>eft Section, click the Font button Ⓐ, double-click Bold italic, and click OK.

   5. Choose a preset footer and modify it by following these steps:

   a. Open the <u>F</u>ooter drop-down list and choose Halfyr3.xls.

   b. Click C<u>u</u>stom Footer.

   c. In the <u>L</u>eft Section, click the Date button 🗓.

   d. In the <u>R</u>ight Section, key your name.

   e. Click OK to close the Footer dialog box, and then click OK again to close the Page Setup dialog box.

6. View the header and footer in Print Preview, and then close the Print Preview window.

7. Save the workbook as *[your initials]***16-11.xls**.

8. Print and close the workbook.

EXERCISE 16-12

Change page order, and print named ranges.

1. Open the file **NESales.xls**.

2. Click .

3. Page through the worksheet, then return to page 1.

4. Change the page order by following these steps:

   a. Click <u>S</u>etup, and then choose the Sheet tab.

   b. Click Acro<u>s</u>s, then Down, and then OK.

   c. Page through the worksheet to confirm that it will be printed in the correct order.

   d. Close Print Preview.

5. Print named ranges by following these steps:

   a. Select cell B1 through cell E23.

   b. Click in the Name box, key **First_Qtr**, then press Enter.

   c. To the cell range F1:I23, assign the name **Second_Qtr**

   d. Choose Page Set<u>u</u>p from the <u>F</u>ile menu.

   e. Click the Sheet tab.

   f. Key **First_Qtr** in the Print Area text box.

   NOTE: Print titles have already been set.

   g. Click <u>P</u>rint, and then click OK in the Print dialog box. The first-quarter data prints.

   h. Click the arrow to open the Name box drop-down list and click Second_Qtr.

   i. Choose <u>P</u>rint from the <u>F</u>ile menu.

   j. Choose Selectio<u>n</u> in the Print dialog box, and click OK

6. Press Ctrl + Home and save the workbook as *[your initials]***16-12.xls**.

7. Print pages 1 and 2 of the worksheet, and then close the workbook.

Lesson Applications

Modify preset headers and footers, add print titles, insert and remove page breaks, scale the worksheet, adjust column widths and margins in Print Preview, and print a named range.

Feestone Electronics wants to print its yearly sales data on two pages, and print its price list separately, as needed.

1. Open the file **Salesyr3.xls**.

2. Widen column A to accommodate the longest title, and set column A to print on each page.

3. Change the header by moving "Year Sales" to the left section and adding the date to the right section. Change the footer by deleting the page number and then entering the following information in the left and right sections:

   Prepared by *[your name]*   **Filename, Page #**

4. Set the worksheet to print in landscape orientation.

5. Remove the page break above the Dollar Sales row, and insert a page break after the Q2 column.

6. In Print Preview, adjust the left and right margins to about 0.5 inches.

7. Scale the worksheet so that the information for the third and fourth quarters, and the Total column, fill page 2.

8. Adjust the columns on page 1 so that the numeric columns are approximately the same width and the data fills the page.

9. Adjust the top margin to 2 inches.

10. Name cells S16 through S23 **Prices**.

11. Print the range Prices.

12. Press Ctrl + Home and save the workbook as *[your initials]***16-14.xls**.

13. Print and close the workbook.

Insert and remove page breaks, add print titles, add a custom footer, change margins and column widths in Print Preview, and print a named range.

Feestone Electronics' personnel manager needs to print the employee information worksheet for a meeting. The lookup data in the worksheet must be printed separately for the manager's use only.

1. Open the file **EmpInfo.xls**, and key the date of birth and the hire date for the last ten employees, as shown in Figure 16-9.

FIGURE 16-9

		Date of Birth	Hire Date
Rodriguez	Marta	6/29/67	4/6/90
Ross	Sarah	4/23/72	5/19/92
Slavitt	Robert	9/17/74	1/18/92
Smythe	Susan	3/25/73	12/12/95
Torrisi	Thomas	11/3/78	3/5/96
Troisi	Stephen	3/5/78	8/12/94
Tyler	Mary	10/14/69	5/15/96
Vu	Tri	8/16/70	12/15/95
Weinstein	David	2/27/75	12/8/93
Wysocki	Mark	6/6/75	6/10/92

2. Remove the page break to the left of column G.

3. Add a page break above the lookup table in row 49.

4. Add the worksheet title and labels in rows 1 through 4 as print titles (Rows to Repeat at Top).

5. Add columns A and B as print titles.

6. Modify the preset footer to include the department name (Personnel), the page number, and the date.

7. Change the top margin to 1.5 inches.

8. In Print Preview, increase the width of column A to about 13 characters.

9. In Print Preview, increase the width of column B as much as possible without moving the column labeled "Weeks Vacation" onto another page.

10. Name cells A49 through C58 **LOOKUP_DATA**

11. Print the range LOOKUP_DATA, and then clear the Print Area.

12. Press Ctrl + Home and save the workbook as *[your initials]***16-14.xls**.

13. Print pages 1 and 2 of the worksheet, and close the workbook.

EXERCISE 16-15

Insert page breaks, set print titles, scale the data, change the print order of the pages, adjust the margins and column widths in Print Preview, modify preset headers and footers, and create and print a named range.

A detailed financial statement of changes in net assets for the retirement accounts of the employees of Feestone Electronics needs to be reformatted for printing. It needs specific page breaks and headers and footers. Each year's data should fit on one page for a total of three pages with the same print title.

1. Open the file **Retracct.xls**.

2. Change the page orientation to landscape and examine the worksheet in Print Preview.

3. Close Print Preview and set page breaks to create three pages, one for each year's data.

4. Set columns A, B, and C as print titles.

5. Change the page order to read the worksheet across, then down.

6. Adjust the column widths to make the data fill one page. Scale the worksheet down, if necessary.

7. Select a header that includes "Prepared by," the date, and the page number. Modify the header to identify the accounting firm, Brown and Brown, that prepared the statement.

8. Select a footer with the filename.

9. Lower the top margin to two inches. Raise the bottom margin to one inch.

10. Set up a named range **CapGrowth_96** for 1996's capital growth, so you can print only this information for clients that request it, without giving them other confidential information.

11. Print the range CapGrowth_96, and then clear the Print Area.

12. Press Ctrl + Home and save the workbook as *[your initials]***16-15.xls**.

13. Print pages from 1 to 3 of the worksheet, and close the workbook.

EXERCISE 16-16

Insert page breaks, scale the data, adjust margins and column widths, modify headers and footers, and print named ranges.

The Feestone Electronics company needs to create an attractive worksheet that shows the net investment returns of the retirement accounts of its employees.

1. Open the file **Invest.xls**.

2. Change the page orientation to landscape.

3. Insert page breaks so that each investment plan (Monthly Dollar Averaged, Single Investment, and Variable Monthly Investments) prints on a separate page.

4. Scale the data and adjust columns so the data fills the page, and center the page horizontally and vertically.

5. Add a centered header identifying the **Feestone Electronics Company Retirement Accounts** in bold.

6. Add a footer identifying the preparer (the investment firm Galax, Hemmings, and Sampson), the date, and the filename and page number.

7. Save the workbook as *[your initials]***16-16.xls**.

8. Create a named range for each page, and then print the pages.

9. Save the workbook again, and close it.

Unit 5 Applications

APPLICATION 5-1

Open multiple workbooks, switch between workbook windows, copy and paste between workbooks and worksheets, modify preset headers and footers, scale the worksheets, protect the worksheets, and print a range of worksheets.

Feestone Electronics currently ships products through United Express. It wants to compare the costs of three other delivery companies. Since the costs might change, Feestone needs a summary worksheet linked to each company's rate card.

1. Open the files **Shipanls.xls** and **Crntship.xls**.

2. Copy the information from **Crntship.xls** to a new first worksheet in **Shipanls.xls**. Use the same formatting and positioning used in the other three worksheets, and name the worksheet **United Express**.

3. Move a blank sheet to be first in **Shipanls.xls**, name it **Analysis**, and in cell A1 key the title **Shipping Costs Analysis**.

4. Key the labels in bold as shown in Figure U5-1. Center the column labels.

FIGURE U5-1

	United Express	CPS Corp.	Packages R Us	Overnight Specialists
Standard				
2-Day				
Overnight				

5. Paste link the shipping rates from each of the four delivery companies in the proper column in the Analysis sheet.

6. In the CPS Corp. sheet, change both the 2-day and overnight rates to **125.00**.

7. For each worksheet, modify the current header with "Shipping Cost Analysis" on the left and the date on the right. Create a custom footer with the worksheet name on the left and **Page** *[page number]* **of** *[total pages]* on the right.

8. Center the worksheets horizontally on the page and scale the worksheets to 125% of their normal size.

TIP: Select all the sheets, then choose the Page Set<u>u</u>p command on the <u>F</u>ile menu instead of setting up each page in Print Preview.

9. Protect only the Shipping Analysis worksheet, using *[your initials]* as the password.

10. Save the file as *[your initials]***u5-1.xls**.

11. Print the Shipping Analysis worksheet, and then print the United Express and CPS Corp. worksheets, and close all files.

APPLICATION 5-2

Copy and paste between worksheets, link between workbooks, insert hard page breaks, set print titles, modify headers and footers, unlock cells, and protect the worksheet.

Employees at Feestone Electronics get paid vacation, sick, and personal time. All employees get 3 personal days and 12 sick days per year. The amount of vacation time each employee receives depends on how long the person has been employed. Employees who have worked at Feestone for 0 to 3 years receive 1 week (5 days) paid vacation. Employees who have worked at least 4 years receive 2 weeks vacation. Employees who have worked for the company 7 years or more receive 3 weeks per year. You need to link the employee list and hire dates to a worksheet that calculates the time off due each employee.

1. Open the files **Timeoff.xls** and **Slryempl.xls**.

2. Paste link the Last Name, First Name, and Date Hired data from **Slryempl.xls** to **Timeoff.xls**.

3. Copy the formula in cell D9 down to calculate the vacation time due each employee.

4. Key the time off already used by each employee, as shown in Figure U5-2 (on the next page). (Hint: Key the vacation time used in column E, the sick time used in column G, and the personal time used in column I.)

5. Create and copy formulas to calculate the vacation time left, sick time left, and personal time left. Remember, sick time and personal time are the same for each employee every year.

6. Set the "Last Name," "First Name," and "Date Hired" columns as print titles.

7. Insert page breaks so the worksheet prints on three pages, one for vacation time, one for sick time, and one for personal time.

8. Protect the worksheets except for the "Used" columns.

9. Set up the worksheet to print in portrait orientation, centered horizontally.

10. Make the header 14-point size.

11. Modify the footer to include the filename at the left, and the page number and total number of pages at the right.

FIGURE U5-2

Last Name	First Name	Vacation Time Used	Sick Time Used	Personal Time Used
Abbott	Martha	3	5	0
Frisbee	John	5	1	0
Garcia	Ramone	10	9	1
LaConte	Danielle	10	12	0
Maplethorpe	Holly	5	0	3
Martin	Jamaica	5	0	0
Needlehoffen	Adrian	9	3	0
Northridge	Leroy	7	2	2
O'Connor	Patrick	12	0	0
Santos	Julia	5	1	0
Tellman	Lowell	5	0	3
Underwood	Marc	1	10	0
Young	Emma	15	11	1
Zimmer	Joseph	5	0	1

12. Save the file as *[your initials]***u5-2.xls**.

13. Print all three pages and close all files.

APPLICATION 5-3

Link data between workbooks, create linked formulas, create custom headers and footers, and protect the worksheet.

Feestone Electronics gives bonuses to its sales managers if they exceed their sales goals for the year. Develop a new worksheet that calculates the bonuses for the managers for 1996. Use Figure U5-3 as a guide for setting up your new worksheet.

FIGURE U5-3

```
                    Feestone Electronics

                  Sales Manager Bonus Plan

Manager              Region   Goal   Actual   Difference   Bonus

H. Maplethorpe       NE

A. Needlehoffen      NW

J. Frisbee           SE

J. Martin            SW

Total
```

The goal for 1996 is a 10% increase over the 1995 total sales. In the "Goal" column, create linked formulas that multiply the regional sales in **95sales.xls** by 1.1. In the "Actual" column, link the regional sales in **96sales.xls**. In the "Difference" column, subtract the Goal from the Actual.

If a manager meets the goal (Difference >=0), he or she receives $10,000. If a manager exceeds the goal by $1 million (Difference >= 1,000,000), he or she receives $20,000 total. Use a nested IF function to calculate the bonuses, and then total the bonuses.

Print the worksheet with a custom header that identifies the purpose of the worksheet and a custom footer that identifies the filename and date. Protect the worksheet from changes.

Save the worksheet as *[your initials]***u5-3.xls**. Print the worksheet and close all files.

Graphics

Charting a Running Success

Harry Hascabar's Hand-Crafted Leather Goods has been in existence for over 20 years. The company makes briefcases, shoes, handbags, and laptop-computer cases and sells them in a five shops in the San Francisco area. But Harry Hascabar's real passion is running. He has often run in the Boston Marathon and is a nationally known sports figure.

For over a decade, the company has been quite successful making special running shoes for long-distance runners. Harry would like the company to continue moving into this market by selling sports drinks that enhance performance for long-distance runners. He's even thinking of creating a new subsidiary called "Marathon Products."

Harry wants to research all the competing sports drinks before he formulates his own. He will keep a detailed log of his distances, times, and the product he drinks before he runs. Harry will be collecting a considerable amount of detailed information, and he needs to summarize it in an attractive format to secure financing for his new company.

To present his results attractively and visually, he needs to:

 Create a bar chart showing the average minutes per mile for each sports drink he tested personally. **(Lesson 17)**

 Create attractive charts that compare the various sports drinks he tested, with drawing objects and clip art. **(Lesson 18)**

Creating Charts and Maps

LESSON 17

OBJECTIVES

After completing this lesson, you will be able to:

1. Identify chart types and chart objects.
2. Use the ChartWizard to create an embedded chart.
3. Size and move a chart.
4. Edit a chart.
5. Save and print a chart.
6. Create a chart on a chart sheet.
7. Create a data map.
8. Enhance a data map.

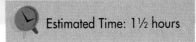
Estimated Time: 1½ hours

A chart is a visual representation of worksheet data. Charts are linked to worksheet data through cell references. This approach enables Excel to update the data in a chart automatically when you change the data in a worksheet.

Identifying Chart Types and Chart Objects

Many types of charts can be created in Excel. Once you have learned the different types, you can determine the purpose of the chart and match it to the data in the worksheet. Each Excel chart consists of various chart objects.

TABLE 17-1   Chart Types in Excel

TYPE	DEFINITION
Area	Area charts show the relationship of parts to a whole and emphasize the magnitude of change.
Bar	Bar charts illustrate comparisons among items or shows individual figures at a specific time.
Column	Column charts show variation over a period of time or demonstrate a comparison among items.
Pie	Pie charts compare the sizes of pieces in a whole unit. Each chart shows only one data series.
Doughnut	Doughnut charts also compare the sizes of pieces in a whole unit. The doughnut chart enables you to show more than one data series, however.
Line	Line charts show trends in data over a period of time at the same intervals, emphasizing the rate of change over time.
XY (Scatter)	XY (Scatter) charts compare trends over uneven time or measurement intervals plotted on the category axis. Scatter charts also display patterns from discrete x and y data measurements.
Radar	Radar charts show changes or frequencies of data relative to a center point and to other data points. Each category has its own value axis radiating from the center point. Lines connect all values in the same series.
3-D Surface	3-D surface charts are useful for finding the optimum combinations between two sets of data. They can show relationships between large amounts of data that would otherwise be difficult to see.
3-D Area	3-D area charts emphasize the sum of plotted values and separate chart data series into distinct rows to show differences among the data series.
3-D Bar	3-D bar charts compare data series over time or against one another.
3-D Column	3-D column charts add visual impact for comparing data series over time.
3-D Line	3-D line charts show the lines as 3-D ribbons, making individual lines easier to view.
3-D Pie	3-D pie charts emphasize the data values in the front wedges.

Excel charts contain many objects you can select and modify individually.

FIGURE 17-1
Excel chart objects

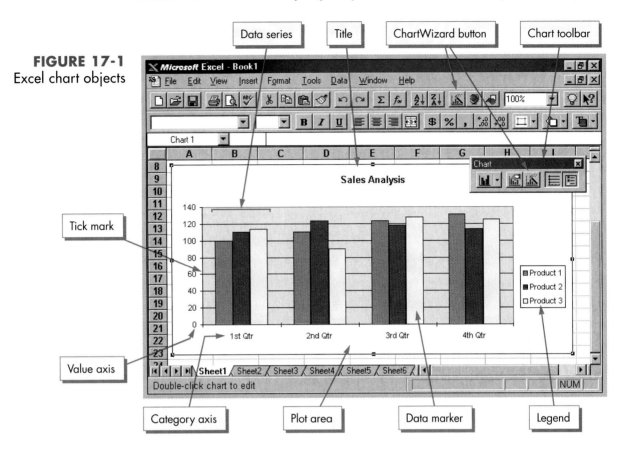

Each Excel chart object is described below:

- The *category axis* is the horizontal (or *x*) axis along the bottom of most charts; it frequently refers to time series.
- The *value axis* is the vertical (or *y*) axis against which data points are measured.
- The *plot area* is the rectangular area bounded by the two axes. It includes all axes and data points.
- A *data marker* is an object that represents individual data points. It can be a bar, area, dot, picture, or other symbol that marks a single data point or value.
- A *legend* is a guide that explains the symbols, patterns, or colors used to differentiate data series.
- A *tick mark* is a division mark along the category (x) and value (y) axes.
- A *data point* is a single piece of data.
- A *data series* is a collection of data points that are related to one another. These values are usually found within the same column or row in the worksheet.
- The chart title gives the name of the chart.

- The Chart toolbar is a available with special charting tools.
- The ChartWizard button starts the ChartWizard, which guides you step-by-step through the creation of a chart.

Using the ChartWizard

The ChartWizard is the easiest method of creating an Excel chart. Using selected worksheet data, the ChartWizard guides you through the process of creating a chart. The completed chart is *embedded* in the worksheet. If you change data in the worksheet, Excel will update the chart automatically.

In the case study, Harry Hascabar wants to chart the effects of different sports drinks on his running speed. Before creating the chart, you'll need to develop a worksheet showing the sports drinks used and the average minutes per mile recorded for each drink.

EXERCISE 17-1 Enter the Chart Data

1. Start a new workbook, and then key the following data in the cells indicated:

A1:	**Drink**	B1:	**Average Minutes**
A3:	**HydraPunch**	B3:	**7.63**
A4:	**SurgeQuench**	B4:	**7.77**
A5:	**AllSport**	B5:	**8.2**
A6:	**CynoMax**	B6:	**8.12**
A7:	**Endrun**	B7:	**7.86**
A8:	**Everlast**	B8:	**8.22**
A9:	**Innergize**	B9:	**7.98**

2. Modify the column widths as necessary.
3. Center the column headings and make them bold.
4. Save the workbook as *[your initials]***17-1.xls**.

EXERCISE 17-2 Use the ChartWizard

1. Select cells A1 through B9.
2. Click the ChartWizard button on the Standard toolbar. A moving border appears around the selected cells and the mouse pointer changes to a crosshair with a small chart object attached to it.

3. Select cells B11 through F25. You've now identified the area where the embedded chart will appear.

TIP: To align a chart with cell edges, hold down [Alt] as you drag across where you want to establish the chart. To make the chart square, hold down [Shift] as you drag.

4. Release the mouse button. The ChartWizard - Step 1 of 5 dialog box appears.

FIGURE 17-2
ChartWizard - Step
1 of 5 dialog box

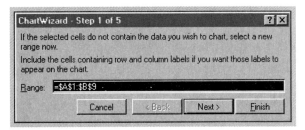

NOTE: The Step 1 of 5 dialog box allows you to verify the selected data. You can edit the data range if necessary by clicking in the reference range.

EXERCISE 17-3 **Choose the Chart Type**

1. Click Next to go to the second ChartWizard dialog box.

NOTE: Clicking Finish in the first step of the ChartWizard creates the chart by using the Excel 2-D column default chart format.

FIGURE 17-3
ChartWizard - Step
2 of 5 dialog box

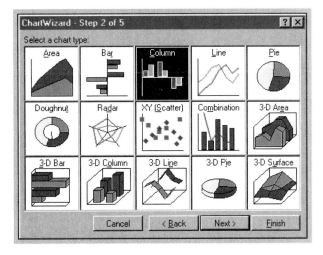

2. Click the Bar chart type.

3. Click Next. The ChartWizard - Step 3 of 5 dialog box displays all available formats for bar charts.

FIGURE 17-4
ChartWizard - Step
3 of 5 dialog box

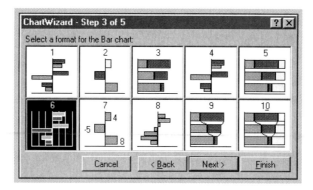

4. Choose format 1, and then click Next.

EXERCISE **17-4** **Enter Additional Chart Information**

The ChartWizard - Step 4 of 5 dialog box allows you to specify certain plotting information to produce the desired chart.

1. Click the Columns option button under Data Series in, if necessary.

2. Use First should be set to 1 Column. This choice indicates that column A will be used as the labels on the x axis (see the Sample Chart in the dialog box).

3. For the next setting, Use First should be set to 1 Row. The data label in row 1 ("Average Minutes") will appear in the legend.

4. Click Next.

EXERCISE **17-5** **Add a Legend and Titles**

---

1. Click the Yes option to add a legend.

FIGURE 17-5
ChartWizard - Step
5 of 5 dialog box

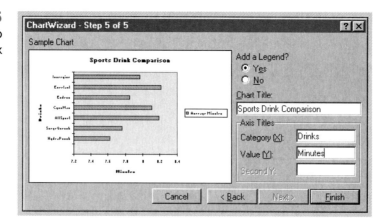

2. Key **Sports Drink Comparison** in the <u>C</u>hart Title text box. The title will appear in the Sample Chart.

3. Press `Tab`, and then key **Drinks** in the Category (X) text box.

4. Press `Tab`, and then key **Minutes** in the Value (Y) text box.

5. Click <u>F</u>inish. The chart is displayed in the worksheet.

Sizing and Moving a Chart

Once you've created a chart, you can change its size, proportions, and position on the worksheet.

EXERCISE 17-6 Move and Size the Chart

1. Select the chart by clicking with the mouse inside the chart. Small black squares, called *selection handles*, appear around the selected chart.

2. Point anywhere within the chart.

3. Click and drag the chart so that the upper right-hand corner is in cell A14.

4. Move the pointer over the bottom right selection handle until it changes to a double-headed arrow.

5. Using the double-headed arrow, enlarge the chart by dragging the bottom right corner to cell G29.

6. Click outside the chart to deactivate it.

7. Save the workbook as *[your initials]***17-6.xls**.

Editing a Chart

After creating a chart, you may want to edit its contents or change the chart type to make it more attractive or easier to understand. Before modifying an embedded chart, you must *activate* it by double-clicking it. The Chart toolbar can then be used to make additional modifications.

EXERCISE 17-7 Activate the Chart and Display the Chart Toolbar

1. Move the mouse pointer inside the embedded chart and double-click. The chart window becomes activated. A hatched border appears around the chart, and the Chart toolbar is displayed.

2. If the Chart toolbar is not displayed automatically, click any toolbar displayed on the screen with the right mouse button, and then choose Chart from the shortcut menu.

FIGURE 17-6
Activated chart in
the worksheet

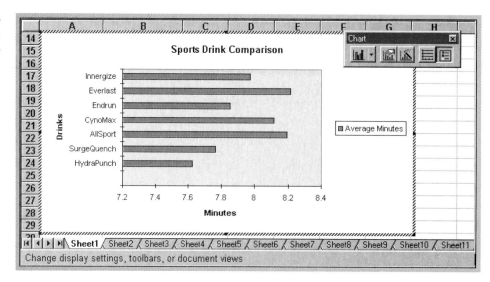

TABLE 17-2   **Chart Toolbar**

BUTTON	NAME	DESCRIPTION
	Chart Type	Displays the different chart types available.
	Default Chart	Applies the 2-D column by default chart type by default.
	ChartWizard	Guides you through the process of creating a chart.
	Horizontal Gridlines	Removes or adds horizontal gridlines.
	Legend	Removes or adds a legend.

EXERCISE **17-8** **Change the Chart Type**

Viewing information arranged in a variety of chart types can provide different perspectives of your data. You can use the Chart toolbar or the menu bar to change the chart type.

1. Click the down arrow to the right of the Chart Type button on the Chart toolbar. Excel displays a drop-down list of chart types.

FIGURE 17-7
Drop-down list of
chart types

2. Click the Area button in the top left-hand corner. The chart is displayed as an area chart.

3. To view another perspective, reopen the drop-down list and click the 3-D Pie button ⬜.

4. Choose Chart <u>T</u>ype from the F<u>o</u>rmat menu.

5. Under Chart Dimension, select the <u>2</u>-D option.

6. Select the Bar chart and click OK. The first chart type you selected is restored.

⭐ **TIP:** Another way is change the chart type is to right-click the activated chart and choose Chart Type from the shortcut menu.

EXERCISE **17-9** **Change Chart Subtype**

Excel offers various formats, called subtypes, for each type of chart.

1. With the chart still activated, choose Bar Group from the Format menu.

2. Click the Subtype tab, if necessary.

3. Choose the second Subtype, stacked bars. The sample chart within the dialog box changes to display the new format.

4. Click Cancel to close the Format Bar Group dialog box.

EXERCISE **17-10** **Change Chart and Axis Titles**

You may want to change titles, axes, or other items in your chart. You can select various chart items in an active chart by clicking the item.

1. Click the chart title "Sports Drink Comparison." The title is selected, and "Title" appears in the Name box on the formula bar.

2. Type **Comparison for Weeks 1-5** and press Enter. The new text replaces the old title.

3. Click the category axis title "Drinks," and change it to **Sports Drinks**

4. Click the value axis title "Minutes," and change it to **Minutes Per Mile**

 TIP: After selecting a chart text item, you can use the I-beam pointer to edit the text. Once a chart text item is selected, you can use the Formatting toolbar to change its font, style, or size.

EXERCISE **17-11** **Use the Legend to Display Categories**

In this chart, you can remove the category labels (the sports drink names) and list them in the legend instead.

1. Select the category axis in the active chart window. (To select the axis, you can either click it directly, click a tick mark, or click one of the drink names.) "Axis 2" should appear in the Name box on the formula bar.

2. Choose Selected Axis from the Format menu.

3. Click the Patterns tab, if necessary. In the Tick-Mark Labels box, click None.

FIGURE 17-8
Patterns options in
the Format Axis
dialog box

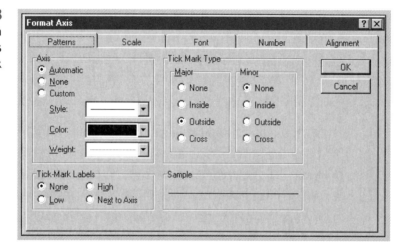

4. Click OK. The sports drink names no longer appear next to the category axis.

5. Choose Bar Group from the Format menu, and then click the Options tab.

6. Click the Vary Colors by Point check box to make each data point in the series a different color.

7. Click OK. The legend displays the category labels and colors corresponding to the labels used in the chart. Because row 2 of the worksheet is blank, the legend includes a blank eighth color key and the category axis shows a blank area below HydraPunch.

8. Click outside the chart to deactivate it. Scroll to row 2 and delete it from the worksheet. The chart reflects the change.

FIGURE 17-9
Options in the
Format Bar Group
dialog box

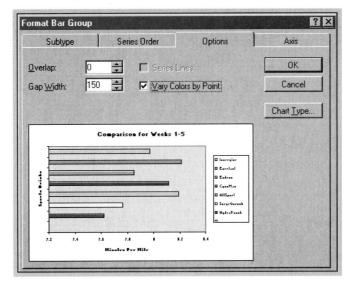

EXERCISE **17-12** **Add Data to a Chart**

The easiest way to add data to an embedded chart is to enter it in the worksheet and then drag it onto the chart.

1. In cell A9, key **PowerEase**

2. In cell B9, key **6.1**

3. Select the new data in cells A9:B9.

4. Drag the data onto the embedded chart and release the mouse button.

 NOTE: To drag the selected data, move the mouse pointer to the bottom edge of the selection. Make sure the mouse pointer appears as an arrow, and not a cross, before dragging.

Saving and Printing a Chart

A chart is saved each time you save the workbook in which it is embedded. Once a chart is completed, you'll want to print it. Embedded charts print with the worksheet. You can preview the chart before printing to see how it looks on the worksheet. You can also print only the chart by first activating it and then clicking 🖨.

UNIT 6 ■ GRAPHICS

EXERCISE 17-13 Saving and Printing

1. Click outside the chart to deselect it.

2. Save the workbook as *[your initials]***17-13.xls**.

3. Click to preview the chart and worksheet.

4. Change the page setup, if desired.

5. Print the worksheet.

Creating a Chart on a Chart Sheet

You can create a chart so that it appears in a separate sheet in a workbook. If you need to print a chart to use in a presentation, for example, creating a chart on its own chart sheet is the best approach.

When you insert a chart in a sheet, you add the chart to the active workbook. Although you can print a chart sheet separately from the worksheet containing the chart data, it is saved with the other sheets in the workbook.

The charts are named Chart1, Chart2, Chart3, and so on by default. They can be renamed by choosing Format, Sheet, Rename, or by double-clicking the tab for the chart sheet and typing in a new name.

EXERCISE 17-14 Create a Chart on a Chart Sheet

1. Select the same data you used for the embedded chart.

2. Choose Insert, Chart, As New Sheet.

3. Click Next to confirm the cell range.

4. Choose the 3-D Pie chart ,and then click Next.

5. Choose format 7, and then click Next.

6. Click Next again, and then click Finish. Chart1 appears as a new sheet in the workbook.

7. Save the workbook again.

8. Print the chart sheet, and then close the workbook.

428

FIGURE 17-10
New chart sheet

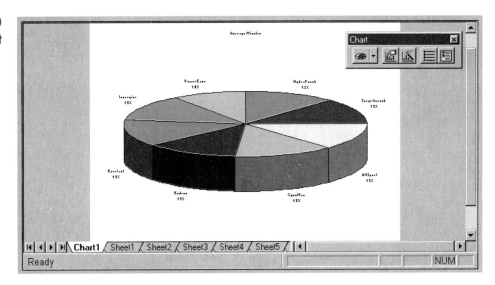

Creating a Data Map

Data Map is a new feature in Excel that is used for charting geographical data. Just as you created a chart based on worksheet data, you can display a map based on worksheet data to analyze information for a particular region.

Before you create your map, you need to organize the data so that the Data Map Feature can read it. The first column must contain names or abbreviations of geographic regions, such as states or countries. The next column or columns contain numeric data related to each region.

When you select the data to create your map, include the column headings. These headings will help Data Map automatically create legends and titles.

EXERCISE **17-15** **Create a Data Map**

For this exercise, you'll create a map showing where in the United States Harry Hascabar has competed in races, and how many races he won in each state.

1. Start a new workbook.
2. Key the data as shown in Figure 17-11 (on the next page).
3. Select cells A1 through B8.
4. Click the Map button on the Standard toolbar.
5. Drag across the worksheet to the position where you want the map displayed.
6. Release the mouse button. Because the Data Map feature cannot determine a unique map to use when it analyzes the left column of data, it displays the Multiple Maps Available dialog box.

429

FIGURE 17-11

	A	B
1	STATES	RACES
2	CA	5
3	FL	5
4	IL	10
5	NY	5
6	WA	3
7	TX	7
8	AZ	2

7. Choose United States and click OK. The map is displayed in the worksheet. The Data Map toolbar and menu appear, and the Data Map Control dialog box appears over your map.

FIGURE 17-12
Using the Data Map feature

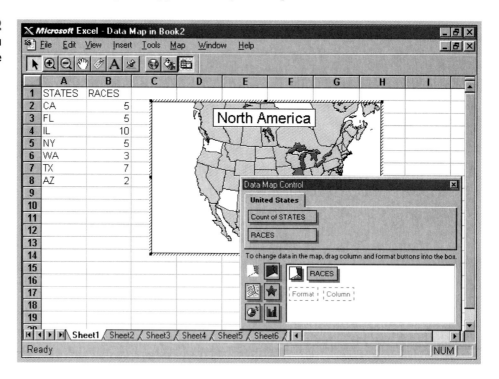

8. Drag the Data Map Control dialog box by its title bar to another location if it covers the map.

Enhancing a Data Map

When a data map is active, you can use a menu and toolbar designed to manipulate the data map object. Use the Data Map Control dialog box to change your map. You can also enhance your map by adding and formatting text and labels, changing fonts, and selecting a different color scheme.

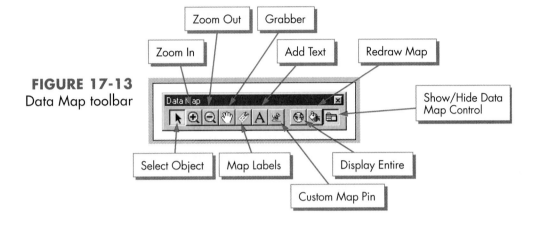

FIGURE 17-13
Data Map toolbar

EXERCISE 17-16 Insert Map Labels

---

1. Double-click the title on the map and highlight the text by dragging.
2. Key **UNITED STATES** as the new title.
3. Click the Add Text button A on the Data Map toolbar.
4. Click the insertion point on California. Key **5** and press Enter.
5. Click the insertion point on Florida. Key **5** and press Enter.
6. Follow the same directions to key the number of races won in each state, as shown in the worksheet.

TIP: After keying a number, you may want to move it for better positioning. Click ▶, point to the number, and click to select it. You can then use the four-headed arrow pointer to drag the number.

EXERCISE 17-17 Change Fonts

---

1. Activate the map by double-clicking, if necessary.
2. Point to the map title and right-click with the mouse.
3. Choose Format Font from the shortcut menu to display the Font dialog box.

4. Choose Arial Black, Bold, 14 point, and then click OK.

EXERCISE 17-18 Change Map Features and Shading

1. Using the Data Map Control dialog box, drag the Category Shading button across into the white box. Each category (state) is now specified by color.

2. Right-click the mouse button anywhere within the activated map.

3. Choose Features from the shortcut menu to display the Map Features dialog box.

FIGURE 17-14
Map Features
dialog box

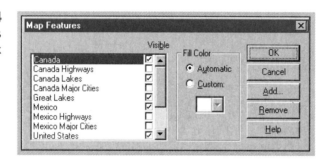

4. Because you want to show a map of the United States and not all of North America, click the following check boxes to deselect them: Canada, Canada Lakes, and Mexico.

5. Click OK. The map now includes just the United States.

6. Click outside the map to deselect it and return to the worksheet.

7. Save the workbook as *[your initials]*17-18.xls.

8. Print and close the workbook.

COMMAND SUMMARY

FEATURE	BUTTON	MENU	KEYBOARD
Create a chart	📊	Insert, Chart	F11
Create a map	🌐	Insert, Map	

Microsoft Excel Help offers extensive help on charts and maps. For example, you can refer to Help for a visual description of chart types and for information about creating and formatting data maps.

Use Help to view examples of charts and maps:

1. Choose Answer Wizard from the Help menu.

2. Key **chart types**

3. Display the first topic under "Tell Me About."

4. Explore the Help window, viewing examples of the different chart types.

5. When you're finished, click Help Topics.

6. Click the Contents tab, and double-click "What's New."

7. Display "Data Map."

8. Explore the Help window, closing it when you're finished.

FIGURE 17-15
Using Help to learn more about data maps

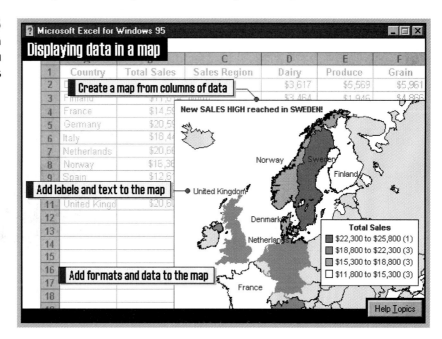

Concepts Review

Each of the following statements is either true or false. Indicate your choice by circling T or F.

T F **1.** Charts are linked to worksheet data through cell references.

T F **2.** A tick mark represents a single piece of data.

T F **3.** The ChartWizard can create an embedded chart or a chart on its own chart sheet.

T F **4.** Once a chart is created, you cannot edit its contents.

T F **5.** The Chart toolbar is displayed when a chart is activated.

T F **6.** Embedded charts do not print with the worksheet.

T F **7.** Organizing your data is the first step in creating a map.

T F **8.** You activate a chart or a map by double-clicking it.

Write the correct answer in the space provided.

1. Which type of chart shows trends in data over a period of time at the same intervals, emphasizing the rate of change over time?

2. Which chart element explains the symbols, patterns, or colors used to differentiate data series?

3. What appears around a chart after it has been activated?

4. What are the various formats for each type of chart called?

5. Which axis is generally the horizontal axis?

6. If you create a chart on a chart sheet, what is the chart named by default?

7. What is the name of the area bounded by two axes on a chart?

_____

8. Which dialog box allows you to select only the features you want to see on your map?

_____

CRITICAL THINKING

Answer these questions on a separate piece of paper. There are no right or wrong answers. Support your answers with examples from your own experience, if possible.

1. Why would a business find the charting feature of Excel advantageous? What reasons could you give your boss for creating charts?

2. If you were working for a large retail store with many different outlets, would the mapping feature be an important tool for you? How many different ways could you use the Data Map feature to illustrate data from your company?

3. Can you think of instances in your own life where you could use both charts and maps? Make a list of those instances.

Skills Review

EXERCISE 17-19

Use the ChartWizard to create an embedded chart.

1. Open the file **Times.xls**.

2. Use the ChartWizard to create an embedded chart by following these steps:

   a. Select cells A2:B6.

   b. Click the ChartWizard button on the Standard toolbar.

   c. Use the crosshair pointer to select cells B9:H20 as the chart area.

   d. Click Next in the first ChartWizard dialog box to confirm the range.

   e. Choose 3-D Bar as the chart type, and then click Next.

   f. Click Next in the third and fourth dialog boxes.

   g. In the fifth dialog box, key **Best Marathon Times** as the chart title and then click <u>F</u>inish.

3. Click outside the chart to deselect it.

4. Save the workbook as *[your initials]***17-19.xls**.

5. Print and close the workbook.

EXERCISE 17-20

Add data to a chart, change the chart type, and size a chart.

1. Open the file **Drinks1.xls**.
2. Enter the following data in cells A9:B11:

   Exceed   7.75

   HydraFuel   8.20

   PurePower   7.87

3. Incorporate the new data into the embedded chart by following these steps:
   a. Double-click the chart to activate the chart window.
   b. Select cells A9:B11.
   c. Drag the selection to the embedded chart.
4. Change the chart type to Column by following these steps:
   a. Click the down arrow on the Chart Type button ![Chart Type button] on the Chart toolbar.
   b. Choose the Column chart.
5. Size the chart to fit the category labels by following these steps:
   a. Click the chart. Sizing handles appear around the chart border.
   b. Scroll to the bottom of the chart.
   c. Point to the middle selection handle at the bottom of the chart.
   d. Using the two-headed arrow, drag the bottom border down until all of the category text fits.
6. Deselect the chart.
7. Save the workbook as *[your initials]***17-20.xls**.
8. Print and close the workbook.

EXERCISE 17-21

Create a separate chart sheet.

1. Open the file **Drinks2.xls**.
2. Create a separate chart sheet by following these steps:
   a. Select cells A1:B11.
   b. Select Insert, Chart, As New Chart from the menu bar.
   c. In the first ChartWizard dialog box, click Next.
   d. Choose the Pie chart, and then click Next.
   e. Choose format 7, and then click Next.
   f. Click Next, and then click Finish.
3. Save the workbook as *[your initials]***17-21.xls**.
2. Print the chart sheet, and then close the workbook.

EXERCISE 17-22

Create a data map, and enhance the map by adding map labels.

1. Start a new workbook.

2. Key the following data in cells A1:B7:

STATES	NUMBER
UT	70
FL	86
TX	75
NY	35
IL	13
CA	96

3. Create a data map by following these steps:

  a. Select cells A1:B7.

  b. Click the Map button 🖳 on the Standard toolbar.

  c. Drag the crosshair pointer from cell A10 to cell G22.

  d. In the Multiple Maps Available dialog box, choose United States and then click OK.

4. Change the map title by following these steps:

  a. Double-click the map title.

  b. Drag to select the existing text.

  c. Key the new title **States Selling Most Drinks**

  d. Click outside the title to deselect it or press Enter.

5. Move the title by following these steps:

  a. Click the title to select it.

  b. Using the four-headed arrow, drag the title to center it across the top of the map.

6. Add labels to the map by following these steps:

  a. Click the Add Text button A on the Map toolbar.

  b. Click in each state and key in the number of drinks sold in that state.

  c. Adjust the position of the number labels, if necessary.

7. Click outside of the map to deactivate it.

8. Save the workbook as *[your initials]***17-22.xls**.

9. Print and close the workbook.

Lesson Applications

Enter data, and use the ChartWizard to create a column chart and enter additional chart information.

After testing eight different sports drinks over an eight-week period, Harry Hascabar has recorded the number of miles he ran and his running times. Enter the data and create a chart to display it.

1. Start a new workbook.
2. Enter the data shown in Figure 17-16, using the alignment indicated. Format all of the times for two decimal places.

FIGURE 17-16

```
            HASCABAR'S RACING RECORD

               Weeks 1-8

  DRINK         MILES    AVERAGE MILE TIME

  HydraPunch      10            7.83

  SuperQuench     15            7.77

  AllSport         8            8.20

  CynoMax         12            8.12

  Endrun          10            7.86

  Everlast         9            8.22

  Innergize       10            7.96

  PowerEase       10            6.10
```

3. Create an embedded column chart using the ChartWizard. Include a legend, add the title **Hascabar's Racing Record**, and add the x-axis title **Sports Drink**
4. Size the chart to include all of the data.
5. Rename the Sheet1 tab as **Column Chart**.
6. Save the workbook as *[your initials]***17-23.xls**.
7. Print the chart with the worksheet, and then close the file.

EXERCISE 17-24

Create a new chart sheet, change the chart type, and add new chart information.

Harry Hascabar has run another eight weeks and has charted his speed and distance using a bar chart. He'd like a different perspective on his data by seeing it displayed in another type of chart.

1. Open the file **Wks9-16.xls**.

2. Create a Combination chart as a new chart sheet. Use format 2, include a legend, and add the chart title **WEEKS 9-16**

3. Use the Chart toolbar to change the chart type to Line and add horizontal gridlines.

4. Right-click the Category axis, and then key the x-axis title **Sports Drinks Used**

5. Save the workbook as *[your initials]***17-24.xls**.

6. Change the chart tab to the filename.

7. Print the chart sheet, and then close the file.

EXERCISE 17-25

Create a data map with map labels, and adjust the map features, font, and shading.

After competing in seven races over an eight-week period, Harry Hascabar wants to analyze how fast he ran in each state. He needs a map that shows where he ran and his running times.

1. Open the file **Map.xls**.

2. Reverse the position of the "Drink" and "Time" column headings and data. Insert a new column at column A. Adjust the column widths and alignment as necessary.

3. Add the following data to cells A3:A10:

STATE

AZ

NC

MT

GA

WY

OR

MD

4. Create a data map using the data in columns A and B.

5. Delete any features that don't belong on a map of the United States.

6. Change the map title to **RUNNING TIME PER STATE**, and then center it.

7. Use the Data Map Control dialog box to display the map with category shading.

8. Add map labels that show Harry's running time in each state.

9. Change the font of the running time labels to Arial Black.

 TIP: Right-click each label and then use the Shortcut menu.

10. Make the map slightly larger.

11. Save the workbook as *[your initials]***17-25.xls**.

12. Print and close the workbook.

EXERCISE 17-26

Choose the appropriate chart type, create a chart as a separate sheet, and add new chart information.

Harry Hascabar wants to see how his running times stack up against three of his colleagues. Using the data for all four runners, create a chart that compares the times and miles for each runner.

1. Start a new workbook.

2. Enter the data shown in Figure 17-17, using the alignment and formatting indicated.

FIGURE 17-17

COMPARISON BETWEEN COLLEAGUES

NAME	MILES	TIME
Harry Hascabar	9.30	7.98
Jose Garcia	10.10	7.51
Mark Yingling	8.97	6.87
George Bunting	9.98	7.45

3. Create the chart as a new chart sheet, using the chart type that will best depict the information.

4. Use appropriate titles for the chart and the chart axes.

5. Enhance the chart by using any method you have learned in this lesson.

6. Rename the Chart tab, giving it an appropriate name.

7. Rename the Sheet tab, giving it an appropriate name.

8. Save the workbook as *[your initials]***17-26.xls**.

9. Print the entire workbook and then close it.

Enhancing Charts and Worksheets

LESSON

18

To make your charts more attractive, you can enhance them by adding colors, patterns, borders, and new fonts. You can also add impact to either charts or ordinary worksheet data by creating drawing objects (such as lines, arrows, or text boxes) or importing clip art.

Formatting Chart Text

Just as you can format the text in a worksheet, you can format any chart text by changing its font, style, color, size, or alignment. Experimenting with formatting can create charts that have greater visual appeal.

EXERCISE **18-1** **Change Font, Style, and Size**

1. Open the file **Sports.xls**.

2. Activate the chart by double-clicking. Because the chart is too large for the window, it appears in its own window with a title bar.

3. Click the chart title, "Sports Drink Comparison." The title is selected, and "Title" appears in the name box on the formula bar.

 NOTE: Each time you select a chart object, the name box on the formula bar displays its name, such as Title, Axis 1, Legend, and so on. Refer to the name box to make sure that you have selected the desired object.

4. Use the Font drop-down list on the Formatting toolbar to change the font to Arial Black.

5. Right-click the value axis title, "Minutes Per Mile." The title is selected, and the shortcut menu opens.

6. Choose Format Axis Title from the shortcut menu. Notice the various formatting options available in the dialog box.

 NOTE: Each element of the chart has its own dialog box, which enables you to change the appearance of that particular element.

7. Click the Font tab, if necessary. Change the font to bold italic, and then click OK.

8. Click the category axis title, "Sports Drinks," to select it. Click $\boxed{I}$ on the Formatting toolbar to add italic formatting.

EXERCISE **18-2** **Change Text Color**

1. With the chart still activated, double-click the chart title. The Format Chart Title dialog box opens.

.

 NOTE: Double-clicking a chart element is another way to open the dialog box to format the element.

2. Click the Font tab, if necessary.

3. Under Color, click the down arrow to open the color palette.

4. Choose red from the top row of the palette.

5. Change the font size to 11 point, and then click OK.

FIGURE 18-1
Formatting the
chart title

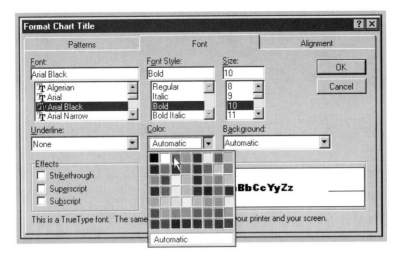

Enhancing the Legend

Legends are a vital component of a chart. They focus the viewer on what the chart is trying to depict. For this reason, it's important to make the legend stand out. You can customize the legend in several different ways:

- Place it in a different area on the chart.
- Use colors and patterns.
- Customize the border.
- Change the font.

EXERCISE 18-3 Change Legend Color, Pattern, and Border

1. With the chart window still active, double-click the legend. The Format Legend dialog box appears.

2. Click the Patterns tab. Check the Sha*d*ow box in the Border area.

3. Under Area, choose a background color from the color palette that appeals to you. (Avoid dark colors.)

4. Click the down arrow next to *P*attern. The Pattern palette allows you to choose a pattern and pattern color. By default, the pattern color is black.

5. Choose the first pattern in the third row (horizontal lines). Notice the black pattern and the background color that appear in the Sample box.

6. Click OK. The legend now has a background color and pattern.

 NOTE: Because the legend is small, you may not be able to see the pattern in the chart window. When the legend is enlarged in Exercise 18-5, the pattern will be more easily seen.

1. Double-click the legend.

2. Click the Placement tab in the Format Legend dialog box, and then choose <u>B</u>ottom.

3. Go back to the Font tab and change the font to Times New Roman, bold, 10 point.

4. Click OK. The legend now appears at the bottom of the chart, below the category axis title.

FIGURE 18-2
Legend with a new format and position

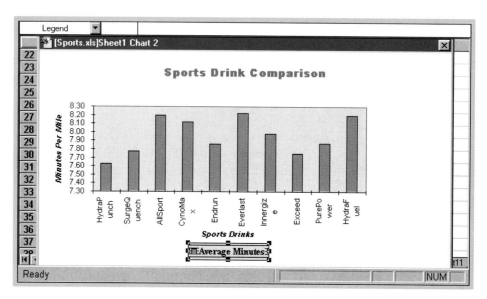

5. Close the chart window by clicking its Close button ☒. Review the new position and formatting of the legend.

6. If the new formatting and placement now occupy space needed by the category labels (check the longest label, "SurgeQuench"), resize the chart. To do this, click the chart once to select it, and then drag the center selection handle at the bottom of the chart down one or two rows.

7. Save the workbook as *[your initials]***18-4.xls**.

Changing Data Series Colors and Patterns

You can change data series colors and patterns for the entire chart or for individual data markers. When you change colors or patterns for individual markers, the legend will reflect those changes by displaying the color key and data point labels.

EXERCISE 18-5 Change Color for a Data Series

1. Double-click the chart to activate it.
2. Click one of the columns in the chart to select the data series.
3. Choose Selected Data Series from the Format menu (or click Ctrl + 1).

 NOTE: The Format menu and Ctrl + 1 are two additional methods for opening the dialog box to format a selected chart item.

4. Choose another color from the color palette, and then click OK. The columns appear in the new color.
5. Click ↺ to undo the color change.
6. Right-click one of the columns in the chart, and then choose Format Column Group from the shortcut menu.
7. Click the Options tab.

 NOTE: The Options tab in the Format dialog box varies according to the type of chart with which you are working. You may remember this dialog box and the one that follows from the previous lesson, in which you worked with a bar chart.

8. Click to select Vary Colors by Point, and then click OK. The data markers appear in different colors, and the legend displays each color and label.
9. Deactivate the chart.
10. Resize the chart to accommodate the new legend, if necessary.

FIGURE 18-3
Legend reflecting
color changes

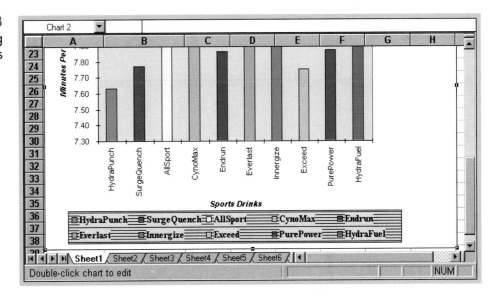

Adding Backgrounds and Borders

To add variety to your chart, you can apply colored or patterned backgrounds and borders. Use the Format Chart Area dialog box, being careful not to make the chart look cluttered.

EXERCISE | **18-6** | **Add Background Color and Borders**

---

1. Double-click the chart.
2. Right-click on the white background of the chart, and then choose Format Chart Area from the shortcut menu.
3. Choose the Patterns tab. Under Border, click Custom.
4. Open the Weight drop-down list and choose the last option (the heaviest line).

FIGURE 18-4
Formatting the chart area

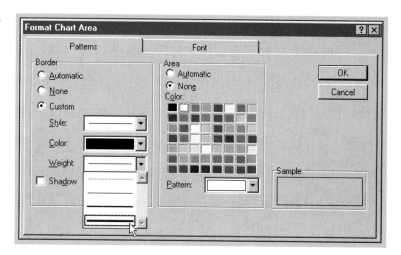

5. Choose a light color from the palette for the chart area, and then click OK.
6. Close the chart window.

Adding Drawing Objects

An effective method for enhancing charts or highlighting important data is to create graphic objects with the Drawing toolbar. You can draw text boxes, arrows, rectangles, and other objects. These items can then be moved, sized, and formatted independently of the worksheet.

EXERCISE 18-7 **Display and Position the Drawing Toolbar**

Use the Drawing button on the Standard toolbar to display the Drawing toolbar. You can then position this toolbar anywhere you want for convenient access.

1. Click ⬚ on the Standard toolbar. The toolbar will appear in the same position in which it was previously placed.
2. Drag the toolbar to place it under the Formatting toolbar, if necessary.
3. Examine each of the buttons on the Drawing toolbar by pointing to it. A ToolTip will identify the button by name, and the status bar will describe the button's function.

TABLE 18-1   **Drawing Toolbar**

BUTTON	NAME	FUNCTION
	Line	Draws a straight line.
	Rectangle	Draws a rectangle or square.
	Ellipse	Draws an ellipse (oval) or circle.
	Arc	Draws an arc or circle segment.
	Freeform	Draws any shape that combines straight and freehand lines.
	Text Box	Draws a text box in worksheets and charts.
	Arrow	Draws an arrow.
	Freehand	Draws any shape.
	Filled Rectangle	Draws a filled rectangle or square.
	Filled Ellipse	Draws a filled ellipse or circle.
	Filled Arc	Draws a filled arc.
	Filled Freeform	Draws a filled freeform shape.
	Create Button	Creates a custom button to which you can assign macros.
	Drawing Selection	Selects an object or drags a rectangle around multiple objects to select them.
	Bring to Front	Brings a selected object above other objects.
	Send to Back	Sends a selected object behind other objects.
	Group Objects	Groups separate objects into one object.

continues

447

TABLE 18-1   **Drawing Toolbar** *continued*

BUTTON	NAME	FUNCTION
🔲	Ungroup Objects	Separates the selected group into individual objects.
🔲	Reshape	Reshapes a freehand line by dragging at points along the line.
🔲	Drop Shadow	Draws a shadow behind text boxes and most shapes.
🔲	Pattern	Adds or changes a pattern or pattern color to a selected object.

EXERCISE **18-8** **Add Text Boxes**

Text boxes can be positioned anywhere on a chart and are often used to provide labels or comments. They are frequently combined with arrows.

This exercise will demonstrate two ways to create a text box: one involving keying text directly into the formula bar, and a second that uses the Drawing toolbar.

1. Activate the chart by double-clicking.

2. Position the pointer in the formula bar. When the pointer changes to an I-beam, click the left mouse button.

3. Key **Best Tasting** and press [Enter]. The text box appears in the chart, surrounded by a hatched border with selection handles for sizing. You can move the text box to any position on the chart.

4. Point to the border of the text box. Use the white arrow pointer to drag the text box so that it's centered below the chart title.

5. Click outside the text box to deselect it. By default, text boxes in charts do not have borders.

6. Close the chart window.

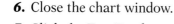

7. Click the Text Box button 📋 on the Drawing toolbar. The pointer changes to a crosshair (or cross).

9. Drag the crosshair pointer to draw a box that spans roughly from cell D2 through cell F3. Release the mouse button.

10. At the insertion point, key **The faster the time, the better the drink!**

11. Click outside the text box to deselect it. By default, text boxes in worksheets *do* have borders.

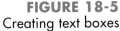
FIGURE 18-5
Creating text boxes

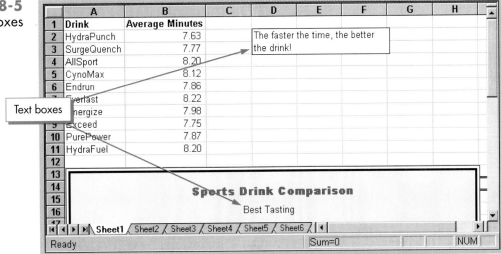

EXERCISE **18-9** **Draw Lines, Arrows, and Shapes**

Use the Drawing toolbar to create lines, arrows, rectangles, and ellipses to highlight specific areas in a chart or worksheet.

Just as you created a text box, you can simply click the desired drawing button, position the crosshair where you want to start drawing, and then drag the crosshair pointer to the desired size. When you release the mouse button, the drawing object is automatically selected and the object name appears in the name box on the formula bar.

NOTE: If you click a drawing button and then decide not to draw, you can press ⎋Esc to cancel the drawing process and restore the normal pointer. In addition, if you draw an object and decide you don't like it, you can delete it immediately by pressing ⎉Delete.

1. Click the Rectangle button ▭ on the Drawing toolbar.

2. Position the crosshair pointer at the upper right-hand corner of cell B2 in the worksheet. Drag diagonally to the left until you have created a rectangle around the numbers 7.63 and 7.77. Release the mouse button. The rectangle is selected, as indicated by the selection handles. (If you're not pleased with the shape of the rectangle, press ⎉Delete and try again.)

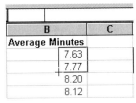
FIGURE 18-6
Drawing a rectangle

3. Click outside of the rectangle to deselect it.

4. Click the Line button ╲.

5. To connect the rectangle with the text box, position the crosshair at the right side of the rectangle you just drew. Drag straight across to the left side of the text box, and then release the mouse button.

> **TIP:** Hold down Shift to keep lines vertical, horizontal, or at a 45-degree angle; to keep ellipses circular; and to keep rectangles square. You can also hold down Alt to align the corner of the object with cell gridlines.

6. Using the arrow pointer, point to the rectangle around the two numbers and click to select it. Press Delete to delete the rectangle.

7. Use the arrow pointer to select the line, and then delete it.

> **TIP:** You can also delete an object by right-clicking it, and then choosing Clear from the shortcut menu.

8. Click the Ellipse button . Position the crosshair just under the "M" in "Average Minutes." Drag diagonally to the right until an oval surrounds numbers 7.63 and 7.77. Deselect the ellipse.

9. Click the Arrow button. Position the crosshair at the left side of the text box in the worksheet. Drag to the left until the crosshair touches the right side of the ellipse. Release the mouse button.

FIGURE 18-7
Drawing an arrow

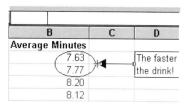

10. Deselect the arrow, and then scroll to the chart (but do not activate it).

11. Draw an arrow that begins just below the text "Best Tasting" and that points to the top of the "PurePower" column (second from the right). Deselect the arrow.

12. Go to Sheet2 of the workbook.

13. Click the Filled Rectangle button . Hold down Shift and draw a square.

> **NOTE:** A fill color or fill pattern is often applied to a filled object.

14. Click, hold down Shift, and draw a circle. Notice the difference between the filled object, which is opaque, and the circle.

15. Save the workbook as *[your initials]***18-9.xls**.

Formatting Drawing Objects

Once you've created a drawing object, you can change its border style, line style, fill pattern, or color. You can also change the font, font style, and font size in text boxes.

EXERCISE **Format Drawing Objects**

1. Return to Sheet1. Click the oval in column B to select it.

2. Choose Object from the Format menu to open the Format Object dialog box.

> **TIP:** You can also open the Format Object dialog box for a selected object by pressing Ctrl + 1.

3. Under Border, choose a bright color from the Color drop-down list. Choose a heavier weight, and then click OK.

4. Click the worksheet text box (to the right of the oval) to select it. Using the Formatting toolbar, change the font style to bold italic, and change the text color to match the oval color. Use the Drawing toolbar to add a drop shadow.

5. Activate the chart. Right-click the "Best Tasting" text box, and choose Format Object from the shortcut menu.

> **NOTE:** The arrow is not visible in the activated chart—it is floating on top of the chart, but is not part of the chart. The "Best Tasting" text box, on the other hand, was created in the chart window and is part of the chart. It can be selected only in the activated chart window.

6. Under Border, click Custom and then check Round Corners. Under Fill, choose black from the color palette.

7. Click the Font tab and choose Bold. Under Color, choose white from the color palette, and then click OK. The text box now has rounded corners with white text against a black background.

8. Deactivate the chart. Right-click the arrow in the chart and choose Format Object.

9. Change the line to a thicker weight, and change the style to the second option on the Style drop-down list. Click OK.

Sizing, Moving, and Copying Objects

Drawing objects are easy to reshape, size, and move. If you need multiple copies of the same object, you draw it once and make as many copies as needed.

EXERCISE 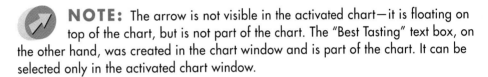 **Size and Move a Drawing Object**

1. Click the text box in the worksheet (not the one in the chart) to select it.

2. Position the pointer on the middle selection handle on the right side of the text box. Using the double-headed arrow pointer, drag the handle to the left so that it fits the text.

> **NOTE:** You may want to resize the text box more than one time to get the perfect fit.

FIGURE 18-8
Resizing the text box

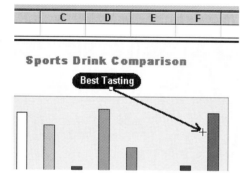

3. Select the oval in column B. Using the white arrow pointer, drag the object down two rows.

4. Click [↶] to undo the move.

FIGURE 18-9
Repositioning
the arrow

5. Select the arrow in the chart. (Remember, if you activate the chart, the arrow won't be visible.)

6. Position the crosshair pointer over the selection handle at the tip of the arrowhead. Drag the handle so that the arrow points to the last column (the data marker for "HydraFuel"). Shorten the arrow as you drag the selection handle.

EXERCISE 18-12 Copy a Drawing Object

After selecting an object, you can Copy and Paste using the Formatting toolbar, keyboard shortcuts, the shortcut menu, or the Edit menu. You can also copy an object using drag and drop.

1. Draw an oval around the HydraFuel number in cell B11 of the worksheet. Use the same style and color as applied to the other oval. Reposition the object as necessary.

2. Select the text box at the top of the worksheet, and click [📋] to copy it.

3. Select cell D10, and click [📋] to paste the text box.

4. With the text box still selected, use the I-beam pointer to highlight the text in the text box. Key as replacement text **Best tasting, but poor performance!** Resize the text box, if needed.

5. Select the arrow at the top of the worksheet.

 NOTE: Use the white arrow pointer to select the arrow—not the cross pointer, which will select cells.

6. With the arrow pointer positioned over the arrow, hold down Ctrl and drag a copy of the arrow down to cell C11.

FIGURE 18-10
Copying drawing objects

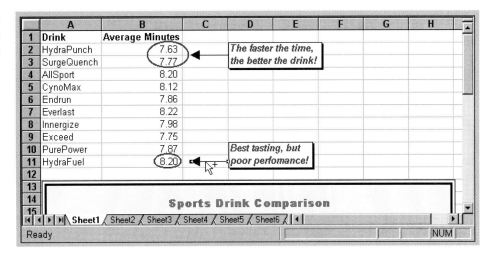

7. Click on the Standard toolbar to hide the Drawing toolbar.

Importing Clip Art

You can further enhance your worksheets by adding clip art. *Clip art* is any graphic image that has already been created and can be imported into a worksheet or chart.

Some programs come with clip art collections. Microsoft Office, for example, includes images that you can use with Excel in the Msoffice\Clipart folder.

EXERCISE **18-13** **Import Clip Art in a Worksheet**

1. Select cell G2.

2. Choose Picture from the Insert menu.

3. Open the Look in drop-down list and locate the Msoffice\Clipart directory.

 NOTE: If you can't locate the clip art folder, ask your instructor for help.

453

4. Scroll in the Name list and choose the picture entitled **Checkmrk.wmf**. Click OK to insert it. The picture appears with a border and is selected. As with any object, you can now move, size, copy, or format the picture.

FIGURE 18-11
Inserting clip art

5. Drag the picture to the left until it overlaps the right edge of the text box.

6. Double-click the picture to open the Format Object dialog box. Under Border, click <u>N</u>one to remove the border. Click OK.

EXERCISE 18-14 Use Clip Art in a Chart

Clip art can be used instead of ordinary data markers in a chart. For example, in a column chart, a clip art image can be stretched across the length of the column or images may be stacked one on top of the other. Experimenting with this capability can produce attention-getting results.

1. Select (but do not activate) the chart. Copy it to cell A1 on Sheet3 of the workbook.

2. Use the Page Setup dialog box (Page tab) to change Sheet3 to landscape orientation, and then return to the worksheet. The dotted line in the worksheet indicates that the right margin now follows column M.

3. Make the chart wider by dragging the middle right sizing handle through column L.

4. Activate the chart. Delete the "Best Tasting" text box and the legend. (To delete an object, select it and press Delete, or right-click it and choose Clear from the shortcut menu.)

5. Click a data marker to select the data series, and then choose <u>P</u>icture from the <u>I</u>nsert menu.

6. From the Msoffice\Clipart folder, choose **1stplace.wmf** and click OK. The data columns are replaced by stretched reproductions of the clip art image.

7. Double-click the data series to open the Format Data Series dialog box. Under Picture Format, choose St<u>a</u>ck and click OK. The images are stacked vertically.

8. Select the plot area of the chart by clicking the background behind the stacked images.

9. Drag the bottom right selection handle down and to the right, resizing the plot area to fit the window.

10. Right-click the plot area and choose Insert Gridlines. In the gridlines dialog box, choose major gridlines for both axes and click OK.

11. Change the chart colors, if you like, and then preview the chart.

12. Center the chart vertically and horizontally.

FIGURE 18-12
Using clip art for
data markers

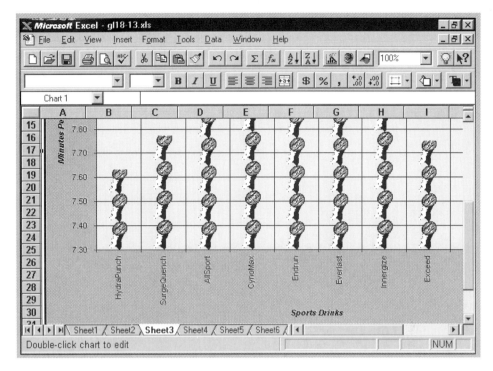

13. Save the workbook as *[your initials]***18-14.xls**.

14. Print sheets 1 and 3 of the chart, and then close the workbook.

Concepts Review

Each of the following statements is either true or false. Indicate your choice by circling **T** or **F**.

T F **1.** The Drawing toolbar is used to create an arrow in a chart.

T F **2.** You can drag a text box to any position on a chart.

T F **3.** You can change the font, style, and size of a chart element, but not its color.

T F **4.** When you finish drawing an object, it is automatically selected.

T F **5.** Legends cannot be placed in a different position on a chart.

T F **6.** The Format Chart Area dialog box is used to add chart borders and backgrounds.

T F **7.** You can use Delete to delete a chart element.

T F **8.** The Formatting toolbar cannot be used to change text objects in a chart.

Write the correct answer in the space provided

1. After clicking the Text Box button on the Drawing toolbar, what shape does the pointer have?

_____

2. When drawing a line or an arrow, what key can you press to ensure that your line is perfectly straight?

_____

3. What appears when you double-click the legend in an activated chart?

_____

4. How do you activate a chart?

_____

5. Name two ways you can customize a legend.

_____

6. How do you use the shortcut menu to delete a chart object?

_____

7. Which shape must the mouse pointer be to select an object?

_____

8. Which dialog box opens when you double-click a drawing object?

_____

CRITICAL THINKING

Answer these questions on a separate piece of paper. There are no right or wrong answers. Support your answers with examples from your own experience, if possible.

1. What advantages are there in using the methods for enhancing charts you have learned in this lesson? Are there any disadvantages? If so, what are they?

2. What advantages are there in adding drawing objects, such as lines, arrows, or text boxes, to a chart? Give some examples of how you might use these objects to present information.

3. If you were submitting a chart to the CEO of a company, what type of enhancements would you apply to the chart? Assuming you had a color printer, how would you use color? Does the amount of chart enhancement depend upon the company? If so, how?

Skills Review

EXERCISE 18-15

Format chart text and enhance the legend.

1. Open the file **MWMin1.xls**.

2. Format the chart text by following these steps:

   a. Double-click the chart, and then double-click the chart title.

   b. In the Format Chart Title dialog box, click the Font tab and choose Arial Black, italic, 14 point, and single underline. Click OK.

   c. Click the categories title "Drinks" to select it, and then click I on the Formatting toolbar. Repeat the process for the values title.

   d. Double-click a category axis label (a drink name), and change its font color to dark blue. Repeat this formatting for the value axis label.

3. Enhance the legend by following these steps:

   a. Double-click the legend.

   b. Click the Patterns tab.

    c. Click the Sh<u>a</u>dow box.

    d. Click the down arrow to the right of <u>P</u>attern and choose the fourth pattern in the top row.

    e. Click the Placement tab and choose <u>B</u>ottom. Click OK.

4. Close the chart window.

5. Preview the chart. If necessary, resize it to accommodate the legend and category labels.

6. Save the workbook as *[your initials]***18-15.xls**.

7. Print and close the workbook.

EXERCISE 18-16

Change data series colors and add a background color and border to a chart.

1. Open the file **MWMin2.xls**.

2. Change the data series colors and pattern by following these steps:

    a. Activate the chart window.

    b. Select the green data series (Men) by right-clicking one of the columns.

    c. Choose Format Data Series from the shortcut menu.

    d. Click the Patterns tab. Under Area, choose a color from the palette.

    e. Open the <u>P</u>attern drop-down list, and choose a pattern from the third row. Click OK.

    f. Repeat the preceding steps for the second data series (Women), choosing a different color and pattern.

3. Add a border and background color to the chart by following these steps:

    a. Double-click the white background area of the chart.

    b. With the Patterns tab displayed, click the Custom option under Border.

    c. Click the arrow to the right of the <u>W</u>eight box, and choose a thicker line for the border.

    d. Under Area, choose a light background color from the palette.

    e. Click OK.

4. Double-click the chart title. Under Border, click Sha<u>d</u>ow, and then click OK.

5. Double-click the legend. Choose white from the color palette to apply a white background, and then click OK.

6. Close the chart window.

7. Save the workbook as *[your initials]***18-16.xls**.

8. Print and close the workbook.

EXERCISE 18-17

Add drawing objects to a worksheet and then format the objects.

1. Open the file **Wks17-24.xls**.

2. Draw a text box in the worksheet by following these steps:

    a. Click the Drawing button [icon] on the Standard toolbar to display the Drawing toolbar, if necessary.

    b. Click the Text Box button [icon].

    c. Using the crosshair pointer, draw a box that covers the cell range F5:G6.

    d. Key **Same performance, different drinks!**

    e. Click outside of the text box.

3. Draw arrows by following these steps:

    a. Click the Arrow button [icon].

    b. Position the crosshair pointer in cell E5, at the left side of the text box. Drag the pointer through cell D5. (Hold down Shift as you drag to draw a straight line.) Release the mouse button. The arrow should point to 8.01 in cell C5.

    c. Draw another arrow from the text box to cell C7. (Because you are drawing a diagonal line, do not hold down Shift.)

4. Format the text box by following these steps:

    a. Click the text box to select it.

    b. Use the Formatting toolbar to center the text and change the font style to italic.

5. Draw an ellipse around the PowerEase numbers by following these steps:

    a. Click the Ellipse button [icon].

    b. Position the crosshair in the upper left-hand corner of cell D12 (diagonally below the number 6.21 in cell C11). Drag up and to the left until the numbers 11 and 6.21 in row 11 are enclosed in the oval. Release the mouse button.

6. Format the drawing object by following these steps:

    a. Right-click the oval and choose Format Object from the shortcut menu.

    b. Under Border, choose a thicker weight and change the border color to red. Click OK.

7. To the right of the oval, draw a text box containing the text **Impressive!** Format the text as centered and italic. Add an arrow that points from the text box to the oval.

8. Save the workbook as *[your initials]***18-17.xls**.

9. Print and close the workbook.

Size, move, and copy a drawing object and import clip art.

1. Open the file **Wks9-16.xls**.

2. Activate the chart window and reposition the legend at the bottom of the chart.

3. Create a text box by clicking the I-beam pointer in the formula bar and keying **Good timing but bad tasting!** Press ⌷Enter⌷.

4. Move, size, and copy the text box by following these steps:

   a. With the text box selected, use the arrow pointer to drag it to the bottom right-hand corner of the chart window.

   b. Using the middle selection handles, drag the right side in and drag the bottom side down so that the text appears on two lines.

   c. Drag the text box to the upper right-hand corner of the chart window.

   d. Format the text box with a rounded blue border and pale yellow fill color. Resize the text box, if needed.

   e. With the text box selected, click 🗐 to copy it to the Clipboard.

5. Close the chart window.

6. Select cell F9, and click 🗐 to paste the text box.

7. Edit the new text box to read **Good tasting but bad timing!** Draw an arrow from this text box to cell C7.

8. Without activating the chart, draw an arrow from the chart text box to the top of the "PowerEase Average Mile Time" data marker.

9. Insert clip art into the worksheet by following these steps:

   a. Select cell F1.

   b. Choose <u>P</u>icture from the <u>I</u>nsert menu.

   c. Locate the Msoffice\Clipart folder, choose the clip art file **Sports.wmf**, and click OK.

10. Resize the picture by following these steps:

    a. With the picture selected, hold down ⌷Shift⌷ and drag the bottom right selection handle toward the center of the picture, until the picture is five rows shorter (the picture width will be adjusted automatically).

    b. Release the mouse button and ⌷Shift⌷.

11. Save the workbook as *[your initials]***18-18.xls**.

12. Print and close the workbook.

Lesson Applications

Format chart text, and add a background color and a border.

Harry Hascabar has created a pie chart showing the breakdown of carbohydrates for one of the sports drinks he has used. Enhance the chart to make it more appealing.

1. Open the file **Pie.xls**.
2. Format the chart title font as 14-point Arial bold underlined.
3. Format the legend text as bold.
4. In the upper right-hand corner of the chart, below the chart title, add a text box with the text **Percentages are Approximate**
5. Format the text in the text box as 10-point Times New Roman bold italic.
6. Add a shadow border to the text box.
7. Add an arrow that points from the text box to the pie.
8. Add a shadow border and a light background color to the chart.
9. Save the workbook as *[your initials]***18-19.xls**.
10. Print and close the workbook.

Format chart text, enhance the legend, add a background color and border, and add and format drawing objects.

Harry Hascabar would like a separate chart sheet that uses a 3-D pie chart to show the carbohydrate breakdown of the sports drink Endrun.

1. Open the file **Pie.xls**.
2. Create a 3-D pie chart for only the drink Endrun as a separate chart sheet. Use format 6 to show percentages, and include a legend.

 TIP: Select the labels and information in rows 1 and 4 of the worksheet.

3. In the new chart sheet, format the chart title as 14-point Arial bold, and format the legend text as 12-point Arial.
4. Create an interesting pattern and border for the legend. Reposition the legend at the bottom of the chart.
5. Add a border and background color to the chart.
6. Draw a circle around the label "21%" (next to the "Fructose" slice). Format the circle using a different weight and color.

461

7. Draw a text box containing **Comparable to PurePower**. Draw an arrow from the text box to the circled chart label.

8. Format the text box as 11-point Arial Black.

9. Save the workbook as *[your initials]***18-20.xls**.

10. Add the completed filename to the right side of the header for the chart sheet.

11. Print the chart sheet and then close the workbook.

EXERCISE 18-21

Format chart text, enhance the legend, add background colors and borders, and add and format drawing objects.

Three new drinks have been added to Harry Hascabar's study. Using a column chart, specify that the data series appear in rows instead of columns, so that the data markers for men and women are displayed as two groups.

1. Open the file **Drinks3.xls**.

2. Create a column chart as a new sheet. Display the data series in rows (step 4 of 5), include a legend, and use the title **AVERAGE MINUTES**. Include a legend but no axis titles.

3. Add a background color and a border to the chart.

4. Reposition the legend at the bottom of the chart. Add a pattern and color to the legend, and make the legend text bold.

5. Make the category labels bold.

6. Below the chart title, create a text box that contains the name **SuperSport**. Draw two arrows starting at the text box and pointing to the SuperSport data markers for men and women.

 TIP: Zoom in to approximately 75% to make the chart sheet easier to work with.

7. Format the SuperSport text box as bold italic with a round-cornered border and a light fill color. Adjust the arrows, if needed.

8. Copy the chart text box and paste it to cell E14 on Sheet1. Change the new text box to read **New Drinks**

9. Draw arrows from the New Drinks text box to the three new drinks in rows 13 through 15.

10. Change the header for both sheets to include the filename and the sheet name.

11. Save the workbook as *[your initials]***18-21.xls**.

12. Print the entire workbook, and then close it.

EXERCISE 18-22

Format chart text, change data series colors, add background colors, add and format drawing objects, and import clip art.

Harry Hascabar and three of his running buddies are always trying to beat their best marathon times. Using the best times from their last marathon, Harry wants to depict the information in two column charts – one of which uses clip art instead of regular column markers.

1. Open the file **Times.xls**.
2. Create a column chart with the title **Best Times**, the y-axis label **Hours**, and no legend.
3. Size and position the chart so that it extends from column A to column H and is approximately 20 rows high.
4. Format the chart title as 12-point Arial bold with a shadow border.
5. Format the chart columns as different colors.
6. Copy the chart onto Sheet2 of the workbook.
7. On Sheet2, insert the clip art file **Motorcrs.wmf** to replace the colored data columns. Use the picture format that stretches the picture.
8. Change the orientation of Sheet2 to landscape.
9. Size the chart so that it extends to the right margin.
10. Add a background color to the chart on Sheet2, and then center the chart horizontally and vertically on the page.
11. On Sheet1, draw an ellipse around the number 4.13 in cell B3.
12. Create a text box with an arrow pointing to cell B3. The text box should read **Still in the lead with best time!**
13. Size the text box to fit the text, and add a red shadow border.
14. Change the header for both sheets to include the filename and the sheet name.
15. Save the workbook as *[your initials]***18-22.xls**.
16. Print the entire workbook, and then close it.

Unit 6 Applications

Add a border to a worksheet, create a 3-D bar chart, format chart text, format and resize the chart legend, and draw arrows.

After completing his experiment on sports drinks, Harry Hascabar is now focusing again on his leather goods business. He wants to chart the costs for each of the items he makes.

1. Open the file **Costs.xls**.

2. Format the first row as 14-point Arial Narrow bold.

3. Format the second row as the same font style but 10-point.

4. Center the first two rows across columns A through E, and apply light gray shading.

5. Center each of the column headings, and resize the columns to fit the text. Format the column C heading as two lines.

6. Place a blue border around the column headings.

7. Format cell ranges as follows:
   - Make cells A9 through A11 bold.
   - Right-align cells A4 through A11.
   - Format cells B4 through E10 in comma style.
   - Format cells B11 through E11 in currency style.

8. Total the costs in row 9 and in column E. Adjust column widths as needed.

9. Create a formula to determine the profit realized in each category.

10. Using the range A3:D8, create a 3-D bar chart with the default subformat (#4) as a new sheet. Use **Mr. Hascabar's Costs** for the chart title, **ITEM** for the category axis title, and **COSTS** for the value axis title.

11. Format the chart title as 16-point Times New Roman bold with a shadow border.

12. Change the alignment of the category axis to the middle vertical choice.

13. Format the legend as follows:
    - Light blue shadow border using the second weight choice
    - 9-point Arial Narrow bold
    - Corner placement

14. Resize the legend so that all text becomes visible.

15. Create a text box that contains the text **Highest Cost**. Format the text box as follows:
    - Round corner border using the heaviest weight and bright yellow fill color
    - 11-point Arial Narrow bold

16. Resize the text box, if necessary, and place it in the fourth column of the plot area, between the longest bar and the top of the chart.

17. Draw arrows from the text box to the bar in each category that represents the highest cost.

18. Format the numbers along the value axis in currency style with no decimal places.

19. Add the tab name to the header on both sheets.

20. Save the workbook as *[your initials]***u6-1.xls**.

21. Print the entire workbook, and then close it.

APPLICATION 6-2

Create a column chart, enhance the legend, add and resize a text box, change the color of the date series, and draw arrows.

To plan his future inventory, Harry Hascabar wants to chart how many of each item has been sold during the past eight months.

1. Open the file **Sold.xls**.

2. Key **August** in cell A4, and then fill in the months down through March (A11).

3. Left-align the data in cells A4 through A11.

4. In cell A12, key **TOTAL**. Format the cell as right-aligned and bold.

5. Calculate the total number of each item sold at the bottom of each column.

6. Create a formula in cell E4 to show how many total items have been sold during each month.

7. Format the data in cells B4:E12 in comma style with no decimals.

8. Rename the Sheet1 tab as **Months**

9. Create a column chart as a new sheet using the cell range A3:D11. Use the default settings for a column chart. Use **Number of Items Sold** for the chart title, **MONTHS** for the category axis title, and **NUMBER SOLD** for the value axis title.

10. Place the legend at the bottom of the chart, and then resize the plot area to fill the area formerly occupied by the legend.

11. Drag the legend so that it is centered under the category axis title "Months."

12. Add a text box that contains the text **LAPTOP COMPUTER CASES ARE THE RAGE!** Move the text box to the top left corner of the plot area, and then format it as follows:

● Add a shadow border and a light background color.

● Change the font to 14-point bold.

● Resize the text box so the text wraps to two lines.

13. Change the data series colors to your favorite colors, making sure that they complement one another.

14. Copy the text box to the top right corner of the plot area. Modify the text box as follows:

465

- Replace the text with **Highest Sales in December**.
- Change the font to 12-point italic.
- Resize the text box to fit the new text.

15. Draw an arrow from the new text box to the "December Laptop Computer Case" column. Format the arrow to have a heavier weight.

16. Rename the Chart1 tab as **No. Sold**.

17. Modify the header on both sheets so that it contains both the filename and the sheet name.

18. Save the workbook as *[your initials]***u6-2.xls**.

19. Print the entire workbook, and then close it.

APPLICATION 6-3

Create three pie charts and add backgrounds to the charts.

Using the sales data for items sold, Harry Hascabar would like to see a pie chart comparison for the months of September, December, and February.

1. Open the file **Pie2.xls**.

2. Change the page orientation to landscape, and make the top and bottom margins .75 inch.

3. Using the cell ranges A3:D3 and A5:D5, create a pie chart on the same sheet as the worksheet for the month of September, as follows:
- Make the chart extend from cell A14 through cell C26.
- Use the chart type 3-D Pie and the default subformat (#7).
- Enter the chart title **SEPTEMBER SALES**
- Add a light background color to the chart.

4. Create a pie chart on the same sheet for the month of December, as follows:
- Make the chart extend from cell D14 through cell H26. (Change the zoom to 75% so you can see more of the worksheet.)
- Use the same chart type and subformat as the existing chart.
- Enter the chart title **DECEMBER SALES**
- Add a different background color to the chart.
- Drag the December chart about one-half column to the right to separate the two charts.

5. Create another 3-D pie chart on the same sheet for February, as follows:
- Create a chart that is approximately the same size as the existing charts, and center it below the two charts.
- Use the chart title **FEBRUARY SALES**
- Add a different background color to the chart.

6. Preview the worksheet. If all the charts do not fit on a single page, reposition the bottom chart so that it overlaps the bottom edges of the other two charts.

7. Create a custom header that contains the filename at the left, the text **Comparison of Months** in the center, and **1997-1998** at the right.

8. Save the workbook as *[your initials]***u6-3.xls**.

9. Print and close the workbook.

APPLICATION 6-4

Create and enhance a data map, draw and resize a text box, add a border, and draw arrows.

Harry Hascabar's business only services the Western states. He would like to see the sales distribution by state per item, and in particular, he'd like a data map of laptop computer case sales so can plan his marketing strategy.

1. Start a new workbook.

2. Key the data shown in Figure U6-1. Use wide columns, so that the worksheet extends almost to the right margin.

FIGURE U6-1

State	Laptop Computer Cases	Handbags	Briefcases
OR	315	175	205
WA	307	212	189
CA	579	343	297
AZ	437	313	278
NM	401	201	312
NV	579	234	277
UT	643	368	415
ID	247	156	217

3. At the top of the worksheet, add the title **Leather Goods Distribution by State**

4. Center the data under the column headings, and center the title across the columns. Add any other formatting desired to make the worksheet attractive.

5. Using the column heads and data in columns A and B, create a data map that shows the distribution of laptop computer cases by state. Draw the map so that it extends the width of the worksheet, and use the United States map.

6. Use the Data Map Control dialog box to change the map to category shading, and then close the dialog box.

7. Use the Map Features dialog box to delete all parts of Canada and Mexico from the map.

8. Change the map title to **Distribution by State**. Right-click the title to change it to 14-point Arial bold, and move it so that it is centered above the map.

9. Drag the map legend to the bottom right corner of the map.

10. Deselect the map, and then draw a text box on top of the map as follows:
    - Placement: Bottom left corner of the map
    - Text: **Time to expand to the Midwest!**
    - Border and Fill: Rounded corners and a shadow light background color
    - Font: 10-point Arial bold italic
    - Alignment: Centered vertically and horizontally within the box

11. Resize the text box so that the text appears on two lines.

12. Draw a rectangle around the laptop computer case data in the worksheet, including the column heading.

13. Format the rectangle with a blue shadow border, and then draw an arrow from the rectangle to the map. (If necessary, drag the map down to allow space for the arrow.)

14. Change the worksheet header to display the filename.

15. Center the worksheet vertically and horizontally on the page.

16. Save the workbook as *[your initials]***u6-4.xls**.

17. Print and close the workbook.

APPLICATION 6-5

Create a worksheet with drawing objects, borders, and clip art.

Harry Hascabar needs a new, professional-looking invoice for his leather goods business. He'd like the invoice created in Excel and enhanced with clip art and drawing objects.

1. On a new worksheet, create an invoice for Harry Hascabar's Handcrafted Leather Goods. Use your creativity to format it with font, borders, colors, patterns, and drawing objects.

2. Import clip art to enhance the invoice.

3. Rename the sheet tab as **Invoice**.

4. Change the worksheet header to the filename and the footer to the sheet name.

5. Save the workbook as *[your initials]***u6-5.xls**.

6. Print and close the workbook.

Using Excel's Database Features

Out of the Frying Pan . . .

Indiana Iron Works was a small foundry started in 1854 by Dexter Peabody. The company produced cast iron frying pans and wrought-iron porch rails. In 1990, the business was taken over by Dexter's great-grandson, Dexter IV, who renamed the company "Indiana Iron Works" and set out to expand and improve production. Young Dexter's background is in art history, and while he was away at school, he became interested in the intricate iron work of the early Renaissance. He now travels worldwide in search of decorative works to reproduce in the foundry.

Dexter is in the process of selling off some of the properties his father acquired for the company over the years. He wants to use the profits to buy new equipment. He also wants to get a better handle on the company's overall profitability.

Dexter needs to do the following to keep track of Indiana Iron Works' customers and property holdings:

✔ Create a database of customer names, addresses, phone numbers, and amounts due, so he can sort by any of these categories as needed. **(Lesson 19)**

✔ Set up his customer database, so he can find specific data quickly and use database functions. **(Lesson 20)**

✔ Set up a database of the property owned by Indiana Iron Works. **(Lesson 21)**

Using Databases

OBJECTIVES

After completing this lesson, you will be able to:

1. Set up a database in a worksheet.
2. Use the data form to enter and edit database records.
3. Sort data in the database.

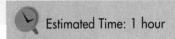

Estimated Time: 1 hour

A *database* is a collection of related information organized in a systematic way. Examples of databases include a company's list of client names, addresses, and phone numbers, or a library's card catalog that records book titles, authors, and publishers. Lessons 19 through 21 explain how to use Excel's database features. This lesson explains how to set up a database, enter and edit data, and sort information.

Setting up a Database

A database begins in Excel with a *list*—a series of worksheet rows that contain data. You create databases by keying lists of data in a workbook. Once you have set up a list of information, you can consult it and work with the data to support your business needs.

In a worksheet, each row corresponds to one database record, and each column corresponds to one database field. A *field* is a category of information, while a *record* is a set of categories. For example, in a card-catalog database, the book title, author, and publisher are fields, while all the information entered for one particular book, constitutes a record. Each field must be as-

471

signed a unique *field name,* which is a column label used to identify the contents of the field. In this example, "Title" or "Publisher" might be field names.

When you create a database in an Excel worksheet, you simply key the information you need into a list, in the same way that you would key it into a regular worksheet.

Keep these rules in mind as you set up your database:

● Field names must appear in the first row of the list.

● Field names must be unique.

● Field names may contain letters, spaces, and numbers, but the first character must be a letter.

● Do not skip any rows or columns within the list. Leave at least one blank row or column between the list and any other data that you enter in the same worksheet as the list, however—for example, between the field names and the title.

● Create only one list per worksheet.

FIGURE 19-1
Typical Excel
database

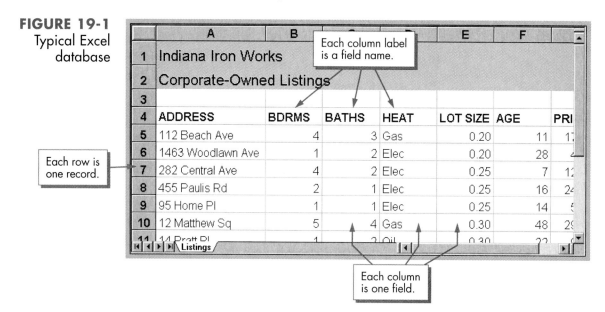

EXERCISE 19-1 Enter the Field Names and Data

Here are a few more points to keep in mind when entering field names:

● If you are using multi-row names, Excel uses the last row.

● Format the field names to make them easier for Excel to differentiate between the records.

● The maximum length of a field name is 255 characters.

1. Open the file **Iron1.xls**.

2. Starting in cell A3, key the following column labels in cells A3 through G3:

Last	First	Address	Suite/PO	City	State	ZIP

3. Make all the column labels bold, and center the labels in cells G3 through I3.

4. To display the leading zeros in the ZIP-code field, format the cells G4 and G5 with the Special Zip Code format, which is found using Format, Cells, and selecting Number, Special.

5. Key the following information in cells A4 through G4, skipping the "Suite/PO" field:

Brown	Gail	97 Old Lyme Rd.	Orange	CT	06477

6. Add another record by keying the following information in cells A5 through G5, again skipping the "Suite/PO" field:

Brawn	Jean	194 Maplewood Rd.	Essex	VT	05452

FIGURE 19-2
Database with bold
column labels

	A	B	C	D	E	F	G	H
1			Indiana Iron Works Customer List					
2								
3	Last	First	Address	Suite/PO	City	State	Zip	Pho
4	Brown	Gail	97 Old Lymn Rd.		Orange	CT	06477	(203) 55
5	Brawn	Jean	194 Maplewood Rd.		Essex	VT	05452	(802) 55
6	Hailey	Linda	12 Garden St.	P.O. 542	Brooklyn	NY	11201	(718) 55
7	Marley	Luke	1028 College St.		Pittsburgh	PA	15206	(412) 55
8	Small	Cathy	11 Pomona Rd		Jersey Cit	NJ	07310	(201) 55
9	Small	Ray	455 Daniels Rd		Lakewood	CA	90715	(310) 55
10	Smith	Betty	12 Putman Ave.		Derby	MA	06484	(508) 55
11	Smith	Ed	1463 Woodlawn Ave.		Kent	OH	44240	(216) 55
12	Smith	Gary	287 Carmel Ave.	Suite 102	Hatfield	MA	01038	(413) 55
13	Wilcox	Wendy	690 Rice Ave.		Portage	MI	49008	(616) 55
14	Zenner	Ann	122 Stuyvesant Rd		New York	NY	10010	(212) 55

Customers

NOTE: To visually differentiate between the first row containing the column labels and the first record containing data, use attributes, borders, and lines to format the column labels row. Do not enter dashed lines in a row, or Excel will be unable to work with the data.

7. Widen columns where necessary.

EXERCISE   19-2   Enter a Series of Data Automatically

You can enter a series of data into a database field automatically by using the Edit, Fill, Series command or the AutoFill feature. Entering a series allows you to assign a number to each record in the database, which can be useful for distinguishing between similar records, such as customers with the same name.

1. Insert a new column to the left of column A.

2. Select cell A3 and key **No.**

3. Select cell A4 and key **1**

4. Format the width of column A for AutoFit. (Hint: Double-click the right border of the column label.)

5. Select cells A4 through A15, and choose F̲ill from the E̲dit menu.

6. Choose S̲eries from the cascading menu. The Series dialog box appears.

FIGURE 19-3
Series dialog box

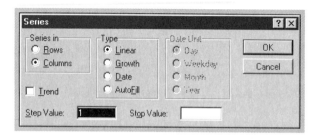

7. Click the C̲olumns button in the Series in category, if necessary. L̲inear should already be selected in the Type category.

8. Click OK. Excel enters numbers in the "No." field for each record automatically.

9. Save the file as *[your initials]***19-2.xls**.

EXERCISE **19-3** **Name the Database**

It is good practice to assign a name to the range of cells that make up your database list. You can name the list using the I̲nsert, N̲ame command or by using the Name box on the formula bar.

1. Select the range A3 through J15 (the entire list, including field names).

2. Click in the Name box on the formula bar.

3. Key **CustList**.

4. Press Enter.

 NOTE: When you add records to the database, you must redefine the range name for the database or insert rows within the existing database.

Using the Data Form

When you work with a list database, you see all of the records in the worksheet simultaneously. Sometimes it is easier to work with one record at a time. In this case, you can use Excel's *data form*. The data form is a dialog box that displays only the fields for one record, in a vertical arrangement.

Even though the data form displays only one record at a time, you can scroll forward or backward, one record at a time, through all of the records you have already entered in the database. You can add and delete records, and search for a specific record using the data form. If a formula exists as part of a record, the data form will copy it to the new record along with any formatting.

 NOTE: If the database contains a large number of fields, all of the fields may not fit on the data form. In this case, you should key the data directly into the rows.

EXERCISE 19-4 View Records with the Data Form

1. Select any cell in the list, and choose F̲orm from the D̲ata menu. The data form appears, displaying the first record.

FIGURE 19-4
Data Form
dialog box

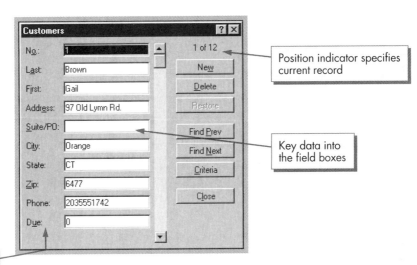

Field names listed vertically

2. To view the next record in the database, click the Find N̲ext button.

3. Locate the position indicator in the top right corner of the Data Form dialog box. The position indicator tells you how many records are entered in the database, and which record is currently displayed. In this instance, it tells you that the current record is 2 out of a total 12.

4. Click Find N̲ext again to scroll forward through several records.

5. Click the Find P̲rev button to scroll backward through the records.

EXERCISE 19-5 Add Records with the Data Form

1. In the Data Form dialog box, click the Ne̲w button.

475

2. In the field box for the "No." field, key **13**

3. Press [Tab] to move to the "Last" field box.

4. In the field box for the "Last" field, key **Mercer**

5. Press [Tab] to move to the "First" field box.

6. In the field box for the "First" field, key **Donna**

7. Press [Shift]+[Tab] to move to the previous field.

8. Press [Tab] twice to move to the field box for "Address."

9. Key the remaining data for the record in the appropriate field boxes. Don't forget to skip the "Suite/PO" field:

   8 Windy Hills Rd.   Dunwoody   GA   30338   4045552552   100

10. Press [Enter] to add the record to the database. Excel displays a new blank data form.

 NOTE: If you want to see the newly added record in the worksheet list, you may have to drag the Data Form dialog box up or to the right.

EXERCISE 19-6 **Edit and Delete Records with the Data Form**

1. Click Find Prev to display the record you just added to the database.

2. Edit the address from "8 Windy Hills Rd." to **800 Windy Hills Rd**.

3. Click Restore. As long as you have not pressed [Enter] or scrolled to a different record, you may revert to the original data.

4. Click Delete. Excel displays a prompt warning you that you are about to delete the record, permanently. Note that you cannot use 🔄 to get it back.

5. Click OK. Excel deletes the record.

EXERCISE 19-7 **Find Records with the Data Form**

You can use the data form to search through all of the records in the database to locate a specific record or group of records. Excel finds only records that match the *criteria*—that is, the data you specify that Excel must match when searching for a record.

1. To find records that have "Orange" in the "City" field, click Criteria in the Data Form dialog box, and then key **Orange** in the "City" field.

2. Click Find Prev. Excel searches backward through the database until it finds a record that includes "Orange" for the city. (You can also use the Find Next button to search forward through the database.)

3. Click Find Prev again. The record does not change because no other records match the specified criteria, and the system beeps.

4. Click Criteria to display the Criteria data form.

5. Click Clear in the Criteria data form, and then key **MA** in the "State" field.

6. Click Find Next to scroll through the records of the customers in Massachusetts.

7. Click Criteria, and then click Clear. All of the criteria keyed in the Criteria data form are cleared away.

8. Click Form.

9. Click Find Next or Find Prev several times to scroll through the records and verify that all records are shown.

10. Click Close to close the Data Form dialog box.

> **TIP:** Use the question mark (?) as a wildcard to search for any character. For example, if you key **Br?wn**, Excel will find last names such as "Brown" and "Brawn." Use the asterisk (*) as a wildcard to find any number of characters. For example, if you key **P.O.***, Excel will find all P.O. box numbers, such as "P.O. Box 543" and "P.O. Box 20."

Sorting Data

Excel allows you to sort data either alphabetically or numerically, in either ascending or descending *sort order*. You can sort any worksheet data using this feature—even data that is not set up as a database.

When you perform a sort, Excel rearranges rows according to the contents of the specified column. When sorting, you must indicate in the Sort dialog box whether your list includes the field names. Excel will include these (referred to as the "Header Row") in a sort, unless you indicate that your list has them, in which case Excel will exclude them.

> **TIP:** To sort a list in ascending order quickly, select a cell in the column you want to sort by, and click on the Standard toolbar. To sort in descending order, select a cell in the column you want to sort by, and then click. If column headings are formatted differently, Excel will exclude them from the sort.

EXERCISE **19-8** **Sort Data**

1. Select any cell in column J, the column for the "Due" amount.

2. Choose Sort from the Data menu. The Sort dialog box appears. Excel automatically places "Due" in the Sort By text box. The sort is also preset

FIGURE 19-5
Sort dialog box

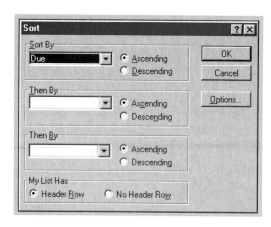

to perform an ascending sort. Header <u>R</u>ow is selected at the bottom of the dialog box, telling Excel to exclude the field names from the sort.

3. Click OK. Excel sorts the records numerically in ascending order by the amount due.

4. To change the sort to descending order, select any cell in the "Due" column, and click [Z↓].

5. Select any cell in the database, and choose <u>S</u>ort from the <u>D</u>ata menu. The Sort dialog box appears. Excel assumes you still want to sort by the "Due" field.

6. Click the down arrow in the <u>S</u>ort By text box to open the drop-down list box.

7. Select State in the list. Excel enters State into the <u>S</u>ort By text box.

8. Click the <u>A</u>scending button next to the <u>S</u>ort By text box, and click OK. Excel sorts the records in ascending order by state.

FIGURE 19-6
Records sorted in alphabetical order by state

	A	B	C	D	E	City	State	Zip
3	No.	Last	First	Address	Suite/PO	City	State	Zip
4	6	Small	Ray	455 Daniels Rd		Lakewood	CA	90715 (31
5	1	Brown	Gail	97 Old Lymn R	The Sort by	range	CT	06477 (20
6	12	Marley	Dave	20 Krammer C	field is State.	ethany	CT	06524 (20
7	7	Smith	Betty	12 Putman Ave.		Derby	MA	
8	9	Smith	Gary	287 Carmel Ave.	Suite 102	Hatfield	MA	Sort order is
9	10	Wilcox	Wendy	690 Rice Ave.		Portage	MI	alphabetical, ascending.
10	5	Small	Cathy	11 Pomona Rd		Jersey City	NJ	07310 (20
11	3	Hailey	Linda	12 Garden St.	P.O. 542	Brooklyn	NY	11201 (71
12	11	Zepper	Ann	122 Stuyvesant Rd.		New York	NY	10010 (21
13	8	Smith	Ed	1463 Woodlawn Ave.		Kent	OH	44240 (21
14	4	Marley	Luke	1028 College St.		Pittsburgh	PA	15206 (41
15	2	Brawn	Jean	194 Maplewood Rd.		Essex	VT	05452 (80

\Customers

NOTE: Excel's default for sorting is not case-sensitive, so it does not matter whether you key capital or lowercase letters when specifying criteria. If you want Excel to be case-sensitive, however, you can choose this option from the <u>O</u>ptions button in the Sort dialog box.

EXERCISE 19-9 **Sort by Multiple Columns**

Excel also allows you to sort within a sort. You can sort by up to three columns at one time.

1. Move to any cell in the database, and choose <u>S</u>ort from the <u>D</u>ata menu.

2. Click the down arrow in the <u>S</u>ort By text box, and choose Last from the drop-down list of fields.

3. Choose First from the <u>T</u>hen By drop-down list of fields, and click OK. The records are sorted initially by last name and then by first name.

FIGURE 19-7
Records sorted by last name, then by first name

	A	B	C	D	E	F	G	H	
3	No.	Last	First	Address	Suite/PO	City	State	Zip	
4	2	Brawn	Jean	194 Maplewood Rd.		Essex	VT	05452	(80
5	1	Brown	Gail	97 Old Lymn Rd.		Orange	CT	06477	(20
6	3	Hailey	Linda	12 Garden St.	P.O. 542	Brooklyn	NY	11201	(71
7	12	Marley	Dave	20 Krammer Ct		Bethany	CT	06524	(20
8	4	Marley	Luke	1028 College St.		Pittsburgh	PA	15206	(41
9	5	Small	Cathy	11 Pomona Rd		Jersey City	NJ	07310	(20
10	6	Small	Ray	455 Daniels Rd		Lakewood	CA	90715	(31
11	7	Smith	Betty	12 Putman Ave.		Derby	MA	06484	(50
12	8	Smith	Ed	1463 Woodlawn Ave.		Kent	OH	44240	(21
13	9	Smith	Gary	287 Carmel Ave.	Suite 102	Hatfield	MA	01038	(41
14	10	Wilcox	Wendy	690 Rice Ave.		Portage	MI	49008	(61
15	11	Zepper	Ann	122 Stuyvesant Rd.		New York	NY	10010	(21
16									

Customers

4. Save the workbook as *[your initials]***19-9.xls** and print it.

5. To restore the database to its original order, select any cell in the database, and choose <u>S</u>ort from the <u>D</u>ata menu.

6. Choose No. from the <u>S</u>ort By drop-down list of fields.

7. Choose [none] from the <u>T</u>hen By drop-down list, and then click OK. Excel sorts the records by the numbers in the No. field, putting them back into the original order.

8. Close the workbook without re-saving it.

**C O M M A N D
S U M M A R Y**

FEATURE	BUTTON	MENU	KEYBOARD
Enter a data series		<u>E</u>dit, F<u>i</u>ll, <u>S</u>eries	
Display the data form		<u>D</u>ata, F<u>o</u>rm	
Sort, ascending order	⬆	<u>D</u>ata, <u>S</u>ort	
Sort, descending order	⬇	<u>D</u>ata, <u>S</u>ort	

Concepts Review

Each of the following statements is either true or false. Indicate your choice by circling **T** or **F**.

T F **1.** You can create a database in any Excel worksheet.

T F **2.** You must leave a blank row between the column labels and the first data record in a list.

T F **3.** You can use AutoFill to enter a series in a list automatically.

T F **4.** You can name a list in the same way that you name other cell ranges in a worksheet.

T F **5.** The only way to add new records to a list is by using a data form.

T F **6.** You can use a data form to view all of the records in a database at the same time.

T F **7.** You can easily restore a deleted database record when it is deleted in the data form.

T F **8.** You can sort lists by as many as five fields.

Write the correct answer in the space provided.

1. Which part of a worksheet corresponds to a database record?

_____

2. Which part of a worksheet corresponds to a database field?

_____

3. What is the name that Excel uses for a database in a worksheet?

_____

4. Which key moves you between fields in a data form?

_____

5. Which aspect of the data form tells you how many records are in the database, and which one is displayed?

_____

6. What kind of sort arranges records from A to Z?

_____

7. What kind of sort arranges records from Z to A?

_____

8. What must you specify if you want Excel to find and display a particular record?

_____

CRITICAL THINKING

Answer these questions on a separate piece of paper. There are no right or wrong answers. Support your answers with examples from your own experience, if possible.

1. How can Excel's database features help a business?

2. Describe three different types of databases you could create with Excel.

3. Suggest some guidelines for setting up a database in Excel that would make it easier to sort and retrieve data.

Skills Review

EXERCISE 19-10

Set up a database of inventory parts by entering column labels, keying data in a list, and automatically numbering records.

1. Open the file **Iron2.xls**.

2. Beginning in cell A3, enter the three following column labels:

Description   **Size**   **Price**

3. Beginning in cell A4, key the following records into the worksheet to create the database:

Ornate Scrolls	Large	55
Ornate Scrolls	Medium	45
Ornate Scrolls	Small	35
Outlet Plates	Standard	15

4. Format the column labels using a larger font size and making them bold. Adjust the column widths accordingly.

5. Add a new column A, and label it as **Part #** by following these steps:

a. Select column A.

b. Choose Insert, Columns.

c. Key **Part #** in cell A3.

d. Apply the same formatting to cell A3 as found with the other field names, and move the worksheet heading to start in column A.

6. Automatically number the records by entering a series in the "Part #" column by following these steps:

   a. In cell A4, key **1**

   b. Select cells A4 through A7.

   c. Choose <u>E</u>dit, F<u>i</u>ll, <u>S</u>eries, and then click OK in the Fill Series dialog box.

7. Right-align cells A3 and D3.

8. Save the workbook as *[your initials]***19-10.xls**.

9. Print and close the workbook.

EXERCISE 19-11

Add records to a database by keying information directly into a list and by using a data form.

1. Open the file **Iron3.xls**.

2. Beginning in cell A8, add a record by keying the following data:

   | 5 | Grates | Large | 45 |

3. Display the data form for the database by following these steps:

   a. Select any cell in the list.

   b. Choose <u>D</u>ata, F<u>o</u>rm.

4. Add a new record to the database by following these steps:

   a. Click the Ne<u>w</u> button in the data form.

   b. Key **6** in the "Part #" field, and then press [Tab].

   c. Key **Railing Cap** in the "Description" field, and then press [Tab].

   d. Key **Standard** in the "Size" field, then press [Tab].

   e. Key **35** in the "Price" field.

   f. Press [Enter] to display a new record.

5. Add another record to the database by keying the following data:

   | 7 | **Door Knocker** | **Medium** | 75 |

6. Close the data form by clicking the C<u>l</u>ose button.

7. Save the workbook as *[your initials]***19-11.xls**.

8. Print and close the workbook.

EXERCISE 19-12

Find, edit, and delete records using the data form.

1. Open the file **Iron4.xls**.

2. Display the data form.

3. Display the data form for Part #6 by clicking the Find <u>N</u>ext button.

4. Change the price for Part #6 from "$35" to **$40**.

5. Restore the original price for Part #6.

6. Find and delete the record for Part #8.

7. Find all records for parts that are in stock, by following these steps:

   a. In the data form, click the <u>C</u>riteria button.

   b. Key **Yes** in the "In-Stock?" field text box.

   c. Click the Find <u>P</u>rev or Find <u>N</u>ext button to display each record.

8. Clear the criteria and display all records by following these steps:

   a. In the data form, click the <u>C</u>riteria button.

   b. Click the <u>C</u>lear button.

   c. Click the <u>F</u>orm button.

9. Click the C<u>l</u>ose button to close the Data Form dialog box.

10. Save the workbook as *[your initials]***19-12.xls**.

11. Print and close the workbook.

EXERCISE 19-13

Name a database, sort by a single field, and sort by multiple fields.

1. Open file **Iron5.xls**.

2. Name the database by following these steps:

   a. Select cells A3 through H15.

   b. Click in the name box and key **Suppliers**.

   c. Press Enter.

3. Sort the records alphabetically from A to Z by supplier name, by following these steps:

   a. Select cell A3

   b. Choose <u>D</u>ata, <u>S</u>ort.

   c. Make sure that Supplier Name is entered in the <u>S</u>ort By text box, and that the <u>A</u>scending option button is selected.

   d. Click OK.

4. Sort the records alphabetically from Z to A by supplier name, by clicking the Sort Descending button on the Standard toolbar.

5. Sort the records by State and then by City by following these steps:

   a. Choose <u>D</u>ata, <u>S</u>ort.

   b. Click State from the <u>S</u>ort By drop-down list of fields.

   c. Click the <u>A</u>scending option button.

   d. Select City from the <u>T</u>hen By drop-down list of fields.

   e. Click the <u>A</u>scending option button, and then click OK.

6. Save the workbook as *[your initials]***19-13.xls**.

7. Print and close the workbook.

Lesson Applications

EXERCISE 19-14

Create a database, add data series, use the data form to add a new record, and sort the database.

Indiana Iron Works wants to create a worksheet of delinquent invoices for its problem customers. The worksheet will be used as a database that can be sorted by invoice number, customer name, invoice date, due date, or amount due.

1. Open the file **Iron6.xls**.
2. Enter the data in Figure 19-9.

FIGURE 19-8

Customer	Invoice Date	Amount Due
Johnson Manufacturing	5/12/97	$1,009.65
Anderson Metal Works	5/15/97	2,376.23
Acme Industries	3/30/97	34,987.22
Anderson Metal Works	4/15/97	203,979
Anderson Metal Works	6/15/97	542.18
Johnson Manufacturing	5/15/97	1,409.67

3. In the "Due Date" column, enter a formula that calculates the dates in column C plus 30 days.
4. Assign invoice numbers to the invoices, beginning with 1000.
5. Use the data form to add an invoice that contains the following information:

   Metalware Design   2/10/97   311.98
6. Sort the database by the amount due, from highest to lowest.
7. Sort the database by customer and invoice date, in ascending order.
8. Save the workbook as *[your initials]***19-14a.xls**, and then print it with gridlines and centered on the page.
9. Return the records to their original order.
10. Save the workbook as *[your initials]***19-14b.xls**.
11. Print and close the workbook.

EXERCISE 19-15

Add records to an existing database with the data form, find and delete records with the data form, and sort the database.

Indiana Iron Works has a database of corporate-owned homes that it wants to sell. The company needs to number the properties, search for specific records, and update the records to include five new properties.

1. Open the file **Iron7.xls**.
2. Add the data shown in Figure 19-10. Add new records by keying them directly into the list or into a data form.

FIGURE 19-9

203 Narrow	4	2	Gas	0.60	12	95,000	08-Feb-97
14 Shaw Dr.	4	2	Oil	1.75	32	135,000	05-Apr-97
12 Franklin	2	2	Gas	0.75	15	12,000	30-Mar-97
690 Rice St.	1	2	Oil	0.60	25	92,000	01-Dec-96
194 Glenwood	1	1	Oil	0.80	35	76,000	23-Dec-96

3. Use the Criteria data form to view records with five bedrooms.
4. Clear this criterion, and return to viewing all records.
5. Find and delete the record for 30 Lake.
6. Sort the list by the number of bedrooms and by the number of bathrooms. Use a descending sort.
7. Add a new field to the left of column A called "Item #." Make it bold and right-align the text. Move the worksheet heading to the left, and add the appropriate shading and borders on the right side of the worksheet over the last column.
8. In the "Item #" field, number the properties in a series beginning with the number 1. Make sure that the font size for the series is the same as for the rest of the data.
9. Adjust all column widths to accommodate data.
10. Sort in ascending order by price.
11. Save the workbook as *[your initials]***19-15a.xls.** Print the worksheet, centering it on the page.
12. Restore the worksheet to its original sorting order, by item number.
13. Save the workbook as *[your initials]***19-15b.xls.**
14. Print and close the workbook.

EXERCISE 19-16

Convert a worksheet into a database, use the data form to find and add records, name and add a data series, and sort the database.

To organize its checking-account transactions, Indiana Iron Works needs a worksheet set up as a database that serves as an electronic checkbook.

1. Open the file **Iron8.xls**.
2. Use the data form to add the checks shown in Figure 19-11.

FIGURE 19-10

Date	Check #	Description	Category	Amount
2/13/97	204	Pyramid Properties	Rent	(1,522.08)
2/19/97		Jacobson & Sons	Acct Rec	500.00
2/20/97	205	Clips Co.	Supplies	(54.86)
2/22/97		Arlington Industries	Acct Rec	652.99

3. Insert a column to the left of column A labeled **Trans #.** Format the new column to display two leading zeros. The format of the new cells should match the format of the existing cells.
4. Number the records in the list, beginning with the transaction number 001.
5. At the right side of the worksheet, insert another column labeled **Balance**, and enter formulas to calculate the daily balance. Assume an opening balance of $2,000. Copy over the formats.
6. Name the list **Checking**.
7. Sort the worksheet by Description. Notice the effect that the formulas have on the balance column.
8. Use the data form to find out how much money was spent on office supplies.
9. Sort the worksheet by transaction number.
10. Save the workbook as *[your initials]***19-16.xls**.
11. Print the workbook, centered on the page, and then close it.

Add records to a database, add a data series column and a field to compute percentage increases, and find and sort records in the database.

A worksheet set up as a database can help Indiana Iron Works keep track of its employees and the payroll budget.

1. Open the file **Iron9.xls.** Key the records shown in Figure 19-12.

FIGURE 19-11

Last	First	Position	Hire Date	1997 Salary	%
Kane	Sam	Operator	9/10/94	25000	3%
Whittier	Chris	Designer	10/11/91	35000	3%
Yang	Li	Designer	6/15/92	32500	4%

2. Sort the records by the date that each employee began working for Indiana Iron Works.

3. Add a new column A labeled **Emp. #**. Format it to display two leading zeros. Format the new cells to match the formatting of the existing cells, and center or right-align them.

4. Number the records consecutively, beginning with number 001.

5. In the "1998 Salary" column, enter formulas that calculate the new salaries for each employee.

6. Sort the records by 1998 salaries, from lowest to highest.

7. Locate the records for all employees who earned $35,000 in 1997.

8. Return to viewing all records.

9. Sort the records by employee number.

10. Save the workbook as *[your initials]***19-17.xls**.

11. Print and close the workbook.

Filtering Data

After completing this lesson, you will be able to:

1. **Use AutoFilter.**
2. **Filter with Advanced Filter.**

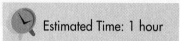
Estimated Time: 1 hour

The process of finding and selecting information in Excel is called *filtering*. After you have set up a worksheet as a database, you can use Excel's filtering features to hide records that you don't want and list only records that you do want. For example, you can list only the records for customers who live in certain states. This option saves time and makes your work easier. Filtering is also convenient when printing, charting, deleting, editing, formatting, or copying a subset of your database. When you print or copy as usual, only filtered data will print or copy.

Using AutoFilter

Use AutoFilter when your criteria for filtering are simple—for example, when you need to view all records with the last name "Small" or all amounts due over $50.

To use AutoFilter, select any cell in the database, and then choose Data, Filter, and AutoFilter. Excel applies down arrows to field names in the list. Click a down arrow to choose from a drop-down list the items that you want to filter. For example, you can click Smith to see only the records (rows) containing the last name "Smith." If you filter more than one field using AutoFilter, Excel will display only the records that meet all specified conditions.

Besides choosing a field like "Smith," AutoFilter allows you to choose from the following options:

- (All)
  Shows all records in the database (this option removes the filter)

- (Top 10…)
  Shows records by number of items or by percent from the top or bottom of the database

- (Custom…)
  Shows records using a simple or two-field comparison

- (Blanks)
  Shows all records with blanks in the field

- (NonBlanks)
  Shows all records that contain data in the field

EXERCISE | **20-1** | **Filter Directly with AutoFilter and Edit Records**

1. Open the file **Iron10.xls**.

2. Select any cell in the 15-record list, and choose <u>F</u>ilter from the <u>D</u>ata menu. A cascading menu appears.

3. Choose Auto<u>F</u>ilter. The AutoFilter down arrows appear at the top of each column.

FIGURE 20-1
Fields with AutoFilter down arrows

	A	B	C	D	E	F	G	H	
1				Indiana Iron Works Customer List					
2									
3	N ▾	Last ▾	First ▾	Address ▾	Suite-PC ▾	City ▾	State ▾	Z ▾	
4	1	Brawn	Jean	194 Maplewood Rd.		Essex	VT	05452	(802)
5	2	Brown	Gail	97 Old Lyme Rd.		Orange	CT	06477	(203)
6	6	Marley	Dave	20 Krammer Court		Bethany	CT	06524	(203)

4. Click the AutoFilter down arrow for the field "Last" that is located in cell B3. A drop-down list appears with all the unique entries in the field.

5. Scroll down the list, and click the name "Smith." Excel filters the list to show only records containing this last name. If you have a color monitor, the AutoFilter down arrow for "Last" becomes blue, indicating that four records were filtered from this field. Row labels 8, 13, 14, and 18 are blue, indicating that they are the result of a filter. The number of records found appears in the status bar.

FIGURE 20-2
List filtered for last
name "Smith"

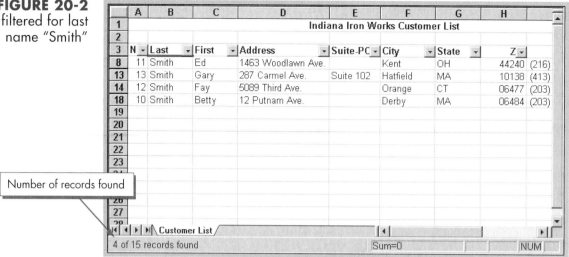

Number of records found

6. Click the AutoFilter down arrow for the "State" field, and choose "MA" from the list. Only two records meeting both conditions (last name of "Smith" and state of Massachusetts) are displayed.

7. Click the AutoFilter down arrow for the "Last" field. Select (All) to show all records. The list is still filtered for the state, so only three records are seen.

8. Click the AutoFilter down arrow for the "State" field. Select (All) to show all records in the database.

9. Click the AutoFilter down arrow for the "Phone" field. Select (Blanks). Excel displays the one record with a blank phone field.

10. To edit a field while filtering, select cell I17, and enter **7185559874**

11. Click the AutoFilter down arrow for the "Phone" field again. Select (All) to show all records in the database.

12. Click the AutoFilter down arrow for the "Suite-PO" field and click (NonBlanks). Two records are displayed.

13. Double-click cell E13, and change the suite number to **105**

14. Click the AutoFilter down arrow for the "Suite-PO" field again. Select (All) to show all records in the database.

15. Choose Filter from the Data menu, and click AutoFilter to turn it off.

EXERCISE 20-2 View Top or Bottom 10 with AutoFilter

One AutoFilter option lets you select records from the top or bottom of the database. You can specify the top or bottom records by number of items or by percentage of items.

1. Select any cell in the database. Choose Data, Filter, AutoFilter.

2. Click the AutoFilter down arrow in the "Due" field that is located in cell J3. Select (Top 10...) from the option list. The Top 10 AutoFilter dialog box appears.

FIGURE 20-3
Top 10 AutoFilter
dialog box

3. Enter **2** in the middle box.

4. If necessary, select Items from the drop-down list on the right of the dialog box and then click OK. The two records listed have the highest balances in the customer database.

5. Save the workbook as *[your initials]***20-2.xls** and print it.

EXERCISE 20-3 Customize AutoFilter

With AutoFilter, you can create custom criteria. You can then use a comparison operator, such as greater than (>) or less than (<), as well as the "and" and "or" operators. Comparison operators can be used to:

- Display the results of a single criterion, such as >500.
- Display either of two items in a field. For example, display all records with either "Smith" or "Jacobs" in the last-name field.
- Display items that meet both of two conditions. For example, display records that contain both the last name "Smith" and the city "New York."
- Display records that fall within a range, such as >500 and <1000.

1. Click the AutoFilter down arrow for the "Due" field, and then click (All).

FIGURE 20-4
Custom AutoFilter
dialog box

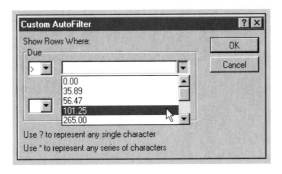

2. Click the AutoFilter down arrow for the "Due" field again, and then select (Custom...). The Custom AutoFilter dialog box appears.

3. Click the top left arrow in the dialog box to open the drop-down list for operators. Select >.

4. Click the top right arrow to open the drop-down menu for the values in the "Due" column, select 101.25, and click OK. Excel displays five records for which the amount due is greater than $101.25.

5. Click the AutoFilter down arrow for the "Due" column and select (Custom…).

6. Key **300** in the top text box, and then click OK. Excel displays four records where the amount due is greater than $300.

7. Click the AutoFilter down arrow for the "Due" field and select (Custom…). Click the bottom left arrow, and select < from the drop-down list.

8. Click the bottom right arrow, select 2,100.00, and click OK. Excel displays two records where the amount due is greater than $300 but less than $2,100.

9. Click the AutoFilter down arrow for the "Due" field, and select (All) to show all records.

10. Click the AutoFilter down arrow for the "Last" field and select (Custom…). Click the top right arrow, and select Smith from the drop-down list. Select <u>O</u>r.

11. Click the bottom left arrow, and select = from the drop-down list. Click the bottom right arrow, and select Small from the drop-down list.

12. Click OK. Six records containing the last names "Smith" or "Small" are displayed.

FIGURE 20-5
Filtering the database for "Smith" or "Small"

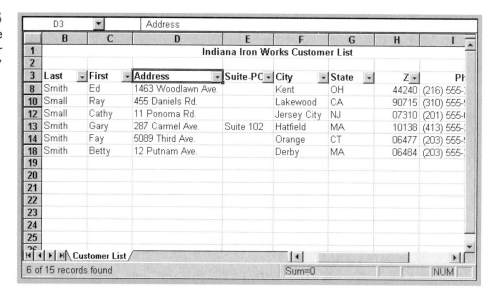

13. Select (All) from the drop-down list for the field "Last" to show all records.

14. Click the AutoFilter down arrow for the "Suite-PO" field and select (Custom…). In the top text box, key **S***

 NOTE: Custom AutoFilter can be used for searching with wildcards. Remember, the question mark (?) is a wildcard for a single character, and the asterisk (*) is a wildcard for a group of characters.

15. Click OK. Excel displays the single record containing a word that begins with "S" in the field for "Suite-PO."

16. Click the AutoFilter down arrow for the "Suite-PO" field, and select (All) to remove the filter.

17. Click the AutoFilter down arrow for the last-name field and select (Custom...). In the top text box, key **Br?wn**

18. Click OK. Excel displays three records with a last name that begins with "Br," ends with "wn," and has any one character in between.

19. Click the AutoFilter down arrow for last name, and select (All) to remove the filter.

20. Choose <u>F</u>ilter from the <u>D</u>ata menu, and click Auto<u>F</u>ilter to turn it off.

21. Save the workbook as *[your initials]***20-3.xls**.

> **TIP:** To redisplay all records at once, select <u>D</u>ata, <u>F</u>ilter, <u>S</u>how All.

Filtering with Advanced Filter

Advanced Filter requires more work than AutoFilter but allows you to filter data based on more complex or calculated criteria. It also allows you to copy filtered data to another location on the worksheet and to display unique records.

Before you use the Advanced Filter, you must:

- Set the list range.
- Set the criteria range.

EXERCISE 20-4 Set the List Range by Naming the Database

As you learned in Lesson 19, the *list range* is the area containing the database. It is easier to set the list range if the database is named. Setting the list range is the first step in using the Advanced Filter.

1. Select cell A3.

2. Click the Name box on the formula bar, key **A3:J18**, and press Enter. The entire database is selected.

3. Click the Name box again, key **Customers**, and press Enter. Click any cell to deselect the database, which is now named "Customers."

> **NOTE:** Once the database is named, you can add records to it by simply inserting a row and keying the new record. This updates the defined range. You can also use <u>D</u>ata, F<u>o</u>rm to add additional records and keep the defined name updated.

4. Press Ctrl+Home to make A1 the active cell.

5. Click the down arrow to open the Name box drop-down list. The name "Customers" is listed. Select it, and the database is again highlighted. Press an arrow key to remove highlighting.

6. Select cell D20, and choose Insert, Name, Paste. Select Customers and then click Paste List. This shows you a list of named cells in the worksheet.

FIGURE 20-6
Pasting the
list range

	A	B	C	D	E	F	G	H	
13	13	Smith	Gary	287 Carmel Ave.	Suite 105	Hatfield	MA	10138	(413)
14	12	Smith	Fay	5089 Third Ave.		Orange	CT	06477	(203)
15	5	Jarman	Lucinda	5 Evonne Ave.		Canton	MA	02021	(617)
16	3	Brown	Trevor	145 E. 15 St.		New York	NY	10001	(212)
17	4	Hailey	Linda	12 Garden St.	P.O. 542	Brooklyn	NY	11201	(718)
18	10	Smith	Betty	12 Putnam Ave.		Derby	MA	06484	(203)
19									
20				Customers	='Customer List'!$A$3:$J$18				
21									
22									

Name box: D20 — Customers

7. Save the workbook as *[your initials]*20-4.xls.

8. Delete the list range in cells D20:E20.

EXERCISE 20-5 Set the Criteria Range

The *criteria range* is the area of the worksheet in which you specify the conditions that the filtered data must meet. The first row of the criteria range must contain the exact field name used in the database. The only exception to this rule is when you use calculated criteria. In this situation, you cannot use the field name if it exists in the database. Most users substitute the name "Calc" or "Formula" to indicate a calculated—rather than a comparison—criterion. In the cell beneath the field name, the condition for each field is keyed. At a minimum, the criteria range contains two rows: one for field names and one for criteria. It is easier to work with the criteria range if it is named. Be sure to include all appropriate field names and conditions in the criteria range.

Two rules to remember when entering criteria for more than one field are as follows:

- If you key criteria for more than one field in the same row, Excel treats them as if they are connected by "and."

- If you key criteria for more than one field on different rows, Excel treats them as if they are connected by "or."

Note that you may have multiple criteria ranges, but you can actually use only one at a time.

1. Choose Insert, Worksheet. A new sheet is added before the Customer sheet.

2. Right-click the worksheet tab labeled Sheet1.

3. Click Move or Copy, and select (move to end). Click OK. The sheet is moved after the Customer sheet.

4. Rename the Sheet1 tab as **Criteria**

 TIP: It is best to place criteria on a separate sheet from the database. If you then add or delete records or field names, it will not affect the criteria.

5. Click the Customer List tab, and copy the Last field name in cell B3 to cell A2 in the Criteria worksheet.

 NOTE: Always copy field names from the list range to the criteria range. The field names must be identical, and copying them ensures that no typing errors or other differences occur between the two ranges, including the use of upper- and lowercase letters.

6. In cell A3 on the Criteria sheet, key **Smith**

7. Copy the field name in cell G3 from the Customer List worksheet (the "State" field name) to cell B2 on the Criteria worksheet.

8. In cell B3 on the Criteria worksheet, key **MA**

9. Click the Name box on the formula bar, key **A2:B3**, and press Enter. The criteria range just entered is highlighted.

10. Click the Name box again, key **Sm_ma**, and press Enter. The range for comparison criteria is named with an And condition.

 NOTE: Be careful not to include blank rows when setting the criteria range. A blank row filters all records in the database.

11. Copy the field name in cell J3 from the Customer List worksheet (the "Due" field name) to cells D2:E2 on the Criteria sheet.

12. Key **>100** in cell D3 and **<2000** in cell E3.

13. Click the Name box, key **D2:E3**, and press Enter. The criteria range just entered is highlighted.

14. Click the Name box again, key **Due_bet**, and press Enter. The second range for comparison criteria is named, using an And condition in the same field.

15. Copy the field name in cell B3 from the Customer List worksheet (the "Last" field name) to cell G2 on the Criteria worksheet.

16. Copy the field name in cell B2 of the Criteria worksheet (the "State" field name) to cell H2 on the same worksheet.

17. Key **Smith** in cell G3 and **NY** in cell H4.

18. Click the Name box, key **G2:H4**, and press Enter. The criteria range just entered is highlighted.

19. Click the Name box again, key **Sm_Ny**, and press Enter. The third range for comparison criteria is named using an Or condition.

20. On the Criteria sheet, copy cell G2 to cell A6, and copy cell D2 to cell B6.

21. Enter the following text in the cells indicated:

A7 **Smith**   B7 **>0**
A8 **Brown**   B8 **>50**

22. Click the Name box, key **A6:B8**, and press Enter. The criteria range just entered is highlighted.

23. Click the Name box, key **SB_Due**, and press Enter. The fourth range for comparison criteria is named using an Or and And condition.

24. Add the filename as a header and the tab name as a footer.

25. Save the workbook as *[your initials]***20-5.xls**. Print the criteria sheet only.

EXERCISE **20-6** **Use Advanced Filter to Produce a Filtered List**

After you have set the list range and the criteria range, you are ready to run the Advanced Filter option. When you sum items on a filtered list, you are actually generating a subtotal.

1. Select cell A4 on the Customer sheet (not the Criteria sheet). You can select any cell as long as it is located within the database.

2. Choose Data, Filter, Advanced Filter from the menu. The Advanced Filter dialog box is displayed.

FIGURE 20-7
Advanced Filter
dialog box

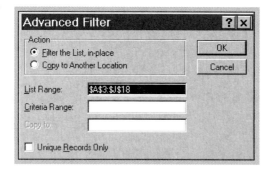

3. If necessary, select the Filter the List, in-place option. This option displays matching records in the database area of the worksheet.

NOTE: To place the filtered data in another area of the worksheet so that the original data remain unaffected, choose Copy to Another Location in the Advanced Filter dialog box. If you use this option, the target area must contain the field names needed. Creating a range name will make the target area more accessible.

4. If necessary, click on the <u>L</u>ist Range edit box. Key **Customers**, the name you assigned to the database. (It is easier to remember a name than a range address.)

5. Select the <u>C</u>riteria Range edit box and then press F3. The Paste Name dialog box is displayed. Click the range name Sm_ma, and then click OK.

6. Click OK in the Advanced Filter dialog box. The database changes to display the only two records that match the criteria.

7. Save the file as *[your initials]***20-6a.xls**. Print the Customer sheet.

TIP: If your filtered list shows duplicate records, you can check Unique <u>R</u>ecords Only in the Advanced Filter dialog box. This option displays only the first record that meets the criteria and eliminates any duplicates.

8. Choose <u>D</u>ata, <u>F</u>ilter, <u>A</u>dvanced Filter from the menu. Select the <u>C</u>riteria Range edit box and then press F3. Select the range name Sm_Ny. Click OK, and then click OK a second time. Seven records are shown in the database area. Print the Customer sheet.

9. Choose <u>D</u>ata, <u>F</u>ilter, <u>A</u>dvanced Filter from the menu. Select the <u>C</u>riteria Range edit box and then press F3. Select the range name SB_Due. Click OK, and then click OK again. Four records are shown in the database area.

10. Select cell J19 and click Σ. Review the formula in J19, noticing that the sum is actually a subtotal.

11. Save the workbook as *[your initials]***20-6b.xls**. Print the Customer sheet.

12. Choose <u>D</u>ata, <u>F</u>ilter, <u>S</u>how All to remove the filter on the database and show all records.

13. Close the workbook.

Concepts Review

TRUE/FALSE QUESTIONS

Each of the following statements is either true or false. Indicate your choice by circling **T** or **F**.

T F   ***1.*** AutoFilter is a quick way to search a list for a set of criteria.

T F   ***2.*** The best method of filtering using complex criteria is AutoFilter.

T F   ***3.*** One method of removing the filtered list in AutoFilter is to click the down arrow and select the option All.

T F   ***4.*** A name for your database should not include the field names in the selected range.

T F   ***5.*** When you set criteria for Advanced Filter, field names must appear in the first row.

T F   ***6.*** Criteria located on the same row are treated as "or" conditions by Excel when using Advanced Filter.

T F   ***7.*** Sums performed on filtered data are actually subtotals.

T F   ***8.*** Filtered data can be copied to another area of the worksheet.

SHORT ANSWER QUESTIONS

Write the correct answer in the space provided.

1. Which menu commands are used to filter a list using simple criteria?

_____

2. Which operator is used to indicate "less than"?

_____

3. Which option is selected when using the AutoFilter to display the top 2 criteria?

_____

4. Which menu commands are used to filter a list using complex criteria?

_____

5. Where should criteria be located when using the Advanced Filter?

_____

6. Which row arrangement should you use to have Excel read the criteria as an "or" situation when using Advanced Filter?

_____

7. Which row arrangement should you use to have Excel read the criteria as an "and" situation when using Advanced Filter?

_____

8. Which menu commands should you select to remove the filter when using Advanced Filter?

_____

CRITICAL THINKING

Answer these questions on a separate piece of paper. There are no right or wrong answers. Support your answers with examples from your own experience, if possible.

1. Your company maintains a customer database with telephone numbers. You have been asked to filter the list on a weekly basis. Would you maintain a separate field for ZIP codes? Why or why not?

2. Name three types of businesses that would find Excel's filtering options useful. Explain what types of information each company might filter.

3. More than one person is using your company's database for advanced filtering. Explain how you would organize the workbook containing the database for ease of use by all users.

Skills Review

EXERCISE 20-7

Use AutoFilter, filter a database using comparison criteria, and then remove AutoFilter.

1. Open the file **Iron10.xls**.

2. Filter the database for all records with the last name "Small" by following these steps:

   a. Choose Data, Filter, AutoFilter from the menu.

   b. Click the down arrow in cell B3.

   c. Select Small from the drop-down list.

3. Save the workbook as _[your initials]_**20-7a.xls** and print the list.

4. Remove AutoFilter by choosing <u>D</u>ata, <u>F</u>ilter from the menu, and deselecting Auto<u>F</u>ilter.

5. Save the workbook as *[your initials]***20-7b.xls**.

6. Print the file and close the workbook.

Use AutoFilter, filter a database using mathematical operators and the Top 10 option, and then remove AutoFilter.

1. Open the file **Iron10.xls**.

2. Filter the database for all records with a balance of less than $500.00 by following these steps:

   a. Choose <u>D</u>ata, <u>F</u>ilter, AutoFilter.

   b. Click the down arrow in cell J3.

   c. Select (Custom...) from the drop-down list

   d. Click the top left down arrow.

   e. Select the less than operator (<) from the drop-down list.

   f. Click the top edit box, key **500**, and then click OK.

3. Save the workbook as *[your initials]***20-8a.xls** and print the list.

4. Filter the database for the four highest balances by following these steps:

   a. Click the down arrow in cell J3.

   b. Select (Top 10...) from the drop-down list.

   c. If necessary, select Top in the first box by clicking the down arrow and clicking Top.

   d. Click the down arrow until the box reads 4.

   e. If necessary, select Items from the last box.

5. Save the workbook as *[your initials]***20-8b.xls** and print the list.

6. Remove AutoFilter by choosing <u>D</u>ata, <u>F</u>ilter from the menu, and deselecting Auto<u>F</u>ilter.

7. Close the workbook without saving it.

Name a list, add a criteria sheet, and set up a criteria sheet with an And criteria; use Advanced Filter and copy the results to another location.

1. Open the file **Iron10.xls**.

2. Name the database by following these steps:

   a. Click the Name box, key **A3:J18**, and then press `Enter`.

   b. Click the Name box, key **Cust_List**, and then press `Enter`.

c. Press the Left arrow key to deselect.

3. Add a new sheet to the workbook and name it **Criteria**

4. Move the new worksheet after the Customer List worksheet by dragging the Criteria tab to the right of the Customer List tab.

5. Set up an And criteria range by following these steps:

a. Copy cell B3 in the Customer List worksheet (the "Last" field) to cell A2 in the Criteria worksheet.

b. With the Criteria worksheet displayed, click the Name box, key **A2:A4**, and then press Enter.

c. Click the Name box, key **Names**, and then press Enter.

d. Key **Zepper** in cell A3 and **Brown** in cell A4.

6. Filter the records using the And criteria and copy the results to the Customer List worksheet by following these steps:

a. Click the Customer List tab and select cell B4.

b. Choose Date, Filter, Advanced Filter from the menu.

c. If the List Range does not show $A$3:$J$18, press F3 and select Cust_List.

d. Select the Criteria Range edit box.

e. Press F3 and select Names. Click OK.

f. Select Copy to another location.

g. Select the Copy to edit box. Key **A22** and click OK.

7. Save the workbook as *[your initials]***20-9.xls**.

8. Print the worksheet and close the workbook.

EXERCISE 20-10

Set up a criteria range using multiple criteria, use Advanced Filter, and remove Advanced Filter.

1. Open the file **Criteria.xls**.

2. Set the And criteria for records in which the last name begins with "S" and the customer lives in the state "MA" by following these steps:

a. Copy cell B3 in the Customer List worksheet to cell A3 in the Criteria worksheet.

b. Select cell A4 and key **S***

c. Copy cell G3 in the Customer List worksheet (the "State" field) to cell B3 in the Criteria worksheet.

d. Select cell B4 and key **MA**

3. Name the And criteria by following these steps:

a. Click the Name box, key **A3:B4**, and then press Enter.

b. Click the Name box, key **S_MA**, and then press Enter.

4. Set the Or criteria for customers who live in Massachusetts or Connecticut by following these steps:

    a. Copy cell G3 in the Customer List worksheet (the State field) to cell D3 in the Criteria worksheet.

    b. Key **CT** in cell D4 and **MA** in cell D5

5. Name the Or criteria by following these steps:

    a. Click the Name box, key **D3:D5**, and then press Enter.

    b. Click the Name box, key **CT_MA**, and then press Enter.

6. Filter for the And criteria called S_MA by following these steps:

    a. Click the Customer List worksheet tab and select cell B4.

    b. Choose Data, Filter, Advanced Filter.

    c. Select the List Range edit box, and then press F3.

    d. In the Paste Name dialog box, select Cust_list from the list and click OK.

    e. Click the Criteria Range edit box.

    f. Press F3. Select S_MA from the list and click OK.

    g. Click OK a second time.

7. Save the workbook as *[your initials]***20-10a.xls** and print the list.

8. Filter for the Or criteria called CT_MA by following these steps:

    a. Choose Data, Filter, Advanced Filter from the menu.

    b. Check the List Range edit box for the entry $A$3:$J$18. If the range is not correct, rekey it.

    c. Select the Criteria Range edit box.

    d. Press F3. Select CT_MA from the list and click OK.

    e. Click OK a second time.

9. Save the workbook as *[your initials]***20-10b.xls** and print the list.

10. Remove the Advanced Filter by choosing Data, Filter, Show All.

11. Save the workbook again and close it.

Lesson Applications

Enter new records in a database, filter and edit a record with AutoFilter, and customize criteria with AutoFilter.

Indiana Iron Works needs to add records to its database of product sales. The company needs to filter the data by item number and company. It also needs to calculate the total units sold and the total sales for each product.

1. Open the file **Iron11.xls**.
2. Key the data as shown in Figure 20-8. Use the data form, or insert six rows above row 13 and key the data directly.

FIGURE 20-8

Date	Company	Item	Price	Quantity
3/14/96	Items Unlimited	2-5000	475.00	34
10/14/96	Parts, Inc.	1-3000	453.21	67
3/14/96	Items Unlimited	1-1100	11.98	18
9/25/96	Parts, Inc.	2-1010	104.00	2
3/2/96	Items Unlimited	1-1100	11.98	1
11/1/96	NERS	2-5000	32.52	45

3. Complete the total column for the new records by copying the formula in the column.
4. Filter the database using AutoFilter for the record dated 11/7/96. Edit the item number for this record to read 2-1010 and change the price to 563. Add a new row between rows 2 and 3. Add a subtitle to the report in cell A2, describing the record shown.
5. Save the workbook as *[your initials]***20-11a.xls**. Print the worksheet.
6. Display all records.
7. Filter the records for the NERS company that are dated after 3/1/96. Add a subtitle to the report in cell A2 based on the records shown.
8. Save the workbook as *[your initials]***20-11b.xls**.
9. Print and close the workbook.

EXERCISE 20-12

Use AutoFilter with multiple conditions and custom criteria; generate reports for top five records, sorting the outcome.

The management of Indiana Iron Works needs some reports showing sales by salesperson and sales amount.

1. Open the file **Sperson.xls**.
2. Filter the records for sales over $25,000 by Linda Brenner. Add a subtitle to the report describing the records shown.
3. Save the workbook as *[your initials]***20-12a.xls** and print the report.
4. Filter the records showing the top five sales amounts. Sort the records in descending order. Add a subtitle describing the records shown.
5. Save the workbook as *[your initials]***20-12b.xls**.
6. Print the report and close the workbook.

EXERCISE 20-13

Set up a criteria worksheet for use with a database. Use the Advance Filter to generate reports with multiple conditions, sorting the outcome.

Indiana Iron Works has two people who must filter the sales database. These two employees produce reports by salesperson and by sales amount. Create a criteria sheet that can be used repeatedly by both workers to filter the same database.

1. Open the file **Sperson.xls**.
2. Create a name for the database.
3. Insert a new sheet for the criteria. Move the sheet after the database sheet and then name the worksheet tab **Criteria**.
4. On the Criteria sheet, create and name criteria to be used to filter for a salesperson.
5. On the same sheet, create and name criteria to be used to filter for a sales amount.
6. Produce a report for Michner using the same criteria range. The named range should include both names. Add an appropriate subtitle to the report.
7. Save the workbook as *[your initials]***20-13a.xls** and print it.
8. Produce a report indicating all sales under $30,000, with records sorted in descending order. Subtitle the report appropriately.

9. Change the footer so that the tab name appears in the center of each worksheet, rather than the page number. Save the workbook as *[your initials]*20-13b.xls.

10. Print the entire workbook, and then close it.

EXERCISE 20-14

Set up a criteria worksheet using multiple criteria, generate different reports using the same criteria, and add formulas computing commissions and totals.

Indiana Iron Works needs reports that determine the commissions for each salesperson. Commissions are based on sales amounts. A 20 percent commission is given on the amount of sales exceeding $5,000.

1. Open the file **Sperson.xls**.

2. Create a name for the database.

3. Insert a new sheet for the criteria. Move the sheet after the database sheet and then name the worksheet tab **Criteria**.

4. On the criteria sheet, create and name criteria to be used to filter for sales of more than $5,000 for any salesperson.

5. Filter the database for Victor's sales over $5,000. Calculate the commission on each sale. (The commission is paid for sales above $5,000, so this amount must be subtracted first before the commission is calculated.) Show a total for commissions. Format cells in currency style with no dollar signs.

6. Save the workbook as *[your initials]*20-14a.xls.

7. Add an appropriate subtitle to the report, and then print it in landscape orientation.

8. Delete the formulas, and then repeat step 5 for Travis.

9. Save the workbook as *[your initials]*20-14b.xls.

10. Add an appropriate subtitle to the report, and then print it in landscape orientation. Print the report again, showing formulas, gridlines, and row and column headings. Adjust the column widths so that the formulas are fully visible.

11. Close the workbook without saving the changes.

Advanced Database Features

OBJECTIVES   After completing this lesson, you will be able to:

1. Use database functions.
2. Work with data tables.
3. Get summary information with subtotals.
4. Create a pivot table using the PivotTable Wizard.

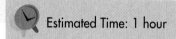
Estimated Time: 1 hour

This lesson introduces four advanced Excel features that provide additional methods of computation and elementary database management: database functions, data tables, subtotals, and pivot tables.

Using Database Functions

Database functions allow you to perform calculations on the values in a specific field of the database. You can calculate the value for all records or just for records that meet specified criteria. All of Excel's database functions use the same format: FUNCTION(database,field,criteria)

The first argument, (database), refers to the database range. You can enter it as a cell range or as a name assigned to the database range.

The second argument, (field), is the field used in the calculation. You can enter the field name enclosed in quotation marks or the field's column number in the database. The first column in the database (starting at the left) is numbered 1, the second column is numbered 2, and so forth.

The third argument, (criteria), is the cell range that contains the criteria for the records to be included in the calculation. You can enter it by either cell address or range name.

 TIP: It's good practice to assign range names to the database and criteria range when working with database functions. You can then use the names in the function instead of the cell ranges.

TABLE 21-1   Database Functions

FUNCTION	RESULT
DAVERAGE()	Averages the numbers in a field
DCOUNT()	Returns a count of the numbers in a field
DCOUNTA()	Counts the nonblank cells in a field
DMAX()	Returns the largest number in the field
DMIN()	Returns the smallest number in the field
DSUM()	Adds the numbers in the field

EXERCISE **Produce Statistical Data Using Database Functions**

1. Open the file **Property.xls**.
2. Select the Name box on the formula bar and key **A5:I29**. The database is highlighted.
3. In the Name box, key **HOMES** to name the database. Select any cell to remove the highlighting.
4. Insert a new worksheet, position it after the Property worksheet, and name the new worksheet tab Statistics.
5. In cell A1 on the Statistics sheet, key **Statistics for Properties over Ten Years Old**
6. In cell A4, key **AGE**
7. In cell A5, key **>10**. The criteria specify homes over the age of 10.
8. Select cells A4 through A5, and name the range **AGE_10**
9. Select cell C6, and key **Average Price**. Widen column C to accommodate the entry.
10. In cell D6, key the following formula to calculate the average price of homes that meet the search criteria:
    =DAVERAGE(HOMES,"PRICE",AGE_10)

Excel calculates the average price of homes over 10 years old. Format cells D6 through D8 in comma style. Widen the column if necessary.

11. In cell C7, key **Highest Price**. Select D7 and key the following formula: **=DMAX(HOMES,7, AGE_10)**. Notice that the field argument here is 7, which is the "Price" field. You can use either the field name in quotes (as in step 10) or the column number.

12. In cell C8, key **Lowest Price**. Select cell D8 and key the following formula: **=DMIN(HOMES,"PRICE",AGE_10)**

13. In cell C9, key **Number of Homes**. Select cell D9 and key the following formula: **=DCOUNT(HOMES,"PRICE",AGE_10)**

14. Select cell A5 and key **>5**. Excel presents the statistics for homes over five years old.

15. Key **>10** in cell A5. Format numbers and widen columns, as necessary.

16. Save the workbook as *[your initials]***21-1.xls**.

17. Replace the tab header with the filename and print the Statistics worksheet.

Working with Data Tables

Data tables are useful for "what if" analyses. They illustrate how different values in a formula affect its results.

Excel offers two types of data tables. A *one-variable data table* calculates a formula containing one variable. A *two-variable data table* calculates a formula containing two variables.

EXERCISE 21-2 **Create a Data Table with One Variable**

When you create a one-variable data table, you must first designate a worksheet cell to be the input cell. An *input cell* is a cell referenced in the data table formula and varied to calculate the data table results. It can be any cell outside the table range. It is best if the cell is left blank. The data table is constructed so that the input values are entered into consecutive cells of one column or one row.

One application of the data table might be to show the monthly payments on a loan, with interest rates varying one-half percent above and below the current rate. The term is 15 years on a loan of $95,000.

1. Insert a worksheet, position it after the Statistics sheet, and name the new worksheet tab **Mort. Payments**.

2. Key **Comparison Payments on Property Located at 203 Narrow Ave.** in cell A1.

3. Key the following percentages in cells B5 through B11:

6.5%
7.0%
7.5%
8.0%
8.5%
9.0%
9.5%

These percentages are the variables that will be used by the data table to calculate different monthly payments. They must be entered in consecutive cells.

 TIP: These percentages form a series that is incremented by .5%. Use Edit, Fill, Series to create the percentages automatically. Or, key the first two percentages, select them, and then use AutoFill and drag to cell B11.

4. In cell C4, key the following formula: **=PMT(A2/12,15*12,95000)**. It calculates the amount $527.78, which is shown in red. This result represents money going out of your pocket. Cell A2 is the blank input cell used by the formula to indicate the different interest rates.

 NOTE: Notice that the formula is located one column to the right of the variables and one row up from the first variable. This setup is required for the one-variable data table.

5. Select cells B4 through C11 (the data table range), and choose Table from the Data menu. The Table dialog box appears.

6. In the Column Input Cell text box, key **A2** as your input cell and then click OK. The formula located in cell C4 referenced the blank cell A2 for the interest rate variable. The monthly payments are calculated to the right of the corresponding interest rate. This method provides a quick way to compare different interest rates on the monthly payment amount.

FIGURE 21-1
Table dialog box

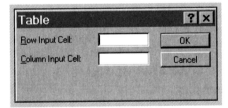

 TIP: The result of the formula in cell C4 doesn't need to be seen. To hide this result, you can change the font color to white. The cell will still contain the formula, but the calculation won't be seen.

7. Format cells C5 through C11 in the same way as cell C4. Save the workbook as *[your initials]***21-2.xls**.

8. Replace the tab header with the filename and print the Mort. Payments worksheet.

EXERCISE 21-3 Create a Data Table with Multiple Formulas

A data table can include more than one formula, as long as all formulas refer to the same input cell and are placed on the same row.

1. Display the Mort. Payment sheet.

2. Select cell D4 and key the following formula: **=PMT(A2/12,30*12,95000)**. The PMT function calculates the amount $263.89.

3. Select the data table range B4:D11.

4. Choose <u>D</u>ata, <u>T</u>able from the menu. Key **A2** in the <u>C</u>olumn Input cell edit box on the Table dialog box. Click OK. The mortgage amounts for a 30-year loan are calculated, along with the 15-year rates.

5. Format the data in column D in currency style, using parentheses for negative values. Add column headings identifying the 15- and 30-year mortgages in cells C3 and D3.

6. Save the workbook as *[your initials]***21-3.xls**.

7. Print the Mort. Payment worksheet.

EXERCISE 21-4 Create a Data Table with Two Variables

You can use two input cells to calculate the result of a formula that depends on two varying input values. To construct a two-variable table, one set of variables must be arranged by row and the other set of variables must be arranged by column. The formula is located at the upper left corner of the table range.

1. Insert a new worksheet, position it after the Mort. Payment sheet, and name the new worksheet tab Mort. Payment 2. The worksheet will compare monthly payments using a different set of interest rates and a different set of terms.

2. In cell A1, key **Comparison of Monthly Mortgage Payments for Different Rates and Terms**

3. In cell B5, key **6.5%**, then select cells B5 through B11, and use <u>E</u>dit, F<u>i</u>ll, <u>S</u>eries with a <u>S</u>tep value of .5% to enter the following interest rates:

   6.5%
   7.0%
   7.5%
   8.0%
   8.5%
   9.0%
   9.5%

4. Key the following payment periods across row 4 in cells C4 through G4:

   10   15   20   25   30

5. Enter the following formula in cell B4: **=PMT(A2/12,A3*12,95000)**. This formula contains two input cells. Cell A2 is the input cell for the interest rates located in the column. Cell A3 is the input cell for terms located on the row. The formula will result in the error message #DIV/0! Hide the result of this formula by formatting the font color as white.

6. Select the data table range B4:G11 and then choose <u>D</u>ata, <u>T</u>able. Key **A3** in the <u>R</u>ow Input cell edit box. Key **A2** in the <u>C</u>olumn Input cell edit box, and then click OK. Calculations appear for interest rates and term.

7. Change formatting as necessary and replace the tab header with the filename.

8. Save the workbook as *[your initials]***21-4.xls**.

9. Print the Mort. Payment 2 worksheet.

EXERCISE **21-5** **Edit, Copy, Move, and Clear Data Tables**

---

1. Display the Mort. Payment 2 worksheet.

2. Beginning in cell C4, edit the term of years in row 4 to read as follows (notice that the table results are recalculated as the payment term changes):

12   17   22   27   32

FIGURE 21-2
Cannot Change Part
of Table message

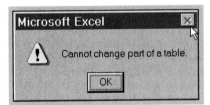

3. Select cell E5. Press Del. A dialog message box appears explaining that the table cannot be changed. You cannot remove individual cells in a data table. To remove such cells, you must first clear all cells in the data table that contain the results.

4. Click OK.

5. Clear the results in the table by selecting cells C5 through G11 and then pressing Del.

6. Select cells E4 through G4 and press Del. Recalculate the results by selecting the new table range B4:D11. Choose <u>D</u>ata, <u>T</u>able from the menu. Key **A3** in the <u>R</u>ow Input cell edit box, and then press Tab. Key **A2** in the <u>C</u>olumn Input cell edit box, and then click OK. The table is recalculated.

7. To move the table, select cell C8 (or click any result cell). Press F5. Choose <u>S</u>pecial, select the Current <u>A</u>rray option, and click OK.

8. Click 🔏, select cell B14, and then click 📋.

9. Return the table to its original location by clicking ↩. Press Esc if the cut is still active.

NOTE: Copying is performed using the same steps as moving, however you click 📋 instead of 🔏. The copy will lose its underlying formulas, and only the results will be copied. The results will not change if new variables are entered.

10. Save the workbook as *[your initials]***21-5.xls**.

11. Print the Mort. Payment 2 worksheet.

Getting Summary Information with Subtotals

Excel's subtotal function provides an easy way to produce subtotals and grand totals based on any specified group or groups. You don't create formulas with subtotals; Excel creates them automatically when you use this feature or when you use AutoSum Σ.

To use the subtotal function, data must appear in a list or database using column labels or field names. The data in the list or database then must be sorted by the group to be subtotaled.

EXERCISE **21-6** **Sort a Database List and Create Subtotals**

1. Activate the Property worksheet by clicking the Property tab.

2. Select cell A6 and choose <u>D</u>ata, <u>S</u>ort from the menu. Click the down arrow next to the <u>S</u>ort By text box. In the drop-down list, select BDRMS, and then <u>A</u>scending. Click OK.

3. Choose <u>D</u>ata, Su<u>b</u>totals from the menu. The Subtotal dialog box appears.

FIGURE 21-3
Subtotal dialog box

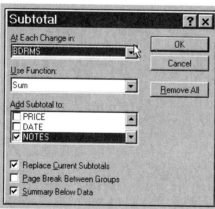

4. Click the down arrow next to the <u>A</u>t Each Change in text box. In the drop-down list, select BDRMS (the group you wish to subtotal by).

5. Click the down arrow next to the <u>U</u>se Function text box. Select Sum from the drop-down list (the calculation you want to perform).

6. In the A<u>d</u>d Subtotal to box, select PRICE (the data you want to calculate). Deselect NOTES.

7. Click OK. Excel inserts subtotal rows at the end of each group and a grand total row at the end of the database, performs the selected calculations, labels each row with appropriate titles, and outlines the data. Outline symbols appear at the far left of the worksheet.

8. Save the workbook as *[your initials]***21-6a.xls** and print it.

 TIP: If you want the groups to print on separate pages, select the <u>P</u>age Break Between Groups check box in the Subtotal dialog box.

9. With cell A6 or any other cell in the database selected, choose <u>D</u>ata, Sub<u>t</u>otals from the menu. Select HEAT from the <u>A</u>t Each Change in drop-down list. Make sure that the Replace <u>C</u>urrent Subtotals check box is selected. This will replace existing subtotals.

10. Make sure that <u>U</u>se Function text box shows SUM and the A<u>d</u>d Subtotal to text box has PRICE selected. Click OK. New subtotals are calculated.

11. Choose <u>D</u>ata, Sub<u>t</u>otals from the menu. Click <u>R</u>emove All to remove all subtotals from the database.

12. Choose <u>D</u>ata, Sub<u>t</u>otals from the menu. From the <u>A</u>t Each Change in drop-down list, select BDRMS. Select Average from the <u>U</u>se Function drop-down list. Make sure that the A<u>d</u>d Subtotal to box shows PRICE. Click OK.

13. Choose <u>D</u>ata, Sub<u>t</u>otals from the menu. Make sure the <u>A</u>t Each Change in text box reads BDRMS. Select Max from the <u>U</u>se Function drop-down list. Make sure the A<u>d</u>d Subtotal to box shows PRICE.

14. Deselect Replace <u>C</u>urrent Subtotals. Click OK. The database includes subtotals for Average and Max.

15. Choose <u>D</u>ata, Sub<u>t</u>otals from the menu. Make sure that the <u>A</u>t Each Change in text box reads BDRMS. Select Min from the <u>U</u>se Function drop-down list. Make sure the A<u>d</u>d Subtotal to box shows PRICE. Click OK.

16. Save the workbook as *[your initials]***21-6b.xls**.

17. Print the database, making sure it fits on one page.

FIGURE 21-4
View of outline
based on subtotals

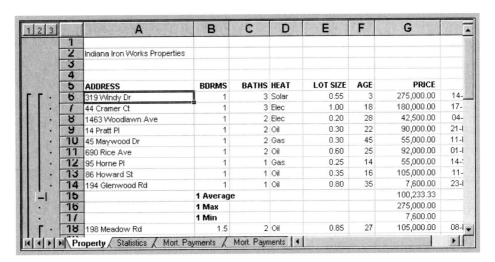

EXERCISE 21-7 Collapse and Expand a Subtotaled Database

Excel creates an outline of different levels based on subtotals that you create. The outline area can be used to collapse and expand the data shown in the subtotaled database.

1. Click the row level 1 symbol (the button located at the top of the outline that contains number 1). This selection displays grand totals and field names only.

2. Click the Display Detail button ⊞ that appears in the gray outline area. The database is expanded.

3. Click the row level 2 button. This selection displays the subtotals and grand total only. For each subtotal group, a Display Detail button is created. Click the first Display Detail button under the row level 2 button area to expand only one subtotal area. The button becomes a Hide Detail button ⊟.

4. Remove all subtotals by clicking Data, Subtotals, and Remove All.

5. Save the workbook as *[your initials]*21-7.xls. Print the Property worksheet.

Using the PivotTable Wizard

In Lessons 19 through 21, you have learned how to sort using Data Sort, how to filter using AutoFilter and Advanced Filter, and how to summarize data using subtotals. Pivot tables perform all three options—sorting, filtering, and summarizing—at once. A *pivot table* allows you to arrange the data in your database in different ways by rearranging rows and columns.

EXERCISE 21-8 Create a Pivot Table

1. Display the Property worksheet. Insert a worksheet and position it after the Property worksheet.

2. Name the new worksheet Pivot Table.

3. Choose Tools, Options from the menu and select the View tab. Deselect the Gridlines check box under Window options, and then click OK. The grids are removed from the worksheet. Select cell B3.

4. Choose Data, PivotTable. The first PivotTable Wizard dialog box appears.

FIGURE 21-5
PivotTable Wizard - Step 2 of 4 dialog box

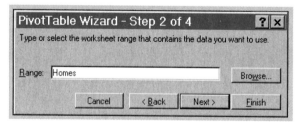

5. Click the Next button. The PivotTable Wizard - Step 2 of 4 dialog box appears. In the Range box, key **Homes**, which is the name of the Property database.

6. Click the Next button, and the PivotTable Wizard - Step 3 of 4 dialog box appears. Click and drag the field BDRMS to the area labeled ROW. Click and drag the field BATHS to the area labeled COLUMN. Click and drag the field ADDRES to the area labeled DATA.

FIGURE 21-6
PivotTable Wizard -
Step 3 of 4 dialog
box

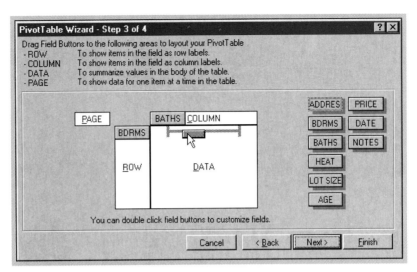

FIGURE 21-7
PivotTable Field
dialog box

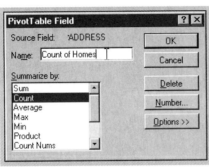

7. Double-click the Count of Address box located in the <u>D</u>ATA area. The PivotTable Field dialog box appears. In the Na<u>m</u>e text box, change "Count of Address" to read **Count of Homes**.

8. Click OK, and then click the Next button. The PivotTable Wizard - Step 4 of 4 dialog box appears.

9. Click the <u>F</u>inish button. The pivot table shown in Figure 21-8 is created. From the table, you can see that Indiana Iron Works owns three properties with one bath and one bedroom. The company owns a total of 24 properties, of which three are two-bedroom homes.

FIGURE 21-8
Completed
pivot table

	A	B	C	D	E	F	G	H
1								
2								
3		Count of Homes	BATHS					
4		BDRMS	1	2	3	4	Grand Total	
5		1	3	4	2	0	9	
6		1.5	1	1	0	0	2	
7		2	2	1	0	0	3	
8		3	1	1	0	0	2	
9		4	0	4	1	0	5	
10		5	0	1	1	1	3	
11		Grand Total	7	12	4	1	24	
12								
13								
14								

Property \ **Pivot Table** \ Statistics \ Mort. Payments

10. Right-align cells C4 through F4.

11. Save the workbook as *[your initials]***21-8.xls** and print the pivot table sheet.

13. Close the workbook.

USING HELP

The Help screens for the pivot table can be especially useful, even for experienced users of Excel. There are many aspects to the powerful tool, and you can learn about many of them via Help. The overview of the pivot table's operations is a good place to start.

To learn more about pivot tables, look up data summaries in the Excel Help Index:

1. Choose <u>H</u>elp, Microsoft Excel <u>H</u>elp Topics.

2. Click the Index tab.

3. Key **data summaries**

4. Double-click PivotTable data.

5. Select the first topic, "Analyzing data with a PivotTable." It provides a good overview of the components of a pivot table.

6. Close Help when you're finished browsing.

FIGURE 21-9
Help screen for
pivot table

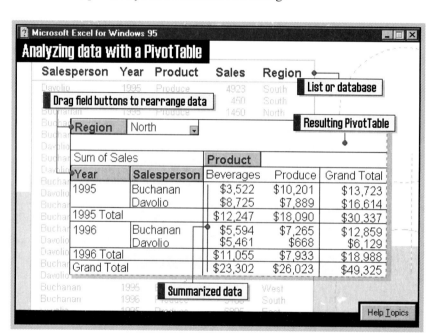

Concepts Review

Each of the following statements is either true or false. Indicate your choice by circling **T** or **F**.

T   F   **1.** All database functions in Excel use the same argument format.

T   F   **2.** When using data tables, you must have an input cell located within the table range.

T   F   **3.** Variables used in the data table can be arranged in nonadjacent cells.

T   F   **4.** A data table can include more than one formula as long as each formula has its own input cell.

T   F   **5.** When using Excel's subtotals, you must create the formulas.

T   F   **6.** To create subtotals, the database must be sorted by the group to be subtotaled.

T   F   **7.** When you create a subtotal, Excel will automatically provide an outline that can be used to expand and collapse the data.

T   F   **8.** Pivot tables allow you to rearrange the data in a database in different ways by choosing field names located in the database.

Write the correct answer in the space provided.

1. Which database function would you use to calculate the average price of one bedroom homes listed in a database?

_____

2. Which database function would you use to calculate the number of homes listed in a database?

_____

3. What kind of data table is needed to calculate a payment at varying interest rates and varying terms?

_____

4. Where must the formula be positioned when using a one-variable data table?

_____

517

5. Which menu commands do you use to create subtotals?

_____

6. Which outline button is used to show grand totals and field names?

_____

7. When would you clear the <u>R</u>eplace Current Subtotals check box?

_____

8. Which menu commands do you use to create a pivot table?

_____

CRITICAL THINKING

Answer these questions on a separate piece of paper. There are no right or wrong answers. Support your answers with examples from your own experience, if possible.

1. Imagine that you maintain a customer database. You need to know the following information: which customers bought how many of what product, what was charged for the product, and what is the balance owed? What is the best method of summarizing the data – subtotals or pivot tables? Why?

2. List some examples of types of calculations that would be best performed with a data table. Remember that data tables provide "what if" analysis.

3. Imagine that you maintain an employee database. The database contains fields for years employed, gender, and pay. What types of data could be calculated and compared by using the database functions?

Skills Review

EXERCISE 21-9

Insert a worksheet, create criteria, and calculate basic statistics using database functions.

1. Open the file **Property.xls**.
2. Insert a new worksheet, position it after the Property sheet, and name it Statistics.
3. Name the database (cells A5 through I29) on the Property worksheet HOMES.

4. Create criteria on the Statistics worksheet to provide statistics on homes with five bedrooms by following these steps:

  a. In cell A3, key **BDRMS**

  b. In cell A4, key **5**

5. Name the criteria (cells A3 through A4) FIVE .

6. Calculate Statistical data for five-bedroom homes by following these steps:

  a. Key **Average Price** in cell C5. In cell D5, key the formula **=DAVERAGE(HOMES,"Price",FIVE)**

  b. Key **Highest Price** in cell C6. In cell D6, key the formula **=DMAX(HOMES,"Price",FIVE)**

  c. Key **Lowest Price** in cell C7. In cell D7, key the formula **=DMIN(HOMES,"Price",FIVE)**

  d. Key **Number of Homes** in cell C8. In cell D8, key the formula **=DCOUNT(HOMES,"Price",FIVE)**

7. Widen column C and format the cell range D5:D7 in currency style, with no decimal places. Widen column D if necessary.

8. Key **Price Statistics for Five-Bedroom Homes** in cell A1.

9. Replace the tab header with the filename.

10. Save the workbook again as *[your initials]***21-9.xls**.

11. Print the worksheet and close the workbook.

Create a one-variable data table.

1. Open the file **Property.xls**.

2. Insert a new worksheet, position it after the Property worksheet, and name it Data Table.

3. In cell A1 of the Data Table worksheet, key **Commission Comparison Table on a Sale of $125,000**

4. In cells B5:B9, key the following percentages:

  3%
  4%
  5%
  6%
  7%

5. In cell C4, key the formula **=ROUND(125000*A2,2)**

 NOTE: This formula calculates the commission on $125,000, rounding it to two decimals, and using the cell A2 for the commission percentage variables.

6. Select the table range B4:C9.

7. Perform the table calculations by following these steps:

   a. Choose <u>D</u>ata, <u>T</u>able from the menu.

   b. Key **A2** in the <u>C</u>olumn Input Cell text box in the Table dialog box. Click OK.

8. Hide the "0" in cell C4 by changing the text font color from black to white. Format the numbers in column C in currency style, with no decimal places. Widen the column if necessary.

9. Replace the tab header with the filename.

10. Save the workbook as *[your initials]***21-10.xls**. Print and close the workbook.

EXERCISE 21-11

Create subtotals, collapse data to show grand totals, and expand data to show subtotals.

1. Open the file **Property.xls**.

2. Sort the database in ascending order by type of heat.

3. Create subtotals showing the average price of a home based on type of heat by following these steps:

   a. Choose <u>D</u>ata, Su<u>b</u>totals from the menu.

   b. Select Heat from the <u>A</u>t Each Change in drop-down list.

   c. Select Average from the <u>U</u>se Function drop-down list.

   d. Select Price from the Add Subtotal to list. Deselect all other items, if necessary, and then click OK.

4. Save the workbook as *[your initials]***21-11a.xls** and print it.

5. Collapse to show only the grand total average by clicking the row level 1 symbol.

6. Save the workbook as *[your initials]***21-11b.xls** and print the grand total average.

7. Expand to show the subtotals by clicking the row level 2 symbol.

8. Save the workbook as *[your initials]***21-11c.xls**, print the subtotals, and close the workbook.

EXERCISE 21-12

Create a pivot table.

1. Open the file **Property.xls**.

2. Name the database (cells A5 through I29) on the Property worksheet HOMES.

3. Insert a new worksheet, position it after the Property worksheet, and name it Pivot Table.

4. Make the grids on the Pivot Table sheet invisible by using <u>T</u>ools, <u>O</u>ptions, View.

5. Select cell B3 and create the pivot table by following these steps:

   a. Choose <u>D</u>ata, <u>P</u>ivotTable from the menu.

   b. In the PivotTable - Step 1 of 4 dialog box, click the Next button.

   c. In the PivotTable - Step 2 of 4 dialog box, key **Homes** in the <u>R</u>ange text box and then click the Next button.

   d. In the PivotTable - Step 3 of 4 dialog box, drag the field HEAT to the <u>R</u>OW area, drag the field BDRMS to the <u>C</u>OLUMN area, and drag PRICE to the <u>D</u>ATA area.

   e. Double-click the Sum of Price box. Change "Sum of Price" to read **Total Value of Property**. Click OK and then click the Next button.

   f. In the PivotTable - Step 4 of 4 dialog box, click <u>F</u>inish.

6. Center the bedroom titles in the cell range C4:H4.

7. Format all price amounts in comma style with no decimal places.

8. Replace the tab header with the filename.

9. Change the width of column A, if necessary, to make the table fit on one page.

10. Save the workbook as *[your initials]***21-12.xls**.

11. Print the worksheet and close the workbook.

Lesson Applications

Name a database, create and name criteria, and calculate basic statistics.

Indiana Iron Works would like to extract some statistics from its database on its New York customers. The company would like to know the number of customers, and the highest, lowest, and average balances among amounts currently due.

1. Open the file **IndCust.xls**.
2. Name the database.
3. Insert a new worksheet, position it after the Customer List sheet, and name it Statistics.
4. Create and name criteria for those customers living in the state of New York.
5. Calculate the following statistics for New York customers: average balance owed, highest balance owed, lowest balance owed, and total number of customers.
6. Add an appropriate title and format the numbers.
7. Replace the tab header with the filename.
8. Save the workbook as *[your initials]***21-13.xls** and print the Statistics worksheet.
9. Close the workbook.

Create a one-variable data table.

Indiana Iron Works offers discounts to its customers. The discount rate ranges from a high of 6% to a low of 2%. Create a table that shows the amount owed after the discount has been applied using the average balance due of $1,208.54. Use an increment of 1% for the discount rates.

1. Open the file **IndCust.xls**.
2. Insert a new worksheet, position it after the Customer List worksheet, and name it Data Table.
3. In cell C4, key a formula that computes the amount due after the discount, using a balance of $1,208.54 as a constant.

 NOTE: Remember that a blank input cell is used in the formula as the variable for the discount rate.

4. Beginning in cell B6, set up the percentage variables that will be used by the formula to compute the discounts in the table. Use <u>D</u>ata, <u>T</u>able to create the table.

5. Hide the formula.

6. Provide appropriate titles for the table and format numbers where necessary.

7. Replace the tab header with the filename.

8. Save the workbook as *[your initials]***21-14.xls** and print the Data Table worksheet.

9. Close the workbook.

EXERCISE 21-15

Create a pivot table.

Indiana Iron Works would like to generate a table from its database that shows total amounts due by state and product item.

1. Open the file **Orders.xls**.

2. Insert a worksheet for the pivot table.

3. Create a pivot table that displays the amount due for each state and for each product item.

4. Format the amounts due in comma style, and center the headings.

5. Save the workbook as *[your initials]***21-15.xls**.

6. Print and close the workbook.

EXERCISE 21-16

Produce statistics and summary reports.

Indiana Iron Works needs a report generated from its Property database showing the age, price ranges, and the number of homes over 20 years of age. The company would also like to see a report generated from the same database showing the properties categorized by heating type, with the highest-priced, lowest-priced, and the number of properties listed in each category.

1. Open the file **Property.xls**.

2. Add a new worksheet, give it a name, and produce statistics (average price, lowest price, highest price, and number) for homes over 20 years old.

3. Produce a summary report by type of heat showing the highest cost, lowest cost, and number of homes.

4. Use the filename as the header and the tab name as the footer on both worksheets.

5. Change formatting where necessary.

6. Print the entire workbook, which should include both reports on the two worksheets.

7. Save the workbook as *[your initials]***21-16.xls** and then close it.

Unit 7 Applications

APPLICATION 7-1

Number records in a database, sort the database, and add a record using the data form.

Indiana Iron Works maintains an employee list. The Personnel Department has converted the employees' salaried pay to an hourly rate as requested by the company president, Dexter Peabody. He has requested reports from Personnel concerning the employee database. The information gathered will be used to assess the company's overall profitability.

1. Open the file **IndEmpl.xls**.
2. In column I of the database, create a field called "Record #." Number each record of the database. Format the heading to match, and adjust the named range "Database."
3. Sort the list by male and female gender, and within the male and female classification by number of years employed, using the ascending sort order.
4. Save the workbook as *[your initials]***u7-1a.xls**.
5. Add an appropriate subtitle, and center both the title and subtitle across the worksheet columns. Print the report in landscape orientation.
6. Using the data form, add the following employee record to the database:

   Jones   Donna   F   244-88-1228   Designer   1   1 $19.99   26
7. Re-sort the list using the same sort categories.
8. Save the workbook as *[your initials]***u7-1b.xls**.
9. Print the new list and close the workbook.

APPLICATION 7-2

Filter the database using AutoFilter.

The management of Indiana Iron Works needs several reports generated from its employee list. Managers would like to see separate reports of male and female employees who have worked for the company over 10 years. They also need a report on the top five pay rates for employees.

1. Open the file **IndEmpl.xls**.
2. Using AutoFilter, produce a list of female employees who have worked for the company for more than 10 years. Sort by years employed using ascending sort order, and add an appropriate subtitle.
3. Save the workbook as *[your initials]***u7-2a.xls** and print it centered horizontally on the page.

4. Using AutoFilter, produce a list of male employees who have worked for the company for more than 10 years. Sort by years employed using ascending sort order, and add an appropriate subtitle.

5. Save the workbook as *[your initials]*u7-2b.xls and print it.

6. Produce a report showing the top five pay rates for employees.

7. Add an appropriate title to the report.

8. Save the workbook as *[your initials]*u7-2c.xls and print it.

9. Close the workbook.

APPLICATION 7-3

Filter the database using Advanced Filter, using multiple selection criteria, and copy the data to another location.

Using the employee list, managers of Indiana Iron Works would like a report showing all designers and all engineers, as well as a report showing all clerks and secretaries earning more than $5.50 per hour.

1. Open the file **IndEmpl.xls**.

2. Insert a new worksheet, position it after the Database worksheet, and name it **Criteria**. Set up all criteria on the Criteria worksheet.

3. Using Advanced Filter, produce a report listing all designers, using the option to copy the filter results to another location. Have the results copied to the bottom of the Database worksheet, beginning in cell A30.

4. Cut and paste the results to the Criteria worksheet, placing them under the criteria beginning in cell A10.

5. Produce a report listing all Engineers. Have the results copied to the bottom of the Database worksheet, and then cut and paste them to the Criteria worksheet, beginning in cell A16.

6. Filter the Database worksheet to list all clerks and secretaries whose pay exceeds $5.50 per hour. (Hint: Use the wildcard character ? to filter both Clerk 1 and Clerk 2.) It is not necessary to copy the results to another location for this filter.

7. Change the footer for both worksheets to reflect the tab name instead of the page number. The header should contain the filename. Adjust the column widths on both worksheets appropriately and set the page orientation to landscape.

8. Save the workbook as *[your initials]*u7-3.xls.

9. Print the entire workbook and then close it.

APPLICATION 7-4

Create statistics with database functions and generate a summary report showing various database subtotals.

Indiana Iron Works needs some statistical information from the employee database concerning gender and pay. Specifically, managers want statistics for the number of female employees and their highest, lowest, and average pay; the same report should show similar data for men. They also want a report generated from the database that summarizes the total pay, average pay, highest pay, and lowest pay by employee class.

1. Open the file **IndEmpl.xls**.

2. Insert a new worksheet, position it after the Database worksheet, and name it **Statistics**.

3. On the Statistics worksheet, use the top right area of the worksheet to set up the criteria. Use database functions to calculate the following statistics for all female employees: average pay, highest pay, lowest pay, and number of female employees. Format, label, and widen the columns appropriately.

4. On the same sheet, calculate the same statistics for men.

5. On the Database worksheet, produce a report that summarizes the total pay, average pay, highest pay, and lowest pay by class.

6. Change the footers on each worksheet to show the tab name instead of the page number; the header of both worksheets should show the filename. Set the page orientation of both worksheets to portrait, and adjust the Database worksheet to fit on one page.

7. Save the workbook as *[your initials]***u7-4.xls**.

8. Print the entire workbook and then close it.

APPLICATION 7-5

Create two pivot tables on a single page.

Indiana Iron Works needs two reports generated from its employee database: one showing average pay as a function of class and gender; and one showing the average years of employment as a function of class and gender. Management would like to see the data in tabular form on a single page.

1. Open the file **IndEmpl.xls**. Create a pivot table for the first report. The table should show average pay based on class and gender. Turn off the gridlines on the worksheet containing the pivot table. Format the pay in currency style with two decimal places. Align the labels and widen the columns where appropriate.

2. Position the cell pointer below the first table, and produce a second pivot table that shows the average years employed based on class and gender.

Format the years to show one decimal place. Widen the columns and align the labels appropriately.

3. Rename the worksheet **Table**. Change the header to show the filename and the footer to show the tab name.

4. Save the workbook as *[your initials]***u7-5.xls**. Print the Table worksheet and then close the workbook.

Appendices

APPENDIX A

Windows 95 Tutorial

If you're unfamiliar with Windows 95, we suggest that you review this Windows 95 tutorial.

If you've never used Windows before, you may need additional help with some basic Windows actions. At appropriate points in this Tutorial, a Note will guide you to one of the two Appendixes covering basic Windows actions (Appendix B: "Using the Mouse," and Appendix C: "Using Menus and Dialog Boxes").

Starting Windows

Individual computers may be set up differently. In most cases, however, when you turn on your computer, Windows 95 will load and the Windows desktop will appear.

The desktop contains *icons*, or symbols representing windows. If you double-click an icon, the window represented by that icon opens. Two icons are especially important:

- My Computer
  Opens a window that contains icons representing each input and output device on your printer or in your network.

- Recycle Bin
  Opens a window listing files you have deleted. Until you empty the Recycle Bin, these files can be undeleted.

 TIP: If you don't know how to use the mouse to point, click, double-click, or drag and drop, see Appendix B: "Using the Mouse."

Using the Start Menu

 The Start button on the taskbar at the bottom of the desktop is probably the most important button in Windows. Clicking displays the Start menu from which you can perform any Windows task.

 NOTE: If Microsoft Office is installed on your computer, additional options may appear on your Start menu.

1. Turn on the computer. Windows will load, and the Windows desktop will appear.

 NOTE: When you start Windows, you may be prompted to log on to Windows or, if your computer is attached to a network, to log on to the network. If you are asked to key a user name and a password, ask your instructor for help.

2. Click on the Windows taskbar. The Start menu appears.

TIP: If you don't know how to choose a command from a menu, see Appendix C: "Using Menus and Dialog Boxes."

FIGURE A-1
Windows 95
desktop

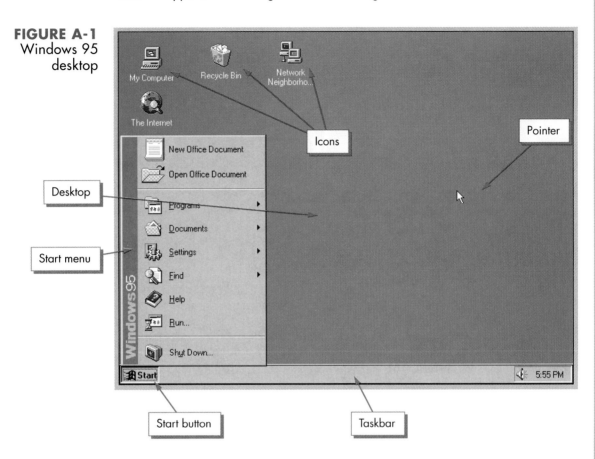

TABLE A-1   Start Menu

COMMAND	USE
Programs	Displays a list of programs you can start.
Documents	Displays a list of documents that you've opened previously.
Settings	Displays a list of system components for which you can change settings.
Find	Helps you find a folder or a file.
Help	Starts Help. You can then use Help to find out how to perform a task in Windows.
Run	Starts a program or opens a folder when you type an command.
Shut Down	Shuts down or restarts your computer, or logs you off (if you are on a network).

Using the Programs Command

The <u>P</u>rograms command is the easiest way to open a program.

1. Click |📷Start|.

2. Point to <u>P</u>rograms. The <u>P</u>rograms submenu appears, listing the programs present on your computer. Every computer will have a different list of programs.

FIGURE A-2
<u>P</u>rograms submenu

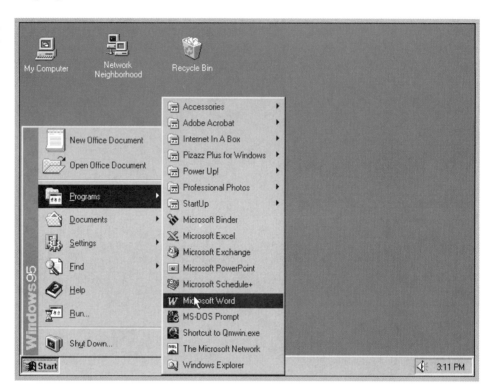

3. Point to a program that you want to open and then click. In a few seconds, the program will load and its first screen will appear. Notice that a button for the program appears in the taskbar. Keep the program open.

NOTE: Many items on the <u>P</u>rogram menu represent names for groups of programs. These group names have an arrow ▶ across from them on the right side of the menu. When you point to the group name, a submenu will appear listing programs that you can click to select.

Using the Taskbar

One of the major features of Windows 95 is that it enables you to work with more than one program at a time. The taskbar makes it easy to switch between open programs.

The window in which you are working is called the *active* window. The title bar for the active window is highlighted, as is its taskbar button.

1. The program you opened in the preceding procedure should still be open. (If it's not, open a program now.) Open a second program using the Program command. Notice how the second program covers the first. The window containing the second program is now active. Its title bar is highlighted and its button on the taskbar is highlighted.

FIGURE A-3
Active window

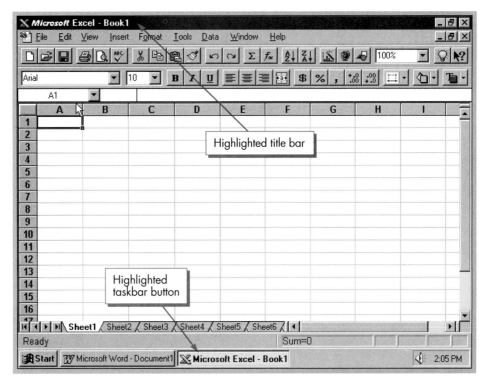

2. Click the button on the taskbar for the first program you opened. The program appears again.

3. Click the button on the taskbar for the second program to switch back to it.

Changing the Sizes of Windows

In Windows it's easy to adjust the size of your windows using the pointer.
You can also use the Minimize button , the Maximize button , and the Restore button to adjust the size of windows.

TABLE A-2

Sizing Buttons

NAME	BUTTON	USE
Minimize button		Reduces the window to a button on the taskbar.
Maximize button		Enlarges the window to fill the desktop.
Restore button		Returns the window to its previous size. (Appears when you maximize a window.)

1. In the open window, click ▣ at the right side of the title bar of the window. (If ▢ appears instead of ▣, the window has already been reduced. In that case, go on to step 2.)

2. Move the pointer to a window border. The pointer changes to a double-headed arrow ↔.

TIP: Sometimes the borders of a window can move off the computer screen. If you're having trouble with one border of a window, try another border.

3. When the pointer changes shape, you can drag the border to enlarge, reduce, or change the shape of the window.

4. Make the window smaller. Notice that the other open program appears behind the currently active window.

5. Click the window that had been behind the first window. It now appears in front of the first window because it has become the active window.

 6. Click ▭ to minimize the window to a button on the taskbar. The other program becomes active.

 7. Click the Close button ⊠ at the top right corner of the window to close the current program. The desktop should now be clean.

8. Click the button on the taskbar for the other program you have open. Close the program by clicking ⊠. You have a clean desktop again.

Using the Documents Command

You can open an existing document by using the Document command on the Start menu. This command allows you to open one of the last 15 documents previously opened on your computer.

1. In the Start menu, point to Documents. The Documents submenu appears, showing documents that have been previously opened.

2. Click on a document. The document opens, along with the program in which the document was written (for example, if the document were a Word document, it would open within Word). A button for the document appears on the taskbar. You could now work on the document, if you wanted.

3. To close the document, click ⊠ on the document window. Click ⊠ to close the program window that contained the document.

FIGURE A-4
Close buttons

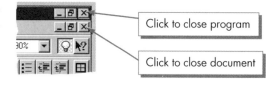

Using the Settings Command

You can change the way Windows looks and works by using the Settings command. Be very careful when changing settings. Don't change them unless it's really necessary.

 NOTE: Before changing any settings, talk to your instructor.

FIGURE A-5
Settings submenu

1. Open the Start menu, and point to Settings. The Settings submenu appears.
2. Click the option that relates to the settings you want to change. Close any open windows and clear your desktop.

TABLE A-3

Settings options	
OPTION	**USE**
Control Panel	Displays the Control Panel, which allows you to change screen colors, add or remove programs, change the date or time, and change other settings for your hardware and software.
Printers	Displays the Printer window, which allows you to add, remove, and modify your printer settings.
Taskbar	Displays the Taskbar Properties dialog box, which allows you to change the appearance of the taskbar and the way it works.

Using the Find Command

If you don't know where a document or folder is, you can use the Find command to find and open it.

FIGURE A-6
Find submenu

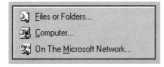

1. On the Start menu, point to Find. The Find submenu appears.
2. Click Files or Folders. The Find: All Files dialog box appears.

FIGURE A-7
Find: All Files
dialog box

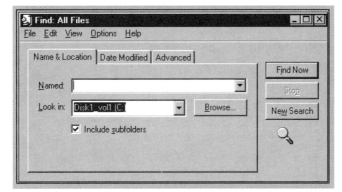

3. In the Named box, key the name of the file or folder you want to find.
4. Click the arrow next to the Look In box to specify where to search. (You could also check Browse.)

TIP: You can use the Advanced tab to search files for specific text.

5. Click Find Now to start the search. Any matches for the file will be shown at the bottom of the dialog box.

6. To open a file that was found, double-click on the filename.

7. When you have finished viewing the file, close all open windows and clear your desktop.

Using the Help Command

FIGURE A-8
Help Topics:
Windows Help
dialog box (with
Contents tab open)

FIGURE A-9
Help Topics:
Windows Help
dialog box (with
Index tab open)

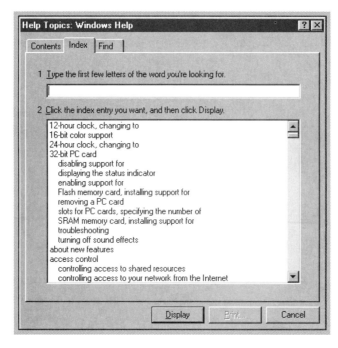

You can use Help to learn more about Windows. There are three ways to receive Help about a specific topic. You can use Help's Contents (like the table of contents in a book), Help's Index (like a book's index), or Help's Find command (like skimming a book for key words).

1. On the Start menu, click Help. The Help Topics: Windows Help dialog box appears.

2. Use the Contents tab to find topics grouped by subject. Double-click a topic, and then double-click subtopics until the desired Windows Help window appears. When you're finished, click Help Topics to return to the Help Topics window.

TIP: If you don't know how to use tabs in dialog boxes, see Appendix C: "Using Menus and Dialog Boxes."

3. Use the Index tab to scroll through the alphabetical index of Help topics. Key the first few letters of the word for which you want to search. When you're finished, click Help Topics to return to the Help Topics window.

4. You can use the Find tab to find all topics that contain a specific word or phrase. Follow the instructions in the Find tab. When you're finished, click Help Topics to return to the Help Topics window.

FIGURE A-10
Help Topics: Windows Help dialog box (with Find tab displayed)

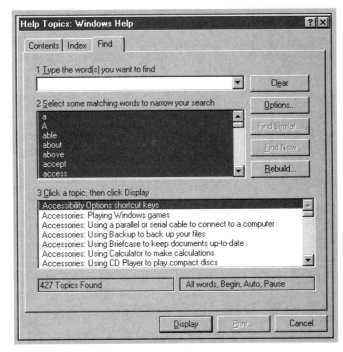

NOTE: The first time that the Find tab is used, the Find Setup Wizard dialog box appears. It will guide you through the initial process of creating a word list that is specific to your computer.

5. Click the Close button when you're finished using the Help Topics dialog box.

Using the Run Command

If you know the name of the program you want to use, you can use the Run command to start it easily. This command is often employed to run a "setup" or "install" program that installs a new program on your computer.

1. In the Start menu, click Run. The Run dialog box appears.

FIGURE A-11
Run dialog box

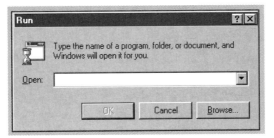

2. If you know the name of a program you want to run, key the name and click OK. The program you specified will start. Otherwise, you can click Browse to look for the program.

3. When you're finished, close the program.

Using the Right Mouse Button

When the pointer is on an object in Windows and you click the right mouse button, a shortcut menu will typically appear. This menu provides you with the commands that would be most useful in working with the object to which you were pointing.

A shortcut menu is available for . The shortcut menu options for Start are described in Table A-4.

FIGURE A-12
Shortcut menu for
the Start button

| Open |
| Explore |
| Find... |

1. Click Start with the right mouse button. The right mouse button Start menu appears.

2. Investigate the options on the right mouse button menu, and then close any open programs.

TABLE A-4

Shortcut menu for the start button

OPTION	USE
Open	Opens the Start Menu window. Double-click the Programs icon to open the Program window. Then, double-click the icon for the program you want to open.
Explore	Opens Windows Explorer (see Appendix E: "File Management").
Find	Opens the Find: All Files dialog box.

Using the Shut Down Command

You should always shut down Windows before you turn off or restart your computer. You can then be sure that your work will be saved and no files will be damaged.

FIGURE A-13
Shut Down Windows
dialog box

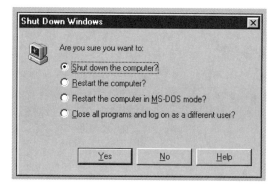

1. In the Start menu, click Shut Down. The Shut Down Windows dialog box appears.

2. Click Yes. Windows will prompt you to save changes to any open documents, and will then shut down your computer.

APPENDIX B

Using the Mouse

Although you can use a keyboard with Windows, you'll probably find yourself using the mouse for most work. Typically, you roll the mouse on a small mat called a *mouse pad* (or on any flat surface). A *pointer* shows your on-screen location as the mouse moves.

To select items on the computer screen using a mouse, you usually press the left button on the mouse.

 NOTE: Whenever you're told to "click" or "double-click" the mouse button, use the left mouse button. In those cases where you should use the right button, you'll be told to do so.

When using a mouse, you'll need to become familiar with the following terms.

TABLE B-1   **Mouse Terms**

TERM	DESCRIPTION
Point	Move the mouse until the tip of the on-screen pointer is touching an item on the computer screen.
Click	Press the mouse button and then quickly release it.
Double-click	Press and quickly release the mouse button twice.
Triple-click	Press and quickly release the mouse button three times.
Drag (or drag-and-drop)	Point to an object, hold down the mouse, and move the mouse to a new position (dragging the object to the new position). Then release the mouse button (and drop the object in the new position).

The mouse pointer changes appearance depending on where it's located and what you're doing. Table B-2 shows the most common types of mouse pointers.

TABLE B-2   **Frequently Used Mouse Pointers**

POINTER NAME	POINTER	DESCRIPTION
Pointer	⌖	The most common pointer. Used to point to objects.
I-beam	I	Used when keying, inserting, and selecting text.
2-headed arrow	⬊	Used when changing the size of objects or windows.
4-headed arrow	✛	Used to move objects.
Hourglass	⌛	Indicates that the computer is processing a command. Generally, you cannot perform any tasks when the hourglass appears.
Hand	🖐	Used in Help to display additional information.

APPENDIX C

Using Menus and Dialog Boxes

Menus

Menus throughout Windows applications use common features to let you know what will happen when you select a command. Figures C-1 and C-2 show examples of two menus. To open a menu, click the menu name (for example, to open the File menu, click File on the menu bar). An alternative method for opening a menu is to hold down Alt and key the underlined letter in the menu name.

 TIP: If you open a menu by mistake, click the menu name again to close the menu.

FIGURE C-1
Edit Menu (Excel)

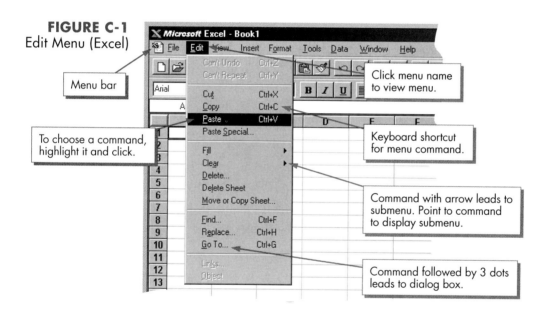

Menu bar

To choose a command, highlight it and click.

Click menu name to view menu.

Keyboard shortcut for menu command.

Command with arrow leads to submenu. Point to command to display submenu.

Command followed by 3 dots leads to dialog box.

FIGURE C-2
View Menu (Word)

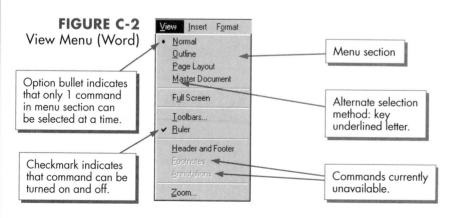

Option bullet indicates that only 1 command in menu section can be selected at a time.

Checkmark indicates that command can be turned on and off.

Menu section

Alternate selection method: key underlined letter.

Commands currently unavailable.

Dialog Boxes

Dialog boxes enable you to view all of the current settings for a command, as well as change them. Like menus in Windows, dialog boxes share common features. The following examples show the most frequently seen features.

 TIP: If you open a dialog box by mistake or decide that you don't want to change any of the information shown there, click [Cancel] to exit the dialog box or press [Esc].

FIGURE C-3
Print Dialog Box
(Word)

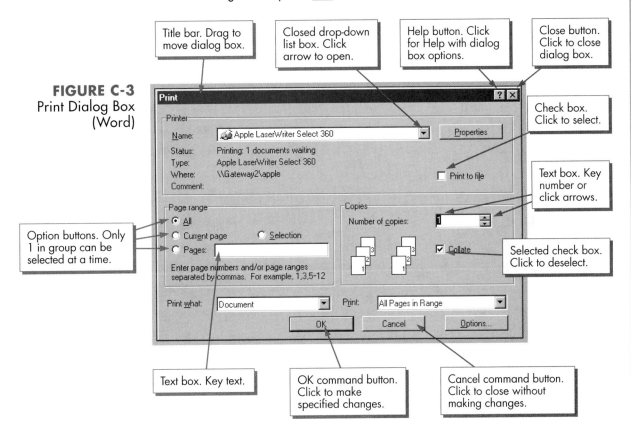

Title bar. Drag to move dialog box.

Closed drop-down list box. Click arrow to open.

Help button. Click for Help with dialog box options.

Close button. Click to close dialog box.

Check box. Click to select.

Text box. Key number or click arrows.

Option buttons. Only 1 in group can be selected at a time.

Selected check box. Click to deselect.

Text box. Key text.

OK command button. Click to make specified changes.

Cancel command button. Click to close without making changes.

FIGURE C-4
Font Dialog Box
(Word)

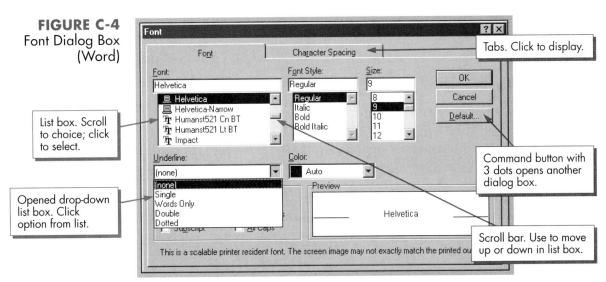

Tabs. Click to display.

List box. Scroll to choice; click to select.

Opened drop-down list box. Click option from list.

Command button with 3 dots opens another dialog box.

Scroll bar. Use to move up or down in list box.

APPENDIX D
Excel Toolbars

The following toolbars are most commonly used in Excel:

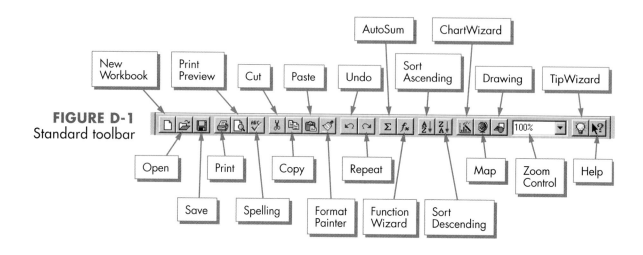

FIGURE D-1
Standard toolbar

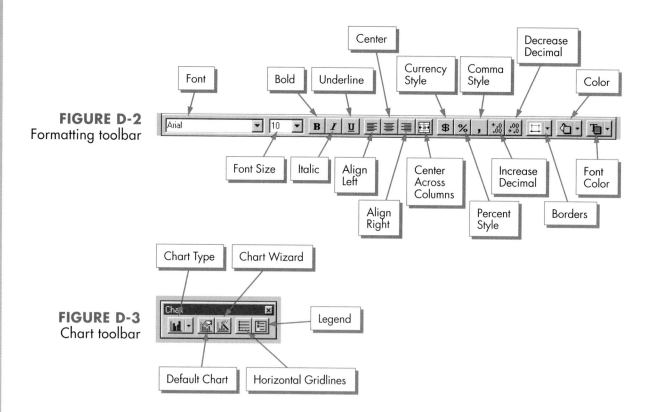

FIGURE D-2
Formatting toolbar

FIGURE D-3
Chart toolbar

APPENDIX E

File Management

This Appendix briefly explains how information is stored in Windows 95. It also introduces one of the most useful tools for managing information in Windows—the Windows Explorer.

Files, Folders, and Paths

In Windows, the basic unit of storage is a *file*. The documents you create and use are files, as are the programs you use. These files are stored in *folders*, which can also contain other folders.

Windows 95 supports filenames that can contain up to 250 characters. A filename also has a three-letter extension, which identifies the type of file. For example, the extension "doc" identifies a file as a Word document. The extension is separated from the filename by a period. For example: "Birthdays.doc."

NOTE: In this course, we assume that your machine displays file extensions. If it doesn't, open Windows Explorer, select Option from the View menu, and make sure that the following option is *not* selected: "Hide MS-DOS file extensions for file types that are registered."

A file's *path* is its specific location on your computer or network. A file's path begins with the drive letter, followed by a colon and a backslash (example: c:\). The path then lists the folders in the order you would open them. Folders are separated by backslashes. The last item in the path is the filename.

For example: c:\MSOffice\Winword\My Documents\Birthdays.doc

Windows Explorer

One of the most useful tools in Windows for managing files is the *Windows Explorer*, which gives you a view of your computer's components as a hierarchy, or "tree." Using Windows Explorer, you can easily see the contents of each drive and folder on your computer or network.

To open Windows Explorer, click the Start button [Start] with the right mouse button. Then click Explore in the Start button shortcut menu.

Table E-1 describes how to accomplish common file management tasks using Windows Explorer and shortcut menus.

FIGURE E-1
Windows Explorer

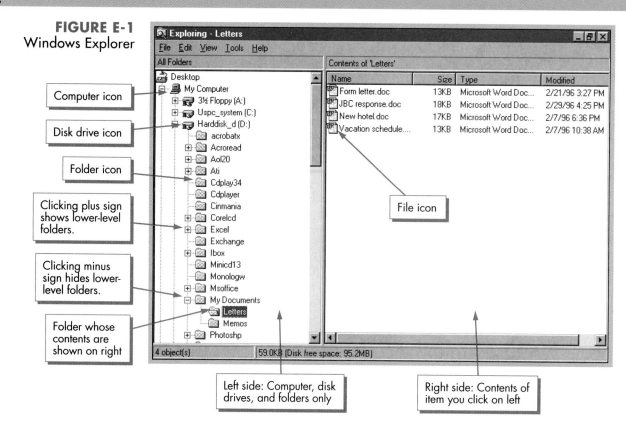

Computer icon

Disk drive icon

Folder icon

Clicking plus sign shows lower-level folders.

Clicking minus sign hides lower-level folders.

Folder whose contents are shown on right

File icon

Left side: Computer, disk drives, and folders only

Right side: Contents of item you click on left

TABLE E-1   **Common File Management Tasks**

TASK	HOW TO DO
Copy file or folder	Point to icon for file or folder to be copied, press right mouse button, and click Copy. Then, point to icon for folder in which you want to copy file, press right mouse button, and click Paste.
Move file or folder	Same procedure as above, but using Cut and Paste.
Delete a file or folder	Point to icon for file to be deleted and press Delete.
Create a new folder	Choose New from File menu, and then choose Folder. Creates new folder at current position within Windows Explorer.
Copy file to floppy disk	Point to icon for file to be copied and press right mouse button. Point to Send To and click floppy disk drive in submenu.
Edit/rename file	Point to icon for file you want to rename, press right mouse button, and click Rename.
Open file	Double-click icon for file.
Print file	Point to icon for file to be printed, press right mouse button, and click Print.

 TIP: You can also drag a file from the left side of the Windows Explorer to the right side to move or copy the file.

Proofreader's Marks

PROOFREADER'S MARK	DRAFT	FINAL COPY
⌒ Delete space	to⌒gether	together
# Insert space	It#may be	It may be
∿ Transpose	beleivable	believable
◯ Spell out	②years ago	two years ago
⋀ Insert a word	How much *is* it?	How much is it?
— OR — Delete a word	it may ~~not~~ be true	it may be true
⋀ OR ⋏ Insert a letter	temper*a*ture	temperature
⌒ OR ⊰ Delete a letter and close up	commit⌢ment to bur⌢y	commitment to buy
— OR — Change a word	~~and~~*but* if you ~~won't~~*can't*	but if you can't
⟨stet⟩ Stet (don't delete)	⟨stet⟩ I was ~~very~~ glad	I was very glad
/ Make letter lowercase	/Federal /Government	federal government
≡ Capitalize	Janet L. g̲reyston	Janet L. Greyston
⊙ Insert a period	Mr⊙Henry Grenada	Mr. Henry Grenada
⋀ Insert a comma	a large⋀old house	a large, old house
⋁ Insert an apostrophe	my childrens⋁ car	my children's car
� quote⋁ Insert quotation marks	he wants a ⋁loan⋁	he wants a "loan"
= Insert a hyphen	a first=rate job	a first-rate job
—— Insert underscore	an issue of Time̲	an issue of Time̲
⟨ital⟩ Set in italic	⟨ital⟩ The New York Times	*The New York Times*
⟨bf⟩ Set in boldface	⟨bf⟩ the Enter key	the **Enter** key
⟨rom⟩ Set in roman	⟨rom⟩ the *most* likely	the most likely
⦃ ⦄ Insert parentheses	left today⦃May 3⦄	left today (May 3)
⊐ Move to the right	$38,367,000 ⊐	$38,367,000
⊏ Move to the left	⊏ Anyone can win!	Anyone can win!

APPENDIX G

Excel Operators, Formulas, and Functions

Mathematical Operators

OPERATOR	DESCRIPTION
+	Add
-	Subtract
*	Multiply
/	Divide
%	Percent
^	Exponentiation
( )	Parentheses—used to control the hierarchy of mathematical operations

Formula Construction

Basic Formulas

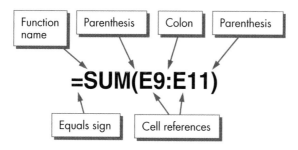

Formula with Nested Functions

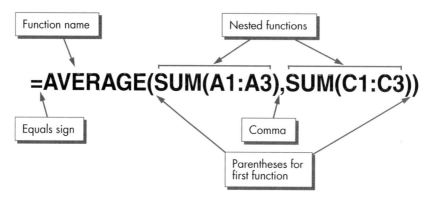

Common Excel Functions

Date & Time Functions

Function	Description
DATE	Returns the serial number of a particular date
NOW	Returns the serial number of the current date and time
TIME	Returns the serial number of a particular time
TODAY	Returns the serial number of today's date
WEEKDAY	Converts a serial number to a day of the week

Database & List Management Functions

Function	Description
DAVERAGE	Returns the average of selected database entries
DCOUNT	Counts the cells containing numbers from a specified database and criteria
DCOUNTA	Counts nonblank cells from a specified database and criteria
DGET	Extracts from a database a single record that matches the specified criteria
DMAX	Returns the maximum value from selected database entries
DMIN	Returns the minimum value from selected database entries
DSUM	Adds the numbers in the field column of records in the database that match the criteria

Financial Functions

Function	Description
FV	Returns the future value of an investment
NPER	Returns the number of periods for an investment
PMT	Returns the periodic payment for an annuity
PPMT	Returns the payment on the principal for an investment for a given period
PV	Returns the present value of an investment
RATE	Returns the interest rate per period of an annuity

Information Functions

Function	Description
CELL	Returns information about the formatting, location, or contents of a cell
ISBLANK	Returns TRUE if the value is blank
ISERR	Returns TRUE if the value is any error value except #N/A
ISERROR	Returns TRUE if the value is any error value
ISNUMBER	Returns TRUE if the value is a number
ISTEXT	Returns TRUE if the value is text

Logical Functions

Function	Description
AND	Returns TRUE if all its arguments are TRUE
FALSE	Returns the logical value FALSE
IF	Specifies a logical test to perform
NOT	Reverses the logic of its argument
OR	Returns TRUE if any argument is TRUE
TRUE	Returns the logical value TRUE

Lookup & Reference Functions

Function	Description
HLOOKUP	Looks in the top row of an array and returns the value of the indicated cell
VLOOKUP	Looks in the first column of an array and moves across the row to return the value of a cell

Math & Trigonometry Functions

Function	Description
ABS	Returns the absolute value of a number
INT	Rounds a number down to the nearest integer
ROUND	Rounds a number to a specified number of digits
SQRT	Returns a positive square root
SUM	Adds its arguments
TRUNC	Truncates a number to an integer

Statistical Functions

Function	Description
AVERAGE	Returns the average of its arguments
COUNT	Counts how many numbers are in the list of arguments
COUNTA	Counts how many values are in the list of arguments
MAX	Returns the maximum value in a list of arguments
MIN	Returns the minimum value in a list of arguments

Text Functions

Function	Description
LOWER	Converts text to lowercase
PROPER	Capitalizes the first letter in each word of a text value
TRIM	Removes spaces from text
UPPER	Converts text to uppercase

Glossary

Absolute cell reference A formula cell address that specifies the exact address of a cell, regardless of the position of the cell containing the formula. Example: $A$1. (11)

Active cell The cell that is current–that is ready to receive information. (1)

Add-In A file that can be installed to add additional commands and functions to the Excel program. (13)

Annuity A constant periodic payment paid over a fixed time period. (12)

Argument A value or other data operated on by a function. (10)

Block A group of adjacent cells. (2)

Category axis The horizontal (or x) axis along the bottom of most charts; it frequently refers to time series. (17)

Cell The unit that is formed by the intersection of a row and a column, which can contain text, numeric values, or formulas. (1)

Cell address The location of a cell in a worksheet, indicated by its column letter and row number. (1)

Character string A sequence of characters in a formula or text. (7)

Circular reference An error condition in a formula in which a cell is both operated on by the formula and serves as the location of the formula. (11)

Clip art Any ready-to-use graphic image that can be imported into a worksheet or chart. (18)

Clipboard Temporary storage in the computer's memory. (3)

Consolidated worksheet A worksheet that contains a consolidation table. (15)

Consolidation table A table that summarizes the data from one or more source ranges. (15)

Constant An unchanging numerical value in a formula. (6)

Criteria range The area of the worksheet where you specify the conditions that the filtered data must meet. (20)

Criterion The specified information that Excel must match when searching for a record. (19)

Cut To clear data from selected cells and store it temporarily on the Clipboard. (3)

Data form A dialog box that displays only the fields for one record, in a vertical arrangement. (19)

Data marker An object that represents individual data points. It can be a bar, area, dot, picture, or other symbol that marks a single data point or value. (17)

Data point A single piece of data. (17)

Data series A collection of data points that are related to one another. These values are usually within the same columns or row in the worksheet. (17)

Database A collection of related information organized in a systematic way. (19)

Database A file containing an organized list of related data. (13)

Dependent worksheet A worksheet that depends the data in another worksheet. (15)

Docked toolbar A toolbar in a fixed position outside the work area. (5)

Dynamic link A formula reference to a different worksheet that is automatically updated when changes to data occur. (15)

Embedded chart A chart that is part of a worksheet. (17)

External reference A reference to a cell, cell range, or defined name in another workbook. (15)

Field A category of information in a database, arranged as a single column of data. (19)

Field name A column label used to identify the contents of a field. (19)

Filename The unique name given to a workbook when it is saved. (1)

Fill handle The small box in the lower right-hand corner of a selected cell or cell range. (5)

Filtering The process of finding and selecting information from a database. (20)

Floating toolbar A toolbar positioned over the work area. (5)

Font A type design applied to an entire set of characters, including all letters of the alphabet, numerals, punctuation marks, and other keyboard symbols. (9)

Footer Repetitive information about a worksheet that is printed across the bottom of the page. (16)

Format Attributes of text or numbers, such as font style, underlining, bold, number of decimal places, or alignment. (8)

Full precision Numbers stored and used in calculations, regardless of how the number is formatted on the screen. (8)

Header Repetitive information about a worksheet that is printed across the top of the page. (16)

Input cell A cell referenced in the data table formula and varied to calculate the data table results. (21)

Interest The amount paid to the lender as profit at a set rate. (12)

Internal reference A reference to a cell, cell range, or defined name in another worksheet within the same workbook. (15)

Label Text that is excluded from calculations and that may include any character. (2)

Landscape A horizontal page-orientation setting. (4) **Print area** A range of a worksheet that is to be printed. (4) **Source range** The cell or range of cells from which data is copied or moved. (5)

Legend A guide that explains the symbols, patterns, or colors used to differentiate data series. (17)

Line break A method to force the movement of the insertion point to the next line down within a cell. (8)

List A series of worksheet rows that contain data. (19)

List range The area containing the database, which includes the field names and all records. (20)

Logical values The values TRUE and FALSE, which are the results of formulas that use comparison operators such as = or >. (10)

Mixed cell reference A formula cell address in which part of the address had an absolute cell reference, with the other part of the address remaining relative. Examples: $A1 and B$1. (11)

Nested function A function that contains another function as an argument. (10)

One-variable data table A table that calculates a formula containing one variable. (21)

Order of precedence The preset order in which mathematical operations in a formula are performed. (2)

Page orientation Vertical or horizontal display of data on a printed page. (4)

Panes Sections of a worksheet shown simultaneously on the screen. (4)

Paste To transfer data from the Clipboard to a worksheet. (3)

Pivot table A table that allows you to arrange the data in a database in different ways by rearranging rows and columns. (21)

Plot area The rectangular area bounded by the two axes; it includes all axes and data points. (17)

Point size The way in which font size is measured; there are 72 points per inch. (9)

Portrait A vertical page-orientation setting. (4)

Precision as displayed An option that stores numbers as the rounded values that appear on the screen. (8)

Principal The portion of a loan that represents the amount borrowed, or the present value. (12)

Range Any group of cells specified to be acted upon by a command. (2)

Range name A name given to a cell or range of cells that can be used instead of its address. (6)

Record A group of fields that comprise one complete set of data in a database, arranged in a single row. (19)

Relative cell reference A cell address characteristic in which the cell reference adjusts to its new position when copied. (5)

Relative cell reference A formula cell address that specifies the address of the cell relative to the cell containing the formula. Example: A1. (11)

Scaling Enlarging or reducing the size of a worksheet's contents. (16)

Selection handles Small black squares appearing around a selected object that are used to resize the object. (17)

Serial number Numbers arranged in order by rank. In Excel, dates are stored as serial numbers, ranging from 1 (for January 1, 1900) to 65,380 (for December 31, 2078). (12)

Sort order The order in which Excel arranges records during a sort. (19)

Source worksheet A worksheet that contains the data being used by other, dependent worksheets. (15)

Split bars Double lines that divide panes on a worksheet. (4)

Split boxes Click boxes on the scroll bars that allow you to create panes by using the mouse. (4)

Style A set of formatting instructions that can be applied to the cells in a worksheet. (9)

Target range The cell or range of cells to which data is copied or moved. (5)

Templates Formatted models of a worksheet. (13)

Test data Simple numbers used to verify the accuracy of formulas. (4)

Tick mark A division mark along the category (x) and value (y) axes. (17)

Two-variable data table A table that calculates a formula containing two variables. (21)

Value A number or a formula. (2)

Value axis The vertical (or y) axis against which data points are measured. (17)

Wildcard A symbol that stands for any combination of letters or numbers. (7)

Workbook An Excel worksheet or group of worksheets saved as a file. (1)

Worksheet The area in which text, numeric values, and formulas are entered. Worksheets contain a grid that defines a series of rows and columns. Worksheets are collected into workbooks, which can contain up to 255 worksheets. (1)

Zoom A sizing feature used to make the onscreen view of a worksheet larger or smaller. (4)

Index

Photo Credits

Pages 4 & 9: Telegraph Color Library/FPG; Pages 5 & 205: Buss/FPG; Pages
6 & 349: Laird/FPG; Pages 7 & 415: Weber/FPG; Pages 7 & 469: Kahn/FPG